Praise for Terry Frei's *Horns, Hogs, and Nixon Coming*

"Frei does a masterful job of weaving in the historical significance of the turbulent times, including Vietnam War protests, the military draft lottery and the civil rights movement that were so much a part of campus life in that era. It's political football at its best."
—**Bob Holt,** *Arkansas Democrat-Gazette*

"Like a Tocquevillian sportswriter in a new world, Terry Frei does the unexpected, if not the impossible: He makes that damn game—and all the cultural, political, and social issues swirling around it like so much red-and-white confetti—seem new again, relevant again." —*Arkansas Democrat-Gazette* **editorial page**

"A great story, well-told, with more delicious details than a linebacker could tackle."
—**David Hendricks,** *San Antonio Express-News*

"I'm impressed that [Terry Frei] took the time to go to so many different players and coaches and to dig into their background and history. When you combine that with the political turmoil that was going on at the time, he really has done a great job of pulling it all together." —**Chuck Dicus, former Arkansas All-American wide receiver**

"I couldn't put it down." —**Red McCombs, owner, Minnesota Vikings and longtime University of Texas football fan**

". . . a superb blending of sports, history and politics." —**Si Dunn,** *Dallas Morning News*

"I most enjoyed the personal stories of the players themselves, a collection of scrubs and stars, hippies and soldiers, partyers and priests who came together as teams amid a unique confluence of events that conspired to make this game one of the most memorable events in the history of sports. Frei possesses the football expertise, the uncanny ability to buttonhook diverse personal anecdotes together, and the appreciation for history to best tell this remarkable tale." —**John Moore, theater critic, *The Denver Post***

"Frei's often humorous telling is much more than a rehash of the game. Attended by both President Nixon and [George Bush], the game was also memorable for its combination of Southern pride and anti-Vietnam War protests. Frei's treatment also serves as a larger history of the social and political climate surrounding the competition. [The book is a] delightful, well-researched chronicle of a turbulent era." —**Larry Little, *Library Journal***

"Some of us codgers on the scene thought we knew all facets of The Big Shootout. But now, 33 years after that climatic Arkansas–Texas game, comes a most intriguing account of whys and wherefores and backgrounds and personality quirks, warts and all, and political implications (Vietnam protests) and whatever. Terry Frei must have worn out a dozen tape recorders in the process." —**Blackie Sherrod, *Dallas Morning News***

"Everyone knows that football today is a far cry from what it was in the days of leather helmets and dropkicks, but it takes a book like Terry Frei's *Horns, Hogs, and Nixon Coming* to show how much the game has changed in just the last three decades. Frei does so by chronicling what might have been the final game of the God-Family-Football era, before shoe companies, superagents, and TV networks turned the muddy old gridiron into a multigazillion-dollar business." —**Charles Hirshberg, *Sports Illustrated***

Horns, Hogs, and Nixon Coming

Texas vs. Arkansas in Dixie's Last Stand

Terry Frei

TAYLOR TRADE PUBLISHING

Lanham • New York • Dallas • Boulder • Toronto • Oxford

Copyright © 2002 by Terry Frei
First Simon & Schuster edition 2002
First Taylor Trade Publishing edition 2004

Published by Taylor Trade Publishing
An imprint of The Rowman & Littlefield Publishing Group, Inc.
4501 Forbes Boulevard, Suite 200
Lanham, Maryland 20706

Distributed by National Book Network

A previous edition of this book was catalogued by the Library of Congress as follows:

Frei, Terry, 1955–
   Horns, hogs, and Nixon coming : Texas vs. Arkansas in Dixie's last stand / Terry Frei.
      p.   cm.
   Includes bibliographical references and index.
   1. Texas Longhorns (Football team)—History. 2. University of Texas at Austin—Football—
History. 3. Arkansas Razorbacks (Football team)—History. 4. University of Arkansas,
Fayetteville—Football—History. I. Title.
   GV958.T45 F75 2002
   796.332'63'0976431—dc21   2002075233

ISBN 1-58979-129-0 (pbk : alk. paper)

⊖™ The paper used in this publication meets the minimum requirements of
American National Standard for Information Sciences—Permanence of
Paper for Printed Library Materials, ANSI/NISO Z39.48–1992.
Manufactured in the United States of America.

TO COACH JERRY FREI, WHO IS MISSED

ACKNOWLEDGMENTS

My wife, Helen, as always, lent her support, tolerating my obsession.

Literary agents Randy Voorhees and John Monteleone of Mountain Lion, Inc., believed in this project—and in a writer they had never met.

Jeff Neuman and Jonathan Malki of Simon & Schuster have my gratitude for taking on this book and prodding me to improve it. Jon's initial editing spared the reader from encountering roughly 1,836 uses of the passive voice.

Fellow journalists Jim Beseda and Neal Rubin gave the manuscript critical readings in the early stages, and they were both helpful and encouraging.

The sports information offices at Texas and Arkansas opened their archives and also helped locate many former players and coaches. The Razorback Foundation and the Arkansas Alumni Association also aided in the searches.

After my father's death in February 2001, the reaction and loving support from his former University of Oregon players and assistant coaches—including Dan Fouts, Ahmad Rashad, Tom Graham, Bob Newland, Ken Woody, and George Seifert—reinforced my faith in college football, warts and all, past and present, as a character- and camaraderie-building experience. It's no myth. The Ducks' loyalty caused me to further understand and value what I generally found to be the respect the Arkansas and Texas players retain for their coaches, and for each other.

It was a difficult year for my mother, Marian, but she was quietly encouraging as I immersed myself in this project. But that's the way she always has been, both as the career coach's wife and as the mother of five.

Finally, this book wouldn't have been possible without the cooperation of the 1969 Razorbacks and Longhorns, including Darrell Royal and Frank Broyles, plus the many others who spoke with me about their experiences.

CONTENTS

PROLOGUE

Good Morning, Mr. President

UCLA DEFENSIVE COORDINATOR BOBBY FIELD loved his three-and-a-half-mile run through the canyons above the Westwood campus on early spring mornings, when he could hear the sprinklers and smell the damp grass. He tried to make it an escape from the Xs and Os of the game, but strategic revelations came in flashes—such as when one arrived shortly after he crossed Sunset Boulevard and started up Stone Canyon Road.

The new safety is going to be quick enough to send after the quarterback on second-and-long, especially against teams with tailbacks who don't check if they're needed to block for the quarterback before drifting into the flat and leaving a lane wider than—

What's this?

On this morning, near the stately, sprawling, and isolated Hotel Bel-Air, where the famous stay to be unseen and where the smell is either of the hotel's plush Gardens or of old money, three men are walking toward Field. It is 6:15 A.M., a time in the Bel-Air Estates for expensive sweatsuits or shorts or golf shirts or cashmere sweaters, or perhaps for a chauffeur's uniform, if the driver is stretching his legs as he waits for his wealthy passenger. But these three men are in dark suits, white shirts, and ties, and they are strolling downhill toward the jogging and sweating football coach who is trying to avoid developing the sort of paunch that fills those coaching shirts and can be so embarrassing on television.

Suddenly, Field realizes the slightly hunched figure between two guards is Richard Milhous Nixon.

It is March 30, 1985, nearly eleven years since the resignation, and a week before the opening of the Bruins' spring practices. Field doesn't know this, but the night before, the ex-president dined with former *Rowan and Martin's Laugh-In* producer Paul Keyes at Chasen's, and Nixon's "Sock-It-to-Me" cameo on the classic television show undoubtedly came up. Later, Nixon would check out of the hotel to leave for Rancho Mirage and the "Sunny-lands" estate of Walter Annenberg, the founder of *TV Guide* and the ambassador to Great Britain during the Nixon administration. Now, Nixon is taking a morning walk with two guards, who check out Field. They conclude he doesn't have a knife hidden in the elastic band of his jogging shorts.

So what's the protocol here, Bobby Field? Whistle "Hail to the Chief" as you pass? Veer off path, as if there is a presidential halo that remains after the exit from office? Hold both hands aloft, signaling "V" for victory over Humphrey and McGovern?

Like a quarterback under siege, Field has only a few seconds to make a choice, and he nods in midstride, and puffs out a greeting.

"Good morning!"

Nixon nods back. It is almost imperceptible, but it is there, the slight acknowledgment. Now Field is past the former president, heading further into the foothills.

Good morning?

Bobby Field comes across Richard Nixon for the second time in his life, and that's all he can say? He choked in the clutch, he lectures himself on the move. He runs for another ten minutes on his uphill portion, passing immaculate homes, then takes one more stride to the north and reverses direction, as if he had stepped on the line at the end of the field during "gasser" drills and must start back the other way. It's time to head back to the UCLA football offices and prepare for the workday—film, practice plans, staff meetings, all the details involved in getting ready for the Bruins' upcoming season.

As Field runs back down Stone Canyon Road, he again approaches the Hotel Bel-Air, on his right. Nixon and his two protectors are standing near the canopied stone footbridge that leads over a pond to the hotel. Field tells himself to be braver this time. He slows and veers toward the former president. The guards' heads turn: It's the jogger again. Field downgrades to a walk, catches Nixon's eyes, and approaches. He reaches out his hand and speaks.

Sir, he says, my name is Bobby Field, and I just wanted to say hello.

Why, thank you, the ex-president responds. He is being courteous, not warm. Nixon's escorts are scanning Field again, making sure.

Field says he is a football coach on Terry Donahue's staff at UCLA, down in Westwood—the defensive coordinator, in fact. Now Nixon is perking up.

"As a matter of fact," Field says, "in 1969, I was playing for the University of Arkansas and you, sir, came to one of our games, the one in Fayetteville against the University of Texas."

In the respectful formality of a conversation with the one-time most powerful man in the world, it just seems right to say "University of Arkansas" and "University of Texas," and not just blurt it out—"the Texas-Arkansas game."

Field also doesn't mention that he has been teased for years because an instant after he fell on a Texas fumble on the second play of the game, the ABC shot switched to a late-arriving president making his way into the stadium—and the distracted announcer later told the millions of viewers *somebody else* came up with the ball! Field doesn't mention that to Nixon because that would be rude, and besides, now the former president is excited. Nixon is so excited, in fact, that the other two men in dark suits are astounded and transfixed as the one-time Whittier College benchwarmer gives the former Razorback, who *played* in the game, a virtual play-by-play account and strategic analysis of that afternoon in Razorback Stadium.

With an amazed Field standing there sweating in the morning sun and hazy smog, the former president goes on and on. "And, oh," he says, "it was such a terrific game, what a shame it was that someone had to lose." As Nixon continues, Field tells himself it's almost as if the former president had watched the game film the night before.

Bobby Field, who as a stunned Arkansas defensive back stood among sniffling teammates in a tiny dressing room at the end of Razorback Stadium when President Richard Nixon told them they should be proud, nods and tells the former president that it indeed was a privilege to be able to say he had been on that field on December 6, 1969.

It was a game Richard Nixon couldn't forget, and he wasn't alone.

Yet there was more to it than four quarters of football, or what Texas coach Darrell Royal dubbed "The Big Shootout." The final regular-season game in the centennial year of college football, it also came in the final days when the faces under the helmets all could be white and the simple question "Why?" could be rank insubordination. Maybe it was why there weren't blacks in the programs sooner, or why workouts sometimes seemed designed to run off the lesser players, or why some of the coaches (and even the trainer!) acted as if a visit to the training room for treatment was a sign of weakness, not sensibility. *"No, son, you shoot it up and you play and you will thank us years later."* (And many of them did! Again and again in later years, the Hogs and Horns would discuss the football mentality of their playing era, shake their heads, and qualify it with something like: *"But that's just how it was then."* Rather than applying twenty-first-century standards retroactively and pervasively, anyone with a sense for the era understood *exactly* what they meant.)

That's just how it was then.

While college football was struggling with its evolution—an evolution progressing at differing paces around the country—the game often served to highlight aspects of national polarization in the late sixties. Many wanted sports to be an escape from turmoil, but by the end of the decade, sports often contributed to the general unrest. The most notorious instance was when sprinters Tommie Smith and John Carlos raised gloved fists during the medal ceremony at the 1968 Olympics, arguing that in fact the nation still wasn't for all its citizens the land of the free, even fourteen years after *Brown* v. *Board of Education* and four years after the Civil Rights Act of 1964 and following epic struggles in the civil rights movement. In 1969, campuses were boiling caldrons, primarily because of anti–Vietnam War sentiment, often angrily expressed, but it was linked also to a general sense of disillusionment and cynicism. John Kennedy, Martin Luther King, and Robert Kennedy were dead and still mourned. In Fayetteville that day, and even that week, the football game provided a focal point for that polarization, although the evidence of its significance was mostly ignored at the time—as if the cheers and martial music drowned out everything else happening both in the nation and on a campus struggling with racial antipathy and divisiveness.

One political protest came off that afternoon in Fayetteville. Another, which would have been far more embarrassing to University of Arkansas officials and disruptive to the national television broadcast, was always one trumpet—or tuba or trombone—note away from beginning. That demonstration, even if angry and prolonged, would have been preferable to the racially charged armed conflict that seemed on the verge of breaking out the night before the game in Fayetteville.

One of Nixon's White House successors was in the Razorback Stadium seats that day. Another was in England, wondering how quickly his angst-filled letter could get from Oxford to Fayetteville. A trailblazing young law student who eventually would interrogate a sitting president in the White House anxiously watched the game on television in a University of Arkansas dormitory—after getting out of the hospital that morning.

On the field, two teams of young men—mostly bright, mostly tough, mostly conventionally grateful to accept the perks that came with being the stars on campus, mostly destined for productive postfootball lives, and all of them white—represented a dying football era. One of them was displaying monumental toughness just by playing—although nobody else knew it at the time, and even he didn't truly yet know the magnitude of his courage.

Many of the imminent changes in sports and the society in which the games were played were shamefully overdue. Yet the men on the field that day were the last, and in some ways the best, of how it was.

ONE

Coach Broyles

THE TALK OF A 1969 SCHEDULE CHANGE started on the day Frank Broyles played golf in Little Rock and attended a Razorback Club gathering in little Lonoke, twenty miles farther east.

The routine was part of the job for any college football coach: Travel the state, usually in a plush dealer-provided car, often with coffee cup in hand, and make speeches, mingle, or play golf with groups large and small. Yet one reason Frank Broyles loved coaching at the University of Arkansas was that *every* gathering around the state could turn into a pep rally. He could scan any sort of group—service organizations, lodges, high school awards banquets—and know these people were *for the Razorbacks!* Unlike his coaching contemporaries in the Southwest Conference and most of them around the country, Broyles didn't need to worry about divided loyalties in his state. He never witnessed half the men standing for the fight song of State U, with the others glowering in their seats, before the roles were reversed for the next song.

In Arkansas, major-league football was the University of Arkansas Razorbacks. There was no "other." If Arkansans—at least white Arkansans, and that's who attended the sort of meetings attended by the coach who still didn't have any black players on his varsity in 1969—were behind any college team, and they usually were, it was the Razorbacks. And from a young age, Arkansas fans learned the proper form for "calling the hogs":

"*Wooooooooooo, Pig! Sooie!*

"*Wooooooooooo, Pig! Sooie!*

"*Wooooooooooo, Pig! Sooie! Razorbacks!*"

The drawback to the coach's goodwill tours in the state involved geography. Tucked in the northwest corner of the state, Fayetteville is closer to Tulsa, Oklahoma (117 miles), than to Little Rock (192 miles), where so many of the power brokers lived. The Razorbacks played at least three "home" games a season in Little Rock's War Memorial Stadium.

In March 1969, when Broyles was visiting Little Rock and Lonoke, he was forty-four years old and a veteran of eleven seasons as the Razorbacks' head coach. He already had won a national championship, in 1964, with a team that shut out its last five regular-season opponents and included heady crew-cut hustlers Jimmy Johnson and Jerry Jones. Alabama was No. 1 in the final Associated Press and United Press International polls, and the Razorbacks were No. 2. Neither wire service conducted a poll after the bowl games. In the Orange Bowl, a hobbled Joe Namath came off the bench to lead an Alabama comeback that came up short and the Crimson Tide lost 21–17 to, of all teams, the Texas Longhorns. The Football Writers Association had a poll then, too, and it took a vote after the bowl games. Arkansas, which beat Nebraska 10–7 in the Cotton Bowl, climbed to No. 1, and that became the accepted and eminently sensible national view, both at the time and in record books.

Especially after that national title the Razorbacks' lanky head coach with the Georgia drawl was as renowned in the state as Arkansas's high-profile politicians. He was as big as or bigger than Senator J. William Fulbright, the former Rhodes Scholar and Razorbacks football player from 1921 to 1924 who also served as the University of Arkansas's president from 1939 to 1941 before entering politics. Broyles was as well-known as Representative Wilbur Mills, feared and courted on Capitol Hill and around the country because he chaired the House Ways and Means Committee. If Governor Winthrop Rockefeller, Nelson's brother, had walked into a room with Broyles, the football coach likely would have drawn more attention.

To his players, Broyles was a Christian southern gentleman above it all, sometimes literally, watching from a tower while the sun set behind him and looking like an apparition. Some of the Razorbacks considered him their Billy Graham, relocated from the pulpit to the sideline and tower. When he addressed his boys, he could have them crying one moment, ready to run through a wall the next. He demanded that his players play tough but clean football, and there was just something about him that made the Razorbacks want to emulate his dignity, at least when they were around him. Yet this always would be an arm's-length relationship, not a full-scale embrace. Broyles wasn't intimidating as much as he was detached, and it was the sort of distance that couldn't be eliminated even when he came down from the tower. Sometimes, it seemed that the southern gentleman was a cold man, incapable of becoming closer to his players. But a few Razorbacks came to believe he held himself back not only to maintain the image of the detached, all-powerful coach with the final authority, but also because Broyles was vulnerable and could be troubled when he had to make tough decisions about players—especially if he had allowed himself to grow close to them. So, his detachment might have been more of a defense mechanism than a calculated coaching strategy. But it all meant that when Broyles did try to be more fuzzy and fatherly as games approached, it made some Razorbacks uneasy because it seemed such a change from the coach's standard operating procedure.

The Razorbacks understood that Broyles was the boss who hired sharp assistants and let them do their jobs—which included the "dirty work" of running off-season conditioning programs, enforcing boot-camp punishment when the boys got carried away, and even pulling strings here and there, including with the National Guard. The head coach as chief executive was not a unique concept, but Broyles already was known to have a brilliance for luring and nurturing bright assistant coaches who could live up to his trust. By the late 1960s, several former Broyles assistants had moved on to be head coaches—Hayden Fry (Southern Methodist), Jim Mackenzie (Oklahoma), Doug Dickey (Tennessee), and Johnny Majors (Iowa State). Barry Switzer, a Razorbacks cocaptain under Broyles in 1959, was on the Broyles staff from 1964 to 1966, then moved to Oklahoma as an assistant in 1966.

In 1969, the Razorback players knew all about the upward mobility of Broyles assistants, too, and they assumed they were working with ascending stars in the coaching profession—including offensive backfield coach Don Breaux, twenty-nine; receivers coach Richard Williamson, twenty-eight; and defensive line coach Charley Coffey, the graybeard at thirty-five. Those were the official designations: In reality, Breaux was the head offensive coach and Coffey ran the defense—the title "coordinator" wasn't yet in vogue.

Broyles was above it all, and not only when he was on that tower.

"He was certainly an excellent coach of coaches," 1969 Razorbacks linebacker Mike Boschetti says. "I don't think he's ever been necessarily a great sideline coach. But as far as behind the scenes, knowing football, and coaching coaches, I don't know how you can have much better. I liked and respected him, but he was aloof and he wasn't the players' coach."

Tailback Bill Burnett says, "Coach Broyles was not a personal guy in terms of his relationship with the players. He was pretty much aloof from all of that. That wasn't his style. If he had tried to be more personable, it wouldn't have worked. That wouldn't have been him. So nobody could really expect it. He worked through his coaches."

Beyond that, as with all head coaches, the players' feelings toward Broyles were dramatically affected by factors such as playing time and individual success. Still, the respect for Broyles was impressively pervasive among the veteran Razorbacks—and has remained strong over the years.

Regardless, most of the Razorbacks knew little of Frank Broyles's background. He was "Coach Broyles," and they didn't really need to know much else.

THE ARKANSAS COACH'S GRANDFATHER, R.A., started a string of small grocery stores in the Atlanta area, and Frank's father, O.T., inherited three of them. Frank was born December 26, 1924, the youngest of five children in the family, which lived in Decatur, adjacent to Atlanta. O.T.'s business weakness was his benevolent extension of credit, and his inability, or unwillingness, to collect. So the stores went under during the Great Depression, and when Frank was about ten, the family lost its house when O.T. couldn't pay the taxes. The clan moved into a rental home formerly owned by R. A. Broyles, and O.T. got back on his feet selling cars.

All along, as Broyles wrote in his 1979 autobiography, *Hog Wild*, Frank immersed himself in sports, memorizing the lineups of all sixteen major-league baseball teams and reading the latest news from the bushes—even the Class D East Texas League—in the back of *The Sporting News*. The gangly teenager became a great athlete at Boys' High in Decatur, and football was his "third" sport, behind baseball and basketball. He got scholarship offers from Georgia, Clemson, and Duke, but then jumped at the chance to stay home and go to Georgia Tech.

He starred for the Yellow Jackets in both basketball and football during the World War II years, enlisting in the Naval Reserves in December 1942—three days before his eighteenth birthday—and staying in school until March 1945. That delay raised some eyebrows among other World War II veterans going over his biography later, but it was neither his fault nor his anticipation that the Navy was the final branch of the service to summon its reserves off the Georgia Tech campus. (College students who based their enlistment choices on predictions about which services would call up their reserves last often discovered that the "scuttlebutt" was off-target.) Broyles was called up, took officer training at Providence, Rhode Island, married his longtime Decatur girlfriend, Barbara Day, and was in San Francisco when the atomic bomb fell on Hiroshima. He was at Pearl Harbor when the Japanese surrendered, rendering moot the question of how many American lives—including lives among the last wave of inductees—would have been lost in an invasion.

Broyles played one more season in both football and basketball with the Yellow Jackets, the former as a quarterback under his mentor, Bobby Dodd. After graduating, he considered an offer from the Chicago Bears, but married players in those days frequently knew it was potential economic suicide for all but the stars to go to the NFL and delay an entry in the "real" job market. Broyles was an assistant coach at Baylor and then Florida before returning to Tech to serve as a Dodd assistant from 1951 to 1956. He applied for the Arkansas head-coaching job in 1955, but Jack Mitchell was hired instead. Broyles's chance came when he was named to succeed a legendary head coach, Don Faurot, at Missouri in 1957. Broyles also was saddled with an idealistic and naive recruiting approach—the "Missouri Plan," which dictated that he could offer scholarships only to high school players from the state. If you wanted the job, you said during the interviews that you could live with the "Missouri Plan," and you maybe even believed it when you said it. But when you tried to work with it in the tough Big Seven Conference, you realized it was a great way to quickly go from being touted as a bright, young coaching prospect to being a fired, failed head coach. He recruited Missouri's first black scholarship players, halfbacks Norris Stevenson from St. Louis and Mel West from Jefferson City, then coached the Tigers to a 5–4–1 record in 1957. He also assumed—correctly, as it turned out—the Missouri Plan soon would be dropped. But when Mitchell left Arkansas to go to Kansas, the Razorbacks hired Broyles away from Missouri. Athletic director John Barnhill, a former Razorbacks football coach himself, hoped Broyles would be both successful and around for longer than his two immediate predecessors, Bowden Wyatt and Mitchell, who had stayed a combined five seasons.

When Broyles arrived, the Razorbacks had a small stadium in Fayetteville and so-so locker-room, training, and practice facilities. They were battling the perception that theirs was a "poor" school in a "poor" state, competing against the seven Texas-based Southwest Conference universities. But Barnhill—"Barnie"—wasn't silly enough to tell his coach he only could recruit in-state prospects. So the Razorbacks' rosters during the Broyles era routinely included players from Oklahoma, Texas, and Louisiana, and occasionally from other states as well.

By 1969, Broyles hadn't only quieted fears that his goal was to return to Georgia Tech as head coach, that he was another mercenary who would use the Razorback job as a stepping-stone; he also had turned the Arkansas job into his empire. Barnhill was easing toward retirement, and he had turned over the decisions about most football program issues to Broyles, including scheduling. Broyles says that when he called his wife, Barbara, that day in March, Barbara told him that ABC Sports executive Roone Arledge had phoned.

Frank was supposed to call him ASAP.

TWO

Shift!

FRANK BROYLES SAYS HE MIGHT HAVE MADE A QUICK CALL to New York from the golf course, but that the substantive conversations about the schedule change took place after he rushed to the small town east of Little Rock, making sure he didn't miss the start of the Razorback Club gathering. He laughs, remembering talking to Arledge, one of the most powerful broadcasting executives in the country, from "a little gym in Lonoke, Arkansas."

Arledge asked if the Razorbacks would move their October 18 game in Fayetteville against Texas to December 6, to serve as the regular-season finale in the centennial year of college football. Somehow, ABC didn't consider a replay of college football's recognized first game, Rutgers' 6–4 victory over Princeton on November 6, 1869, a palatable option. Arledge made the proposal because Carroll "Beano" Cook, the ABC publicist and behind-the-scenes college football guru, had pored over the schedules, sketched out likely scenarios, and suggested Texas-Arkansas be the season-ending game.

"My recommendation involved Penn State and Arkansas finishing the regular season with perfect records and then playing for the national title," Cook says, meaning a possible Nittany Lions–Razorbacks matchup in the Cotton Bowl. "I said we should move Texas-Arkansas to December 6, because I thought Texas *might* be undefeated then, too."

Cook also guessed that Arkansas would beat the Longhorns and finish the regular season undefeated, but the accuracy of that specific prediction wasn't important. His pinpointing of the Texas-Arkansas game itself was brilliant, and he even anticipated that the defending national champion, Ohio State, would be knocked off. "I thought Ohio State would lose to Minnesota, and that's what I told Roone. I was pretty sure Ohio State would lose a game."

Arledge also consulted ABC's top game analyst, Bud Wilkinson, the former University of Oklahoma coach who ran for the United States Senate as a Republican in 1964, but lost to Fred Harris. Moreover, during the transition period following his 1968 election, President Nixon appointed Wilkinson a special consultant.

Broyles remembers Arledge's phone pitch this way: "Frank, Bud Wilkinson is convinced that you and Texas may be playing for the national championship next season and if you would move the game to December, he'll get President Nixon to come."

The *president*? The *new* president?

Broyles says Arledge told him: "President Nixon will be there. Bud has guaranteed us that. If you'll do that, I'll put you on national TV for the opening game next year."

(The other issue was that while ABC would have been attracted to the Texas-Arkansas game, regardless, in the original October 18 afternoon slot, Arledge and network officials noted it would have been scheduled to go up against Game Six of the World Series on NBC. Razorback Stadium didn't have lights, so the game couldn't be moved to that night, either. In theory, the game could have been played at night in War Memorial Stadium in Little Rock, but ABC didn't consider those lights strong enough to ensure a quality telecast. By moving the game back to December 6, it would be further isolated as a special attraction.)

The switch intrigued Broyles, and Arledge told him the NCAA television committee had agreed that the late game would be an "extra" TV appearance, exempt from counting against the limited number of times each team could be on ABC each season. Provisionally, Broyles said OK, as long as Texas agreed and nobody in the university administration strenuously objected. Broyles called his friend, Texas coach and athletic director Darrell Royal (an Oklahoma quarterback under Wilkinson), and after a couple of phone conversations, both coaches conditionally agreed to the switch.

"One of the things I liked about it was we always played them after Oklahoma," Royal says. "My immediate thought was it would be better to catch them in December than right after Oklahoma. Another thing is, if we happened to have injuries, we might have time to get over them by December 6. I quickly agreed to it. As I said, ABC came out looking smarter than a treeful of owls to postpone that game."

Broyles also conferred with Barnhill, telling him, "They think we might be number one and two at the end of the season and playing for the national championship."

"Well, Frank," Barnhill said dryly, "what if you're only playing for the championship of Washington County? Suppose you lose three or four games before that, and it's supposed to be on national TV, and President Nixon is supposed to be there, and he cancels? Wouldn't that be rather embarrassing?"

Perhaps, said Broyles. But Texas had gone 9–1–1 in 1968, winning the final nine after getting the hang of the new triple-option wishbone offense. Arkansas's only loss that season was to Texas, 39–29, and the Razorbacks embarrassed the previously undefeated Georgia Bulldogs, 16–2, in the Sugar Bowl.

Nixon wasn't mentioned when the schedule change was announced. Broyles quickly and successfully lobbied for the installation of Astroturf at Razorback Stadium, saying that it was the only way to guarantee a good playing surface that late in the year in Fayetteville. When the two schools went into spring practice—or into what was called "spring training" throughout southern college football—the big Texas-Arkansas game, usually played in midseason, was isolated at the end of their 1969 schedules.

Nobody knew *how* big it would be.

THREE

Coach Royal

A NATIONAL CHAMPIONSHIP bought you only so much time at the University of Texas, and by the spring of 1968 Darrell Royal was five years removed from coaching the Longhorns to an undefeated season and the No. 1 ranking. That 1963 defense, led by sophomore linebacker Tommy Nobis and senior defensive lineman Scott Appleton, was dominating. The Longhorns lost their best offensive threat, halfback Ernie Koy, to a shoulder separation at midseason, and still went undefeated and beat Roger Staubach and the Navy Midshipmen in the Cotton Bowl. The national championship came in Royal's seventh season in Austin, when he was only thirty-nine.

Yet that raised the standards even higher. More than ever, winning at Texas didn't mean winning seasons, it meant dominating the Southwest Conference and lording it over every one of the six other Texas-based schools in the league. It meant providing the best punchlines of all for Texas Aggie jokes (e.g., "27–0"). It meant going to the Cotton Bowl every January 1 and landing virtually every high school prospect the Longhorns sought in the state, whether the prospect was going to play or ultimately just be kept away from Texas Tech or Southern Methodist or even Rice. And it meant beating the Big Eight Conference's Oklahoma Sooners every year in the heated Red River rivalry in Dallas, enabling the UT boosters to continue forgiving Royal for being an "Okie."

The Longhorns' coach had been forced to grow up fast in Hollis, Oklahoma. His mother, Katy, died in October 1924, when Darrell—her sixth child—was only three months old. When he was sixteen, his father moved the family to California. Darrell hated the West Coast and got permission from his dad, Burley Ray, to return to Oklahoma on his own. After his high school graduation in Hollis, Darrell had an offer to play football at Oklahoma, but he went into the Army Air Corps in 1943 and eventually was trained as a tail gunner on a B-24 bomber. His crew was held back from being sent overseas to be trained for photo reconnaissance missions, and he still was in the United

States when the war ended. In the fall of 1945, he played for the Third Air Force football team, based in Tampa, and was heavily re-recruited by the college coaches. He was a prized prospect, although he weighed only 158 pounds, and he went to OU to play for Jim Tatum. As a senior All-American quarterback in 1949, Royal was twenty-five years old and playing under Tatum's young successor, Bud Wilkinson. To the press, Wilkinson touted his quarterback as a heady coaching candidate, and writers willingly ran with the suggestion, as when Walter Stewart of the *Memphis Commercial-Appeal* wrote after the 1950 Sugar Bowl that Royal "owns one of the most brilliant masses of football cerebellum we've seen caged in one skull. . . . [T]hat night, he gave us a clinical critique which was magnificently lucid and economically complete. He'll make someone a game-winning coach."

Royal's first college job was as an assistant at North Carolina State in 1950. In 1973's *The Darrell Royal Story*, author Jimmy Banks wrote that even before Royal was on the sideline for his first game, he considered quitting the business because he discovered he was petrified of public speaking, which was part of the job for even assistant coaches. As dynamic as he could be in informal situations, or with small groups, standing on a podium was torture for him at first. But he managed to keep his poise and get through a lecture about his experiences as a Split-T quarterback, and about the offense itself, at a coaching clinic on the University of Tennessee campus that July, and the big-name coaches in attendance—familiar with him as a quarterback—found they agreed with the Memphis columnist's assessment. Royal was stamped as a hot coaching prospect before he had coached in a game, and his knowledge of the hot offense of the period—the Split-T—was coveted.

After that season, Tulsa coach Buddy Brothers offered Royal a raise and a promotion to a No. 1 assistant's job, and Royal verbally accepted it. Before he signed a contract, though, Bud Wilkinson called and offered him a job on the OU staff. Royal wanted to take it, but when Brothers made it clear he believed Royal would be going back on his word, the young coach swallowed hard and went to Tulsa. As it turned out, Royal loved the experience, because Brothers allowed him—a college QB only two seasons earlier—complete freedom to run the offense, and the Hurricanes lost only once. Royal's bona fides as a precocious coach were solidified, and Mississippi State coach Murray Warmath hired him away.

Then Royal took the unusual step of accepting the head job with the Edmonton Eskimos of the Canadian Football League's forerunner, the Western Interprovincial Football Union—for a garish $13,500. North of the border, football was a game of limited resources, twelve players, legal forward motion at the snap, a 55-yard line, and a "rouge" single point when the opposition couldn't get the ball out of the end zone. It also was Royal's chance to get his legs as a head coach, and the Eskimos were 17–5. Royal cited the experience when he talked with Mississippi State about returning—this time as the head coach. He went 12–8 in two seasons in Starkville, then 5–5 in a salmon-out-of-water season at the University of Washington in 1956. When the Texas job opened up, Royal left Washington with three years remaining on his contract and became the Longhorns' head coach in 1957—a year ahead of Frank Broyles's move to Arkansas. Royal was 17–13 as a college head coach when he went to Texas, but he was only eight seasons removed from being an All-American quarterback and had only solidified his image as an offensive genius.

One of the naïve assumptions in sports, whether expressed in the media or in the casual chatter of fans, is that players on any team have a monolithic, easily summarized opinion of their coach. Particularly in the late 1960s, it was difficult to be a beloved and winning college football head coach at the same time. Some of the best molders of young men and best-loved coaches *weren't* aloof and did heavily invest their emotions in their players. But that could eat them up, and when they were fired or they resigned, it could be said: *Just not tough enough to be a great head coach.*

Above all, it was—and is—perilous to overgeneralize, even about Frank Broyles. That said, summarizing the players' views of the Arkansas coach for the most part painted a fair picture. With Royal at Texas, it was far more complex. The Longhorns felt a mixture of fear, respect, hatred, anger, confusion, and reverence—and all of those emotions could swirl within one player. Over the years, those who stuck it out in the Royal program tended to forget the rest and remember the respect, and add to it. It's a fair exchange: If they stuck with Royal, he stuck with them, moving mountains for his former players over the years.

"If he never said your name the entire time, you'd be very happy," 1969 guard Mike Dean says of him. "You were scared to death of him, literally scared to death of him. I don't know anybody who wasn't scared to death. Afterward, I realized what he was doing. He told me one time that he practiced a system he called intermittent reinforcement. You never knew if he liked you or he didn't like you. He told me, 'If I was down on you all the time, you'd quit the team. If all I did was praise you, you'd let up.' You never knew where you stood with him. One day he would praise you and the next day he'd make you feel like a piece of dirt. Because of this, we all feared him. To be honest, we didn't really like him. We certainly respected him. I love the man now, but at the time, I just knew if he said my name, it wasn't going to be good."

Linebacker Scott Henderson, a junior in 1969, says of Royal, "Some people thought he was ruthless. Some people thought he was unfair. I always found him to be fair—tough, but fair."

Tight end Randy Peschel says Royal "was a psychologist and motivator second to none. He knew what buttons to push to get you to do what you needed to. I know my appreciation grew for him exponentially after I was done. Maybe others did, but I know I didn't realize at the time what he was doing and how he was doing it and how he was helping me and all of us as a team."

Royal, meanwhile, earned his players' complicated opinion of him by overseeing a sometimes brutal regimen: The "shit" treatment for the scrubs in the Texas program, involving extra practice work, wasn't unique in college football in the 1960s, and it generated bitterness in those who felt they were being punished—or run off. The Monday "Turd Bowls," matching those who hadn't played on Saturday against the freshmen, were legendary for both their sharp-edged competitiveness and their implicit punishment. The upperclassmen were angry at having to play on Mondays and not Saturdays. "It was the freshmen against everybody in the world," says 1969 All-American tackle Bob McKay, who went through the Turd Bowls as a freshman in 1966. "The sophomores were the worst because they had just gotten out of it, and they treated you like shit anyway. They just took delight in trying to kick your ass, so you had to learn pretty quick that you had to stand up for yourself, and the only friends you had were the other freshmen."

Similarly infamous were the off-season conditioning drills under veteran trainer Frank Medina—drills that some players concluded were tougher for the marginal players. "Medina was somewhat of a henchman," guard Bobby Mitchell says. "He was running people off, really." Others thought Medina's workout program was egalitarian hell. "He was the one who kept us in shape," Mike Dean says. "We were in incredible shape and he deserves some credit for our success." Regardless, Medina considered the workouts biblical trials, challenging the Longhorns to measure their faith. It also was rationalized as a Darwinian test in a tough sport: Only the strong would survive, and maybe they even would contribute to the program. If they stuck it out but didn't play, they still would be stronger and better men for it, wouldn't they? And if they didn't survive, if they quit or dropped out of the program, they weren't strong enough to be missed.

That's just how it was.

———————

THE NUMBERS GAME WAS COLD: Texas annually brought in about fifty scholarship freshman players, the elite of the state's prospects. Even when the lack of a ceiling on the total number of scholarship players in the program lessened the need for attrition, the numbers were unmanageable if all the scholarship players remained in the program. If they left cussing your program, that wasn't a tragedy. They hadn't been playing for anyone else in the league. If they transferred, it often was to where they could play right away, and that wasn't possible within the Southwest Conference because of the transfer rules. It's naïve to assume that everyone who left did so *only* or even primarily because of the physical rigors; players didn't like seeing their name on a little circular disk hanging in the seventh slot below the position name on the depth chart board, and they often wanted to go somewhere they could play. Or they decided to end their college football careers on the spot. But if they stayed with Royal and the Longhorns, they knew they were subject to exhausting physical workouts and caustic reviews.

"When Coach Royal came off his tower at practice, you hoped to hell he turned right because that meant the defense screwed up and it wasn't us," McKay says. "The thing is, it was a different time. We didn't ask questions. When we were told to do something . . . hell, there were three hundred people on the field at any one time. If you didn't like the way things were going, they didn't give a shit, you were more than welcome to leave. It wasn't, 'Well, do we think this is going to work, do we really want to do this?' It wasn't up for discussion."

As the head of that Texas program, Royal *was* universally respected, if the definition included the understanding that he was the supreme power. When the Longhorns gathered on Sunday to watch game film as a full team, there was plenty of collegial chatter in the room as players filed in, sat down, and waited. Then, as Royal walked in from the back, the silence followed him up the aisle like a wave, until those in the first few rows sensed it and shut up even before the coach passed them.

And the odds were pretty strong that none of the players in the room would have a personal conversation with Royal any time soon. In Fayetteville, Frank Broyles seemed uncomfortable with closeness; in Austin, Darrell Royal seemed disdainful of it. Everyone understood that, including Bob McKay and defensive tackle Leo Brooks, both stars. "A guy from a newspaper out in West Texas, where we were from, talked to us, and he couldn't understand that we just didn't walk in and talk with Coach Royal," McKay says. "That would be like me going to play with rattlesnakes. I'm smart enough to know that you don't do that. Coach Royal was always nice, but he was Coach Royal. I didn't stop in to shoot the shit. It wasn't something you did for fun. I told that kid I was in his office five times in my college career and four of them weren't worth a damn." The fifth, McKay said, was late in the 1969 season when Royal called him in and told him he had been named an All-American, but that he needed to keep it quiet until the official announcement. At the Thanksgiving game at Texas A&M, Royal saw McKay's parents after the game and congratulated them. They asked why.

Later, Royal approached McKay.

"You didn't tell 'em?"

"No, sir, you told me not to tell anybody, so I didn't tell anybody."

Royal's authority was unquestioned. Yet by Texas standards, Royal's program struggled mightily from 1965 to 1967. At Texas, 6–4 records were abominable, and that was their record in each of the three regular seasons. The Longhorns beat Mississippi after the '66 season in the Bluebonnet Bowl to finish 7–4, but Royal vetoed any thought of going to a bowl game after the '67 season. The Longhorns didn't deserve to go anywhere, he declared. It really didn't matter all that much that the Texas boosters—the men with the money and the influence—were applying heat, because Royal was plenty hot himself. He was going to do something about it, ordering that the 1968 spring training and the 1968 fall practices be living hell. He didn't even try to pretend it was something other than a test. The candy asses, those who couldn't take it, those who didn't want it bad enough, were going to be gone, one way or another.

"We were coming off three 6–4s," Royal says of the 1968 practices. "You bet it was hard. You always do that. You always had it stern enough to find out who wanted to and who didn't. Who wanted to late? Who wanted to when you were behind? Who wanted to when they were tired? Who wanted to, when it would be easier to take a lazy step or two? You have to push them hard enough to find that out."

By 1968, Royal was ahead of his time in one area, disdaining water deprivation, which was a part of the testing mechanism for so long, from coast to coast: In 1962, reserve sophomore guard Reggie Grob suffered heatstroke during fall practice, went into a coma, and died four days before the season opener in Austin against the Oregon Ducks. Royal's angst was palpable, and he openly talked and agonized about whether he and his staff should have been able to prevent Grob's death.

"Coach Royal had gone through a tough time, when that kid had died," guard Randy Stout says. "We always had water, all the time."

In 1968, they weren't thirsty, but they were so sore they often couldn't even make the walk from the stadium to the football dorm, or vice versa, on the way to the second practice of the day in the fall, without stopping or lying down to rest. Royal's pride and his job were on the line, and if he was going to go down, he was going to go down with the toughest.

"I wasn't surprised that it was that tough," Scott Henderson says of 1968 spring ball. "I *was* surprised that so many guys quit and left. But Royal made it very clear it was going to be whoever wants to play." Henderson had undergone knee surgery after his freshman season, so he was watching the practices, not participating. The rehabilitation from his surgery to repair a torn anterior cruciate ligament was difficult, but Henderson wasn't sure it was any worse than what he witnessed on the field.

Bob McKay was more certain. He had to drop out of spring ball to have rotator cuff surgery. "I swore to God, I was the happiest man in the world when I got to go to the hospital."

Bill Zapalac, then a sophomore-to-be tight end who turned into a star linebacker for the '69 team, says those spring drills were "hellacious, and they weeded out some of the upperclassmen. I don't know if it was intentional, but a lot of people quit."

The survivors added it up: About thirty players quit, and about thirty more were hurt in spring ball. They weren't just the scrubs, either. Tommy Orr was expected to challenge to start at tackle. *Gone.* Jack Freeman, the guy in the dorm room next to McKay, had played for Odessa Permian High School, where they were as tough as they come. *Gone.* McKay managed to say goodbye, but star tight end Deryl Comer—McKay's roommate—was so drained he couldn't even get up. Freeman understood. Comer himself "quit" during spring drills, but came back after a day. Everyone understood that the staff wouldn't have let him come back—he paid for his impudence with extra sprints—if he had been a Turd Bowl regular.

Survivors, such as undersized and unheralded guard Mike Dean, saw themselves move up the depth chart without doing all that much except making it through practice and not throwing up on Royal when he came down from the tower. "That was one of the most difficult times I have ever, ever had," Ted Koy, eventually the cocaptain and starting right halfback for the 1969 team, says of the 1968 spring drills. "We would hit from the time we broke from calisthenics. Coach Royal was going to go the next year with the survivors."

James Street, a backup quarterback in 1967 as a sophomore, also was fortunate enough to miss the '68 spring practices: He was pitching for the Longhorns baseball team, under first-year head coach Cliff Gustafson. Street came over to watch the football workouts and wince. He remembers Royal saying, "The circle's getting tighter, we're losing a lot of players, but the ones staying here want to play ball."

Yes, that was 1968, but it was crucial in the development of the 1969 team. Royal and the staff knew they had "The Worster Bunch"—featuring fullback Steve Worster—coming into their sophomore years for the 1968 season, to go with a holdover starting quarterback, Bill Bradley. The Texas coaches were pondering installing an offense that suited the prospects' talents and also took advantage of the skills of the upperclassmen survivors. The fact that the Longhorns didn't come up with the new offense until *after* spring ball was one indication that those workouts primarily were designed as a screening process. The survivors had the guts to stick around, and they weren't always the biggest and the most talented, but they had spunk and, in most cases, brains. Sometimes it seemed sane young men wouldn't have put up with the hell the Royal staff put them through, but they did, and he was going to take advantage of the thinning ranks.

After that cornerstone '68 spring training, Royal told his new offensive coach, Emory Bellard: *Come up with a scheme that takes advantage of what we're gonna have left.*

AS A HIGH SCHOOL HEAD COACH, BELLARD won Texas state championships at three different schools. After San Angelo High won the 1966 Class AAAA title under Bellard, he finally made the jump to the college game, joining Royal's staff as linebackers coach. Following the third 6–4 season, Royal reorganized his staff, making Bellard the offensive backfield coach—effectively the coordinator.

Bellard doodled and tinkered in his office for hours, pondering splits and formations and pitchouts and belly rides and quarterback improvisations. He was barely a year removed from coaching high school, yet he eventually went into the office of one of college football's legends and said: *This is what we should do.* Bellard suggested a four-man backfield, a variation of the full-house "T" formation with the fullback within arm's length of the quarterback and the halfbacks a couple of yards back on each side. The "T" had become a "Y," and the basic triple-option play would start with the quarterback "riding" the ball in the fullback's belly before deciding—quickly—whether to more emphatically jam in a handoff, or pull the ball out and go down the line himself. Then the quarterback's second and third options would be to cut upfield himself or pitch out to the trailing halfback—the halfback who had started on the other side of the formation. The basic formation would call for a tight end on one side (the "strong" side), a split end on the other.

"It took some guts on his part to do it," Bellard says of Royal. "We got a bunch of guys together who had completed their eligibility who were in summer school to look at it. One time, I played quarterback and another time I found one. I messed with it to see if the quarterback could do the things we were going to ask him to do, and I felt if I could do it, I knew darned well I could teach it to an athlete."

In late July, James Street got a call in his hometown of Longview. James, he was told, it might be a good idea to be back in Austin by August 1, so you can be a part of the first look at a new offense.

The introduction was low-key. "We were out there working out," Street says, "and they said, 'Let's set up here and see how this works, see what y'all think about this.'"

With the fullback so close, the quarterbacks—Bill Bradley and Street—found it impossible to "ride" the fullback long enough to survey the defensive reaction. "Bradley and I kept saying we could do it," Street says, "but neither of us thought it would work. You just didn't have enough time."

After the coaches moved the fullback a yard farther back, the timing began to work. Street and Bradley discovered the offense wasn't complicated. All it required was intuitive and intelligent reaction on the fly and taking care of the ball.

The Longhorns had a terrific holdover halfback, Chris Gilbert, and putting *both* Steve Worster and Ted Koy—each previously listed as fullbacks—in the backfield with Bradley and Gilbert was an astute deployment of resources, not just a strategic wrinkle. The split end was going to be Charles "Cotton" Speyrer, a speedy sophomore from Port Arthur who wasn't able to play freshman football because of shoulder surgery. He was a highly recruited running back in high school and wasn't sold on the position switch. "I thought that was a demotion because UT was notorious for not passing the ball," Speyrer says. "I had my head down a little bit." As it turned out, though, with the Longhorns overloaded with running back talent, it was the best thing for Speyrer—and his future.

Royal considered the wishbone a "modernization" of the Split-T he rode into coaching and up the ranks. "You make it a triple option instead of a double option," Royal says. "It's kind of unique that the side you're running the ball to, you can leave two guys totally unblocked and turn them loose."

Indeed, that was revolutionary: The offense allowed the reactions of one or two unblocked defensive players to help determine the quarterback's decision. That freed an offensive lineman or two to charge and block elsewhere, going after linebackers or defensive backs.

There were variations, though: On counter options, the fullback went one way and the quarterback did a reverse pivot and headed the other. On simple power plays, the fullback led the way through the hole for the halfback, who took a handoff, or the halfback took a handoff from Street after the usual "belly" ride with Worster. Passes usually came off play-action fakes to the fullback, with Speyrer typically the primary receiver.

Bellard didn't even think the offense was revolutionary enough to give it a pretentious name: To him, it was a variation of the veer option offense, using three running backs instead of two. He says the original name for the package was "right-left," which he thought emphasized that the triple-option principles could work to either side—meaning not just right and left, but also to either the split-end or tight-end side. To Bellard, that was "balance."

Bellard and the staff taught the system to the Longhorns in the fall of 1968. And as with all experiments, there were early problems that had to be worked out in games. Bradley struggled and lost the No. 1 quarterback job after the Longhorns tied Houston 20–20 in the 1968 opener (in front of the Houston writer Mickey Herskowitz, who coined the name "wishbone-T" for the Texas offense), and then lost 31–22 to Texas Tech in the second game. In that Tech loss, Worster, Gilbert, and Koy combined for over 300 yards on the ground and Street replaced Bradley in the third quarter. Street was named the starter in the middle of the next week, while Bradley's handling of the demotion earned him the respect of his teammates. When the change seemed imminent, he broke the tension at practice by running pass patterns as a wide receiver, loosening the cord on his sweatpants and allowing them to drop down in midroute. Within two weeks, he was a full-time safety, where he almost immediately was one of the best at the position in the country.

What was going on here? Three straight four-loss seasons, an 0–1–1 start, a new offense, and a switch to an unproven quarterback? Was this time for panic, time for the assistant coaches to get their résumés ready or hope that Royal would get another job and take them with him if he got fired?

But then the Longhorns raced through the rest of the 1968 season undefeated, setting conference records for total offense, rushing yardage, and average points in conference games. Each week, as one of the senior leaders, Bradley would say something along the lines of: "Don't worry, boys, Rat'll get it done," "Rat" being James Street, the little quarterback who replaced him. The Longhorns beat Arkansas, finishing in a tie with the Razorbacks for the Southwest Conference title and going to the Cotton Bowl because of the head-to-head victory. Texas drilled Tennessee 36–13 in that game, finishing 9–1–1. Although Chris Gilbert's career was over, the Longhorns were certain their period of mediocrity had ended. And much of the optimism was based on the success of the wishbone, and on the records of the backs returning for 1969.

FOUR

Slick and Company

IT BECAME A CLICHÉ. James Street? *Winner.* He wasn't big, listed charitably at five-foot-eleven, stretching the truth by at least two inches, and at 175 pounds. He wasn't startlingly fast. Even his decision-making in the wishbone wasn't perfect, but he always seemed to make it work—if not on one particular play, then eventually. As a passer, he could look like the star baseball pitcher he was in the spring, throwing a fastball through traffic. He also, occasionally, could look like a Hungarian placekicker screwing around on the side of the field. But there was just something about the man his teammates called not just "Rat," but "Slick." His shiny black hair and long sideburns were reminiscent of an Elvis Presley impersonator. And when he got talking? He was a high-energy filibuster, a boulder rolling downhill, Niagara Falls, Jim Brown on a sweep: unstoppable.

With so much emphasis placed on his "winning" qualities, some could mistakenly infer that was a way of downplaying his shortcomings as an athlete. On the contrary, he was a terrific all-around athlete. An undersized dynamo without a powerful arm, he wasn't the prototypical quarterback. It was a huge upset that he beat out Bradley, one of the most highly touted recruits in 1960s college football. He did because the new offense worked so much better with the chatterbox calling—and then running—the plays. That's how it was with Street: You measured him not only by what he did himself, but by how others reacted to his presence.

He had been scrambling all his life, growing up on what passed for the wrong side of the tracks in Longview, Texas, about fifty miles from Shreveport, Louisiana. James's father, Grover, had health problems and was a paranoid schizophrenic, convinced someone was lurking behind the next tree and hoping to ruin his life. "He was pretty smart and he would come up with all these plans about how people were trying to get him," James says. Grover zealously coached his two boys, Sewell and James, building a little backstop in the backyard with a cutout of the strike zone and telling them they *must* hit each corner of the rectangle. "I never can remember him saying I did any-thing good," James says. "It was always expected of you to do good. But the reason you did good was because you were prepared. He would make you prepare."

Sewell was older, and he felt the brunt of the attention, but when James came home after pitching a no-hitter as a ten-year-old, Grover chewed him out because he couldn't remember every "out" pitch.

"What does it matter?" snapped little James. "I struck him out!"

"It doesn't matter today," his father said sharply. "But it will matter some-day! Someday, it will come back to haunt you if you don't understand what you're doing!"

Grover left and returned several times. Ultimately, he said he had to go back to his native Oklahoma—alone. "The world was just trying to get him and he had to move off," James, who was about twelve, says. "I didn't under-stand it, and I got used to him not being there. I learned a lot from him be-fore he left, though."

James's mother, Helen, and Grover divorced, and she started working at a department store most of the day, then on the telephone for a home products firm for a few hours, then frequently baby-sat at night. "The amazing part about her was the next morning at six-thirty, she would have breakfast cooked," James says. "So when I got up, there were eggs or pancakes. She seemingly never tired. I think I got a lot of my work ethic from her."

In junior high, James worked in the school cafeteria to earn free meals. "I didn't look at that as a bad thing because I could get all the food I wanted!" James says. "We didn't have much at home, but I didn't know we didn't have anything."

The Streets didn't have a television. James's treasured possession was his little radio, and he listened to the scratchy broadcasts of the St. Louis Cardi-nals games at night, dreaming of someday being in the rotation and hearing Harry Caray calling his strikeouts.

He was a running back until ninth grade, when he switched to quarter-back. When Ty Bain, a new Longview High Lobos football coach, showed up, he blanched when he saw one of his quarterbacks still working in the school cafeteria. "I need you to quit working," said Bain, who had grown up poor himself. "A quarterback shouldn't be working back there in the back."

James quit, and each Monday, Bain handed Street an envelope. Inside were two one-dollar bills and two quarters. "That was fifty cents a day for my sister and me to eat on," Street says. "I thought I was rich!"

The owner of a local restaurant, Jackson's Café, also tried to help the fiery little quarterback. "Mr. Jackson said he wanted to give me some money so I could buy some clothes," James says. "I never thought I didn't have clothes. What did I need clothes for? I wouldn't take it. So they came back to me and asked if I would work weekends. I said I'd love to, and I'd work from seven in the morning until two in the afternoon on Saturday and Sunday. He always paid me cash and I might have gotten ten dollars for the weekend. It seemed like a million at the time."

James's older brother, Sewell, by then was playing minor-league baseball, and James was hoping to do the same thing. College? No way could the family afford it, and he didn't dream anyone would offer him a scholarship. Longview's biggest star was Loyd Phillips, who had gone off to play football at the University of Arkansas, and Loyd's younger brother, Terry Don, was a year older than James and one of his closest friends. Both the Phillips boys were big enough to attract the attention of the college coaches and good enough to keep it; coaches had to look beyond Street's size—to his heart and his competitiveness.

As a junior at Longview High in the spring of 1965, Street was pitching at Texarkana when an errant between-innings toss by a teammate nailed him in the face. Blood poured from his nose, coming in intermittent floods. All Street did was take a towel to the mound and put it down by the resin bag. Terry Don Phillips and the rest of Street's teammates were incredulous. Years later, Street and Phillips still have a friendly disagreement over that incident. "He should remember it," Street says. "He threw the ball that nailed me!"

Responds Phillips: "I *know* he thinks that, but I'm innocent! The point is, he got hit right in the nose and the cheekbone and he's bleeding all over. I mean, *all* over. He had a towel, his nose is bleeding, and he'd wipe off his nose between pitches and go right on. He was just a great, great competitor."

When James was a senior at Longview, Terry Don was an Arkansas freshman. With the Phillips boys gone, the Longview Lobos didn't have much talent around the holdover quarterback. As his senior season began, the scrambling Street was regarded as one of the top quarterbacks in East Texas, but a marginal college prospect. Loyd and Terry Don tried to convince the Arkansas coaching staff to recruit him, but even Street still was thinking baseball first and was surprised when Southwest Conference football coaches started contacting him during the Lobos' 5–5 season. He weighed 155 pounds. He was going to play baseball, and when a Texas A&M coach showed up at Longview High and asked him if he would play football for the Aggies, Street responded: "Naw, I don't want to cut my hair off."

Oklahoma State and Texas Tech also contacted him, and he started to figure out that college was a bona fide alternative to signing a pro baseball contract right out of high school. Texas—the Longhorns!—asked him to make a visit to Austin. It wasn't that Street lacked confidence; he just didn't picture himself as a football player.

Street also was considering another school—the University of Arkansas. The Phillipses' lobbying efforts finally worked: The Razorback staff contacted Street, and then Frank Broyles called. It wasn't an all-out blitz, and it might have been a case of Broyles getting Loyd Phillips—one of the top players in the country—off his back, but Broyles asked James to add the Razorbacks to his list of possibilities. "You have some friends here, James," Broyles said, "and we wish you'd consider becoming a Razorback."

The thought was comforting: He could rejoin the big Phillips boys, his pals, in Fayetteville.

James sat down for a chat with his surrogate father, Mr. Jackson, at the café. Street said he was leaning toward going to Arkansas, or at least making an official visit there.

"What about baseball?" Jackson asked. "Isn't baseball what you want to do?"

Texas's baseball program, then still under longtime coach Bibb Falk, was much higher-profile than the one at Arkansas. Jackson's daughter was a UofA student, but he told Street that Texas sounded like a better fit for a dual-sport athlete. Street went to Austin for his official tour and visited with Darrell Royal. The Texas coach challenged him, bringing up the name of the all-everything quarterback the Longhorns had landed the year before—Bill Bradley.

"I guess a lot of schools are throwing Bradley up to you," Royal said.

"Yes, sir."

"You know," Royal said slowly, "if you start running away from competition now, you'll never know if you could have played with the best or competed against the best. You'll *never* know that."

It was as if Royal was daring Street to keep pitching as the blood ran down his face. Street never took that recruiting visit to Arkansas, and by the time he was a senior at Texas, he was the entrenched starter, the established master of the triple option, and a cocaptain—along with halfback Ted Koy and linebacker Glen Halsell. He also was the baseball program's ace pitcher, and on baseball trips he roomed with another dual-sport player—outfielder/tight end Randy Peschel. "He just did not take defeat in anything," Peschel says. "He wouldn't accept it and wouldn't let anybody around him accept it."

WHEN 1969 PRESEASON PRACTICE BEGAN, Street had just returned from a summer of playing semipro baseball in Colorado with the Boulder Collegians, a team of college all-stars. The Longhorns' Press Day came after a few days of daily double practices, and Street was wearing shorts and a bandage on his leg when he went through a mass interview with reporters.

"What's that bandage for? Does it hurt?" a writer asked.

Street couldn't help himself. His mouth got going, and he couldn't stop it.

Well, as you guys know, I was in Colorado for the summer, playing baseball, and I worked as a substitute mail carrier on the side, and just the other day, a dog bit me, and now they're checking it for rabies and they're a little worried that I may go mad . . .

The writers were scribbling. As he continued, Street was starting to let saliva drip from his mouth, and he was on the verge of laughing, too.

Just kidding, fellas.

He was so adept at scraping the line of scrimmage as he ran the triple option, Street often was kicked by his linemen. That's why he often had a bandage on his leg.

Royal was in the room, and he was livid.

"Nobody likes a smartass," Royal snapped after the session.

Street resolved to follow the coach's guidelines for dealing with the press: Be polite, be classy, compliment your opponents, don't say anything controversial, and then compliment your opponents again to make sure everybody got the point.

But to James Street, life was a revival meeting, a filibuster, a soapbox. "I tell you what, I can't stress enough that James Street was such a catalyst, not only with his play, but with being in the huddle," Cotton Speyrer says.

"James was a guy you couldn't ever get to shut up," a laughing Steve Worster says. "He was a great guy, and there was just something about James Street you didn't see until you put him on the football field. He was just a winner, plain and simple. The guy obviously had talent, but he threw a pass like a wounded duck. I mean, he threw it kind of like I would. That was fine, because we didn't have to throw it very often."

Once the wishbone got rolling, in fact, the Longhorns hammered everyone. With Street usually starting the play by extending the ball into Worster's belly, and with the Texas offensive linemen making the decisions easier because they were blowing away the defensive front, Texas looked unstoppable.

———————

BRIDGE CITY, TEXAS, is in Bayou Country, and it's as much Cajun as Cowboy. Steve Worster had been one of the top high school players in Texas since he was a sophomore—and in Texas, that's saying a lot. His future Longhorns teammate, defensive tackle Carl White, played against Bridge City and Worster in the state championship game in Waco when Worster was a senior. White played for McKinney High.

"I twisted Worster's foot all the way around backward in a pile," White says. "He got up and he didn't even limp. I went back to the huddle and I told the guys, 'Guys, we're in trouble.' They beat us 30–6 and he just ran over us all day long. He was the strongest and toughest two-hundred-pounder I ever saw."

So when Worster was one of the most highly recruited high school seniors in the country, it wasn't automatic that he would go to Texas. The other schools came hard, and this was a time when "hard" meant that coaches or—more often—boosters might offer many enticements beyond a scholarship.

Steve's father, R.B., was a pumper on the oil rigs for Sun Oil, and he had preached to his son for years about the principle of hard work—even get-oil-in-your-hair and under-your-nails and every-muscle-aches hard work—so the offers of riches were incomprehensible to the seventeen-year-old.

At first, Fred Akers—then the offensive backfield coach—recruited Worster for Texas. Almost everyone liked the affable Akers, who had been a quarterback and defensive back for Frank Broyles at Arkansas. As a high school junior in Blytheville, in fact, Akers represented Arkansas at the American Legion–sponsored 1954 Boys Nation convention in Washington, D.C., winning an appointment in the convention's mock government to the directorship of the Federal Bureau of Investigation. (Akers met both President Dwight Eisenhower and Vice President Richard Nixon; a few years later, another Arkansas representative to Boys Nation, Bill Clinton, met President John Kennedy.) But Akers and Worster didn't hit it off. Worster considered Akers "a little Napoleon." Finally, Royal stepped in himself and was the point man in the recruiting of Worster.

Worster swears that Texas was "the only school that . . . didn't try to buy me. With my background—small-town and blue-collar family—that impressed me a lot."

There was an underground system of perks at Texas, too, but it wasn't as overt as at some other schools. It often involved boosters cozying up to players more than "buying" them. Some of the benefits, such as free movie passes for the players and their dates at Austin theaters, were commonplace (and legal) in the era. The NCAA hadn't clamped down on what players did with their game tickets, either, so when players around the country sold theirs for huge profits, that didn't get the program in trouble. It was the players' spending money for the year, and it could be the buyers' way of sponsoring specific players. At Texas, the middleman often was the owner of a particular clothing store on the "drag"—Guadalupe Street—adjacent to campus. Some players took their tickets to him and the clothier sold them, passing the money—minus a cut presumably—back to the players. The players knew him as a bit of a con man, but he also cut deals to help keep them dressed nicer than the typical college student. Again, the significant point is that the Texas coaches weren't involved in the players' ticket business (at some schools, they were, and the ticket profiteering was part of the recruiting spiel and a staff mechanism to keep star players happy). At Texas and Arkansas, where the players also sold their tickets for spending money, the players didn't feel as if they were doing anything wrong, and in the context of the times, and the NCAA rules of the time, they weren't.

Even by 1960s standards, though, the offers Steve Worster heard were extraordinary. Louisiana governor John McKeithen invited the "Bridge City Bomber" to breakfast at the mansion in Baton Rogue. "And then he takes me into the little sitting room," Worster says, "and he puts his arm around me and says, 'Don't you worry, I know your background, as long as you're here you'll be working for me here at the state capitol.'"

Of course, that meant *if* he went to LSU.

Worster says LSU boosters "offered to relocate my dad to Baton Rogue with a better position through his company." A Texas A&M booster, Worster recalls, told him: "You'd be assigned to an alum, and you become his and he'll take care of you. . . . We assign you a number. There's a clothing store and there's a gas station and there's this and there's that, and all you have to do is go in and sign that number."

Worster also sat down with one well-known head coach, from a school outside the Southwest Conference. "He didn't pull any punches," Worster says. "He came right out and handed me a pad and a pen and told me to write down what I wanted. It got really ridiculous. They insulted me."

Did he write anything?

"No, I didn't," Worster says. "And he got pissed off when I didn't, too! He really got upset. I didn't understand him. He said, 'I'm going to take care of you like we took care of [a star player]."

Worster says the head coach took back the pad and started "writing things down. 'Apartment, money, your own car.' Then he says, '[Star player] even had his own tailor, you want a tailor?' 'Tailor?' I said. 'Hell, I don't even own a suit or a sport coat. What would I do with a tailor?'"

With offers swirling and the pressure mounting, Worster met with Royal. Worster says Royal told him: "Look, I know what you're going through. I know that you're getting a lot of things thrown at you. Let me tell you something, if we bought people, believe me, you'd be the first person we bought. But we don't buy people. We've offered you a phenomenal scholarship, a great education at a wonderful university. You come here, I promise I'll do everything in my ability to see you graduate."

Worster took him up on the offer, lending his name to the recruiting class and showing up at Texas in the fall of 1967. By the 1969 season, Worster already had shown he would live up to the hype. "Worster was the toughest son of a bitch I ever saw in my life," tackle Bob McKay says. "He was a real incentive to get the hell out of the way because if you didn't, he'd run right up your ass. He'd knock the shit out of you. Every time we snapped the ball, he got hit, he took a beating. It didn't even faze him."

"I really never looked at it that way," Worster says. "I looked at it like I got my hands on the ball first, before anyone else did, and if the hole was there, I got the ball."

When he reported for fall practice in 1969, his hair was shaggy—shaggier than Royal liked. By then, even coaches were growing their hair out a bit, but Royal touched Worster's locks and "suggested" a haircut. Worster got one: To him, it wasn't a big deal, but at other schools around the country, players were arguing for the right to wear their hair longer and battling against ridiculously arbitrary and increasingly out-of-date standards of appearance. For some coaches and boosters around the country, the primary standard of discipline was hair length. If it was short, you had "discipline," even if your nights were spent drinking beer, playing pool, and beating up "hippies." If it was long, if you looked like a damn drummer for a rock band, you were "undisciplined," even if you had a 4.0 grade-point average and were headed for medical school. In many places, black athletes were battling for the right to wear the wider "Afro" style, but at Texas, nobody had to worry about whether a big-time "Afro" showed up on one of the players in the 1969 team picture. There were no black players in the 1969 team picture.

That fall, the Longhorns moved from the former athletic dormitory, Moore-Hill Hall, across the street from Memorial Stadium, to a nearby new high-rise, Jester Center. The athletes occupied a few floors on the men's wing of the Jester complex, but not the whole building, as was the case at Moore-Hill. One thing, though, didn't change from Moore-Hill: Worster loved to load rock albums on the stereo of his buddy and roommate, backup tight end Jay Cormier, and blast the place. (His teammates, many of whom were into country music, would scream: *What's with that shit?* The "shit" was the Rolling Stones, Led Zeppelin, Jimi Hendrix.)

Worster was part of a Woodstock fringe among the Grand Ole Opry. But when he wanted a real good smile, he would take a walk through the halls and notice the Playboy Playmate posters and all the conventionally collegiate jock adornments, including the Dr Pepper bottles that doubled for spittoons for the many tobacco chewers. And then he would come to Ted Koy's room. Ted had pictures up, too—of his prize livestock.

––––––––––––

KOY WAS THE SENIOR COCAPTAIN IN 1969, and he *looked* like a captain, standing there with his hands on his hips with his jostled dark hair and Hollywood looks. He was very earnest and serious, and the guys just couldn't get him to lighten up, and after a while, they gave up trying. None of this boozing for him, and when the women were throwing themselves at the players, especially after games? Nope, that wasn't for Ted, not the Boy Scout. If he went to the parties, he drank soft drinks or maybe Shirley Temples—and didn't blush. He didn't lord that over anyone, either; there was no air of superiority.

He was a tough bastard on the field, though.

His name was famous in Texas, even before he arrived. Ernie Koy, Sr., was a Longhorns star from 1930 to 1932 before going into professional baseball, playing five seasons as an outfielder in the major leagues, with Brooklyn, St. Louis, Cincinnati, and Philadelphia. When his baseball career ended, Ernie went home to Bellville, Texas, and bought a five-and-dime store and enough acreage to provide a working environment for his sons—Ernie Jr. and Ted. The sons built fences, hauled hay, handled the animals, and then—and only then—got to play football or baseball.

"I wore blue jeans, a shirt, a hat, and was outside all day," Ted recalls. "It was so humid and I sweat so much, my leather belt *never* dried."

Ted was in high school when Ernie Jr. started at halfback for the 1963 national champions. When Ted was a high school senior, coaches from other schools came calling.

"I thought, 'You know, I know nothing except the University of Texas, how do I know that's where I want to go?'" Koy says. He liked Baylor coach John Bridgers and the school. He investigated Texas A&M because of its veterinary school. And he scheduled a trip to Notre Dame for January of his senior year, but his trip sponsor called and said it was snowing like crazy in South Bend, and they might need to make alternative travel plans.

Snow? "So I said thank you, but I had eliminated Notre Dame," Koy says. "And I got to thinking that we were a close-knit family and I didn't know if my parents would be able to traipse across the states to my games."

He ended up where everyone thought he would end up—in Austin. As a sophomore in 1967, he was the backup fullback and tailback, going back and forth between positions, and then settled in as the starting right halfback in the wishbone for 1968. Although he was a captain in 1969, the guys knew to be a little careful what they said around Koy, because they had a *reporter* in the huddle. Koy majored in journalism and hoped to go into public relations, or maybe even a sports information office, after his graduation. He was fascinated with the work the athletic department's sports publicists did: Jones Ramsey and his assistant, Bill Little, entertained the press, and they wrote features on a Texas letterhead that ended up in newspapers around the state, billed as "special" stories. ("AUSTIN [Special]—Darrell Royal looked around . . .")

So during the 1969 season, the Longhorns' captain wrote a sports column that appeared every Wednesday in *The Daily Texan*. It wasn't a case of a jock talking to a writer, and the writer using those words—approximately—to produce a story under the athlete's name. Koy sat down at the manual typewriter, slid the sheets of paper—with carbon paper between them—into the roller, and wrote his column himself.

In the November 5 *Texan*, three days after the Longhorns beat SMU 45–14 to go 4–0, Koy's column was about James Street. Koy wrote of the Longhorns' huddle:

"Street is a master at 30-second psychology. To understand the Texas huddle, one must know the Texas quarterback. Street is controlled bedlam. He is an excitable and emotional personality who completely thrives on competition.

"Street has never been defeated in his life—outscored perhaps, but never defeated. He is the type of fellow you would want on your side if you were fighting the guys down the block. It's not that he's physically imposing, but that he never quits. He's gutty, nervy and explosive; a real fireball of seething energy."

Koy quoted his own quarterback:

"'Aw, I'm no different than any other quarterback,' retorts Street when quizzed about his tactics. 'Well, maybe I might talk a little more than the other quarterbacks. I like to get things moving.'"

Koy also told of a huddle during Street's first start, against Oklahoma State in the third week of the 1968 season:

"During one of Texas' offensive drives against the Cowboys, a penalty and a busted play put a temporary damper on things. When the ten offensive men stuck their heads in the huddle to receive the next call, they were met with a barrage of words from a wild-eyed Street. He was yelling about guts and pride and integrity and you could feel everyone's adrenaline begin to flow. All at once, he said, 'OK, on two, ready, break.' People went storming out of the huddle ready to run through a wall and then it dawned on everyone. In the course of his 'talk,' James had forgotten to call the play."

Koy didn't use the first person, or otherwise spell out that he was something other than a carbon-stained wretch, sitting in the press box at games. Nor did an editor's note spell out why this writer with the mug shot at the top of the column seemed to have so much inside information. It wasn't necessary, everyone knew Ted Koy. And they also knew that it wasn't Ted Koy's style to tell *all*, which in this case would have meant mentioning that there were other occasions when Street got so wound up, speechmaking and exhorting, one of his teammates would pipe up: *Shut up and call the play!*

If it had been up to Ted Koy to corral Street's orations, he would have said, "James, please . . ."

The other halfback wouldn't have said anything at all.

SOME OF LEFT HALFBACK JIM BERTELSEN'S TEAMMATES would have had to guess which state "up there" was Wisconsin on a map. Bertelsen's father, Arved (or "Art" to his friends), ran a nightclub in Hudson, Wisconsin, just across the Mississippi River from Minneapolis.

Bertelsen found himself down south because his aunt, a nurse in Irving, Texas, called the Longhorn office and said her nephew was one great high school football player, and he wanted to get out of the snow for college.

Royal had heard that sort of recommendation before, and would hear it again. He says that in twenty years as the Longhorns' head coach, he had only ten lettermen from non-Texas high schools. In this case, however, something about the pitch from Bertelsen's aunt piqued Royal's interest, and the Texas staff requested game films from Bertelsen's high school. What a tough runner this Wisconsin kid was: He could either be a running back or a linebacker. So Royal sent assistant R. M. "Pat" Patterson to visit Bertelsen, and then arranged for a campus visit.

Bertelsen told Royal he had narrowed his choices to Texas and Colorado, and Bertelsen signed a Big Eight Conference letter of intent with the Buffaloes. That only meant Bertelsen couldn't go to another Big Eight school. Texas still was in the running. Royal knew this kid had good grades and test scores, but had he studied geography? "Jim, Jim," he told Bertelsen, "you're trying to get out of snow and ice, and you can't make up your mind between

Colorado and Austin? Son, have you looked at the map? If you draw a line across, we hit North Florida! Have you checked the weather in Colorado?"

Royal won out, visiting Bertelsen to watch him sign a national letter of intent. The Longhorns' coach, at a news conference with a high school kid outside Texas? Snow falls more often in Austin.

At Texas, Bertelsen set a freshman rushing record in 1968, gaining 685 yards in only five games, and the Longhorn boosters already were talking him up as a worthy successor to the three-year star Chris Gilbert. In the 1969 spring intrasquad game, Bertelsen ran for 156 yards, but in part because he missed most of spring practice with a pulled muscle, Bertelsen still was listed as the No. 2 left halfback, behind Billy Dale, as the 1969 fall practice opened.

When the season started, he was No. 1. Bertelsen was only a sophomore, but despite his elevation to starting halfback, his famous stoicism didn't abate at all. Many of his teammates decided he was the inspiration for the phrase "He wouldn't say shit if he had a mouthful."

His major was communications.

FIVE

The Colonel, the Tailback, the Rhodes Scholar, and the Disillusioned Vet

In July 1969, Arkansas tailback Bill Burnett was worried. The Razorbacks' preseason practices were beginning in less than a month, and he wasn't yet able to run hard after undergoing winter surgery on his left foot. Adding to his frustration, he wasn't willing to put himself in the hands of the Arkansas team physicians—literally or figuratively—and ask what he should do to accelerate his recovery. He didn't trust them.

Although his two older brothers had played for Frank Broyles a few years earlier, and his father, Clell, was a prominent Arkansas high school coach, Bill Burnett already had shocked almost everyone with his strong sophomore season in 1968, gaining 859 yards and scoring sixteen touchdowns. He had an unassuming look and a soft, sometimes squeaky voice that could cause him to be mistaken for the student manager. He did have an abiding faith that he could be every bit as good as his brothers Bobby, who in 1969 was a member of the Denver Broncos, and Tommy. But at first, almost nobody else did.

Because of heart problems, Clell Burnett took a step back from the pressure of head coaching and moved the family to Bentonville, where he accepted a job teaching math while helping out with the football program. Bill was about to enter the ninth grade. Bentonville was a small hamlet with a town square on Main Street. One of the local families—the Walton clan—was trying to build up a regional string of discount department stores, and Bill Burnett spent a lot of time in the home of his buddy, Jim Walton, Sam Walton's third son. Jim and Bill went hunting and fishing together, and Jim's blocks helped Bill gain over 1,000 yards as a senior halfback at Bentonville High.

Yet Bill wasn't flashy and he weighed only 155 pounds. He wanted to follow his brothers to Arkansas, but not with anything but a four-year scholarship. That was how Frank Broyles discovered, in the spring of 1966, just how darned tough this kid with the squeaky voice could be.

"My brothers kept after Broyles, and he finally offered me a one-year, make-good scholarship, which is what they did with a lot of guys back then," Bill recalls. "If you didn't make good after a year or two, they just didn't renew the scholarship."

Meanwhile, Tulsa coach Glenn Dobbs thought Bill would be a good fit as a pass-catcher in the Hurricanes' wide-open offense. "My brothers were livid and they went back to Broyles and said, 'You need to offer this kid a scholarship or he's going to go to Tulsa,'" Bill says. "So Frank called me up one day and said, 'Come down to my house and see me.' On a Sunday afternoon! Gee, if you don't think that's intimidating!"

Burnett says Broyles paternalistically told him that a one-year scholarship would make him a better player, keeping him hungry. With assertiveness that makes him laugh years later—*who did he think he was?*—Burnett told this coach who already had won a national championship that a one-year scholarship wasn't good enough. If the Razorbacks didn't come through with a four-year scholarship, ensuring his entire college stay would be paid for, he would go to Tulsa, a school that played Arkansas every season and occasionally knocked them off. Burnett believes that Broyles pondered how embarrassing it would be for the youngest of the Burnett boys to go to nearby Tulsa, less than two hours away, and maybe play for the Golden Hurricanes—or even worse, help them beat the Razorbacks. It was a longshot, but why take a chance?

Broyles maintains Bill Burnett and his brothers originally were satisfied with the one-year offer to the runt of the litter. Bill says that never was the case. Regardless, the stubborn Burnett got his four-year scholarship.

In his first season, Bill didn't get off the bench much for the Razorbacks' *freshman* squad, spending most of his practice time running on the "scout" team, imitating opponents with the sophomores and juniors on the B squad. (Texas didn't have a B squad and just dropped players down the depth chart; Arkansas formalized the scrub status.) Some of the B team Razorbacks were redshirt prospects, held out of varsity action for a year without loss of a season of eligibility, but most were far enough down the depth chart to have little hope of getting in a game, or even of suiting up for a conference matchup. A freshman on loan to the B team—colloquially called the "Meat Squad"—

was not a prospect, even if his name was Burnett. When Burnett was red-shirted as a sophomore in 1967, it was mostly because backfield coach Johnny Majors let it be known he considered Bill a hopeless washout, not anywhere near the player his brothers were. His future wasn't bright and his family was fuming.

When Burnett reported for spring practice in 1968, he checked the depth chart on the bulletin board. He was listed as the *ninth-string* tailback. Out of ten. At least Johnny Majors was gone, after getting the head-coaching job at Iowa State. Majors's successor as the offensive backfield coach was the young Don Breaux, who had been an American Football League quarterback with the Denver Broncos (for whom he threw four touchdown passes in a 1963 game) and with the San Diego Chargers as John Hadl's backup in 1964–65. Breaux came to Arkansas from the Florida State staff and was trying to install a pro-style passing offense. Broyles was enamored of the Florida State attack and believed the wide-open, multidimensional offense would give the Razorbacks a better chance to remain among the nation's elite programs. So when Majors left (former players joke that Broyles fired assistants by getting them head-coaching jobs), the Razorbacks' head coach recruited Breaux, promising him considerable power to design and run the offense.

During the first scrimmage of spring training, Breaux watched the top tailbacks fail repeatedly to get through the holes and threw down his hat in frustration. Charley Coffey, the tobacco-chewing defensive line coach, remembered the tailback who at least had tried and had been able to quickly pick up opponent plays when the scout team was going against the first-team defense. "Put Burnett in there," Coffey said. "He'll run it!" He pointed at the ninth-string tailback.

At that moment, Burnett was lounging in the pole-vault pit at the side of the field.

Him?

But Breaux called over Burnett, and he at least got his assignments right and showed some potential, and Breaux especially liked the way he intelligently followed and used his blockers. By that fall, the redshirt sophomore had gone from ninth string and the pole-vault pit to stardom. "If it was Johnny Majors, I never would have played a down at Arkansas," Burnett says. "I grew to truly love Don Breaux."

Breaux says, "If you look at Bill, you certainly wouldn't say: 'This is the stud who's going to lead us.' But he certainly was a better player than we first anticipated. We should have known, though, because he had some pretty good genes in that family."

Burnett would have cracked 1,000 yards in 1968 if he hadn't come down with the big-toe problem that kept him out of one game, against Rice, and hampered him in the Sugar Bowl victory over Georgia, when he had twenty carries for only 31 yards.

He was hurting that day in New Orleans, but he remembered to wink at the camera when he was introduced on television. Burnett had just taken a local high school senior, Linda Holmes, on a blind date and he told her he would wink at her on national television. That came after he asked out an Arkansas coed who, declining, said, sorry, she had a boyfriend. She said Burnett should go out with her boyfriend's sister instead and offered to set up the blind date. Burnett was the kind of guy girls set up with their friends.

When Bill picked up Linda and took her to the Christmas party at the athletic dormitory, Wilson Sharp House, he was smitten. But when his teammates learned who she was, they asked: *Are you nuts?* Linda's father, Colonel Eugene Holmes, was the head of the University of Arkansas ROTC program. He also was a World War II hero who had survived the Bataan Death March and three years as a prisoner of war, a man who didn't put up with any shit from these long-haired war protesters who tried to disrupt the ROTC drills, and who certainly wasn't going to stand by quietly if a football player brought home his daughter four minutes after her curfew. On a land-grant campus where two years of ROTC was mandatory for all male students without some sort of medical excuse, everybody knew Colonel Holmes—or knew of him. So Burnett probably would be wise not to let Colonel Holmes know that he had promised several other girls—not just Linda—a wink on national TV, wouldn't he?

After the Sugar Bowl, as Burnett started to seriously date Linda Holmes and become friends with the colonel himself, the area around Burnett's big toe continued to hurt. Late in the '68 season, team doctors had diagnosed it as "a foot problem." No big deal. It would heal. In the meantime, they gave him shots in the foot before each game and sent him out. "I played four or five games with Novocain in my foot," Burnett says. "That's the only way I could play."

Before school started again, Burnett's mother skirted the team doctors and made an appointment for Bill with a podiatrist. The podiatrist looked at the X-rays and said Burnett's big toe was out of joint, and it had been out of joint long enough for adhesions to develop, and what the hell had he been doing playing on that? Burnett underwent surgery in Oklahoma City, and, shaking his head, the surgeon walked in to meet with Bill's parents. He said they had done all they could, but he wasn't sure Bill would be able to play football again on that toe. But because he wasn't dealing with the team doctors, the gloomy prognosis remained Bill's painful secret. He would have to skip spring practice, he said, but he would be OK for the fall. That's what he was hoping, anyway.

Burnett kept visiting the equipment room, working with the equipment staff to design a metal insert to put in his shoe and protect his toe. That helped, but because it made him feel unbalanced, he had them make a wedge for the shoe on his *good* foot. He still wasn't able to do serious conditioning work, and as the summer of '69 continued, he still had his doubts. At least he was falling deeper for Linda Holmes, who was going to be a UofA freshman that fall, and he was becoming a regular at her parents' home. The colonel, Burnett discovered, was all right. He saw life in absolutist terms, involving duty and love of country, and among other things, that meant sending Linda's two brothers off to Vietnam. But when you've suffered barbaric treatment in the clutches of the Japanese on the Bataan Peninsula, and won a chestful of medals, and grieved over the death of a pilot brother in the European Theater, nobody is going to accuse you of insincerity. And if you're Colonel Eugene Holmes, you'll also talk with a Rhodes Scholar asking about an ROTC draft deferment—then keep quiet about it for years, or until the thought of the kid becoming the commander in chief turns your stomach.

THE STUDENT HOLMES HELPED WAS BILL CLINTON, who, emulating so many young men of that time, was doing his best to manipulate the system however he could to keep from ending up in Vietnam. It could be considered simple cowardice, but more often, it was a combination of fear and confusion and varying degrees of conviction. Were the cause and the South Vietnamese government worthy of American military support? Were they worth fighting—or dying—for?

Like a lot of Americans, Bill Clinton didn't think so. When he visited Colonel Holmes in Fayetteville, the young Arkansas native had attended Georgetown University, spent one year as a Rhodes Scholar in Oxford, and was a Senator J. William Fulbright protégé. But the selective service system, a maze of exemptions and deferments and corruption and notes and winks and standards that changed from draft board to draft board, and was prone to snare blacks and the poor, was about to snare Clinton. In 1969, he received a draft notice, facing an induction date of July 28. He was desperate to avoid being inducted then—and avoid it without sabotaging his political future.

Holmes and other ROTC officials heard from representatives of Governor Rockefeller and Senator Fulbright, a former Rhodes Scholar himself and one-time UofA president. The ROTC brass was asked to help Arkansas's Rhodes Scholar find an alternative to immediate induction. Nobody was stupid enough to try to order Colonel Holmes to do anything, and they didn't use the words "avoid" and "draft" in the same paragraph—much less the same sentence.

In July, during the week of the launching of the history-making Apollo 11 mission to the moon, when Bill Burnett was showing up almost daily to pick up Linda Holmes and still wondering if he would be able to play football that fall, William Jefferson Clinton knocked on the colonel's front door.

When Clinton was running for president in 1992, Holmes issued a statement Linda helped him write. In the statement, Holmes said the 1969 conversation with Clinton lasted two hours. By 2002, Holmes understandably is incapable of precise recall, but his disdain remains sharply focused.

"He didn't want to come inside," Holmes says. "He wanted to sit out on the curb. I had just met him. I thought he was just a normal, young American guy who would fulfill his duty to his country if it came up."

They talked about Clinton attending the Arkansas Law School, and, after taking basic training in the summer of 1970, participating in the school's advanced ROTC program. A commitment to the ROTC and three years of active duty would enable Clinton to obtain a 1-D draft deferment in 1969.

On July 17, three days before Neil Armstrong became the first man to walk on the moon, Holmes signed off on Clinton's eventual enrollment in the ROTC program, leading to the Garland County draft board granting Clinton the 1-D deferment. Still unclear over three decades later was whether Clinton ever spelled out to Holmes, that night or over the next two months, that he still might spend the next academic year in Oxford before returning for basic training, the ROTC program, and law school. It's even possible that they never went over the agreement point by point, and that Holmes drew inferences about Clinton's intentions—correct or otherwise. But Clinton's plans were a work in progress and the issue of whether he would spend the 1969–70 academic year in Oxford as a Rhodes Scholar or at Fayetteville as a law student is unimportant. The crucial point was whether, in order to get the 1-D deferment and void his July 28 induction date, he deliberately misled Holmes about his professed intention to take basic training in the summer of 1970, which was the earliest he could have done so, and then enter the advanced ROTC program as he took law school classes at Arkansas. At one point, Oxford officials weren't expecting him to return for the 1969–70 school year and his friends believed he would be in the Arkansas law school that fall. Other ROTC officials believed Clinton would be on campus by the end of the year. Clinton managed to get his draft notice quashed on the basis of his ROTC and Arkansas law school plans—and those plans changed.

As the Razorbacks' season began, as Bill Burnett's toe began to come around and Linda Holmes began college, Clinton agonized over his draft status, and the steps he had taken to avoid induction. The Nixon administration was issuing periodic leaks about its plans for draft reform. At one point, as David Maraniss wrote in the 1995 Clinton biography *First in His Class*, Clinton seemed "safe" if he again exposed himself to the draft because news stories quoted administration sources hinting that because of imminent troop withdrawals, soon only nineteen-year-olds might be draft-eligible and Vietnam service might be voluntary for draftees. In mid-September, in fact, Nixon disclosed the November and December draft calls would be canceled. At his request, Clinton was reclassified 1-A on October 30, after giving up his 1-D deferment and declaring he wouldn't join the ROTC program. He was back in Oxford, and he participated in the October 15 Moratorium protest against the war outside the United States Embassy in London. Yet soon he knew he wasn't completely "safe": The Nixon administration's draft reform was a push for a draft lottery system, which would apply to all able-bodied men from nineteen through twenty-five, including Rhodes Scholars and college football players.

As all this was happening, a young man who flunked his way out of school and into the draft—as so many had done—was thrilled to be getting a second chance in college. Don Donner was thrilled not because he loved academia, but because it meant he was still alive. Some of his buddies weren't so lucky.

———————

WHEN HE WAS IN FIRST GRADE, Don Donner's family moved from Southern California to northwest Arkansas. One of his first Arkansas memories is being anointed General Ulysses S. Grant on the playground, then getting pummeled by boys pretending to be the Confederate troops of Robert E. Lee. "I was a very confused little boy," Donner recalls. "I had never heard of these Grant and Lee guys."

His father, Carl, was first a chicken farmer, then the live-in head maintenance man at the Methodist Assembly grounds on Mount Sequoyah—actually a big hill—in Fayetteville. When Don was ready for college, the natural choice for the Methodist boy was the state's Methodist school, Hendrix College in Conway, despite the fact that the Donners lived near the UofA campus. Donner was smart but was a conventional party animal who loved beer and didn't need much else. "They had to give you three semesters before they kicked you out of there," he says of Hendrix College. "I did my three semesters and got kicked out."

After getting his draft notice, Donner tried to coax his blood pressure to unacceptable levels for the induction physical in July 1966. A tall man who tended to be chunky, he had been warned by his family doctors to take better care of himself. So wouldn't too much booze shove him off the charts—and out of the military? "I drank heavily before the physical," he says. "But if anything, it lowered my blood pressure. I went through the whole experience slightly tipsy, and that meant I woke up at Fort Polk, Louisiana, with no hair on my head."

He ended up learning to be a combat engineer outside Washington, D.C. Waiting for his orders, he worked on a harbor patrol, and one day in 1967, an officer approached him, smiling. "Hey, Donner, guess where you're going?" he asked.

"I don't have to guess," Donner said.

He spent ten months in Vietnam with the U.S. Army Corps of Engineers. He wasn't there long when the Corps finished rebuilding a bridge, and Donner watched as an officer groused that while it was perfectly suitable for traffic, it wasn't quite straight. Nudge it with bulldozers, the officer said, get the damn thing straight. The bulldozers nudged the bridge, it fell into the river below, and two soldiers drowned. For the next three months, Donner and the Corps rebuilt it—again.

On January 31, 1968, during the early hours of the Tet holiday, Donner and his friends were joining in the celebration and were mostly drunk or otherwise out of it when the skies lit up in the distance. "There were tracers and rockets going off everywhere, and we're going, 'Man, these guys know how to celebrate! This is great!'" Donner says, laughing. The next morning, the engineers discovered that the noise hadn't been a Tet celebration, but a major offensive, and it had left them temporarily cut off from their supply base. C-rations had to be dropped to them for days.

When the bridge was completed, the engineers moved to the Mekong Delta, where they patched the oil road from the south of the country to Saigon. One day, Donner looked around and concluded that, at twenty-one, he was the oldest man in his unit, other than career officers. He even did volunteer minesweeping duty, before he figuratively slapped himself: He had reached "short-time" status, and his ass still was in one piece, so why add to the risk?

By then, he was convinced the war was a waste. Civilians didn't seem to know or care about which factions were in power. And he saw death—too much of it. He talked with South Vietnamese soldiers, including one who had been drafted back into the army for a second time—*and had six years left in his second stint!* "I was not a gung-ho type when I went over, never was," Donner says. "But I was not an anti-type, either. I went over with a sense that it was my duty, that you do these things when your country calls upon you. While in Vietnam, I started seeing that there was no likely probability of a good outcome, that it was a senseless thing, that whatever we did was not going to work and we were not going to change the situation. And once that realization started sinking in, then it became sort of a waste of life to continue when no real change could be accomplished."

In mid-1968, Donner finished his tour. He still was twenty-one. Landing in San Francisco, he went to Portland, Oregon, picked up the yellow Corvette convertible he had ordered while in Vietnam, and wandered the country. Every noise, every look, every question made him suspicious. He couldn't shake that hypervigilance, the survival mechanism learned in Vietnam, and the "Dear Don" letter he received from his girlfriend didn't improve his mood, either.

He landed a job with a soil lab for a quarry in Tulsa. After a year, he was ready to try college again, and he enrolled in summer school at Arkansas in June 1969. By mid-August, he was restless and considered taking a week off to attend the Woodstock music festival in upstate New York, but decided against it.

He was different from other students: He was older, he didn't have to take ROTC classes, he didn't have to worry about the draft. And he didn't give a damn about football.

In the fall of 1969, while the Razorbacks won game after game, after other tensions simmered on campus, Donner met other Vietnam veterans at the local Presbyterian Center, the flashpoint for the anti–Vietnam War movement in Fayetteville. He became an outspoken campus protester, and newspaper reporters—whether from the *Arkansas Traveler*, the campus newspaper, or the *Northwest Arkansas Times*—learned to seek him out for comment. He could stand in front of other students in a fatigue jacket and a headband and say the war was useless, and announce that he wasn't some head-in the-clouds idealist, speaking as if he was reading off a poster or out of a pamphlet. He had been there.

On October 15, when anti–Vietnam War Moratorium protests were held around the country, Donner spoke for about ten minutes at the gathering on the steps of a classroom building in the middle of campus. He said his experiences convinced him American troops should be withdrawn. He made a quick trip to Washington to participate in the Capitol Mall version of the Moratorium in mid-November. His bitterness and disillusionment showed, but he was also trying to make a new life for himself, living on the Methodist Assembly Grounds; getting cozy with his new, young girlfriend, Star; and starting work toward a geology degree. Shortly after he came back from Washington, the buzz was beginning: What if Nixon came to the Big Game?

Well, shit, Donner thought, if Nixon did, they just might have to stage a protest for him.

SIX

Texan Razorbacks

THE TEXANS ON FRANK BROYLES'S ROSTER often were the most vehemently loyal Razorbacks. "It seemed like half the guys on our team were Texans, refused by Texas," tackle Mike Kelson says, exaggerating. "So we went to Arkansas to do one thing—kick their ass. We had total respect for Darrell Royal, but we had complete respect for Frank Broyles and what he had done."

When the Razorbacks' Texans told their friends they were going to Arkansas, it might as well have been Alaska, it was such an outpost. The goal for the Razorbacks' Texans was to force the boosters of the Texas schools, and especially of UT, to ask: *How the hell did that kid get away?*

The six major contributors from Texas among the 1969 Razorbacks—quarterback Bill Montgomery, split end Chuck Dicus, offensive linemen Kelson and Ronnie Hammers, defensive back Bobby Field, and defensive tackle Terry Don Phillips—spanned the recruiting spectrum, from the highly sought to the afterthoughts. Every time Montgomery completed a pass to his favorite receiver, Dicus, the extremes of that spectrum came into play.

Montgomery and Dicus were star quarterbacks and basketball players at rival high schools in the Dallas area and had competed against each other since junior high. "I didn't particularly like him," Dicus says, smiling. "I thought he was a little cocky."

Montgomery was at R. L. Turner High in Carrollton, Dicus at Garland High on the north side of the Dallas area. Montgomery *could* be grating, because he was so good and didn't pretend he didn't know it. Or at least that's the way it seemed: As happens with most gifted all-around high school athletes, the jealousy of others unfairly distorted his undeniable cockiness into intolerable arrogance. Still, there was no doubt that Montgomery displayed no false humility. His gravelly voice, even as a teenager, dripped with confidence. At R. L. Turner, he was the star in everything—football, basketball, baseball, golf—and was the student body president. Though he wasn't imposing physically, at six-foot-one and maybe 170 pounds coming out of high school, his magnetism and leadership seemed to add stature.

When Bill pondered his college choices and narrowed them to Texas, Alabama, and Arkansas, everyone understood his recruitment was a package deal: You get Bill, you get Catfish. Catfish was Carl, Bill's dad, and the fact that only someone with a legal document in hand called him Carl was illustrative of his outlook on life. Catfish sold chemical and cleaning products, mostly to schools, and his passion was watching his son play. (Eventually, when Bill was a Razorback, his teammates scribbled an addendum to a notice posted on the locker-room door. "PLAYERS AND PRESS ONLY," the sign announced. Somebody took a pen and added, ". . . and Catfish." The security guards, managers, trainers, and anyone else inclined to act as cops already knew that's the way it was.) Besides, everybody liked Catfish; it was as if he was the team chaplain.

Texas was tempting for Bill, because it was the marquee school and Bill's older brother, Baker, already was enrolled at UT, and the Longhorns wanted him. In his senior high school season, Bill attended nearly every Texas home game in Memorial Stadium with his brother, and he estimates he saw seven of Texas's ten games in 1966. But quarterback Bill Bradley—a Longhorn sophomore during Montgomery's senior year of high school—was going to be all-world, right? (Nobody mentioned freshman quarterback James Street.) The consensus was that if Montgomery stayed at quarterback, his first chance to play might be 1969, either as a junior or redshirt sophomore, but he wasn't one to shirk from a challenge. Bill had nosed around, though, during his visits, and noticed how many of the former high school quarterbacks found themselves switched elsewhere. The Longhorns tended to want and get the best athletes, and move them around. That Montgomery was better suited to play quarterback in a multiple attack than Texas's one-dimensional offense didn't help his chances of eventually becoming the Longhorns' starting QB; more likely, he would end up at defensive back.

The day after R. L. Turner lost to San Angelo Central in the state semifinals, Montgomery's high school coach called him down to the fieldhouse. He said one college head coach wanted Montgomery to visit his campus as soon as possible, had arranged for a plane ticket, and thought it would be great if Bill Montgomery could come the next *day*. That didn't shock Montgomery; he knew the recruiting season, which didn't begin in earnest until after a player's senior season, was going to get hectic. But he said he needed to report to basketball practice, because he already was far behind, and he would prefer putting off visits for at least a bit. *But you don't understand,* said his high school coach, who had enjoyed delaying the punchline. *This is Bear Bryant!*

So Montgomery visited Alabama, shortly before the Crimson Tide played Nebraska in the Sugar Bowl.

He also went to Fayetteville. Bill's mother, Kay, was raised in Little Rock, and many members of her family still lived in Arkansas, so Bill had visited the state many times. When he met with Broyles, Montgomery was savvy enough to know that he wasn't the only prospect being courted with promises, but he did like what he heard from the head coach. Broyles said that he wanted to go to a more wide-open, pro-style offense. "I want you to run it," Broyles told Montgomery.

As the time for decision approached, Catfish finally stepped in. Uh, Bill, it's your choice, he said. He had stayed out of it, hadn't he? But if it was coming down to Texas, Alabama, or Arkansas, Catfish just had to say it sure would be nice if Bill ruled out Alabama and stayed within easy driving distance. Kay was taking college classes again, and she eventually would obtain a doctorate in nutrition. Fayetteville was only five and a half hours away, not intolerably longer than the three-and-a-half-hour drive to Austin.

Bill picked Arkansas. Broyles was so excited to land him, the coach traveled by private plane to Dallas to get Montgomery's signature on a letter of intent, and the picture of Broyles stepping off the plane made the wire services and newspapers in Texas and Arkansas. The kid's got to be good, everyone realized, when Frank's there to close the deal, when the coach walks off the plane and flaunts this recruiting victory right in the heart of Texas. (And Broyles kept his word to change his offense, eventually hiring Don Breaux and former Alabama receiver and assistant coach Richard Williamson to oversee the more passing-oriented attack.)

So Bill Montgomery was a big catch for the Razorbacks, but Chuck Dicus was a different story. Dicus's father had coached high school football in Texarkana, and sent several players to Broyles's program and stayed close to them. Chuck, though he lived in Dallas, considered himself a Razorbacks fan, but Arkansas didn't seem interested. Chuck's scholarship offers were from Oklahoma State and McMurry College in Abilene. Finally, after some prompting from an Arkansas booster who saw a newspaper story in which Dicus mentioned he had been a Razorbacks fan but hadn't heard from the coaching staff there, Johnny Majors began recruiting Dicus.

"They didn't talk much about the offense they would be running," Dicus says. "They didn't even have to tell me that they had a stadium. I would have paid my own way if they just said they wanted me to come up here and play football."

Dicus and Montgomery, the former high school rivals, talked that summer at the orientation session in Fayetteville. Much to their surprise, they found they liked each other, and agreed to travel together back and forth to Fayetteville and pair up as roommates in the athletic dormitory, Wilson Sharp House. They realized there was going to be culture shock in going from the Dallas area to Fayetteville, which then truly was a small college town of about thirty thousand dropped into the Ozark foothills, and they would cope together. They also knew from the start that they wouldn't be competing with each other for a starting job at Arkansas, because Dicus expected to be switched to another position; he just didn't know which one. Montgomery and Dicus got along well as roommates long before they were a formidable passing combination.

During workouts with the Arkansas Shoats—the freshman team—Dicus first was a defensive back, then a halfback. It wasn't until early in the five-game freshman season that Dicus was switched to receiver. The next spring, after the new offensive coaches arrived, Richard Williamson was intrigued by Dicus, who ran disciplined routes, quickly picked up the nuances of the offense, and seemed to share a kind of telepathy with Montgomery.

Dicus is convinced their friendship was critical in the development of their on-field relationship, and that his own experience at quarterback in high school gave him a step up in grasping the intricacies of the passing game—even though he was catching the ball, not throwing it.

"Our two egos in the same quarters could get crowded," Dicus says, laughing. "I'm probably the only player on the team who could have roomed with Bill. I've joked with him that the only reason I got a scholarship up here was because they had to have someone to room with him. But we got along great.

"He is a unique person, so competitive. I understood that. I think I probably put up with a whole lot nobody else would. He brings a little swagger to the table. Bill wasn't a great talent at throwing or running but he was good at both. What elevated him above someone else was his extreme competitiveness. He was smart and he knew the offense like the back of his hand. And his will to win was second to none."

In the new offense, the roommates starred as sophomores, with Montgomery completing 57 percent of his passes and throwing for a school-record 1,595 yards and ten touchdowns. "He had something special about him," Don Breaux says. "He was a great student of the game. He understood it. I think people were willing to follow him, and he led by example. I think he just had 'it'—whatever 'it' is. He had touch as a passer, and he just made plays when it was critical."

Dicus caught fifty passes, including twelve in the Sugar Bowl against a Georgia defensive backfield that included All-American Jake Scott. After one season, Dicus already was well over halfway to the Razorback career record for receptions—eighty-three.

In the Sugar Bowl victory, Montgomery took a hit from Georgia defensive lineman Bill Stanfill and suffered a slight right shoulder separation when he hit the ground. The hope was that it would heal on its own, but when it didn't, he had surgery in mid-February and missed spring training. During the 1969 season, some reporters mused that Montgomery didn't throw the ball with as much velocity as he had the previous year, but Bill insists that isn't true. However, he also suffered a rib injury and a concussion during the 1969 season and sat out one game completely. Backup John Eichler was effective in the 52–14 victory over Wichita State.

Montgomery was back in the lineup the next week. The Razorbacks rolled along, heading toward that showdown with Texas.

UP FRONT ON THE OFFENSIVE LINE, Texans Ronnie Hammers and Mike Kelson were doing well in their first seasons as Razorback starters. Hammers, a redshirt junior listed as a six-three, 230-pounder, came from Marshall, Texas, where he played high school ball for coach Ralph Brooks, who had started his career in Arkansas. Brooks helped point Hammers to the Razorbacks, saying that his high school offensive system was similar to what Arkansas used, and the transition would be easier. (Then, of course, the Razorbacks changed their system.) That pitch hadn't worked on the other Marshall High cocaptain, Tommy Asaff, who by 1969 was a senior reserve defensive halfback for Texas.

The son of a cabinetmaker who owned a home remodeling company, Hammers was an all-around athlete, and because Marshall and Longview both were in northeast Texas, he played everything against Longview's James Street. "I played four sports in high school and he did, too," Hammers says of Street. "When you're always playing against a guy in everything from eighth grade through the twelfth grade, you might not go have a beer with him, but you know him. He was such a tremendous pitcher and I played in the outfield. James had the worst curveball I had ever seen in my life. It was that good. He'd throw it at your head and you'd think it was going to hit you, and then it would fall off the table. He'd screw up every once in a while and throw me a fastball, but I don't think I ever hit his curveball."

Street and Hammers visited Texas the same weekend, and traveled down on the same plane. In his session with Royal, Hammers got the impression the Texas coach wanted him to sell himself; Hammers thought it was past that stage. He says that when Royal pressed him for a reading on how close he was to committing to Texas, he was uneasy. "This is my first trip," Hammers told Royal. "I have about five or six other trips to go." The small-town boy also felt Austin and UT might be too big for him, and he wouldn't commit to the Longhorns. Hammers was more comfortable when—on his fourth or fifth stop on the circuit—he visited Fayetteville and talked with Broyles. "It just felt right."

As a redshirt sophomore in 1968, Hammers backed up a star senior, Webb Hubbell, at left tackle and got a lot of playing time as Hubbell fought a knee injury. Hubbell was hurt in the '68 opener, missed a game, and played the rest of the season after taking pregame injections in the knee, but Hammers spelled him often.

(Hubbell underwent surgery after the Sugar Bowl and was on the field as a graduate assistant coach the next spring, hoping to recover and play in the NFL. The Chicago Bears drafted him, and he attended training camp, but the knee still wasn't strong enough. The Bears put him on injured reserve for a season before he gave up on the notion of a pro career and settled for law, politics, and a close friendship with Bill and Hillary Clinton.)

For the 1969 season, the Razorbacks moved Hammers to right guard and installed Kelson, a sophomore who sat out '68 as a redshirt, as Hubbell's successor at left tackle. Kelson was heavier than his listed 225 pounds, and both Hammers and Kelson seemed huge.

Kelson had toughness and football in his blood. His father, Ed, was a high school coach in a rough refinery town, Texas City. "There were killers and priests there, and darned near nothing in between," Mike says. Ed fit in, too: He left a Jesuit orphanage in Alabama to enlist in the Marines, and was a member of underwater demolition teams at Iwo Jima, Saipan, and Tinian. He was one tough football coach after he got home. One time at Texas City, a star player challenged him to a fight, and Ed said, "Form a circle, boys." And after Ed had scored a knockdown, the coach said, "Oh, by the way, I was an NCAA boxing champion at Southern Mississippi." Then he told the player to go run, and all would be forgotten.

"I just thank God he retired from coaching before he got to coach me!" Mike says. "But he was my hero. I've had three attorneys tell me he made them what they are today. The head of Monsanto at one time, same thing."

Mike, the tough coach's son, was an all-Houston high school choice and made a handful of recruiting visits, but Texas didn't seem interested. Mike visited Oklahoma State the same weekend as Dicus and took a campus tour. "At the end, they brought us way back to the stadium, and there was a little brick cement wall around a dirt floor," Kelson says. "They said they threw the linemen in there to see who wants to start. I said: 'OK, next plane ticket!'"

Mike chose Arkansas, and Ed drove him to Fayetteville and dropped him off in front of Wilson Sharp House. "Son," Ed said, "this is the best time you'll ever have." The tough Marine's eyes got red. He wiped away a tear. Then he drove away.

Before long, Kelson discovered that his father had a kindred spirit on the Arkansas staff. Wilson Matthews, a Broyles staff member, had been a Marine before he got into coaching at the high school level. The players liked him—once practice started. But the off-season conditioning work he conducted, called the "Fourth-Quarter Program," was horrendous. Did this guy think they were going to storm the shores of Tripoli? And when someone screwed up in the dorm, or didn't go to classes, the punishment could be Matthews's infamous "five and five"—a five-mile run back into Fayetteville at five in the morning.

Why all of this fanatical conditioning and punishment?

"We never asked why," Kelson says. "You started in February, and by the time April rolled around for spring training, you were saying, 'Dear God, thank you!'"

Three days a week in the winter, when the Longhorns were going through similar trials under Frank Medina, the Razorbacks put on Keds tennis shoes, shorts, and T-shirts, and went through hell. They spent a lot of time in a sawdust pit—maybe thirty feet by forty feet—in Barnhill Gym. There, they did crabwalks and other drills, and they did them through all the heaving.

When Dicus puked? "Puke on your own time, not mine!" roared Matthews. Then the Razorbacks ended up running the stadium stairs, for thirty minutes. This was *after* the crabwalks, which could leave you feeling as if your spinal cord had been tied in knots.

"We had a good off-season program," Matthews says. "A lot of them say I was the meanest man they ever knew. I didn't think so. We knew it was tough enough that if they came in and stuck with it, they'd be leaders and not quit in the fourth quarter. That's why we called it the Fourth-Quarter Program. We always felt like if we got to the fourth quarter and we were in it, hell, we were going to win it. And we did—a lot of times."

Kelson showed up in the best condition of any lineman for 1968 fall practice, in part because the coaches mistakenly mailed him cards listing workouts designed for the backs and receivers. When Kelson ran the timed mile on the first day of fall practice, the rest of the linemen got steamed at him, because he ran it like some skinny squirrel on the track team. But Hubbell was an All-American, and the Razorbacks wanted Kelson to be available for three full seasons after Hubbell left.

When offensive line coach Merv Johnson, the captain of Frank Broyles's only Missouri team, tossed Kelson a red shirt—the message was literal, he was going to sit out a season—the big sophomore called his dad. Screw this redshirt stuff, Mike said. He was going to join the Marines.

"Don't be an idiot," Ed snapped.

Mike stayed—and waited. He also got married. His wife, Linda, was a Texas sorority girl, of all things, but moved to Fayetteville and gave birth to a daughter on September 13, exactly a week before the '69 season opened. That day, the Razorbacks were going through their final scrimmage, and the film—or so Kelson had been told—would help decide whether Kelson would be the starter in Hubbell's old spot. Kelson was thrilled and scared to be on the verge of fatherhood at age twenty. But the scrimmage!

As Linda was in labor that morning, Mike called a team trainer and said he was too scared to tell Coach Johnson himself, but he would have to miss the scrimmage. Johnson almost immediately called the hospital and tracked down Kelson. Kelson came to the phone, shaking. *"What's this scared to tell me crap, Mike? You're having a baby, congratulations, stay there, kiss your wife, have a great baby, and don't sweat it: You've got the starting job."*

After that, Kelson would have run up and down the stadium stairs every day for Merv Johnson.

That season, Mike, Linda, and their infant son, Carey, were living in an off-campus apartment, for $250 a month. Mike was learning to change diapers, going to class—including ROTC—and playing football. For sticking with ROTC beyond the first two years, Kelson got a housing allotment, and also $115 a month through the NCAA for being married. It wasn't a carefree campus life, "but I was a good Catholic boy," he says.

He was developing into a pretty good tackle, too, playing next to senior left guard Jerry Dossey.

"When Kelson won that starting job in the spring, I knew he had a world of talent," Dossey says. "It was raw, but he was like a kid, his feet would fly. He would kick me, step on me—and that was in the huddle. He was like a clumsy pup, but he played with such intensity [that it] made up for a lack of speed. I had to help him learn the offense a little bit. He'd ask every once in a while, 'What do I do on this play?' But just the year before, Webb Hubbell did the same for me."

BOBBY FIELD AND CHUCK DICUS had this ongoing argument. Dicus claimed he received the final scholarship available in their Arkansas recruiting class. No, said Field, *he* was the guy on the bottom of the list! It really didn't matter which of them was right, if either was; it was true that neither was considered an elite prospect.

Way out west, in tiny Farwell, Texas, Bobby Field was the star in everything at his small high school. There were thirty-nine in his graduating class, barely one thousand residents in the entire town, and nothing but flatlands as far as the eyes of West Texans could see. Bobby's dad, Billy, was a rancher who was hired to live on the land, oversee the cultivation of wheat, cotton, and grain, and tend to cattle. As Bobby was leaving high school, his beloved Longhorns weren't interested in him, and that hurt. He was a quarterback, but the Texas staff didn't even consider making him one of those seven or eight QBs they brought in every year. Texas Tech and Texas Christian were recruiting him when his high school coach, disgusted by the lack of interest in his star, sent films to the Arkansas staff. The Razorbacks, down to a final handful of scholarships, and maybe the final *one*, decided to offer him a scholarship. After he signed a letter of intent, he guessed his days at quarterback might be over: Broyles's personal trek to get Bill Montgomery's signature in the big city, Dallas, was splashed all over the papers, even in the Amarillo and Lubbock papers trucked over to Farwell. Field didn't even know that the Razorbacks also had landed a highly touted Arkansas high school quarterback, Jerry Moore of Benton. He just knew his own quarterback days were numbered.

"I didn't know one person in Arkansas and I felt like I was going to a foreign country," Bobby says.

After three days as a quarterback in the freshman practices, Field was switched to defensive back, and the Razorback staff quickly decided that this tough little kid from West Texas was a pretty good safety. He was a part-time starter as a sophomore, then as a junior was named the No. 1 "monster" back—essentially a strong safety who occasionally played tight to the line of scrimmage, but more often dropped back into conventional coverage. At Wilson Sharp House he roomed with the Razorbacks' standout defensive halfback—Jerry Moore, the other former quarterback. The two grew close, although Field was so quiet, the friendship was cemented with understanding more than words.

Field was listed at five-eleven and 180. Dripping wet and still holding the towels, he *might* hit 165. "But I tell you what, he'd knock your head off," Moore says.

As the year went along, the Arkansas staff spent the open weeks looking ahead to Texas, and the coaches decided they might have a special role in mind for Field when they came up against the wishbone. Even then, Field seemed a heady extra coach on the field, a quick (if very quiet) study, and they were going to take advantage of that.

BY MIDSEASON, the coaches concluded that they would be without Longview's Terry Don Phillips against the Longhorns. Phillips had been fighting a bad back for three years, and he hadn't even suited up since early October for the Razorbacks in 1969. It felt an anticlimactic way to end the Phillips boys' run in Fayetteville.

Loyd Phillips was an All-American at Arkansas in 1965 and '66 and won the Outland Trophy as the nation's top lineman as a senior; as the 1960s wound down, he was playing for the Chicago Bears. Other schools had gone after Terry Don, too, but after the Phillips boys' parents divorced, the sons were brought up by their mother, Verna, who worked in the meat department at Kroger's in Longview. Verna gently suggested to Terry Don that she didn't want to go to two different campuses to watch her sons play, and that settled it. They were on the Razorback varsity together in '66—Terry Don as a sophomore, Loyd as the highly decorated senior. "He was the left defensive tackle and I was the right defensive tackle," Terry Don says. "He was the Outland Trophy winner. I was far, far, far, far from that level." He laughs. "You *knew* where they were going to run."

The next summer, Terry Don's back began hurting as he worked in construction, and it got so bad that he was redshirted for the 1967 season. During that fall, Phillips wasn't a Razorback as much as he was a party animal, and after one nocturnal incident, Broyles called Terry Don into his office. Like all the Razorbacks, Phillips knew this sort of summons wasn't a social invitation. Other coaches dispensed punishment; Broyles handed down banishment. This was, in fact, the *only* time Phillips was in Broyles's office as a player.

"He told me I needed to leave and come back in the spring, and see if I was going to be willing and able to rejoin the team," Phillips says. "I went down to Little Rock and got a job and came back in the spring. That was the best thing that could have happened to me, because it allowed me to really think about what was important."

He was playing well again in 1968, his junior season of eligibility, when his back problems flared up. Back surgery after the Sugar Bowl didn't eliminate his pain, and he was resigned to being a backup at best in his senior season. He wasn't especially bitter: His life was straightened out and he was a newlywed. After a three-year courtship, Phillips married Linda Butler, the Arkansas head cheerleader, and they lived in Beverly Manor, near the stadium.

"I played the first three or four games, and I wasn't a very good player or very effective," Phillips says. "I was having a lot of problems with the surgery. My back wasn't fused the way it was supposed to have been, and I had four screws [there]."

Phillips and the coaching staff agreed: He wasn't physically fit to play, but Broyles told Phillips he still was a part of the program and he could travel with the Razorbacks for road games. He prepared himself to do that all season, deciding he wasn't going to be able to play against Texas—and his buddy James Street—again.

He was wrong.

SEVEN

. . . and Nixon Coming

RICHARD NIXON LOVED FOOTBALL. He would have been the scrub willing to go through Wilson Matthews's Fourth-Quarter Program at Arkansas, or Frank Medina's virtual boot camp at Texas, and neither complain nor quit the team.

Without intellectually analyzing it, he had elevated football to a metaphor for the American experience and a supreme test of mettle. He agreed with Teddy Roosevelt, the old football coach, who argued that the critics didn't matter and that the "credit belongs to the man who is actually in the arena." In the contentious political career of Richard Nixon, that meant there were far more important souls than critics in the media who took what he said—and twisted it.

Nixon had been heeding the old Roughrider for years. Another Roosevelt line was posted on the football dressing-room wall of Nixon's first high school, Fullerton High: *Don't flinch, don't foul, but hit the line hard!*

In 1969, when Nixon surveyed college football, he mostly saw clean-cut, All-American boys whom he believed were saying "yes, sir" and "no, sir" to authority figures such as Frank Broyles and Darrell Royal as well as other coaching luminaries.

Nixon himself, as he made no attempt to conceal in later years, hadn't been a very good player. He was a scrub at Fullerton and Whittier high schools, and he tried football as a freshman at Whittier College because the team needed an eleventh body to field a full lineup. On the Whittier varsity, he was nothing more than an end-of-the-bench reserve who wouldn't sit down because he was excited just to be on the team. During practice, he would exhort the scrubs, just before they got their teeth kicked in—sometimes literally, in the game of leather helmets and no facemasks—by the regulars, and he would come away unbowed and as determined as ever. If you were a teammate of his in the early 'thirties, you didn't know whether to say, *Nixon, it's a scrimmage, for God's sake!* or, *Nixon, if we all tried like you we'd be undefeated!* But you did know that it didn't seem all that strange that this scrub could get up and give the pep talks in the dressing room—and be taken seriously. At Whittier, a scrambling little curly-haired student leader who seemed to be involved in everything on campus—except the football team's starting lineup—could rally the boys.

So thirty-five years later, football was both an escape for Richard Nixon and, he believed, the source of a sympathetic constituency for the new president during a tumultuous time.

SO MUCH OF IT WAS THE VIETNAM WAR, especially in that first year of the Nixon administration. The Eisenhower-Nixon White House—in which the vice president had minimal decision-making power—had sent advisors, not ground troops. When he assumed the presidency in January 1969, Nixon inherited a legacy, a strategy, and a commitment from John Kennedy and Lyndon Johnson. His campaign position on the war—he would get us out, somehow, eventually, but with honor intact—was interpreted as a perpetuation of the status quo. Nixon was not going to have America abandon the Nguyen Van Thieu government and the South Vietnamese people and with the snap of his fingers instantly withdraw our troops. Nixon did implement a gradual withdrawal—one which, he made it clear, could be reversed if North Vietnam escalated the aggression in the South.

The much-hyped October 15 Moratorium protests against the Vietnam War around the country were passionate. The White House and the nation wondered if the United States would virtually come to a halt for a day, and that didn't happen. Despite impressive raw numbers, the vast majority of Americans hadn't participated, and it still was possible to portray the anti–Vietnam War movement as being in the minority—hampered by an ill-behaving fringe that diluted its credibility and hurt, rather then helped, the cause. In Austin, the angriest anti–Vietnam War voice was *The Rag*, a counterculture weekly newspaper issued out of the YMCA on Guadalupe Street. It sold for twenty cents and looked as if it came off a press in somebody's garage, or was typed on an old Remington directly onto the newsprint. The style was *Berkeley Barb* Southwest, the tone right out of the underground. Its stories cautioned readers about bad LSD and mushrooms hitting the market, glorified the Black Panthers, made the Chicago Seven, defendants in the trial involving violence during the 1968 Democratic convention, sound as if they were the spiritual successors to the twelve disciples. It also parroted the mindless rhetoric of the moment ("outasight, groovy and far-fucking out, brothers and sisters"). So as eloquent as some of the writers were (and some of them were), it was easy to dismiss anything in the weekly—including the anti–Vietnam War voices—as "out there." But that didn't prevent UT students from handing over their two dimes, and the university administration from lobbying the police to enforce the laws about peddlers' licenses against those selling *The Rag* on campus. The paper could be a cheap diversion—*how far will they go this week?*—and a call to action. In that environment, the left-leaning *Daily Texan* seemed the campus equivalent of the notoriously arch-conservative *Manchester Union-Leader.* The same scenario was being played out in college towns across the country; the difference in Austin was that the revolutionary sentiment seemed to come out of nowhere. The Texas capital was as segregated as the Deep South in the 1950s, when questioning an administration's military policy seemed inconceivable. And now the "Drag"—or Guadalupe Street—at times could have served as a Berkeley stand-in for a filmmaker. Generally, the busy football players—most immersed in the game, most at least nominally (or more) concerned with their classes, and many enamored of a college social life that took advantage of athletic notoriety—dismissed the anti–Vietnam War activists as drugged-out extremists. That, however, was myopic: Anti–Vietnam War sentiment was becoming widespread, bordering on predominant, on campus. One didn't need to drop acid and sing the praises of free love to buy into it. Conversely, though, many of the war critics lumped together the football players, an eclectic group, as *jocks* who all thought and acted alike. That was just as misguided.

On Moratorium day in Fayetteville, Don Donner—the former combat engineer in Vietnam—made his speech, and the crowd for that and the other events was sizable. Yet the vast majority of students, including Bill Montgomery, went about their business as usual. "You're taking care of your studies and doing football, and reading the newspaper," Montgomery says. "You know about the war and you know about the body counts, but at that point, you're still thinking that everything the government tells you is the truth. So you're going with the party line. I was figuring that if that's what the leadership wants us to do, we should do it. I was still able to think that we had this great obligation to save the world from communism and it was a noble cause."

The Razorbacks' defensive secondary represented a cross-section of views. Maybe it was appropriate: The left defensive halfback, Terry Stewart, opposed U.S. involvement; safety Dennis Berner, who played on either side of the field, was skeptical; and right defensive halfback Jerry Moore was vehemently supportive of the American presence in Vietnam.

Terry Stewart was the senior class president in the 1968–69 school year. "I was against the war," Stewart says. "I wouldn't say we were active participants in the protests, though. We were kind of there. None of the athletes were ringleaders, let's put it that way."

Dennis Berner says, "Compared to the rest of the country, we were protected and innocent. I think when you're involved in athletics, you're focused and you don't have time for the other stuff. But I guess I was disillusioned that there were people dying without a full effort and support by the country. It was lip service. The people of the United States were not behind the war at all, and it was the military and political leaders that had us there. I wasn't a protester or anything like that, but I think everyone questioned it, what we were trying to accomplish, whether we were successful at it, and at what price."

Jerry Moore's father, J.P., had retired from the Air Force only three years earlier, leaving the service as a lieutenant colonel. "I was very much pro-Vietnam, promilitary," Moore says. He adds he "resented" the protesters.

The Austin Moratorium protests drew larger crowds than those in Fayetteville. At UT, many professors didn't show up to teach their classes. A crowd of about forty-five hundred gathered beneath the campus's landmark, the 307-foot-high Bell Tower, for a noon rally. Professor of government David Edwards was one of the speakers. "Unthinking support of one's country, right or wrong, is not patriotic," he declared. Edwards already was a prominent and popular figure on campus, and the UT administration knew better than to attempt to stifle him.

Joe Krier, the president of the Student Association, told the students that their protest was "a demand to this nation, this state, and this university that we have the right and the duty to question the course of this nation. . . . The war is not a question of what will happen to our prestige if we pull out. What has hit rock-bottom can't go lower."

The Longhorns weren't wearing their jerseys, so maybe nobody noticed, and there's no way of knowing whether they were counted in the official estimate. But on the fringe, a few of the Longhorns—including linebacker Scott Henderson and safety Freddie Steinmark, staunch Catholics and close friends, and Henderson's roommate, reserve defensive end Jimmy Williamson—stood and watched. Most of their teammates dismissed the protesters as unpatriotic, and a few even heckled the activists. But Steinmark and Henderson were a lot like the Razorbacks' Terry Stewart in the sense that they didn't consider themselves participants, but at least were caught in a swirl of their own emotions and confusion. "We were still young enough and impressionable enough and still in that football mentality, so authority meant something," Henderson says. "There was so much discussion about whether it was the right thing to do, and you start thinking about things. There were some very bright antiwar students that made a lot of sense. I didn't know what to think.

"I guess probably at that time I thought the war was OK. These protesters were wrong. I don't think any of us felt like it was our movement or we were participating in it."

Placekicker Happy Feller also was agonizingly ambivalent as he watched the protests on the campus. He was from Fredericksburg, a town in the only Texas county where Barry Goldwater outpolled Lyndon Johnson in the 1964 presidential election. "So I came from a background where it was whatever the government said, by golly, you do it without exception," he says. "And then I come to Texas, I listened to that rhetoric. I'm an American and I have a real strong belief system, and I feel very proud of what we did in World War I and World War II, and I felt if we hadn't played the role we did in those wars, Lord knows what kind of predicament we'd be in. But there was some puzzlement on my part about what was going on in Southeast Asia and what could be so valuable."

(Nixon did have many other supporters among the students. One group, the Young Americans for Freedom, set up a table and held "dialogues" with students and faculty members.)

On October 15, many of the protesting students marched to the state capitol, south of campus, for another rally, and the crowd estimates there ranged from seventy-five hundred to twelve thousand. Ronnie Dugger, a UT grad and a former editor of *The Daily Texan*, was an editor-at-large of the liberal *Texas Observer.* "On Monday, President Nixon said there is nothing new we can learn from these demonstrations," Dugger told the crowd. "President Johnson thought that, too, and he is no longer president."

(That day, the New York Mets beat the Baltimore Orioles to take a 3–1 lead in the World Series. If New York won the next game, one of the secondary reasons for moving the Arkansas-Texas game out of the October 18 slot—a conflict with Game Six of the World Series—would be moot.)

At the time of the Moratorium, the Razorbacks were 3–0 after beating Oklahoma State 39–0, Tulsa 55–0, and Texas Christian 24–6. The Longhorns were 4–0. They opened with a 17–0 defeat of California—at Berkeley, no less, the hotbed of dissent and counterculture. Then the Longhorns beat Texas Tech 49–7, Navy 56–17, and Oklahoma 27–17 in Dallas. The Ohio State Buckeyes, the defending national champions, also were undefeated, behind quarterback Rex Kern, fullback Jim Otis, and defensive back Jack Tatum, and still were ranked No. 1. Eastern independent Penn State, under Joe Paterno, also remained unbeaten.

On October 16, the day after the Moratorium, Jerry Koosman threw a complete-game five-hitter, and Donn Clendenon and Al Weis homered, as the Miracle Mets finished off the Orioles with a 5–3 Game Five victory. Fans tore up turf at Shea Stadium in the wild celebration, and the World Series championship came only seven years after manager Casey Stengel lamented of his expansion team: "Can't anybody here play this game?" It also meant there would be no World Series game on Saturday, October 18.

———

IN HIS JOURNAL (published in 1994 as *The Haldeman Diaries*), White House Chief of Staff Robert Haldeman wrote that on the day after the Moratorium, Nixon "got going again on necessity for hard line and no concession to the left."

Meanwhile, in the October 28 issue of *The Rag*, the Student Mobilization Committee asked that students report the names of any UT professors who held classes on Moratorium day. "SMC members will use the information in a constructive manner by visiting these professors and talking to them about the war," and why they should support the upcoming November Moratorium, the SMC declared. The faculty was caught in the middle, as professors also received a scolding letter from Dr. Norman Hackerman, UT's president, a preemptive strike against the second Moratorium, which featured a march in Washington. Hackerman declared that faculty members couldn't just pick and choose when to show up for their classes, and then he got to his main message: "A point related to the above matter is the question of whether or not the university should be a political action agency. I believe not, particularly in view of the effect such a tack could have on the educational process itself. In any event, the university shall not take political positions." He did add, though, that individuals were free to express their private views—on their own time.

On October 29, when the Longhorns and Razorbacks both were 5–0, the U.S. Supreme Court reaffirmed a Johnson administration policy of denying federal funds to school districts that didn't immediately integrate. The Nixon administration had backed off that policy. "There are those who want instant integration and those who want segregation forever," Nixon said. "I believe that we need to have a middle course between the two extremes."

On November 1, several weeks after being presented with a plan for escalation of the war by General Alexander Haig (Operation "Duck Hook"), which would have included an invasion of North Vietnam, Nixon went along with the recommendation of national security advisor Henry Kissinger and rejected that plan. But a strident speech was in the works for November 3, and that speech, especially viewed in retrospect, seemed to have a bit of everything for everyone—if only everyone would have looked hard enough.

Sitting at a desk in front of a gold curtain, with a family picture behind his right shoulder, Nixon stumbled over the words in a critical passage, but this is the text as released that night in official transcripts: "I have chosen a plan for peace. I believe it will succeed. If it does succeed, what the critics say now will not matter. If it does not succeed, anything I say then will not matter."

Nixon didn't reveal his earlier rejection of re-escalated U.S. involvement. While emphasizing the U.S. plan to continue the gradual withdrawal of troops and turn over combat responsibility to the South Vietnamese, Nixon appeared defiant to those who had marched and protested on October 15—and perhaps supported Eugene McCarthy or Robert Kennedy in the 1968 Democratic primaries. Considered years later, his statement that the "Vietnamization" process could be reversed if North Vietnam escalated the war seems a prudent threat—a form of protection for the Americans still in Southeast Asia. But at the time, his statements were viewed as bellicose, raising concerns among the disillusioned that the onetime "Red-baiter" would jump at the opportunity for escalation.

Nixon asked for the support of "the great silent majority of my fellow Americans," and was adamant that bailing out—and blaming the fiasco on LBJ—would have been easy but dishonorable and damaging to U.S. prestige. Nixon didn't mention dominoes, but parts of the speech advanced the old theory: A cut-and-run agreement ultimately would have encouraged communist aggression on other fronts. Yet amid the defiance were the assertions that he still planned to get U.S. troops out of Vietnam. Eventually. "The more support I can have from the American people," he said, "the sooner that pledge can be redeemed; for the more divided we are at home, the less likely the enemy is to negotiate in Paris. Let us be united for peace. Let us also be united against defeat. Because let us understand: North Vietnam cannot defeat or humiliate the United States. Only Americans can do that."

Nixon's tacit condemnation of the antiwar movement was a shameful encouragement of polarization in a nation watching its college campuses racked by protests, by occupations of administration buildings, by bitter denunciation of authority. America was divided, confused, and angry. But Nixon appealed directly "to the young people of this nation," saying: "I want peace as much as you do."

David Hawk, the inappropriately named cochairman of the National Moratorium, was among those who took Nixon's speech as a reaffirmation of U.S. involvement in Vietnam and not an endorsement of a course of withdrawal. "It's clear that we have to redouble and intensify our efforts," Hawk said.

With the National Moratorium scheduled for November 15, anti–Vietnam War leaders around the country were of like mind. As Nixon neared the end of his first year in office, it was apparent that the president's secret plan to end the war didn't involve an immediate or quick withdrawal.

In his memoirs, Nixon later wrote that the November 3 speech "bought me more time." He wrote that Sir Robert Thompson, a British expert on guerrilla warfare, told him "that within two years we would be able to achieve a victory—either in the sense of an acceptable negotiated settlement or of having prepared the South Vietnamese to carry the burden of fighting on their own." In that light, Nixon wrote that he was "prepared to continue the war despite the serious strains that would be involved on the home front. Two years would bring us to the end of 1971 and the beginning of the 1972 campaign, and if I could hold the domestic front together until then, winning an honorable peace would redeem the interim difficulties."

But the domestic front was heating up. Haldeman wrote in his journal that reconnaissance photos showed that 325,000 attended the November 15 protest march in Washington. Although those within the administration continued to tell themselves that anti–Vietnam War dissent had been discredited as only coming from a dropout, psychedelic, unpatriotic fringe, the reality was not that simple. Far from all of those who questioned the justification for American involvement in Vietnam were marching—or stoned. In Fayetteville, former combat engineer Don Donner laughed when he read that a state senator had labeled the Vietnam War protesters on the Arkansas campus "a bunch of draft dodgers." He pondered wearing the four medals he had earned in Vietnam to the next protest.

The week of the Washington march, writer Seymour Hersh and the Dispatch News Service broke the news of a possible massacre of South Vietnamese civilians by U.S. troops at My Lai in March 1968.

ON SATURDAY, NOVEMBER 22, Ohio State met Michigan in what was guaranteed to be the Buckeyes' final game of the season. The Big Ten had a no-repeat rule for the Rose Bowl, and conference teams couldn't go to any other bowl game. So the Buckeyes, who had been in the Rose Bowl the season before, knew they could clean out their lockers after this game—and celebrate the virtual clinching of a second straight national championship if they won.

They lost.

The Wolverines' 24–12 upset changed everything: In the Thanksgiving week Associated Press media poll, Texas was No. 1, Arkansas No. 2, and still-undefeated Penn State No. 3. The United Press International coaches' poll had Penn State No. 2 and the Razorbacks No. 3. But the possible Cotton Bowl matchup between the Southwest Conference winner and Penn State had been derailed before the Ohio State loss. Penn State—in part because the Nittany Lions had assumed that Ohio State would be undefeated and have the top spot wrapped up after the Michigan game—had rebuffed tentative overtures from Cotton Bowl officials and accepted an Orange Bowl bid. The Penn State players, who had been in the Orange Bowl the year before and enjoyed the experience, voted that they would rather go to Miami for New Year's than Dallas. In terms of climate, it was a wise move; in terms of maneuvering for national title consideration, it was a bad call.

After both Southwest Conference teams won on Thanksgiving to go 9–0, the issue became whether President Nixon indeed would attend a game between the top two teams in the nation (at least according to the AP poll), two all-white teams from southern states, and a game to be nationally televised from one of the nation's most peaceful campuses of five-figure enrollment. Arkansas's congressional delegation, including Wilbur Mills and J. William Fulbright, the former UofA president, had influence far out of proportion to the state's stature and population. Fulbright was one of the most ardent "within-the-system" critics of the Vietnam War, and he was a Fayetteville icon who kept getting elected, but northwest Arkansas still wasn't a hotbed of dissent.

If the president's trip to Fayetteville hadn't already been in the works, somebody would have recommended it. And when all the political considerations are thrown out, this is indisputable: Richard Nixon, the football fan, was excited about watching these two teams play.

EIGHT

The Good Die Young

IN EARLY 1969, in the Denver suburb of Wheat Ridge, Marie Mitchell picked up the phone and called her son, Longhorns guard Bobby Mitchell, at Moore-Hill Hall. She had horrible news: Mark David Mitchell, Bobby's older brother, an Army helicopter pilot in Vietnam, was dead.

Mark was one of the last Americans to die in Vietnam during the Johnson administration. His helicopter was shot down at Tay Ninh on January 17, three days before Richard Nixon's inauguration. The annual American death toll in Vietnam was dropping—from 14,589 in 1968, the final full year of the Johnson presidency, to 9,414 in 1969—but that was no consolation to Bobby and his family.

After he graduated from high school in La Puente, California, Mark Mitchell explored whether he could qualify to fly helicopters if he enlisted. Sure, said the Army, and in 1967, Mark was in Officers Candidate School, learning to operate the jet choppers so important in the war. He had married his high school sweetheart and wasn't itching to fight. He hoped the conflict would be over or winding down by the time he finished training, but if it came to flying helicopters in combat, he could accept that. In Vietnam, Mark twice survived being shot down. "He would send me pictures of him standing next to helicopters with bullet holes in them," Bobby says.

When he was killed, Mark David Mitchell was twenty-one.

The day he got the news, Bobby walked out of Moore-Hill Hall and went for a long walk, thinking, crying, questioning. Bobby was no anti–Vietnam War activist; in fact, he had reacted bitterly to the actions of some of the protesters in Austin.

"It was a weird feeling because I'd see hippies spitting on the soldiers, and see the tremendous harassment of anyone who was in the service," Bobby says. "Here you have a brother halfway around the world getting shot at, thinking he's doing the right thing for his country. And you see that." (Mark and Bobby's father, Charles E. Mitchell, was in the Battle of the Bulge, and later was a prisoner of war.)

As strongly as Bobby believed in the lure of democracy, he never was completely convinced committing American troops in Southeast Asia, so near China, was wise. He wondered if the South Vietnamese people really grasped these concepts. But, damn it, as long as the Americans were there, they should be supported. To young Bobby Mitchell, civilized debate about the war was tolerable; the most virulent expressions of dissent and a lack of respect for those wearing the U.S. uniform were not.

"I was upset with the way our government was playing the war," he says. "It was the old, 'Fight it to win or get out,' and it was this political war of attacking and pulling back. You're either in it or you're not."

Later, Bobby shared the news with his roommate, Longhorns safety Freddie Steinmark. Freddie didn't pretend to have all the answers, but he knew where to seek them—in his faith. Bobby was used to Freddie kneeling by the bed every night, saying his prayers, or getting up every Sunday morning and going to mass, trying to avoid disturbing teammates who had barely stumbled back into the dorm by then.

Not even Freddie could come up with a good answer for why the good die young. But he and Bobby talked about it, just as they had talked about so many things for several years—and not just in their cramped dorm room.

———

BOBBY MITCHELL'S FAMILY moved from California to the Denver area in early 1965, and Bobby enrolled at Wheat Ridge High School in the middle of his sophomore year. The sign carved into marble above the entrance proclaimed that WRHS was founded in 1896, when the farming community of Wheat Ridge was one of the major food baskets for Denver and the surrounding small towns. The building Bobby walked into was less than a decade old, and it was at least the third incarnation of WRHS. Across the street from the high school, a holdout family still was working a huge farm—a farm surrounded by Crown Hill Cemetery, the high school, and other suburban development. Downtown Denver was only about a fifteen-minute drive to the southeast. As a Wheat Ridge Farmer, Bobby would be competing for a school with a logo showing a hayseed in overalls, with a pitchfork in hand.

For his final two high school football seasons, Bobby Mitchell, the star fullback, played in the same backfield with a smaller halfback, Freddie Joe Steinmark. Freddie was raised in North Denver, near his mother's Italian-American neighborhood in the "Bottoms" adjacent to downtown, before the family moved to the suburbs. Freddie's father, Freddie Gene, a hard-driving, strict, and attentive former minor-league baseball player, was a Denver police officer.

As seniors, Steinmark and Mitchell were unstoppable in the pro-style offense installed by new Wheat Ridge coach J. W. "Red" Coats, who played center at Texas Tech and started his coaching career in El Paso. Mitchell was a much-sought prospect; Steinmark was the well-known, all-around athlete who won *The Denver Post*'s Gold Helmet Award as the top scholar–football player in the state. But Steinmark wasn't rabidly recruited because of his size—*maybe* five-eight and 154 pounds.

Coats touted Mitchell and Steinmark to Texas defensive coach Mike Campbell, whom Coats had met while coaching in El Paso, and the Wheat Ridge coach sent game films to Austin. Mitchell was excited because his family had lived for one year in Dallas, coinciding with Texas's 1963 national championship team, and the memories of the Longhorns stayed with him. The Texas staff liked Mitchell, and with some further prompting from Coats, they also looked closer at Steinmark, who ran for a 77-yard touchdown against the Lakewood Tigers in one of the game films. The Texas coaches decided Steinmark had potential as a safety, and they recruited both Wheat Ridge stars, causing University of Colorado coach Eddie Crowder—who previously hadn't given Steinmark the time of day, much less a scholarship—to eventually jump in with an offer to Steinmark, too. Mitchell heard from scores of schools, and he was considering Colorado and California when he and Freddie took their official recruiting visit to Austin together in the spring of 1967. Ted Koy was their escort for the weekend, taking them to dinner at a steakhouse and then to see *The Man with No Name*, starring Clint Eastwood.

On Sunday, Koy waited outside the office when the two Wheat Ridge Farmers visited Darrell Royal in the coach's inner sanctum. By then, Freddie had given up on his dream of playing at Notre Dame; the Fighting Irish weren't interested. Texas was.

"I asked Freddie how it went," Koy says. "He said, 'Well, I'm very impressed and very excited because he was the only coach who didn't talk about my size. I think I can play anywhere!' That was Freddie. He wasn't being arrogant. Just confident."

In his autobiography, *I Play to Win*, written with Blackie Sherrod, Steinmark later said he asked Royal directly if his size bothered the Texas coach. Steinmark said that Royal came back with: "Why should it?" Royal told Freddie he weighed 158 when he arrived at Oklahoma, when he already was twenty-one.

At Texas, Steinmark and Mitchell were roommates from the start. The Longhorns were a bunch of Texans—and two Wheat Ridge Farmers. (When Jim Bertelsen came in from Wisconsin a year behind them, they didn't feel quite so isolated as "outsiders.") Steinmark's Wheat Ridge girlfriend, Linda Wheeler, also enrolled at Texas. Mitchell bought his first car— a junker '52 Ford—for $350 to drive to Austin. Steinmark didn't trust that car to get them to the campus in time for the opening of freshman practice, so Mitchell drove alone. When he arrived, he was told that freshmen couldn't keep cars on campus. He sold it to a dealer for fifty dollars.

One reason Mitchell and Steinmark got along so well as roommates was that they had separate circles of friends, and they didn't feel the need to have to do *everything* together. Surprisingly, Steinmark found his football niche sooner than Mitchell. Although at least one teammate thought Freddie was a shoeshine boy the first time he saw him, Steinmark started at defensive halfback for the Longhorn freshman team. Mitchell, however, mostly watched. He made his mark as a versatile back at Wheat Ridge, but his pass-catching abilities out of the backfield were all but worthless at Texas. He was a reserve halfback and fullback on the freshman team, which was Steve Worster's showcase. "It was really discouraging and I almost left, to go back to Colorado, where they loved me," Mitchell says. "I was going to take my toys and go home."

During that notoriously tough spring practice period in 1968, the coaches asked Mitchell if he was interested in trying to play guard. He was smart enough to know that this "request" wasn't a *request*. It was a proclamation: *If you want a chance to play, you'll play guard.*

The next fall, when the Longhorns went to the wishbone for Mitchell's sophomore season, the need for smaller, quicker, smarter guards was even more pronounced. Mitchell was doing better in the classroom than he was on the field, and he eventually settled on anthropology as his major. He backed up Danny Abbott as a sophomore, then moved into the starting lineup for 1969. He found he enjoyed playing guard, given the aggressive freedom the linemen had in the wishbone, and he liked playing for offensive line coach Willie Zapalac.

"I loved Coach Zapalac," Mitchell says. "Along with that fear of your coaches, I feared him losing respect for me. He had a real magic at getting the most out of you, of pushing you to the limit, but when it was all said and done, you admired and thanked him for it. I think it was a fear of not just losing your position, but the fear of the disappointment he would have in you, that you let him down. In those years, we had tremendous assistant coaches, and that's not to take anything away from Royal, because he was the one who put it all together."

Mitchell even got over the surprise of seeing his roommate start before he did. In 1968, Steinmark was a starting safety and had five interceptions, and also returned punts. Everyone marveled at his determination and his clean living.

"Freddie was a model, a hustler, a real peppy guy," says Fred Akers, who switched from the offensive side of the ball and became defensive backfield coach in 1968. "He never took a lazy step—never. He was always doing more than you asked. And he had that infectious smile. Every time you said anything to him, he'd break out into this huge smile."

Defensive end Bill Atessis calls Steinmark "the kind of guy you'd want your sister to marry. Just a fantastic, upbeat, courteous guy. He was smart, intelligent, well-mannered, and pound for pound, I don't think there was a more talented player in the league. Freddie did more with what he had than anyone I had met before or since."

There was a toughness to the undersized safety, both on and off the field. Freddie was outspoken, the legacy of his grandmother from the Bottoms of Denver, where you never thought twice about saying exactly what you meant—and didn't expect it to be taken personally. "Freddie was kind of a funny Italian and wore his feelings on his shirtsleeve," says linebacker Scott Henderson, the fellow Catholic who was probably the closest to Steinmark of all the Longhorns. "He was a very, very good friend."

Steinmark and Mitchell still shared that Wheat Ridge bond. About the only tension between the two roommates came when Steinmark chased Mitchell and the card games out of their room because he wanted to study, or when he gently chided Mitchell for his occasional partying. In all the other rooms, if a roommate complained about the card games because he wanted to study, the comeback was, "Go to the library!" But not with Freddie. Everybody understood Freddie *was* that serious, and that he sometimes struggled with his engineering courses. And everybody knew that Coach Royal never had to worry about Freddie's actions off the field.

The Texas team rules, roughly, were: *Don't drink, but if boys must be boys, don't embarrass the program.* Bobby Mitchell was perfectly willing to be one of the boys, as were most of his teammates, and he still laughs when reminiscing about the one time he tested Royal's parameters of discipline.

Mitchell was in an Austin bar after 1969 spring ball with teammates Steve Worster, linebacker Glen Halsell, defensive tackle Greg Ploetz, and a reserve offensive player. A couple of girls the players didn't know sat down with them. Next thing the players knew, some men were showing Liquor Control Board badges and saying the players were contributing to the delinquency of minors—the girls. (The players weren't twenty-one, either, but that didn't seem to be the issue.)

The players were scared because they realized this might be a textbook case of *embarrassing the program* if someone wanted to make a big deal out of it. They quickly tried to invent aliases and agreed to claim they didn't have their IDs. The players were divided up and placed in cars for interrogation, and their stories fell apart, because the girls knew who they were—and named names. (The whole thing smelled like a setup; the players never found out if it was.) After they were allowed out of the cars, the reserve panicked and slipped out the back door, jumping into the river behind the bar and spraining both ankles before limping back to the dorm. The LCB men told them not to sweat it and asked them to tell the reserve the girls had said who he was, and if he and all of them cooperated, it wouldn't get back to Darrell Royal.

The boys cooperated, and they were relieved. It wouldn't get back to Coach Royal.

The *next morning*, Coach Royal called them into his office and reiterated the policy. Once this stuff was called to his attention, he couldn't ignore it. He said if they were drinking in public and involved in an "incident," they had a choice: Either be thrown off the team or do some, ahem, "extracurricular activity" with Frank Medina.

Royal said he would take their word as men, and he asked each one of them if they had been drinking. "Yes, sir," said Steve Worster. "Yes, sir," said Bobby Mitchell, Glen Halsell, Greg Ploetz, and the reserve.

The five Longhorns who said yes, sir, did their extra work with Frank Medina every night for so long, they forgot how long it had been since they started. They ran stadium stairs, and if they didn't puke then, they sure as heck puked after the dummy drill. It was a familiar punitive routine for the Longhorns: Two dummies were placed about ten yards apart. You hit one, rolled three times, got up and hit the other one, rolled three times, got up and hit the other one . . . and at some point, all the rolling would sabotage your equilibrium and you would lose whatever was left in your stomach, or get the dry heaves. Then you were reminded that you weren't done, and that maybe you should have been thinking about this when you *embarrassed the program!*

Frank Medina also was the man you were supposed to trust to get you well when you were injured. The diminutive Medina had been with the Longhorns since 1945, and served as a trainer for U.S. Olympic track and field teams. He could give football players such withering looks of disdain when they came into the training room for treatment, they felt the same way they did when they missed a block on the film and the coaches kept playing it over and over. Medina's ability to make them feel tiny was a screening mechanism for traffic to the training room. If they went into his room, they'd better be hurt. Really hurt. Or they'd better prove to him that they were tough enough to be worthy of his treatment or the use of his facilities. He treated "legitimate injuries" efficiently and brusquely, but by god, the Longhorns should be finding a way to stay on the field or to get back on it as soon as possible. He wasn't there to mollycoddle or soothe or cater to guys who came in at every instance of pain. But that was the players' fraternal mentality as well. The tough guys played through the injuries, unless the bone was showing through the skin, or the ligament was torn, or the pain was excruciating and uncontrollable. And the Longhorns knew they might as well be punching in and out on a time clock when they visited Medina's training room to do anything but have their ankles taped, even for something as "innocent" as a soothing whirlpool. The news about the visit would get around to both teammates and coaches—right down to the minutes and seconds.

Steinmark and Mitchell both needed Medina's services during the 1969 season. Mitchell suffered a sternum injury against Rice, in the Longhorns' fifth game, but missed only one game. Over the next few weeks, Mitchell shared time at left guard with Randy Stout as Royal often used them to send in plays. For Mitchell, getting back in the starting lineup by the final game was most of all an issue of pride, because his girlfriend, Honor Franklin, from Mesquite, was attending the University of Arkansas. They were introduced by friends and stayed in touch, and in the fall of 1969, they found themselves getting closer, talking on the phone, writing letters, missing each other.

Mitchell was going to be full-strength for the Arkansas game, but Steinmark wasn't. He couldn't seem to get better, and he couldn't understand it.

It was Steinmark's left leg, the spot between the thigh and the knee exposed between the pads jammed in the pants. Glen Halsell, the linebacker and captain, remembers sitting next to Steinmark on the flight back from the opener at California and hearing Freddie say that his leg was bugging him. Even earlier, Mitchell knew Steinmark was hurting, but they both thought it was a bruise or a calcium deposit. Bobby got used to seeing Freddie rubbing his leg. "Everybody had a bone bruise or a knee or hip pointer or something, so we didn't really think it was all that unusual," Mitchell says. Steinmark wrote that as early as right after that opener at California, he confessed to Akers that his leg was bothering him, saying it was a pulled muscle. Steinmark wrote that he told Medina and Dr. Joe Reneau, the team physician, about the injury during the season, and spent a lot of time in the whirlpool. He took some teasing from teammates for that. "We said Frank should take Freddie under his wing and adopt him," tackle Bob McKay says.

Freddie's father asked him at midseason if he was hurting, because he seemed to have slowed down a bit. Freddie played on, and because he played with such intelligence and instinct, and on such a dominating team, he got by. Scott Henderson told him it might be the same bone disease that slowed Mickey Mantle. In his book, Steinmark said he joked: *They might have to cut it off.*

With Arkansas looming at the end of the schedule, Steinmark knew that the Razorbacks' pro-style offense would challenge him and the two defensive halfbacks—Danny Lester and Tom Campbell—more than any other attack in the Southwest Conference. Because he was a two-year starter in the secondary and he was the safety with the wider view of the action, Freddie was considered the nominal leader of the group on the field. Off the field, he didn't know Danny Lester well. But then again, almost nobody did.

DANNY LESTER WASN'T A SPHINX as much as he was a brooding mystery. His hair and his clothes were getting into "hippie" territory, which in the football dorm and coaches' offices didn't exactly take anything outlandish. You could be a "hippie" to the coaches, and still be suspected as a narc among the real counterculture in Austin. Defensive end Bill Atessis, one of Lester's better friends on the roster, says, "When they had protest marches, sometimes we were out there harassing the hippies. Danny was probably a little more sympathetic to their cause."

His teammates learned that if they asked Danny how he was, just making conversation, he either would be monosyllabic and brief, or suddenly unleash a litany of woe. Ohhhhh, this kind of hurts, or that test didn't go well. They were not filibusters, they weren't particularly revealing, but he frequently seemed to be bothered by something. There was something very refreshing about that, though. He might not tell you much beyond the surface, but what he told you, you knew it was the truth. Danny was genuine. He was close to his roommate of three years, reserve linebacker Buddy Hudgins, and he ran some with Steve Worster and split end Cotton Speyrer. "I had seen so much bullshit by then and so much plastic and so many groupies and so many hangers-on," Worster says. "I appreciated that Danny was just such a *real* human being."

For example, Atessis once received a shotgun for a birthday present and turned around and sold it to Lester for fifty dollars. Danny told his mother about it, and she chewed out Danny for taking advantage of Atessis and paying far less than the gun was worth. Lester tried to get Atessis to take more money, but Atessis refused. A deal was a deal.

The next year, when Cotton Speyrer suffered a broken arm, he was touched when Lester made him a get-well present—a hand-woven leather belt.

And, oh, the girls loved Danny Lester. Teammates would watch, open-mouthed and even jealous, as the belles of the campus—"good" girls! beauty queens!—chased him, shamelessly and relentlessly. The Longhorns were envious of something else, too: Danny could party up a storm one night, and run them all into the ground the next day at practice or in the off-season conditioning workouts. You would think he was a teetotaler, a monk, a fanatic training to climb Mount Everest or run a marathon. Those who were with Lester the night before would be sucking air, just dying, even puking, saying they never would drink again, so help them god, and there would be Danny, charging right along—and maybe with Freddie Steinmark, who probably was in bed the night before at nine. Freddie and Danny often did extra sprints together.

Glen Halsell says Lester "was a little bit sad and lonely. He was a deep person, there was some part of him that looked like he had been hurt, and you didn't want to violate it. There was a sincerity about him that kind of touched your heart."

So there always seemed to be something he wasn't talking about. *What's the story with Danny, anyway?*

———————

DANNY KNEW ALL ABOUT the good dying young.

When he was less than a year old, his mother, Kathy, got one of those phone calls. Her husband, John David Lester, had come in contact with a power line on his job with the electric company and was electrocuted. In later years, Danny would be a ringer for the father he never knew.

Kathy met and married T. A. Paul, who was wonderful with his stepson, and Danny adored him. T.A. would have the patience of Job with the young boy, who already was showing eye-catching natural talent as an athlete in their West Texas hometown of Hereford. But T.A. came down with cancer and died when Danny was eleven. Danny had two fathers, one he never really knew, and one he worshiped. Both died young.

Two years later, Kathy married again. George Pulley was going to move the family from Hereford to the big city, Amarillo, and Danny was scared. All his friends were in Hereford, and how could he get along in Amarillo? He was starting junior high and he didn't know a soul! The coaches didn't know him! His mother remembers telling him: "Oh, Danny, the coaches are going to notice you, and the other kids are going to be starting into junior high, just like you are. The coaches don't know them. So if you want to play, be the best there is. Or else you can sit on the bench and cry." Kathy Pulley laughs. "Well," she says, "he *never* sat on the bench."

For the first six months after the move, he bugged his mom to take him back to Hereford whenever she could, to visit friends and relatives. After that, Kathy couldn't *drag* him back to Hereford. Danny was the star, and he became one of the greatest all-around athletes in the history of Amarillo high school sports. Football, basketball, baseball, he made it all look so easy at Tascosa High. Everyone in the Southwest Conference recruited him, and so did the Naval and Air Force academies. He and his buddy, Tascosa quarterback Monty Johnson, thought of either Oklahoma or Texas, and chose to stay in-state. Their Tascosa High coach, R. M. "Pat" Patterson, joined Royal's staff at Texas following their junior seasons, so they knew one coach already. (Johnson transferred to Oklahoma after his freshman year; Danny stayed.)

Lester played both offense and defense, and he backed up Speyrer at split end as a sophomore. But by his junior year, he was the starting right defensive halfback, the position that later would be known as "cornerback."

"Danny was a tough-as-nails ranch kid," Fred Akers says. "He was very quiet. I mean *very* quiet. After you got to know him, he was *still* quiet. But tough! Very, very tough."

As Akers worked with defensive backs Lester, Steinmark, and Tom Campbell, he was pondering how they might be tested by Arkansas quarterback Bill Montgomery in Fayetteville. Akers, the former Razorback quarterback, could have told his Longhorn charges that their goal was to shut down the offense, limiting the number of times the Arkansas Razorback Marching Band got to play the song that traditionally followed moments of triumph on the field.

"Dixie."

NINE

Dixie's Last Stand

Oh, I wish I was in the land of cotton
Old times there are not forgotten
Look away! Look away! Look away!
Dixie Land.
In Dixie Land where I was born
Early on one frosty mornin'
Look away! Look away! Look away!
Dixie Land.
Oh, I wish I was in Dixie!
Hooray! Hooray!
In Dixie Land I'll take my stand
To live and die in Dixie!
Away, away, away down south in Dixie!
Away, away, away down south in Dixie!

—From "Dixie," by Daniel Decatur Emmett, 1859

No blacks played in the 1969 Texas-Arkansas game. No blacks were in uniform. Every player in both 1969 team pictures is white. But the *programs* were integrated.

Arkansas B team defensive back Hiram McBeth III, an eighteen-year-old sophomore, watched the game from the stands. He believed he and other black students, plus sympathizers both black and white, might end up storming the field during the climactic Texas-versus-Arkansas game, lying down, delaying the game. And all of this in front of the president of the United States of America and a national television audience.

McBETH WAS FROM PINE BLUFF, and was one of perhaps a hundred black undergraduate students on the Fayetteville campus. The University of Arkansas had black students during Reconstruction, before segregation took hold and black graduate students were admitted after 1948 if equivalent programs weren't available at the state's black schools. The first black undergraduates enrolled in 1955, but the UofA dormitories weren't integrated until 1963. Until then, blacks had to live off-campus.

McBeth wasn't a great football player, and he didn't have any illusions that he ever would be. He showed up to football practice in the spring of 1969, when he was only seventeen and in the second half of his freshman year.

He had been *drafted.*

A student group, Black Americans for Democracy, met and decided it would appoint members to integrate various organizations and activities on campus. They laid out all the possibilities. This club, that club, this group, that group. And then: *OK, who's the absolute fool? Who's going to go out for the football team?*

McBeth played high school football and wasn't a bad athlete. His friends knew that, and eyes turned to him. *Hiram?* It was as if a colonel had asked for volunteers, and everyone else had taken a step back. "It was a mission I was sent on," McBeth says.

And who was the absolute fool?

Hiram McBeth, Jr., Hiram's father, was an Army rifleman in World War II, in both the European and Pacific theaters. He was sent into Hiroshima after the atom bomb was dropped. "You know who they sent in there first, don't you?" his son asks. "Yes, the blacks! He was with that group. He had some pictures that showed bones stacked up."

When Hiram, the father, returned to Pine Bluff, he worked for the Pine Bluff Armory and later was head of the ROTC department at Arkansas AM&N. For years, he was either summoned or driven in a government car to the veterans hospital in Little Rock for checkups and treatment of minor ailments. The McBeth family thought that was very nice of the government. "That was a big deal in a black neighborhood," Hiram III says. "White men coming down to pick up a black man and bring him back! People would ask, 'They going to come and get your daddy again?'"

(Years later, Hiram III got a call from one of his college roommates, a doctor who had just started his residency at the VA hospital. *Hey, Hiram, is your dad's name Hiram, too? Yes. Well, I just saw all this paperwork. You know the government's studying him and the other soldiers who were sent into Hiroshima, don't you?*)

The Pine Bluff schools had officially integrated a few years earlier, but the racial lines still were pronounced. The Pine Bluff High Zebras were the white kids. At Townsend Park High, one of the city's four predominantly black schools, Hiram played clarinet in the band, was on the football team, and served as the student body president, graduating at sixteen. The spring of his senior year, he was in a car with the principal, coming back from a meeting in Newport, Arkansas, when the news of Martin Luther King's murder came over the radio. Shortly after his May commencement, Hiram got up one morning and heard that Robert Kennedy had been murdered in Los Angeles. "So I went off to college with a bad taste in my mouth," Mc-Beth says.

His parents, Hiram and Mary, were insistent: He was going to Fayetteville, and he was going to become a doctor or a lawyer. There were about thirty-five blacks in Hiram McBeth's freshman class at Arkansas in 1968. "These were cream-of-the-crop people," McBeth says. "We were groundbreakers and we generally were children of upwardly mobile, educated black people."

On campus, McBeth says, the usual reaction to the black students was neither warm nor overtly hostile. It was frosty resignation. The black students were there, the world was changing, and most seemed able to accept that, but there were exceptions. "You would have the occasional guy pass by in the 1955 Chevy and holler out the 'N' word, waving the Confederate flag," Mc-Beth says. The black students also learned that it was risky to walk past fraternity row on weekend nights, because the epithets flying from some fraternity members got uglier with every beer. Sometimes, even the beer bottles themselves flew.

In that atmosphere, BAD held one of what it called "sensitivity" meetings in a house on Buchanan Street rented by the students. That was when Mc-Beth was drafted to go out for football. "I walked into the offices and said to the first white face I saw, 'I think I'd like to play football,'" McBeth says.

That same spring, the Arkansas coaching staff recruited running back Jon Richardson from Little Rock's Horace Mann High School, where he also was the student body president. Darrell Royal and Texas sought Richardson as well, but lost out to the Razorbacks. In the fall of 1969, Richardson was on the Arkansas freshman team. But when McBeth went out for 1969 spring training, Richardson was finishing up high school, and McBeth was the only black player in the program. (He wasn't the first, but that's another story.) The basketball program was a year ahead of the football team: Almer Lee, from Fort Smith, became the Razorbacks' first varsity basketball letterman in the 1969–70 season. Thomas Johnson was the Razorbacks' first scholarship player, in 1967, and he played for the Shoats freshman team before transferring to Central Arkansas after the first semester of his sophomore year, saying he didn't want to redshirt.

Broyles long has said the state board informally made it clear to him when he arrived at Arkansas that he could not recruit black athletes, but that he felt integration was inevitable and right. His 1957 recruiting of Missouri's first black scholarship players, Norris Stevenson and Mel West, backs up his words. Broyles says he asked Don Faurot, who coached the Tigers for nineteen seasons and still was the athletic director, if the Broyles staff could begin recruiting black players. At the time, Jim Crow laws and traditions still ruled at Columbia restaurants and public facilities. "He said go after it," Broyles says. In January 1957, Broyles sent assistant coach John Kadlec to look at Stevenson, who graduated from St. Louis's Vashon High School after the first semester of the academic year and was leaning toward attending Indiana. Broyles then met with Stevenson himself in St. Louis. Stevenson went to Missouri. That spring, the Broyles staff landed West from Jefferson City, and he and Stevenson became the Tigers' first black football lettermen in 1958 under Broyles's successor, Dan Devine.

On the Arkansas campus, Broyles in some corners was regarded as unenthusiastic, or worse, about trying to integrate the Razorbacks. One reason was that when he was challenged in the mid-1960s at a faculty senate council meeting about why he wasn't recruiting black players, Broyles lashed out, making it clear he felt ambushed by faculty members intruding on his turf. His role in recruiting the first blacks to the Missouri program was on the record. But Broyles's angry reaction quickly got around the campus, including to the black students, and, fairly or otherwise, they considered him an obstructionist on the issue of athletic integration. It didn't help that the football program was slightly behind the basketball team in terms of having black scholarship players.

In 1966, Southern Methodist's Jerry Levias became the Southwest Conference's first black varsity player. The rest of the conference, including

Arkansas and Texas, soon were recruiting black players, and Jon Richardson was the Razorbacks' first black scholarship football player. "The timing was right," Broyles says. "It wasn't my doing. SMU already had brought in Levias. It was the right thing to do and everybody knew that. It was an easy transition." Broyles says he didn't ask the university or athletic administration for permission to begin recruiting blacks. "I think I just told my people what I was going to do, and they said, 'Fine.'" (And there can be no disputing the fact that as the years passed, Broyles generally was given credit for decisively advancing the cause of athletic integration, both as a coach and as an athletic director. The 2002 controversy over the firing of Razorback basketball coach Nolan Richardson, hired by Broyles in 1985, shouldn't change that. Documents showed Broyles generally had defended Richardson to his critics—including racist critics—over the years. Richardson's hypersensitivity to the inevitable heightened criticism any coach receives when a program regresses, as the Razorbacks' had, and his tendency to attribute it all to racism, was tiresome. When he virtually dared the university to buy out his contract, UofA officials had no choice but to fire him. Broyles hired another African-American, Stan Heath, as Richardson's replacement.)

In the spring of 1969, though, Hiram McBeth was the lone black working out with the Razorbacks. "The individual football players were very supportive," McBeth says. He occasionally felt the frost, but there was little open hostility. One exception, at least in one angry argument, was when McBeth, then playing running back, blocked a varsity player in a drill and the player suffered an injured knee. The player's buddy, Webb Hubbell, was the senior starting tackle on the 1968 team and was helping out on the field as a graduate assistant. Hubbell angrily confronted McBeth. "He kind of meant it in terms of I hurt his friend. He turned out to be a good guy," McBeth says.

McBeth admits he wasn't a good running back and preferred to play defense, where he was a decent bump-and-run halfback. Still, it was apparent that he was little threat to take any of the scholarship players' jobs.

Lon Farrell was the B team head coach and the football program's academic counselor. He lived in Wilson Sharp House, and he and Wilson Matthews were considered the godfathers of the program. From day one, Farrell supported McBeth, with words here and there, with an arm around the shoulder, with urgings to stick at it. Farrell made a point of making sure McBeth saw articles in the Little Rock paper about how he was on the verge of becoming the first black Razorback to play in the Red-White spring game. At that point, McBeth was vacillating on whether he would come back out in the fall. "I was thinking about quitting because it was hard, it was tough, I was getting beat up pretty bad," he says. "I was linebacker meat. That's the way it was for the scrubs. We used to have to run up into the hole and let the linebacker hit you. Bam! Then Lon Farrell came to me on the bus with the papers I saw that and said, 'Oh, my god, I'm in it now.' That was my mission, anyway."

In fact, he was useful to the Razorbacks: He was good enough, the coaches knew, to be a B team—or scout team—defensive halfback, and work against Chuck Dicus as he "imitated" the opposing team's defensive backs each week. McBeth says Dicus and Bill Montgomery both encouraged him. He also appreciated the "hang-in-there" words he got from the young offensive coaches—Don Breaux and Richard Williamson. He wasn't costing the Razorbacks a scholarship, he was helping integrate the program—which the young coaches, at least, knew was inevitable—and he was a bright student who wasn't going to cause them any trouble. Or so they thought.

But McBeth and his BAD contemporaries hated that the football program was linked to the song "Dixie," which the black students on campus considered an abhorrent throwback. Ohio native Daniel Decatur Emmett wrote the song for a minstrel show in New York in 1859. The Confederate States of America, including its army, considered the song its informal anthem during the war; a century later, the Arkansas band played it as a fight song, as a celebration of touchdowns and points, as a rallying cry for the moment. Some of the most vehement proponents of continuing the use of the song by the university viewed it as an expression of heritage and tradition and regional pride, not an endorsement of slavery or racism. Others just wanted the "*niggers*" to shut up and get the hell out of the way. But to the black students, there was no avenue for compromise: If the UofA band continued to play the song, and the university continued to approve its use as a quasi-official school anthem, the black students would not put up with it.

McBeth wasn't a vocal leader of the black student community. Those roles went to others, including law students Darrell Brown and Eugene Hunt. Although Brown's name was mentioned in a few news reports the week of the Texas-Arkansas game, it wasn't disclosed then that he briefly had integrated the Razorbacks football program—in the fall of 1965, the same season Jerry

Levias was on the Southern Methodist freshman team. That was four years before McBeth was on the B team and Arkansas made Jon Richardson its first scholarship player. "Oh," McBeth says, waving his hand in self-deprecating dismissal, "Darrell Brown was a *way* better athlete than I was."

BROWN'S HIGH SCHOOL in tiny Horatio, Arkansas—the Sevier County Training School—didn't even have a football team. It also didn't have white students. The Horatio schools weren't integrated until the fall after Brown graduated. "The word 'training' has significance when you're black," Brown says. "You never will run into a school designed to treat whites called a training school."

In 1965, Brown was encouraged to go to one of the state's traditionally black schools—Arkansas AM&N or Philander Smith—but he decided on the UofA. "I was obsessed with the need to attend an institution that served across the board regardless of race, creed, and color," Brown says. So he went to Arkansas, which had been admitting black undergraduates for only ten years.

"There were probably a lot of students who would have been happy if I hadn't been there," Brown says. "Yet I found some Caucasians who appreciated my situation and befriended me and encouraged me."

And when he showed up for the Shoats' practices?

"On the football side, I found there existed that same kind of makeup of people who wanted me and people who didn't want me," Brown says. "Many of the players received me well." Two of them, he says, were quarterback John Eichler and Webb Hubbell. (Eichler was a redshirt in 1966, then played three varsity seasons and was Bill Montgomery's senior backup in 1969.) Brown also says "a lot of the players" called him "nigger," and so did one coach. "I didn't feel welcomed on the field by the coaches," Brown says of the freshman team staff. He says Wilson Matthews, the Fourth-Quarter Program czar then listed as the varsity linebackers coach, was at some freshman practices and encouraged him. Matthews had played at Arkansas and joined the Razorback staff in 1958 after coaching at Little Rock Central High.

Because Little Rock Central's 1957 integration crisis was front-page and magazine-cover news around the nation for weeks, Matthews already had worked under a spotlight. Under orders from Governor Orville Faubus, National Guardsmen prevented nine black students from integrating the school on September 4, the second day of classes. President Dwight Eisenhower federalized the Arkansas National Guard and sent one thousand Army paratroopers from the 101st Airborne Division to Little Rock to enforce integration and protect the students. The nine black students finally attended classes on September 25 after being escorted into the building by the paratroopers.

"We had a long winning streak going at the start of that season," Matthews says. "If I didn't have a group of young men with a lot of character and a lot of 'womp' to them, there were a lot of things that could keep them from concentrating and playing." But Central, which played games in several surrounding states against top teams, also was undefeated in 1957, extending its winning streak to thirty-three games. "Hell, there were pup tents on the practice field and things like that," Matthews says. "They were always trying to question me about what effect this and that had, and my answer was that if a bunch of damn soldiers hadn't showed up and got a crowd around, there wouldn't have been any problems. I know they tried to interview some of the players. 'What went on in school today?' They'd say, 'I can't tell you until I get home and watch the news tonight.'"

After coaching Central to ten state championships in his final eleven seasons, Matthews joined the Broyles staff. Brown says Matthews was his ally as he went out for the Shoats. "He would say, 'You can do it, Brown! Keep your head up! Go after them!' Those words were pregnant with encouragement to me." Matthews says he doesn't doubt any of that, but that he doesn't remember it, or Brown, either.

Brown says one freshman team coach was openly derisive all season, and it boiled over in one practice. "We were in a tipping drill and one of the players had tipped the ball, and I missed it, and he said, 'Get that ball, nigger!'" Brown says. "I just bowed my neck and went after it again. I was not raised to be a quitter. I was probably too young and hardheaded to believe that was going to stop me."

Brown worked at several positions, and he says he never was given a playbook. Late in the third game of the season, a 17–0 victory over the Oklahoma State freshmen in Fayetteville, he was sent in at running back and John Eichler and other teammates were determined to get him the ball. Brown hadn't been able to study the plays at the position, so he had to ask where he should go on the play Eichler called.

Eichler laughs when he tells the story of miscommunication.

"I said, 'Darrell, now you go right to the left,'" Eichler says.

Brown heard the "right"—and that's the way he went.

Eichler went left.

"It was his chance to get the ball," Eichler says. "We just missed connections and I had to eat it."

Brown was on the field for a few other plays in the five-game season, but the official Shoat rushing statistics don't credit Brown with any carries.

He still was determined to go out for the varsity the next season as a sophomore when he suffered knee and thumb injuries participating in the off-season conditioning work. "I think it probably woke me up," Brown says. "It was a red light coming on and it said, 'Maybe you should think about something that at this point realistically you can do, be welcome in, and succeed at—and it's not going to be playing football out here.' It was hard, but I used that to move to the next level of my life."

Brown gave up his dreams of integrating the football program and didn't go out for the varsity. By the fall of 1969, he was in his first term of law school, living with his wife as a resident advisor in Razorback Hall, one of the main dormitories. He was encouraging both McBeth and Richardson in their attempts to become the first blacks to play for the Arkansas varsity. He also was bitter and prepared to join in the protest over "Dixie." There, he was following the lead of another first-year law student. No, not Bill Clinton, who hadn't enrolled in the UofA law school that fall, after all. It was a professorial twenty-four-year-old from Pine Bluff, Eugene Hunt.

THE SON OF LAUNDRY WORKERS in Pine Bluff, Hunt sailed through Arkansas AM&N and studied at Harvard under a Rockefeller Foundation program designed to recruit black students for the law. When he entered the Arkansas law school in January 1969, he was one of three blacks enrolled. That fall, Brown joined him, and the black students—including the other BAD leaders, Jimmy Wilson and R. D. Rucker—were fed up with "Dixie."

"We had some of the brightest people in the state of Arkansas in our ranks, the African-American students," Hunt says. "We were glad to be there at Fayetteville. But regardless of the situation, you don't sacrifice your dignity or your integrity. 'Dixie' was seen as a racist call to arms, and I don't think I can put it any better than that. We felt the university was very insensitive when it countenanced the playing of 'Dixie' at the pep rallies."

As the 1969 Razorbacks kept winning, there was much to celebrate and many Razorback scores, which triggered the playing of the song by the Arkansas band. BAD campaigned all fall for the banishment of the song. BAD also demanded more black faculty members and students, more financial aid to black students, a black culture center in the planned new student union, and the hiring of a black campus police officer. At the time, the UofA had *one* black faculty member, sociology associate professor Gordon D. Morgan, who had received his doctorate from Washington State and had taught in Africa and at Lincoln University in Jefferson City, Missouri. He joined the UofA faculty in the fall of 1969, and Morgan and his family lived in a house the university owned, virtually adjacent to the BAD house.

The black students considered Morgan their intermediary to the university administration, headed by President David W. "Moon" Mullins. An Arkansas native, Mullins was an executive vice president of Auburn University when he assumed the UofA presidency in 1960. He was an adept politician, often working behind the scenes and keeping negotiations—or any other events—out of the public eye. But the black students believed Mullins ignored their concerns in the fall of 1969, despite several meetings. "He was always gracious," Eugene Hunt says. "But there was a question whether he understood the predicate of the concerns. He was not in touch with us."

The tensions grew on November 25, the Tuesday before the Thanksgiving Day game against Texas Tech in Little Rock. Pep rallies traditionally were held at the Chi Omega Greek Theatre, an outdoor amphitheater several blocks east of Razorback Stadium. This rally was going to follow the time-honored form—the UofA band would march in and play "Dixie." The BAD students decided they wouldn't let it happen this time. "Things evolved to the point where we felt we had to engage in some overt action—peaceable overt action, but overt action," Hunt says. The plan was to occupy the stage until the black students were promised the band never would play "Dixie" again.

Hiram McBeth says he tried to talk Jon Richardson into coming with him, but failed. "He was a recruited player," McBeth says. "If I got him to come with me, that would kind of get me a little cover, too."

McBeth rushed off to the Greek Theatre. Shortly before the pep rally was scheduled to begin, a group of black students, including Hunt and Darrell Brown, occupied the chairs onstage reserved for the band. "I guess you could say we took over the Greek Theatre," Hunt says. "I'm not bragging about that. We wanted to avoid a fight, we were not into that business."

Darrell Brown says, "We were a bunch of young, hungry black students. We were hungry, I guess, in the sense of wanting to take a stand and let it be known. We bravely, and in retrospect without much foresight, stepped in front of that crowd and said it was not going to happen. We were not going to have 'Dixie' played."

McBeth arrived just in time to jump into another group that blocked the path of the band as it marched into the Greek Theatre. "The band got stopped and they started stepping on each other," McBeth says.

The black students said they would leave the stage if they were promised that the band never again would play "Dixie." Student organizers announced the pep rally would be held outside Wilson Sharp House, so the students walked to the nearby athletic dormitory.

In the next issue of the *Arkansas Traveler*, which didn't appear until December 2 because of the Thanksgiving holiday, Hunt said: "All we asked was a chance to explain our position. The most disgusting thing is that they didn't allow us to say it."

On the day after the pep rally, November 26, or Thanksgiving Eve, Hunt led a delegation of about sixty black students into Mullins's office. "We left a list of grievances, didn't have a discussion, and walked out," Hunt says. The *Northwest Arkansas Times* reported: "Eugene Hunt, one of the black students, said they had not remained to talk with Dr. Mullins because 'we've been talking to him for a year and half now.' . . . Dr. Mullins was not available for comment late Wednesday and Hunt declined to say if students intended to take further action."

As it happens, they did. They already were talking about pushing for a ban on "Dixie" before the Texas game, and about what they might do at Razorback Stadium that day if the band played the song at the confrontation between the two all-white teams.

Like the Razorbacks, though, the Longhorns were on the verge of varsity integration.

Darrell Royal was no crusader, but by the mid-1960s, he also knew he couldn't win much longer with all-white teams. The University of Texas had integrated in 1950, the result of a lawsuit filed on behalf of Heman Marion Sweatt's attempt to be admitted to the law school.

"It might come as a shock to some people," Royal says, "but football coaches don't decide when you integrate."

It's fair to say that Royal didn't aggressively push for integration, even when his teams were competing against teams with black players in the late fifties and sixties. But he also was a pragmatist who wanted to win—and annually beat Oklahoma—not only to keep his job, but because he was miserable when his teams lost. Plus, his later insistence that he had coached black players in previous stops, including at Edmonton and Washington, and had black friends, was true. As Jimmy Banks noted in *The Darrell Royal Story*, the coach's star player at Edmonton, Rollie Miles, and two other starters were black, and a white starter, Tom Stolhandske, later said Royal had blistered several white players for making racist remarks and said he wouldn't tolerate them. Especially because of his friendship with Lyndon Johnson, the coarse pragmatist who, for all his faults, developed a genuine concern for the plight of the disadvantaged and the cause of civil rights, Royal also came to frankly acknowledge that he should have been more concerned about racial equity sooner—and not just in sports—and that candor gives him credibility.

But Texas was behind the curve. His alma mater, Oklahoma, had its first black letterman, Prentice Gautt, from 1957 to 1959, after Bud Wilkinson—who came to be respected as a courageous proponent of integration and was called a "father figure" by Gautt—had been the Sooners' head coach for a decade. Gautt was one year ahead of Frank Broyles–recruited Norris Stevenson at Missouri, OU's fellow Big Seven Conference school.

A decade later, in terms of integration the Southwest Conference was lagging behind the rival league, the renamed Big Eight, not to mention the other conferences around the country that had been playing blacks for years. When Texas successfully recruited Julius Whittier (and, unsuccessfully, Jon Richardson) in early 1969, three blacks had been in the Longhorn program the season before, and the Royal staff had been *trying* to land black players for several years. E. A. Curry and Robinson Parsons both "walked on" without scholarships and practiced with the Longhorns' 1968 team, but didn't letter and didn't return the next season. Leon O'Neal, a scholarship player, was on the 1968 freshman team before transferring to Blinn Junior College and eventually to Southwest Texas State.

So when Julius Whittier committed to attending Texas, he didn't know he would become the Longhorns' first black letterman.

"I didn't go there with that as a goal," he says. "I went there because I wanted to play big-time football, take a shot and see how I stacked up against guys like me. If I was an icebreaker, I didn't feel the breaking ice."

Whittier says he never felt as if Darrell Royal had to be dragged screaming into the era of integrated college football. "There may have been those coaches who made it their goal to make sure college football stayed white," Whittier says. "I didn't see that in Coach Royal, didn't see it as a burning issue with any of the white football players, and even in looking back I don't see it.

"I think the guys I played with felt comfortable they had the skills to compete with anyone, whether that guy was white or black. So, no, I don't see Coach Royal as a fiber in the fabric of the part of football that may have wanted to keep it white. Coach Royal basically came to a school that got its personality from the state it served. Not that he was some big social revolutionary or anything, but I think he recognized that to stay who we were, we were going to have to use black athletes.

"There's a strength that was added to the team by adding different ethnic backgrounds. I think Royal appreciated that and was unafraid. [But] he had a board of regents that thought maintaining racial purity was more important for a long time."

UT's first black letterman came from San Antonio. Julius's father, Oncy, was a doctor, and his mother, Loraine, was a teacher. As he was being raised, Julius was somewhat naïve, because the San Antonio schools were a Texas oasis, integrated for years. White kids and black kids and brown kids went to school together, and from junior high up, students got "bus cards" and could attend any school in the district. But it was as if the city couldn't quite figure out how far to extend this progress.

One example of San Antonio's reticence was that blacks still had to enter the historic Majestic Theater through the back door and sit in the back. Julius's sisters, Cheryl and Mildred, worked at the Handy Andy market, and discovered that they wouldn't be allowed to advance to cashier's jobs; those were reserved for the white girls. Loraine, active in the NAACP, helped organize a protest march on the store; eventually, Cheryl and Mildred and other black girls were allowed to handle the money, too. Julius's older brother, also Oncy, set the example for Julius—one he didn't always pretend to match. Oncy was meticulous in his dress, polite in manner, and studious to an extreme. "He was the gentleman," Julius says. "I was the renegade." But Oncy also was involved in the Black Guerrilla Theatre group, which was in the same building as the militant Student Non-Violent Coordinating Committee and was raided at one point by San Antonio police. "My brother got clubbed in the head, along with several other people, and we had to get him out of jail," Julius says.

At Highlands High School, predominantly white, Julius took part in a protest of the dress code, wearing a dashiki he borrowed from Oncy. Oncy could argue with teachers and win them over, at least earning their respect; Julius could say what was on his mind and be tossed from class. Oncy was an all-city offensive lineman in football, and he ended up at Howard University in Washington, D.C. Julius was surprised when he discovered his options included attending the University of Texas and playing football—with all those white boys! At the end of his senior season, he discovered that his parents and his high school coach had cut a deal to lessen the recruiting pressures. "When the season was over, we were tearing down our lockers and my coach called me into the office," Julius says. "There were three bags of letters on his desk."

"This is for you, as a reward for the year you had."

"What is it, Coach?"

"They're letters from different colleges and universities, Julius. And I want you to read this one first."

Coach Darrell Royal was telling Julius Whittier the University of Texas Longhorns wanted him.

"I didn't know who he was," Whittier says. "I don't say that to minimize who he was, I say that to show how sheltered I was."

Royal's head defensive coach, Mike Campbell, came to San Antonio, met with Whittier, and helped schedule a visit to the UT campus. "I bought into Campbell's honesty," Whittier says. "He was straightforward. He was just an old white man who knew how to play football. He turned out to be just what he showed me—a straight shooter."

As Julius also set up visits to North Texas State and SMU, and he sifted through the letters from Big Ten schools, his mother's NAACP friends were aghast that he was considering UT. "They had this fear that I wouldn't get a fair shot, that I would be just suiting up and holding a dummy," Whittier says. "My mom was fascinated by the challenge, though."

Royal didn't make the kid from San Antonio any promises about how much he would play. "That part's up to you," Royal said. Like James Street and others before him, Whittier took that as a challenge. "You know the bumper sticker that says 'Hire a teenager while they still know everything?' That was me," he says. And he wouldn't be the only black player in the program, he was reminded. On his recruiting visit, Whittier was shown around by the freshman halfback, Leon O'Neal. "He told me the white folks were OK," Whittier says, smiling. "Then he left. It didn't bother me at first, until I thought about it later and he kind of left me there. I was expecting to go there and be real good friends with him for the next two, three years. We got along real well on my recruiting trip."

As he settled in at UT during that 1969 season, Whittier became increasingly bothered because his teammates seemed blinkered and insulated from the events swirling around them. And, no, at times he *didn't* feel welcome. "It's almost a southern gentleman kind of racism to the extent that I never got invited out on the drinking sprees," Whittier says. "Everybody knew I didn't drink. But there were also white boys invited out on these sprees who didn't drink."

He was quoted in the February 15, 1970, *San Antonio Express-News* as saying: "The problems I've had have been with some of the players. Texas seems to recruit a lot of boys from small towns, and most of them have small minds just like their fathers. I've gotten the message from them. It's subtle, but to them I'm definitely an outsider."

Years later, Whittier can repeat his "small-town boys" newspaper statement almost verbatim. You bet he heard about it, and he hasn't forgotten. He doesn't seem to give the Longhorns, even when all except Whittier were white, enough credit for their wide spectrum of attitudes, viewpoints, and level of seriousness, but it's understandable why.

"By that I meant they weren't out to change the world in any way," he says. "They were out to play first-class football at a first-class football school. Race didn't get in our way. The social change that I was into and used to in my home life, through my mom's stewardship, was not part of what they were about. They were about playing football and stepping into the life that a solid football career at a solid football school gets you."

But in 1969, Whittier was just a freshman linebacker, anyway, not a part of the varsity. The tricky part was freshmen were considered lower life forms in the football area of Jester Center, subject to the usual hazing rituals of being ordered to shine shoes, do laundry, go out for hamburgers or beer at two in the morning, or make beds. The freshman season was a plebe experience, and the tradition was that the first-year players couldn't even enter through the main door of the dining hall until they had beaten the Texas A&M freshmen.

Whittier regarded a few upperclassmen as his protectors—including sophomore Randy Stout, who shared time at left guard with Bobby Mitchell, plus backup running backs Billy Dale and Bobby Callison. He felt they were watching out for him, making sure the freshman indoctrination pranks didn't go beyond the norm, to racial harassment. (When Dale was a senior and Whittier was a sophomore, they roomed together in Jester.) Whittier also came to like defensive tackle Greg Ploetz.

"It didn't appear that I was being treated any different than any other freshman," Whittier says. "I think I was respected, too, because I was aggressive and got after it. I didn't slink to the back of the line when it was time for shit drills. In fact, I had made a promise to myself that when they said to line up I always would be first in line, even if I had to push and shove to get there. I wanted the coaches to know they didn't have to worry about me being willing to stick my face in there."

During that fall, the other Longhorn freshmen and a few of the upperclassmen noticed a few other things about the black kid: He could be late for lunch *because he was at a protest!* He would hang out *with the hippies!* He went to the Moratorium march, and he was sympathetic when students protested a Memorial Stadium and street expansion project that forced the bulldozing of Waller Creek between the stadium and the main part of campus. The administration and many students couldn't understand why moving the channel thirty feet was such a problem. So what if it killed a few trees and a few turtles?

"I had to walk by this fight to go into the stadium to get dressed to play football," Whittier says. "I was having to face the fact that what I was doing and the system I was playing in was the dynamite behind the movement to move Waller Creek. I'd have to walk past Frank Erwin"—the chairman of the board of regents—"and the other regents observing the protesters to make sure they didn't interfere with construction. Kids tied themselves to trees to stop the bulldozers."

Whittier says that while coaches made snide remarks every once in a while—*Heard you were up there with all the hippies!*—they never attempted to tell him he couldn't take part in protests or be politically active, either that freshman year or later. In fact, he says, trainer Frank Medina surprised him by saying, "If you take care of business here, you're fine with us."

The 1969 freshman team went 5–0, finishing off with a victory over Texas A&M in Austin on November 21. Then the first-year players settled in to watch their "heroes" close out the varsity season against Texas A&M and Arkansas.

"Those guys were like gods to us!" Whittier says. "You could tell that there was never a thought in their mind that anyone was going to beat them."

Certainly not Arkansas.

TEN

Loose-Cannon Captains

THE THREE CAMPUS POLICE CRUISERS, Glen Halsell could handle. The cop cars were up on the sidewalk, lights flashing, surrounding him. He after all had only been a gentleman and obliged the girl who asked him to deliver her back to the dormitory after the party. Halsell, the Longhorns' linebacker, made sure she didn't have too far to walk, pulling his car up over the curb, onto the sidewalk, up onto the front steps of the dorm's entrance. *Bump, bumpety-bump, crash.*

The humorless cops, and whoever called them, didn't appreciate his chivalry. He was pulled into one of the squad cars. He was in the backseat, waiting, figuring he could handle the wrath of the law, regardless of what these campus flatfeet decided to do with him. But *all* they were doing was sitting and waiting.

Then Halsell's heart damn near stopped. Suddenly, he *knew* he was in trouble. The orange Cadillac convertible was pulling up. *The Car.* It was three in the morning, long past bedtime in the home of Edith and Darrell Royal. Having to get out of bed and pull on clothes and go kick one of the boys in the ass wasn't going to thrill the head coach.

The cops pointed. Halsell climbed out of the safety of the cruiser's backseat and got into the car with one angry football coach.

Halsell was scared sober.

Glen, said Royal, *what are we going to do with you? You can't go through life this way. STRAIGHTEN YOURSELF OUT! You only get so many chances in life, son, and you're running out of them.*

Royal drove Halsell—the toughest, meanest damn football player on his roster—back to his dorm.

AT THE START OF TWO-A-DAY PRACTICES in Fayetteville in 1968, Razorbacks assistant Wilson Matthews—ex-Marine, ex-coach at Little Rock Central, czar of the Fourth-Quarter Program—was in front of the players in the lounge at Wilson Sharp House and was going through the team rules.

No drinking.

No smoking.

No booze or tobacco in the dorm.

Go to class.

Matthews knew that many of the Razorbacks talked about their relationship with the Lord and whether mass should be in English or Latin. There almost were two camps—the hell-raising beer drinkers and the Christians. There were getting to be so many Christians that it could really bug a football coach to whom it seemed second nature to snap off a "goddamn" every once in a while—or every other sentence—when Frank Broyles, the southern gentleman, wasn't around to hear it.

Matthews looked right at round-faced fullback Bruce Maxwell, the toughest, meanest—and maybe even the best—damn football player on the team, the man who just flat-out scared many of his teammates.

Goddammit, Maxwell, Matthews roared, *I know you smoke and drink, and I know you're going to smoke and drink, but here's what you do! You get yourself a goddamn mayonnaise jar lid and you go in that room and lock the door and you smoke those damn cigarettes and then you take that to the bathroom and you flush it down the damn toilet. If I find a cigarette butt or ash in your room, your ass is mine!*

Bruce Maxwell just smiled.

On December 6, 1969, a little after noon, Maxwell walked to the center of the Razorback Stadium field with the other Arkansas captains and shook hands with the Texas captains—James Street, Ted Koy, and a guy who drove his car up the dorm stairs and his coach a little nuts.

Cap'n Maxwell, Cap'n Halsell.

"BRUCE MAXWELL WAS AWESOME," Razorback quarterback Bill Montgomery says. "You might not want him teaching Sunday school class, but I'm telling you, if you're ever in a foxhole, you want him next to you."

Maxwell was the six-foot-one, 218-pound fullback, entrusted to block most of the time, and that was fine with him. He would lead the slight tailback, Bill Burnett, through the hole and steamroll defensive ends, linebackers, safeties, anybody who got in his way. When Montgomery dropped back to pass, Maxwell often protected him. Maxwell loved to pop people. Every play.

You knew he had to be good, because Frank Broyles put up with him. There was nobody on the team more universally respected. Feared, maybe, but respected.

When Maxwell showed up at Arkansas, he hadn't played much football. His daddy was a paper mill worker, transferred from Florida back to his native Arkansas when Bruce was ten. Bruce loved baseball, not football, and one of the reasons was that he couldn't stand the Pine Bluff High School coaches.

"The coaches back then were terrible," Maxwell says. "They were the kickers and the slappers. My daddy told me if I needed my ass whipped, that was his job."

Bruce finally went out for the Pine Bluff varsity as a senior in the fall of 1964, and was one of the stars. One weekend, the Zebras struggled to a tie, and that wasn't good enough for the coaches. "We came in the stadium the next morning and we just did grass drills all morning," he says of the traditional football workouts that included "crab walks" and "bear crawls" and other torture. "They were taking guys who passed out back across the street. They'd throw them in the showers and bring them back out."

Maxwell didn't work very hard to hide his disdain for the coaches, and he was "caught" drinking late in the season. *Drinking?* Hell, Bruce Maxwell was going to the Pine Bluff beer joints since he was fifteen, and everyone knew it. "Hey, Bruce," was ID enough in those places, and liquor control agents would have been treated like KGB agents—if they ever bothered to show up. Bruce was drinking, sometimes fighting, growing up, making friends with rough mill workers twice his age and as tough. So why was football season going to be any different?

"Of course, after the games, we'd go out and have a beer, and they kicked me and two other seniors off the team," Maxwell says.

He played all of six games of high school football, but that was enough to attract the attention of Wilson Matthews, who recruited the Pine Bluff area for the Broyles staff. "My dad was a pretty rough man and Wilson was one of the roughest I've ever met, and they hit it off really good," Maxwell says.

If a coach other than Matthews had been assigned the area, it's unlikely Maxwell would have gotten the chance. "He'd had some differences with his coach, but I'd seen Bruce play a number of times and I knew he could play," Matthews says. "He'd knock your ass off, I know that. Back in those days, if I was in an alley fight, I'd like to have had him on my side."

One night that winter, Bruce came home and found his dad and Wilson Matthews sitting in the living room, waiting for him. "Son," said J. R. Maxwell, "Coach Matthews here wants you to go to the University of Arkansas and that's where you're going."

OK, said Bruce. He was thinking of trying to go to Mississippi State to play baseball, but as tough as Bruce Maxwell was, he knew better than to argue with his daddy about something like this. The Pine Bluff coaches were incredulous, telling Broyles and other coaches that Maxwell was trouble.

For five years, Broyles and Maxwell had a contentious relationship, primarily because Broyles couldn't abide Maxwell's complete lack of deference. "I guess he mostly didn't like me because of reputation," Maxwell says. "I wish I had been a better person in some ways." He didn't care about much except playing the games, drinking beer, smoking, and having a good time, and that didn't make him unique among the Razorbacks as much as the fact that he didn't try to fool anybody about it. But he also found how much he liked Wilson Matthews.

"Coach Matthews was the type that if you were a turd, he'd say you were a turd and that you'd never play," Maxwell says. "But he'd say if you want to go through school, he'd help you. He'd say he wasn't running you off, but that you're not going to play."

Not even Matthews could keep Maxwell interested in the classroom. Maxwell was a wingback as a freshman and was the starting tailback as a sophomore, gaining 376 yards in six games, until he suffered a torn hamstring in a late October practice. He was done for the season.

"The dumbass that I was, once I knew I was out for the year, I just quit going to school," Maxwell says. "I hung out playing pool and drinking." When he flunked out, he packed up his belongings, left Wilson Sharp House, and was about to drive home to Pine Bluff and prepare to get drafted. But first, there was one more farewell mission, so he went down to Maxine's Tap Room, on North Block Avenue, between the campus and downtown. It was a long, dark, skinny beerhole, with a jukebox and a shuffleboard bowling machine near the front door. Maxine Miller sat at the bar and along about last call told the students—in a voice that could peel paint—to start thinking about getting their sorry asses out of there.

In short, Maxine's was Bruce Maxwell's kind of place, and Johnny Majors—then the Razorbacks offensive backfield coach—knew it. The phone rang, and Majors asked for Bruce Maxwell. Majors told Maxwell he needed to get over to such-and-such place to take a physical, then go down to Fort Smith and be sworn into the National Guard. Then he would be leaving on the bus the next morning to Fort Polk and six months of National Guard duty, which was a hell of a lot better than getting drafted, going into the Army, and getting sent to Vietnam, wasn't it? (That was the same Fort Polk where Don Donner entered the Army.)

Maxwell took it all to mean, among other things, that he still would be able to play the next season, 1967. Instead, though, he got out of the Guard and was redshirted that season. Then, in 1968 and '69, he formed the complementary running back combination with Bill Burnett, who seemed like a church mouse compared to Maxwell.

Maxwell was a legend for a lot of things, and one of them was his ability to throw up on the fly. During off-season drills, when he was around for the off-season, teammates learned to never, ever, be the guy behind Maxwell as they ran the stadium stairs, because he'd just lose it and keep right on going, wiping his face.

He tended to show up in such woeful condition each season, he would vomit himself into shape and sometimes just keep losing it all the way through the season, even on poor, unsuspecting opponents in games.

In 1968 spring practice, the new young offensive coaches—Don Breaux and Richard Williamson—were astounded. "Here's a guy who between the plays was lifting up his helmet behind the huddle and puking, but didn't want to come out and still was storming up through there," Breaux says. "I remember telling Richard, 'Man, we got ourselves a good ballplayer there.'"

Earlier, on the first day of 1968 fall practice, Maxwell made it through about a half-lap of the mandatory mile run. He spent the summer working in the Pizza Hut managed by his brother, and he weighed 240 pounds—about twenty-five over his playing weight. He was running—well, at least for the first 220 yards—with fellow fullback Glen Hockersmith, when Maxwell lost breakfast.

"God damn it, Maxwell!" hollered Hockersmith, who had been caught in the spray.

Maxwell pulled up and started walking toward the dressing room, which brought Frank Broyles scrambling out of the bleachers.

"Where you goin'?" Broyles asked sharply.

"I'm just sick," Maxwell said, "I don't know what the problem is."

Broyles sent Maxwell to the team doctor, who promptly delivered the diagnosis. "Hell," the doctor said, "there's nothing wrong with this boy!"

Maxwell made it through the 1968 season, then dropped out of school for the 1969 spring term. "I think the coaches liked that because they were afraid I'd flunk out again," he says. (The 1969 Arkansas press guide said Maxwell had "worked in a business at home" during that semester. "Yeah," Maxwell says. "Pizza Hut.") So on the first day of the 1969 practice, the Razorbacks went through the mile run again. The backs were supposed to crack six minutes, or there would be hell to pay. There was some hope for Maxwell, because his mother had put him on a diet over the summer and he hadn't eaten too much of the Pizza Hut profits. Also, he came up to Fayetteville a couple of weeks early and worked out with his former roommate, the newly married Terry Don Phillips.

In the running backs group, Bill Burnett crossed the finish line in about 5:45, then turned around to check on his buddy, "Bruno." Heck, Burnett concluded, Bruno was so far back, there was no way he was going to beat six minutes.

About thirty seconds passed. Maxwell came chugging along, well beyond the time limit. Don Breaux held up the stopwatch and started calling out the time as Maxwell struggled through the last 20 yards. He tried to keep the grin from showing, but it was there, visible to those close enough (but not to Frank Broyles, up in the stands).

Five fifty-six . . . fifty-seven . . . fifty-eight . . .

Maxwell crossed the finish line, triggering cheers. All the Razorbacks knew exactly what had happened. "He wasn't going to flunk Bruno," Burnett says, laughing. "They would have been afraid to do that."

Frank Broyles had something else to get mad at Maxwell about that fall, during practice. The Razorbacks had installed Astroturf in the stadium over the summer, in part to guarantee decent field conditions on December 6, and to Broyles it was no different from new carpet in the living room.

"Maxwell!" he hollered. "Stop throwing up on my Astroturf!"

During the 1969 season, Maxwell was nominally living in Wilson Sharp House, which was mandatory for all except the married Razorbacks. Maxwell and senior reserve linebacker Richard Coleman also rented a house south of campus, just off Dickson Street, where most of the action was. Sometimes, the action was at their house, and it was the refuge from the dormitory. It was where the boys went to drink beer and play cards, and they decorated the windows with pumpkins as Halloween approached. They carved peace signs into the pumpkins, and it was more a timely joke than a statement of anti–Vietnam War sentiment. One night, they were playing poker when there was a knock on the door. "It was a hippie, a dirty little fellow," Maxwell says. "He said, 'I just wanted to tell you I like your pumpkins over there,' and he rolled out about three joints. We all just panicked and went and flushed the damn things right down the toilet."

THE COACHES weren't the only ones scared of Maxwell, of course. In one 1968 practice, he was blocking a stumpy linebacker, Guy Parker. Parker rose up at the perfect—or imperfect—moment, and his helmet caught Maxwell underneath the facemask, driving his helmet up and knocking out a couple of Maxwell's teeth.

"Maxwell gets up on one knee," guard Jerry Dossey says. "He unsnaps his helmet, flips his helmet up, spits his teeth out, flinches a little bit, stands up, pulls that helmet down, snaps it, and says: 'Let's do that again.' And Parker's eyes get *really* big. Parker ran from him, I think. Maxwell was going to kill him."

Bobby Field, the Razorbacks' "monster" back, says the most stupid thing he *ever* did in college football was spear Bruce Maxwell on the ground during a spring scrimmage in 1968, when Field still was a freshman.

"He's got a stubbly beard, he's missing eight teeth, he's legendary, and I've just speared him," Field says, laughing. "He rolls over and we're face-to-face on the ground there. He has no idea who I am. He looks at my jersey number then says, 'Number 41, huh?' And he gets up and walks back to the huddle. I was looking at the sideline, for a coach to get me out of there. I was scared out of my mind."

Field doesn't remember if Maxwell retaliated, but he assumes the fullback went out of his way to run over him a few times—and that hard football was his way of getting back. And Field never has forgotten how scared he was.

Maxwell was voted a captain for 1969, and got along with both his buddies in the backfield and his backfield coach. "Don Breaux was one swell fellow," Maxwell says. "I loved Bill Montgomery. He was like a coach on the field. People didn't realize how skinny he was. He was a macaroni noodle, he was a leader and he was so tough. And little Billy Burnett, he was so smart. You'd just say follow me, and he knew exactly how to play off your block."

During the games, Maxwell usually played mute, but he had his moments. "Maxwell was the best blocking fullback God ever invented," tackle Mike Kelson says. "He was the meanest guy on the team. He told me he was going to kick my ass on national TV at the Sugar Bowl if I ever got ahead of him again."

During the Rice game in 1969, as the Razorbacks were struggling early in what turned out to be a 30–6 victory, Maxwell went over the edge. He had puked about three times already. The vertical bar on his facemask was dripping, his teammates were trying to stay away from him in the huddle, and Bill Montgomery picked that moment to deliver an emotional harangue to his teammates. It was nothing unusual, nothing out of line, nothing James Street wasn't saying to the Texas Longhorns all the time as well. Montgomery lectured that it was time for the linemen to block better and keep the Owls out of his face and he was getting sick of it and the offense needed to get going and . . .

Maxwell, leaning over, sucking air, had enough. He reached up and grabbed Montgomery's facemask, yanked it down, and snarled: "Shut the fuck up!" *And this was his friend!*

Montgomery quickly signaled timeout and headed over to the sideline as his teammates tried to keep from laughing. They were playing *Rice*, for heaven's sake, and they weren't going to lose. Breaux and Richard Williamson were upstairs in the coaches' box, so Montgomery approached offensive line coach Mervin Johnson, who was wearing the headset and talking with the coaches upstairs. "What's going on?" Johnson asked.

"Well," Montgomery told Johnson, "Maxwell just grabbed my facemask, cussed at me, and told me to shut up."

"Then you probably ought to shut up," Johnson said.

Cap'n Maxwell, Cap'n Halsell. Like Maxwell, Glen Halsell wasn't classic "captain material" on the behavioral front, but he was well-liked, respected, and a damn good linebacker, especially against the run, although he was listed at only five-eleven and 202 pounds. Halsell always had won—including at Odessa Permian. Odessa, Texas, was a football town, and Halsell began taking a football helmet and shoulder pads to school in the third grade, to wear in recess games with the older guys. Permian won the state championship in 1965, when Halsell was the captain, and he could have gone and played anywhere—including Arkansas. He visited the Fayetteville campus and "felt it was a little bit hillbilly," he says. "I just hit the UT campus right, I guess. There was a guy or two I knew down there at UT, and I went to some parties, and I was really impressed with the environment."

Austin had about fifty Maxine's Tap Rooms, it seemed, down on Sixth Street, just south of downtown, or along the Drag. Halsell, majoring in business and aiming for a career in law to emulate his attorney father, found them, with the help of his buddies. The word got around: *That guy's crazy! He bit the heads off frogs! When everyone was wearing bird pins, he pinned a dead bird to his shirt! And, man, how about that drive up the dormitory steps!*

He hung out with the team's unofficial social director, kicker Robby Layne, who came by his carousing instincts naturally; he was the son of Bobby Layne, the former Longhorn and NFL great who set a relentless pace off the field. Layne was one of Street's best friends, too, but Street knew when to slow down. Halsell sometimes didn't.

"Robby took me down to Mexico and I had my first good time, you know," he says.

Halsell was unfortunate enough to have his twenty-first birthday fall during the 1968 season, on October 24, on the Thursday before the Rice game in Houston. Halsell went to Charlie's, a bar on Sixth Street, and one of Rob Layne's friends bought him a fifth of Scotch. It's an acquired taste, but Halsell tried to acquire it in one night. "I came in a little bit tipsy," he says. A senior turned him in to the captains, including All-American linebacker Corby Robertson and Chris Gilbert. Halsell didn't miss a game, but he was put on probation, kicked out of the dining hall for a few weeks, and made to run the dummies during practice the next week. It was the second time that fall he had to go through that torture. Nobody can quite remember the exact reason—these things tend to run together for Halsell and his teammates, and it might have been a delayed punishment for his dormitory stairs escapade. But during fall daily doubles, Halsell ran the dummies, threw up, got the dry heaves, and took a swing at Corby Robertson, who was badgering him. Halsell was so sick and exhausted, it wasn't much of a fight.

But he won his way back into the good graces of his teammates, and nobody ever denied his talent or desire. The next spring, he had to run the stadium stairs and the dummy drills (again!) with Bobby Mitchell, Greg Ploetz, and Steve Worster under Frank Medina's supervision after the incident with the LCB men and the "underage girls" sitting at their table. But his wildest days were behind him, and he was elected a captain for 1969.

"I tried to straighten up," he says. "I was one of those guys who had to learn things the hard way."

So in 1969, Halsell was the left inside linebacker, starting next to junior Scott Henderson, who took the hand signals in from the bench and called the defensive signals. "Glen was a tough, tough guy," Henderson says. "He would never quit. He was very coachable. If Coach Campbell were here now, he'd say Glen was a little wild, a little undisciplined, but Coach Campbell really thought he was a top-notch football player."

Halsell was the only defensive representative among the captains, grateful even then that Royal and defensive coach Mike Campbell hadn't thrown him out of the program. "I always had a lot of respect for Coach Royal," he says. "He scared me. I was not as good as I should have been, and he had good reason to bust me."

And Mike Campbell could be gruff and rub some players the wrong way—even to the point of causing them to quit. But among the survivors? "He won all our hearts," Halsell says. "He was a real fine southern gentleman, and that's what I used to tell Tom and Mike."

Tom and Mike? They were Coach Campbell's sons, and both were starters on the 1969 defense. Like almost everyone else, Halsell had trouble telling apart the identical twins, but he knew the Campbell boys were the biggest surprise success stories on the Texas roster—even to their father.

ELEVEN

Coaches' Sons

WHEN TEXAS DEFENSIVE COACH William Michael Campbell III went on recruiting trips to West or South Texas, he often piloted a private plane himself. He buzzed the high school gym—in Seguin and Beeville and all the other small towns that produced big boys and big stars—and the coaches knew: *Mike's here! Who wants to pick him up at the airport?*

Mike owed his pilot's license to Uncle Sam: A Tennessee native, he was a B-24 bomber pilot in World War II before enrolling at the University of Mississippi and playing football, starring as an end. He met and married a feisty coed, and he and Mary began a nomadic existence as a coaching couple. Mike coached at several Mississippi high schools, including in Vicksburg, where their young twins—William Michael IV and Tom—rode their bikes behind the DDT trucks, darting in and out of the insecticide mist. Campbell was about to join Darrell Royal on the Mississippi State staff when Royal took the Washington job. So Mike, Mary, and their three young sons—Tom, Mike, and Rusty—spent a year in Seattle before moving to Austin when Royal became the Longhorns' head coach. "It didn't take long before we had orange blood running through us," Tom Campbell says.

Mike was old school and didn't apologize for it. "Mike was tough, he was demanding, but he did it with a personality that was very pleasing to the players," Darrell Royal says. "They got a big kick out of it when somebody else was receiving his firm corrections. They thought it was funny and they'd be laughing until it was their turn. Then everybody else got to laugh."

Player after player from the '69 team agrees. They were among the survivors, of course, and they were the ones who had decided they could live with the physical regimen, with the gruff coach, with the life of a football player. Among this group, Mike Campbell was respected both as a tactician and as a man. "Coach Campbell was a great defensive coach," says Scott Henderson, the linebacker who took the defensive calls from Campbell in 1969. "I thought he was a genius."

By that season, Mike's two sons were in the defensive huddle—and every time he went home, he expected his wife, Mary, to tell him: *Told you so!*

When Mary's eldest sons, Tom and Mike, were finishing up at Austin's Reagan High School, they still were seventeen years old and each weighed about 155 pounds. "We were just very average, fighting to make the first team in high school, on a very average high school football team, too," Tom says. "Truth is, we never talked about getting a scholarship to play football. Not that I expected it, but we never received a single call from any college football coach."

They had good grades and as they pondered their options, they decided that if they went to Texas, they would "walk on"—go out for the team without scholarships—and play football, and their own father had mixed feelings about that. "No, he was horrified," Mike IV says. "He was stupefied. He did everything but tell us that we weren't nearly good enough. He asked us why and we just said we weren't ready to quit playing football. If that meant walking on at Texas and being on the scout team for four years or whatever, that's the way it was going to be."

Their daddy was flying all over Texas, recruiting guys who made them look tiny and whose scrapbooks were about eight times as thick. Coach Campbell took a call one day from Texas Tech coach J. T. King, asking if he would be offended if King talked to the two boys about coming to Tech. Campbell didn't even tell the boys about it for several years. "I think what he was telling J. T. King was that he didn't want any favors from him," Mike IV says. "He probably didn't want us to go up to Texas Tech and bomb out. Really, I don't think he thought we were good enough to play anywhere—and at that time we weren't."

Royal and Coach Campbell talked about the boys' determination to walk on. In the era of fifty scholarships a year, there was room for flexibility, and awarding scholarships to the Campbell boys would be a way to give the veteran coach a bonus.

"I told Mike we'll give them scholarships," Royal says, "and if they get out there and find it's over their heads, I'd get something figured out so the kids could stay in school. So I said we'd just go ahead and let them play freshman football, and if they decided they wanted to drop out, we'd work something out. Mike didn't think they'd play. I didn't think they'd play."

Their attitudes set off Mary Campbell, who frowned at Royal.

"They'll play," she snapped.

One night during their senior year at Reagan High, Tom and young Mike were in their bedroom, studying at their desks, when their father came home and marched in.

"Well," he announced, "Darrell said he had a couple of scholarships left, and you two can come out and stay out as long as you want."

To this day, young Mike isn't sure it ever was official. He says he never signed the standard scholarship agreement. However it worked, the coaches' twins soon were out for UT football, and—apparently—they were on football scholarships.

Mary Campbell had only one rule. "You're going out," she told Tom and Mike, "but you're *not* quitting."

They had recently turned eighteen when they started college and were small guys lost amid the freshman mobs. Yet everyone knew they were Mike Campbell's—Coach Campbell's—twin sons. "We had to play hard," Mike says. "Literally every snap of the ball we ever took there, [we] never took a slow step. Not one time, not one play. We couldn't because we knew people were watching us. And it wasn't just the coaches. We knew other players were watching us. We had occasional problems with some guys who had some bad attitudes."

The Campbell boys got in a couple of fights as freshmen when they responded to the "coach's sons" taunts. "Then people realized that we played hard and we weren't going to back down," Mike says. Their teammates came to admire their grit and their work ethic, but *nobody*—well, except for Mary—thought they would develop into anything but practice fodder. "We were so far down the depth charts, we couldn't be found," Mike says.

The Campbell boys played for the freshman team only when games were out of hand, and as sophomores, they started out as fourth-team defensive ends. They couldn't understand why, at about 178 pounds each, they couldn't play in the defensive backfield. That darned defensive coach insisted that the boys stay at defensive end and take on the much bigger offensive linemen, even in the Turd Bowls and "shit" drills involving scrimmage work for the scrubs.

"At other schools, their shit drills were to punish people, but that was never the object at Texas," Tom insists. "If you were on the first or second team, you were getting worked out in practice, but if you were below that, you really never got that much work in practice. So at least once a week, we had shit drills, and I always knew it was instructional stuff. But it was my dad that was running the shit drills."

And his sons were among the "shits."

"His deal was he was going to find out who down here might be able to play football," Tom says. "He wanted to know who down here wearing a blue shirt on the third or fourth team might be able to play football. Well, I'm 178 and I might find myself lined up against someone who was 220 or 230. You're just knocking heads. You had to be optimistic to call this instructional, but you learned. Daddy was down there teaching fundamentals, and all of a sudden you're 180 and you learn that if you have the right fundamentals, and you're going against somebody 220 or 230 who doesn't, you can hold your own."

If Coach Campbell noticed right away, he didn't say so. "Daddy's deal was that if you were doing something right, you knew it and he didn't need to say anything," Tom says.

"Early on, you knew they were going to compete," defensive backfield coach Fred Akers says of the Campbell twins. "They didn't back down from anyone. I mean, those guys really had their jaws set to prove something, to prove that they deserved to be on that team. They earned the respect of everybody pretty quickly, just because of their toughness."

As the boys got better, as they gradually moved up the depth chart, their teammates took them more seriously—and started to ask them why their dad was so tough on them. "He treated us just like the rest of 'em," Mike says. "Like dogs."

"Mike and I never thought he was harder on us than anyone else, because we were used to it," Tom says. "The worst was if you screwed up and he wouldn't say anything to you. He'd given up on you."

As the attrition continued around them—others left school, flunked out, or just gave up on football—the twins were promoted to second-team defensive ends midway through the 1967 season. And they still were only 180 pounds! It helped when the Longhorns changed their defense slightly, bringing the defensive ends out of the three-point stance, which semantically—and practically—changed them into left and right outside linebackers, which had them more often involved in pass coverage.

As a junior, Tom started after star Mike Perrin's injured knee didn't come around. At that point, Coach Campbell again modified the defense to have outside linebacker Corby Robertson always go to the side of the tight end, and Tom go to the weak side as a "rover"—in effect, the weak-side outside linebacker. Mike was backing up Robertson at first, then he was made a rover, too—backing up his own brother.

"I got to start before Mike, and I know it bugs him to this day," Tom says. "We both know he was a much better rover than I was. The only reason I was the one who got to first team first was because the guy playing in front of me ruined his knee."

Mike laughs and agrees. "I didn't like the idea of having to play behind my brother. I knew I was better than him! By this time, I'm up to 185 and I'm a little bit bigger. Tom was a little faster."

One Sunday night, Tom was visiting his parents when his father took a phone call. Tom didn't pay much attention at first, but soon, he figured out his father was listening to the parent of another player complain about Tom starting.

Finally, Coach Campbell had heard enough.

"He said, 'Lady, I know that Tom is no damn good, but he's the best I've got.' When he said that," Tom says, "I knew I was OK. And that was the only compliment that I've ever received from Daddy playing football."

Playing rover suited Tom; in that 1968 season, he had three interceptions, including two in the Cotton Bowl, where he was named the defensive player of the game. Fred Akers approached him and said, "Tom, I didn't know you were that fast!" Responded Tom: "You never raced me!"

Akers lobbied to change Tom to defensive back for the next season, and Tom's father went along. Going into 1969, Tom was in the defensive backfield, joining Danny Lester and Freddie Steinmark, and Mike moved into the starting rover spot. The boys kept the uniform numbers from their days as defensive ends—Tom had No. 84 and Mike No. 86—and they spent the 1969 season chasing receivers.

"They were both strong safety types," Fred Akers says. "One was a rover and one was a defensive back, but that's just terminology. They feared no one and no situation, and they felt like they would find a way to beat anyone."

For his *Daily Texan* column on the day before the Thanksgiving Day 1969 game against Texas A&M, halfback Ted Koy asked all the other starting seniors about their "biggest thrills." Tom Campbell told Koy, the carbon-stained sportswriter: "I hope my biggest thrill hasn't come yet. I'd like to win the national championship and go 11–0."

The Longhorns also had a third coach's son starting on defense, and his was a different story. Everybody wanted Bill Zapalac—from the start.

UNLESS FOOTBALL COACHES ARE FORTUNATE, their children find themselves being teased by military brats about moving around so much. In fact, that was one of the reasons Mike Campbell turned down the chance to be the head coach at lesser programs; he knew he would be battling the odds, the salaries wouldn't be that much better, and he would have to uproot Mary and their three boys.

Willie Zapalac, the Longhorns' offensive line coach, was more nomadic. Like Campbell, he had served in World War II and was one of the many football players with military service gaps between seasons. A native of Bellville, Texas—the home of the Koy family—Zapalac was a fullback at Texas A&M in 1941 and '42 before becoming a navigator on Pacific bombing missions. Then he returned to A&M, playing his senior season in 1946, and got into coaching. He was a Bear Bryant assistant for eight years at Texas A&M, when Bryant thought football was a boot camp, then served short stints at Texas Tech and Oklahoma State before joining the Royal staff in 1964.

By then, his oldest son, Willie Jr.—Bill—was a big-time prospect. Royal didn't need to "find" a scholarship for Bill, who also was an excellent student and planned to study engineering.

"I grew up idolizing John David Crow and Jack Pardee," Bill says of the A&M stars, and as Willie Zapalac moved on to Oklahoma State and Texas Tech, young Bill's attitude about the Texas Longhorns didn't change: They were the elitist bullies who beat his dad's teams virtually all the time. "I always wanted to be good enough so Texas would offer me a scholarship, and then I could turn 'em down," Bill says.

His dad's move to the Royal staff before his sophomore year of high school changed everything. Willie started out as the defensive backfield coach, then switched to the offensive line when Texas assistant Jim Pittman got the head-coaching job at Tulane. Bill was among the enemy, but they were the enemy no more. He grew, he became a star at Austin's McCallum

High School, and his college options were plentiful. He did strongly consider playing for his father's former boss, Bryant, at Alabama, but eventually signed with UT.

At Texas, Bill was one of the Worster Bunch recruiting class, an eclectic group that formed the bulk of the junior class on the 1969 team. Zapalac, Scott Henderson, Greg Ploetz, Freddie Steinmark, and Bobby Mitchell were the intellectual wing of the class; the players a year ahead of them marveled at these guys. They *studied!* They said *"sir"!* Hell, most of them even went to *church!*

The infamous 1968 spring drills might have been tougher on Bill Zapalac and the Campbell boys than anyone else. They not only had to go through them, they had to go through them under their fathers. Zapalac played tight end that spring, and was directly under his father's authority.

In one drill, Bill banged up his shoulder. In pain, he started walking over to the sideline, to join the other injured players—including tackle Bob McKay, who was out with his rotator cuff problem. A coach hollered at Bill. "Where the hell you going? You get your ass to the end of the line!"

The coach also happened to be Bill Zapalac's father. As Bill went to the back of the line, the injured McKay, the dry West Texan who always tried to be helpful in such situations, walked over and offered a suggestion. "Why don't you tell that son of a bitch to go get fucked!"

Bill played through that, but then he suffered a broken hand in a Thursday drill. After the Saturday scrimmage, the Longhorns were scheduled to take a week off for spring break, then return for two more weeks of spring practices. The doctor put Bill's hand in a cast and told him not to return to the field until at least after spring break.

On Saturday, Willie Zapalac walked through the dressing room before the scrimmage and spotted Bill sitting in street clothes, with the cast on his hand.

"What are you doing?"

"Well, I don't think I'm supposed to go."

"The hell with that!"

Bill Zapalac played in the scrimmage, catching passes with the cast on. He didn't miss any more practices. But when the defense started having injury and attrition problems, Bill was switched to defensive end, away from his father's authority. "That was the happiest time of my life," Bill says, smiling.

Zapalac started every game in his Texas career. There never was any estrangement between him and his father. Why should there be? Willie was just being a coach, and Bill knew that was the way it worked. Bill started out the 1969 season at defensive end, but was switched in the middle of the season to strong outside linebacker. Bill's younger brother, Jeff, was a sophomore center on the '69 Longhorns, but he didn't letter until the next season.

So the Longhorns' defense that would try to shut down Bill Montgomery and the Razorbacks was starting three tough SOCs—sons of coaches.

TWELVE

Hogs Up Front

JERRY DOSSEY WAS AN OKLAHOMA FARM BOY. More than that, he was a *big* Oklahoma farm boy, whose father, Clifford, had a spread near the small town of Geronimo. Jerry was raised working in the family dairy, and on the tractor, hay baler, and combine. Oklahoma farm boys were expected to attend Oklahoma State University, perhaps bemoaning the gentrification of the school name from its original designation of Oklahoma A&M—Agricultural & Mechanical. Oklahoma farm boys who also happened to be among the most highly sought high school football players in the Southwest might be offered extra incentives to do the expected. During Dossey's senior year at Lawton High School in 1965, he took a call from a Cowboy alumnus and booster.

"Jerry," the booster said, "if you go to Oklahoma State University, you can pick out any automobile General Motors makes."

At seventeen, Dossey drove an old Mercury, pocked with hail damage, and there were days when the tractor on the family farm was faster—and easier to drive.

"*Any* car?"

"If General Motors makes it, son, any car."

"A Cadillac?"

"Any car, son."

After he hung up, he rebuked himself: *Why didn't I say Corvette?*

His parents, especially Clifford, considered this a done deal. "I was going to Oklahoma State," Jerry says. "I didn't have any option. I'd be shot."

He visited virtually all the Texas schools, but at first nobody—Jerry included—believed he would wind up anywhere but Stillwater. That was true even after his campus visit, when Cowboys players told him the OSU head coach, Phil Cutchings, was a tyrant, and that the only men who made the football experience moderately tolerable were the assistant coaches. But then he felt more and more wary. *Is that how I want to spend four years of football?*

So he started pondering his other choices, including the University of Oklahoma. New Sooners coach Jim Mackenzie, the former Arkansas assistant, came to the Dossey farm, taking off his coat and helping Jerry load fermented feed from the silo into the truck. "OU was like a cussword in my home," Dossey says. "They were the cake eaters, the doctors and lawyers. We were the farmers."

He visited Arkansas on a lark, after a Lawton teammate talked him into it. "I remember thinking, 'Hillbillies' and all that," Dossey says. "So I went over and it had the smallest stadium, plus the least impressive and the smallest campus of any place I visited. But there was an atmosphere, an aura, of the hills. The townspeople were just so friendly. By the time I met Coach Broyles, I was a seasoned recruit. I had heard a lot about how good I was, and I believed every word of it."

Dossey was waiting to be begged.

"Jerry, we've watched your high school films, and we think you can play," Broyles said. "If you come to the University of Arkansas, you will have a chance to play."

That's it?

"I left his office a little miffed," Dossey says. "I'm thinking he really doesn't know how good I am!"

On the trip home, Dossey pondered playing for Frank Broyles. "I was struck by his demeanor," Dossey says. "He was just a very dignified gentleman, with this southern drawl, which just captivated me."

To keep peace in the Dossey home, Jerry signed a Big Eight Conference letter of intent with Oklahoma State, which ruled out only other schools in that league. One morning before school, he was feeding the family cattle, and as always, he had a little plug in his ear and was listening to the news on a transistor radio. Farm prices, Americans in Vietnam, President Johnson . . . and five Oklahoma State assistant football coaches had resigned en masse. And one of them was Tom Ellis, the popular defensive line coach recruiting Dossey.

Dossey finished feeding the cows, then walked into the house and approached his mother, Mildred.

"Mom, I'm going to the University of Arkansas."

His mother was making breakfast, and she stared at him across the kitchen bar.

"*Why?*"

"It's where my heart wanted to go all along, since my trip, and Coach Ellis resigned yesterday! I'm not going to go to Oklahoma State to play for a loser!"

Jerry searched out a piece of paper, and with his shocked mother watching, he dialed a long-distance number. It wasn't yet seven in the morning. He called Frank Broyles. At home. Barbara Broyles answered the phone.

"Mrs. Broyles, is Coach Broyles there?"

"He's still in bed."

"Mrs. Broyles, my name is Jerry Dossey and I'm an Oklahoma football player and he offered me a scholarship and I just want to see if he still has one."

A minute later, a groggy Broyles came on the line. "Jerry? You really want to be a Razorback?"

"Yes, I do, Coach."

Broyles and assistant Bill Pace were at Dossey's high school that afternoon, with a Southwest Conference letter of intent. A week before the national letter of intent date, Oklahoma State still believed it was in the running because of the Big Eight letter of intent, but Dossey had promised Broyles and made his choice.

Clifford Dossey told his son that if he went to Arkansas, he never would come to a game. Jerry was told the family also was offered scholarship aid for Jerry's two brothers and his sister, who already attended OSU.

"Arkansas had not offered me a darned thing except a scholarship," Dossey says. "The more Oklahoma State piled on the table, I'm thinking, 'You have to buy players? People don't go to your school because they want to play football for you?' It became a negative thing."

In a letter, Oklahoma governor Henry Bellmon lectured him that Oklahoma taxpayers had financed the first twelve years of his education, and he owed it to them to play football in the state. "My teachers, my girlfriend, my girlfriend's parents, my girlfriend's brothers, my cousins . . . everybody was saying, 'Why are you saying you're going to Arkansas? You can't do that!'"

The night before the national letter of intent signing date, an Arkansas assistant called just to check. *Get the letter? Everything all set?*

Yes, sir.

A new Oklahoma State assistant came to the Dossey home on the morning of the signing date. As the minutes ticked down, he was sitting at the family breakfast table, eating with Jerry's parents and saying how the Cowboys were moving in the right direction—and would get there faster if Jerry just signed that darned letter.

Jerry insisted: *Sorry, it's Arkansas.*

"At the risk of being divorced by my father," Dossey says, smiling, "my mother signed the Arkansas national letter with me—and the Oklahoma State coach was still sitting there!"

Jerry and his girlfriend broke up.

At one point after Dossey went to Arkansas, Oklahoma State complained that Dossey was driving a new Mercury Comet Cyclone purchased from a Fayetteville dealership, and NCAA investigators showed up. Dossey says he asked Broyles about Ford dealers in Fayetteville, and that Broyles gave him a name. But Dossey financed the car through the Oklahoma Dairy Farmers Credit Union and made the payments with money earned through the sale of his own cattle, other work, and, eventually, the sale of his game tickets. The NCAA found no wrongdoing, and the Razorbacks never were on probation during Broyles's coaching tenure. The joke on Oklahoma State was that the Dairy Farmers Credit Union's office was in Stillwater.

Dossey suffered a minor knee injury as a freshman and underwent surgery. In the hospital, his nurse was Martha Matthews, the wife of Wilson Matthews, the Fourth-Quarter Program czar. "She brought me my crutches, and she said, 'I'm Wilson Matthews's wife, and, freshman, if you're going to play ball you're going to get out of that damn bed, get on those crutches, and get that leg moving!' She was just like he was! The worst thing that could happen to you at the University of Arkansas was to get labeled by Wilson Matthews as a pissant. So I got on those crutches."

Recruited as a defensive lineman, Dossey found he detested Charley Coffey, the old-school defensive coach. Others liked Coffey, but the thoughtful Dossey was completely incompatible with the defensive line coach. Dossey hated the hollering, which sometimes came with sprays of tobacco juice. Coffey was an overachieving, five-nine star nose tackle at Tennessee. A superb teacher of textbook fundamentals and strategy, Coffey expected everyone to appreciate being coached as he had been coached—in the old-school, screaming style.

"Fifteen minutes before the first game," Dossey says, "Charley Coffey told me, 'Goddamn it, Dossey, I hate to play sophomores, but I don't have any choice. You better not embarrass me.' I took the field for my first game against Oklahoma State, of all people, with that kind of encouragement. I played a good game, but I graded miserably. Everything was about technique. I led the defensive line in sacks and tackles and never graded higher than a D because of my technique. My defensive style was not vicious. I had a knack of knowing where the ball was and getting to the football. He wanted that fight across the face of the block, never leave your hole a void."

The Arkansas press guides even bragged that Dossey led the interior line in tackles in 1967, but that didn't do much for Coffey. Shortly before the opening of the 1968 season, the Razorback coaches sensed two things: They needed a guard, and Dossey either was going to punch Coffey right in the kisser or walk out of the program. Offensive line coach Merv Johnson, the man who later would earn Mike Kelson's gratitude on the day Kelson's daughter was born, approached Dossey and asked: *How about playing offensive guard?* "I said, 'OK, Coach, I'm ready to do anything, anything that doesn't involve playing for Coach Coffey,'" Dossey says. "I walked onto the offensive field not knowing a play and they put me at the number one left guard and gave me a crash course."

Dossey grew militantly loyal to Johnson. Still feeling his way, Dossey was coached through the season by the tackle next to him—Webb Hubbell—and Johnson. "Jerry was a tremendous athlete and a smart guy," Johnson says. "A lot of the better linemen I coached were guys who started their careers out on defense. Jerry was very athletic and very competitive." But Dossey started having more serious injury problems, and he says he played the 1969 Sugar Bowl with a fractured sternum, going against Georgia All-American defensive tackle Bill Stanfill. Stanfill made one big hit on Bill Montgomery, but Dossey otherwise controlled him. "I couldn't button my shirt, I couldn't tie my shoes," Dossey says. "I took a Novocain shot before the game and ten minutes after the injections, I could have run into that wall."

So as the 1969 season approached, Dossey was settled into the offensive line's routine, and he took it upon himself to help coach the young tackle next to him, Mike Kelson, who became his close friend. Dossey also was married by then, as was center Rodney Brand, so three of the five starting 1969 Razorbacks linemen were living off-campus with their wives. Dossey was listed at 230 pounds, but he weighed at least 250. His listing stood in contrast to the common practice of adding inches and pounds to the real numbers for the roster, which the Razorbacks did for smaller players, such as Bobby Field. Reversing the practice for the big guys was unique. "I believe Coach Broyles was responsible for that," Dossey says. "It was a psychological thing. We'd come up to the line for that first play, and the guys across from us would be thinking, 'Wow, he's a lot bigger than I thought.'"

In one October practice, the Razorbacks were running a sweep when Dossey heard a loud pop, felt a stinging sensation in his foot, and collapsed. He tried to get to his feet, but couldn't. At the hospital, the physician looked at the X-rays and said he had a broken bone in the joint behind his little toe.

"We have two options," the doctor said. "We can operate on it now and you might be well by the bowl game. Or plan B is to put Novocain in it and see if you can play."

So, from the fourth game on in the 1969 season, Dossey was playing on a broken foot.

Dossey emphasizes that he chose Plan B himself. He tried to avoid putting weight on the ball of his foot during practice, and he sometimes looked downright silly—or crippled.

"It was odd to try to learn to run when you couldn't feel that foot," Dossey says of the numbing and pain-killing injections he took for the games.

"It was like running downhill all the time. That foot would go out and it was like there was a delay before it hit. It didn't affect me at all in the games, but when it wore off, I had to go find a place to be off by myself because the tears were going to run."

But his college career was winding down, and he wasn't about to say: *Enough.*

———

CENTER RODNEY BRAND came from tiny Newport, in northeast Arkansas, where his father owned an auto body shop. His high school coach, Don Horton—whose brother, Harold, eventually joined the Broyles staff in 1968 as the linebackers coach—told any college coaches who asked about Brand not to waste their time, because he was determined to go to Arkansas. "For a boy from Arkansas, the dream of a lifetime was to play for the Razorbacks," Brand says. "I used to ask the guys in my freshman class from other states why they would go to Arkansas if they were going to move back home. They said Arkansas was the national champion in '64 and it was the best place in America to play. To me, we were the national champions, but it was home, too. For me, it would have been an honor to go to the University of Arkansas no matter what the record was."

He was a redshirt in 1966, then started three straight seasons, and was the unanimous choice of the league's coaches as the all-Southwest-Conference center in 1968 as a junior. And as a senior, he ended up a consensus All-American. So, the Razorbacks' offensive line in 1969 had two Texans (guard Ronnie Hammers and tackle Mike Kelson), an Oklahoman (Jerry Dossey), a Pennsylvanian (tackle Bob Stankovich)—and one home-grown Arkansan All-American (Brand) who always asked the others why they had come to Fayetteville.

Stankovich had taken the most circuitous route. He was from Bentleyville, south of Pittsburgh, where his father was a coal miner turned police officer. Nobody knocked down Bob's door with scholarship offers; his high school coach had a buddy out in Kansas, who knew the Pratt Junior College coach, who heard he should give this big kid from the Monongahela Valley a chance. So big Bob Stankovich played two seasons in Pratt, Kansas, before transferring to Arkansas. It wasn't a case of the Razorbacks "hiding" him in JC, either; Stankovich went there to be noticed, and although he was a junior-college All-American, his only other offers when he left Pratt were from Southern Illinois and Texas–El Paso.

"I felt at home when I went to Arkansas, and I thought the people were very friendly—probably more friendly down south than up north," Stankovich says.

He sat out a redshirt year, then started in both '68 and '69. The Razorbacks decided he could have worked in the coal mines, no problem. "He was a tough kid," Merv Johnson says. "I don't know that I ever saw him hurt."

———————

RAZORBACK JUNIOR TIGHT END Pat Morrison was born in Elgin, Illinois, before his father—Robert, an Elgin watch salesman—was assigned the Arkansas territory and the family moved to Little Rock. Pat was a multiple-sport star at Little Rock's Catholic High and didn't consider going anywhere but the UofA. "I wasn't highly recruited, but when I did get letters from anyone else, I just threw them away," Morrison says. He was a backup as a sophomore, then inherited the starter's role. The Razorbacks played the weight game with him, too; he was listed at 205 pounds but was fifteen pounds heavier. "I had average speed, but my expertise was I could block pretty good," he says.

The Arkansas tight end in theory could be a major passing-game threat. But in most ways, he was another Hog lineman—and that was a badge of honor.

THIRTEEN

Horns Up Front

ON NOVEMBER 19, 1966, Bob McKay was about to suit up for the Long-horn freshman team against Texas A&M, hoping to beat the Aggies and win the right to enter the dining hall through the front door. The Notre Dame–Michigan State game—the "Game of the Century"—was on a radio in the dressing room. When the Fighting Irish meekly accepted the 10–10 tie, with coach Ara Parseghian directing the Irish to run out the clock after taking over on their own 30 with eighty-four seconds remaining, McKay led the jeers. "We all cussed Parseghian for not going for the win," McKay says. "Why would you not play for the win if you're out there?"

Three years later, the Longhorns remembered their disdain for Parseghian's take-the-tie-on-the-road mentality in a No. 1 versus No. 2 showdown, and recalled McKay's outspoken derision. But by then, they all were accustomed to McKay's inability to camouflage his feelings. He might have been scared of Darrell Royal—and Royal's power—but he was liable to say exactly what he thought to just about anyone else. He wasn't a chatterbox like James Street, but when McKay talked in that West Texas growl and got that sardonic smile on his face, he would make everybody laugh—in the huddle, on the sideline, in the dressing room, even while running wind sprints. He was "Big 'Un," the giant offensive tackle who manhandled defensive ends and relished aggressively chasing down other defensive players in the wishbone attack.

He came from Crane, a West Texas oil-field town where his dad worked for ARCO. Through grade school, Bob rode his bicycle to the high school football practices, watching and counting down the years to when he could *play*. The college recruiters began dropping in at Crane High School when Big Bob was a senior. They came from all over the Southwest Conference, but only one mattered.

Mike Campbell flew his private plane into Crane and, within an hour, was at the high school, watching film of the big tackle in the Crane coaches' tiny offices. McKay was summoned from class. *The Longhorns are here! Want to talk with Coach Campbell?* "I was more scared of him than I was of a man with a loaded shotgun," McKay says. "He asked me if I'd be interested in coming to visit him, down there in Austin. That was like asking a dying man if he wanted a meal and a glass of water. When I got there, Coach Royal said they had a scholarship for me and if I wanted it, I could have it; but if I didn't, they needed to know."

That approach turned off Texan Ronnie Hammers, which was one reason Hammers played guard for Arkansas on December 6, 1969. But it was exactly what Bob McKay wanted to hear. *Sure, Coach, count me in!* "People like Texas Tech wanted me to come visit there, but hell, I have kinfolks there and I knew what Lubbock looked like," McKay says. "J. T. King didn't understand why I didn't want to go. I had been there, done that, even had the T-shirt. I wasn't smart enough to know I wasn't supposed to be able to play at Texas. Most people I knew were saying, 'Ain't no way in the world he can play there,' but I was too stupid to know better."

After battling a shoulder injury that required surgery in the spring of 1968, McKay was starting by the time he was a junior. He is one of the handful of Longhorns who say the 1968 squad—which had senior All-Americans Ken Gidney at guard, Chris Gilbert at halfback, and Corby Robertson at linebacker—might have been better than the '69 team. But the winning streak continued through '69, and it was so easy, McKay was darn near disgusted. "Hell, halfway through the season, the second team had lettered and we hadn't yet," he says of the system that required players to participate in a certain number of plays to become varsity lettermen that season. "We had to come out so early, and Coach Royal wasn't going to let us embarrass anybody."

That also meant that when the coaches believed the starters hadn't played enough to be physically tested, they had to run conditioning windsprints on Sundays. "Guys," McKay asked his teammates, "could you imagine if we had *lost* this game?"

When Royal told McKay he had been named to the *Look* magazine All-American team, selected by the Football Writers Association, it meant he would get a free trip to New York the weekend after Thanksgiving for pomp and circumstance and a filming of an appearance on the "Bob Hope Special." McKay and fullback Steve Worster were on the *Look* team; the other tackle,

Bobby Wuensch, was on the American Football Coaches Association's All-American team, sponsored by Kodak.

At six-six and 245 (really), McKay was imposing even before the ball was snapped. Wuensch, the other tackle, was a six-three, 221-pound junior, and was scary in a different fashion. A soft-spoken teddy bear away from the field, Wuensch would say "sir" to professors—and sometimes even to the guy across the aisle in the class. He fooled his coaches, too, because it was hard to imagine that this meek kid on campus could be so devastatingly mean on the field. The transformation on game day astounded his teammates, until they got used to it.

"Wuensch was a football player," Bob McKay says. "I happened to be masquerading as a football player. Bobby was good and I happened to be following him around."

Wuensch loved making one block on or near the line of scrimmage and then, once the back was in the open field (which happened a lot in 1969), sprinting downfield and nailing some poor sap safety trying to close in on the ballcarrier. He often just took off, not worrying about the defensive end across from him, and until the whistle blew, anyone was fair game. It was unusual to see a *tackle*—Wuensch—flying into the picture on the film and blowing a linebacker or defensive back right off the screen. The Longhorns howled as they saw Wuensch work in the Sunday movies.

But they were wary of him, too, especially when he was getting himself pumped up. "If you could get out of the dressing room without getting killed by Wuensch, you had a chance to play all right," McKay says. Wuensch would prowl the locker room, banging guys on the shoulder pads, hollering, going crazy. "Nothing they could do to me on the field could hurt me as bad as Wuensch in the dressing room," McKay says.

Wuensch says, "Yeah, I'd get a little pumped. But it was honest-to-goodness adrenaline, I assure you. I just loved being in that state and I loved playing football and I loved hitting people. We had a steak table and if you had a great play or a great hit, you could make the steak table for Monday night. So maybe it was my eating."

Actually, part of his explosiveness came from his conditioning. When the Longhorns took treadmill tests at the beginning of the season, they were supposed to run fifteen minutes. Most guys ran fifteen minutes and maybe four-tenths of a second. But Wuensch—*an offensive tackle*—and Danny

Lester stayed on the treadmills and kept running. For forty-five minutes, showing off, enjoying themselves, competing. Finally, someone had to step in and say: *All right, already!*

Wuensch was a linebacker when he came to Texas from Houston, where his father owned a small sales company. Growing up, his hero was Tommy Nobis. Although an uncle, Les Richardson, played for Texas A&M's 1943 national champions, the lure of getting a shot to be the next Nobis was too strong when Texas offered him a scholarship. Unfortunately, Wuensch jammed his neck as a freshman in 1967 spring practice. He was in traction for a short time and doctors even raised the question of whether he would ever play again. He sat out '67 as a redshirt, but practiced as a center, and his neck healed. The Longhorns switched him to tackle for the '68 season, and they found that the linebacker's mentality worked well for a tackle in the wishbone. "In the wishbone," Wuensch says, "we started using our heads and started popping people right in the nose. That was how I knew how to play football."

THE LONGHORNS between the two All-American tackles were undersized, even for their era. With left guard Bobby Mitchell, the former Wheat Ridge Farmer star fullback, fighting injuries, Randy Stout got a lot of playing time in his place. Stout was six-two and 241, but the other three men between the tackles—Mitchell (five-eleven, 206), center Forrest Wiegand (six-one, 200), and right guard Mike Dean (six-foot, 195)—all were lighter than Steve Worster, the fullback they were blocking for.

Also, if there were a College Bowl quiz show for offensive lines, the Longhorns might have advanced to the semifinals with Princeton. Dean was the president of the Math Club at his high school in Sherman, and was set to go to Texas A&M until Darrell Royal won over his mother, Nadene. To Nadene, UT football was the bully, the bogeyman. "She was adamant that I wouldn't be going to UT," Dean says. "She hated Coach Royal and hated everything about UT. She didn't even want to meet Coach Royal."

Royal knew how to read the various challenges presented by prospects and occasionally hostile mothers. Royal took Dean and his parents out to dinner, and the coach made a point of sitting next to Nadene. "I was sitting down at the end of the table and he was sitting up there next to my mother and before she even got the salad, she was cooing and trying on his T ring," Dean says. "After that dinner, he had her in the palm of his hand. I wasn't going anywhere else."

Dean suspects Royal took the unusual step of visiting him personally in his hometown because he also was after one of Dean's high school teammates, defensive lineman Greg Ploetz. Ploetz, another strong student, and Dean were close friends, and they ended up going to UT together. Dean also acknowledges that the attrition from the 1968 spring practices moved him up the depth chart and gave him a chance, but he was suited for the wishbone blocking approach.

"Quickness was the whole thing," Dean says. "We only had about four pass plays, and all of them were off the option. I didn't even know if we had a dropback passing blocking scheme. If I had to take a step back and block on a guy 255 or 270, I was history. But we never had to do that."

He backed up Ken Gidney as a sophomore, then stepped in as the '68 starter at right guard. During the '69 season, he went home to Sherman on Sunday, November 2, the day after the Longhorns beat SMU to go 6–0, to get married, and was back at practice on Monday.

LIKE MIKE DEAN, Randy Stout once planned to go to Texas A&M. He was the star lineman of Coach Emory Bellard's Texas state championship team at San Angelo Central High School, and when Bellard accepted Darrell Royal's offer to join the Longhorn staff, Stout headed for Texas. "With Coach Bellard," he says, "you never thought you were going to lose."

Stout's UT career started slowly, though, because he suffered a knee injury in the Big 33 high school all-star game between Texas and Pennsylvania in Hershey. While in the toe-to-hip cast necessary following major knee surgery at the time, he lost seventy pounds—going from 270 to 200. He redshirted in 1968, with the understanding that if either Wuensch or McKay suffered a significant injury, he would play. He didn't have to give up that redshirt year, but when 1969 started, he still was a backup tackle. He also attended a couple of the antiwar protests, as an observer and not a participant, until his brother, a Secret Service agent, told him that if he was positively identified in three pictures, he would get an FBI file.

"As the season begins, I'm second team behind two All-American tackles, and the only way I'm going to play is if one of them dies," Stout says. "When Mitchell got hurt, they didn't have anybody to move to guard." Stout was nominated, although he didn't fit the prototype of the small, quick wishbone guard. But he played well, and when Mitchell came back, he continued to spell Mitchell and also serve as the messenger bringing in plays. For example, "53 veer pass."

In Edna, a small town about one hundred miles south of Houston, Forrest Wiegand, like so many other future Longhorns, including Bobby Wuensch, idolized Tommy Nobis and dreamed of succeeding him as a UT linebacker. That dream could get you in fights in rural Edna, where the majority of the kids were Texas A&M fans.

At his small high school, Wiegand was the star, but he hadn't had to learn very much about defense: He just ran around and made all the tackles. At Texas, it was different: He laughs and says that Coach Mike Campbell's lectures about scraping here and scraping there, taking the block on a shoulder, and filling gaps, all went right over his head. "I had no earthly idea what they were talking about," Wiegand says. But he was a strong athlete, and he was switched to center. The Longhorns finally gave up on the thought of redshirting him in 1967 and made him the starter for the final five games of that season. The primary reason was injuries, but he also had shown he could handle the position—and he was even better when UT went to the wishbone. The blocking schemes were about scrambling, and letting certain men go while double-teaming others to create avenues and gaps and mismatches for Street to read, creating dilemmas for the defenders left unblocked. To do it all right, it took smart linemen. And the Longhorns up front did it right.

FOURTEEN

Happy Thanksgiving

WHEN TEXAS A&M beat the Longhorns 10–7 in 1967, the Aggies left the score up on the scoreboard until the next fall. The Longhorns were disgusted, thinking: *How pathetic! Was one win over the Longhorns so monumental as to make the Aggies act as if it was the best damn thing ever to happen on the College Station campus, where there were no girls and nobody had any hair?*

The Longhorns whipped the Aggies 35–14 in 1968 in Austin, but the Thanksgiving Day return to College Station in 1969 was going to be catharsis for the seniors who had been on the same field two years earlier. If that wasn't enough, now the stakes were higher because of Ohio State's loss to Michigan and the Longhorns' ascension to No. 1.

Despite the rivalry and the incentive, captain Ted Koy was worried that the Longhorns might be looking past the 3–6 Aggies and already thinking about the showdown with Arkansas. He even made a little speech about it. *Fellas, we have to take care of business!* Then before the game, when the Texas A&M band began playing the Aggie War Hymn—to Aggies it was glorious, to Longhorns it was obnoxious—Koy looked around and noticed the steely looks of anger among his teammates, especially Tom Campbell and Bob McKay.

Hullabaloo, Caneck! Caneck!

Hullabaloo, Caneck! Caneck!

It was like putting the '67 score back up on the scoreboard.

The Longhorns led 39–0 at *halftime*. Jim Bertelsen ran 63 yards for the first touchdown, Steve Worster scored twice, James Street ran one in, and—what the heck was this?—split end Cotton Speyrer threw a 37-yard touchdown pass on an end-around to tight end Randy Peschel. Texas had 337 yards of total offense at halftime, the Aggies had four first downs.

At one point, the Aggies actually lined up in the *wishbone!* They hadn't done that before, and Tom Campbell took it as a sign of desperation. Besides, the Longhorns had the best defense in the country at stopping the wishbone because they worked against it in practice. In the next defensive huddle, Campbell turned to Freddie Steinmark. "We got 'em right where we want 'em," Campbell said. Steinmark gave a slight grin.

By halftime, Steinmark was just hoping to make it through the game. In the first half, while tackling A&M running back Larry Stegent, Steinmark was nailed on his sore leg by the Aggie's helmet. The flash was excruciating, and Steinmark momentarily thought his leg was broken. He stayed in until Royal called off the starters early in the third quarter. Bob McKay, to whom holding down the score was some sissy cricket crap that shouldn't come into play in *football*, especially against the Aggies, again was mad as hell. "We wanted to just kick the living shit out of them," McKay says. "We still wanted to play. I wish it had been 139–0."

The Longhorns had to settle for 49–12. As they came off the field after the game, Tom Campbell and McKay still were so keyed up that they got in a scuffle with some taunting members of the Aggie band on the field. Royal was livid: "That's not the way we do things here," he barked in the tiny visiting dressing room. The Longhorns were getting the hell out of there, he said, and setting their sights on Arkansas.

To the press, Royal gave no hint of his anger and, instead, got downright folksy—as he often did, even to the point of obvious contrivance—when the Arkansas game came up. "It's not just another ballgame," Royal said. "It's been button, button, who's got the button and we happen to have it right now. But it's just who's got it next week. We can stop playing footsy next week."

Aggies coach Gene Stallings sounded as if he would have bet his house on the Longhorns against Arkansas, who beat Texas A&M 35–13 on November 1. The Longhorns, Stallings said, "are as great as I've ever seen. The best I've ever played against." His pick? "I don't want to compare them. I've already said Texas is the best we've ever played against."

The first move Randy Peschel made when he reached the visiting dressing room after the game was to check his open stall.

The engagement ring still was there.

Some of the Longhorns, including James Street and Ted Koy, were preparing to go hunting with groups of teammates. Also, linebacker Glen Halsell had a standing Thanksgiving tradition: He joined a bunch of his friends for a duck-hunting trip near Texarkana. Other Longhorns went home for a late Thanksgiving dinner with their families. Bobby Wuensch,

McKay, and Worster were heading to New York for All-American festivities.

Peschel had another mission. His touchdown catch against the Aggies was just the start of a ten-day period that changed his life. He was about to become "Hey, aren't you the guy who . . . ?"

———————

THE LONGHORNS didn't have to go far to recruit Peschel—just across town. His father worked at a printing company, and Randy was a star quarterback at Austin's Lanier High School. Like Street, he also was a fine baseball player, and he wanted to play the outfield in college. He mused to friends that he might want to go to Southern California, perhaps the top football-baseball school in the country, but in the back of his mind, he knew he would end up at Texas. "Besides," he says, "I didn't get a call from USC." The Longhorns were his heroes; he had been going to Memorial Stadium since he was a little boy, and it was what he knew.

Darrell Royal brought his wife, Edith, with him for the visit to the Peschels' house. If they were Catholic, the pope's visit couldn't have been any bigger. Lea Peschel, Randy's mom, made special cookies, and Darrell and Edith raved about them. Randy's younger sister, Laurie, was scared to come into the living room. *Coach Royal's in our house!* Finally, she was coaxed out and shyly met the Royals. Royal said Peschel could play both sports, that it was fine with him. The stipulation was that Peschel would participate in spring practice his freshman year; after that, he could play baseball. That clinched it.

On the first day of freshman practice, Peschel was one of seven quarterbacks. He wasn't bothered when freshman coach Bill Ellington—one of the most revered coaches in the program, who later became an assistant athletic director—matter-of-factly said, "We're going to try you out at different positions." Peschel ran at halfback and fullback, then settled in at wingback and worked up to the No. 1 spot on the freshman team by the end of the season. He got into five games of freshman baseball before spring football started, and was a little late getting on the field the first day of practice because he had just been issued his equipment and was stuffing in his pads on the run. He started out with the second team, then was on the first team the next day.

"Mind you, this is after going through football drills, running ropes and running through tires and falling on my face because I wasn't in football condition," Peschel says. "I think what they were doing was Ronnie Ehrig was listed as first-team wingback and they wanted him to play defense, so they were looking for a way to move him to the secondary. But then I had a great spring, I really did."

He started for most of his sophomore season, 1967, but suddenly there was a problem with being a wingback. In the new wishbone, there was no wingback. As a junior, Peschel began the season as a backup split end to Cotton Speyrer, but he knew he wasn't fast enough for the position. After two games, he was switched to tight end, where he backed up Deryl Comer, one of the best tight ends in the country when healthy. Plus, at six-one and 195 pounds, Peschel was undersized for the position even then. In the Cotton Bowl rout of Tennessee, Comer suffered a horrific knee injury, and the question became whether he would be able to play extensively in 1969. As it happened, he couldn't. Peschel and Tommy Woodard both started games early in the season, but then Woodard went out with a knee injury suffered against SMU on November 1. Peschel was the undisputed starter by default. He worked at improving his blocking and he tried to get open when the few passes were called. He developed into a solid tight end—a good athlete not perfectly suited for the position determined not to hurt his team.

In the A&M game, he caught the gadget-play TD pass from Cotton Speyrer, then asked Royal for permission to ride home with his girlfriend, Sue, a UT sophomore he had been dating since he was a freshman and she was a high school junior in Austin. He had the plan down: He brought the engagement ring with him to College Station, put it in his shaving kit bag, and stashed it in the open locker. OK, so that wasn't the smartest thing he had ever done, leaving a diamond ring in an open locker in the middle of Aggie country. The proposal wasn't going to be a shock, since Sue and Randy had been talking about it and even made ring-shopping trips together. But the timing was open.

They drove to the Peschels' home and had Thanksgiving dinner, and then Randy and Sue headed to campus. Randy suggested taking a walk before he returned to the dorm, so they went to look at the Bell Tower—lit up in orange to celebrate the victory—and the nearby Littlefield Memorial Fountain. At the foot of the three-tiered fountain, with the bronze goddess

Columbia statue watching the young couple, Randy pulled out the ring and officially proposed.

Sue said yes.

IN LITTLE ROCK ON THANKSGIVING, the Razorbacks also had no trouble with Texas Tech, winning 33–0. Bill Burnett scored three touchdowns and Bill Montgomery was 13-for-22 for 220 yards.

Frank Broyles exhaled. He always appeared unflappable, but says he had felt pressure all season "to live up to what Roone Arledge thought might happen. Every game that we won that year, I said to myself, 'One more, one more; and please, please, keep us getting better.' It went on and on and on, and we just agonized over every game we played, and once we got there it was a relief."

The Razorbacks' defensive line, though, was getting banged up. Terry Don Phillips hadn't played in six weeks, but was traveling with the team, thinking his career was over and that this was a reward. At pregame meals, if he spotted a teammate putting down his fork, Terry Don would ask, "Hey, you gonna finish your steak?" He was sitting in the dressing room after the Tech game in Little Rock when Broyles approached.

"Do you think you could be ready?"

"For what?"

"For Texas."

Broyles asked Phillips to stay in Fayetteville through the Thanksgiving weekend and work out under the tutelage of Charley Coffey. Broyles said it would be great if Phillips could suit up against Texas—at least as insurance.

Earlier in Thanksgiving week, the word circulated that the Razorbacks would practice that weekend. A group of seniors approached Broyles and asked to be given Friday and Saturday off before reporting to watch the game films Sunday—which would make it a normal work week. Broyles went along, in part because it would seem like standard operating procedure, and he didn't want his team to get *too* keyed up for this one. Plus, like Texas, the Razorbacks had a delegation heading for New York—Chuck Dicus and linebacker Cliff Powell, who were on the Kodak team selected by the Coaches Association. Broyles gently put his foot down, though, to center Rodney

Brand, who was on the *Look*/Football Writers Association team that would be in New York through Monday to film the "Bob Hope Special" appearance. "They asked me not to go," Brand said, and he didn't fight the coaches on it.

This was the Razorbacks' second appeal of the season to Broyles about practice issues. After the 30–6 victory over Rice, Broyles roasted the Razorbacks for their lackluster performance in the humidity. The next day, at a team meeting, senior defensive back Terry Stewart served as the diplomatic spokesman for the team. His point was that the tough in-season practices on the Astroturf were draining the Razorbacks.

"I think we had the feeling that we were being pretty successful and they were still working us pretty hard, being pretty tough on us," Stewart says. "Coach Broyles came in and we talked in front of the team. I don't remember it being confrontational at all. I think maybe the coaches were feeling the pressure of the season as it went along, as we [kept winning]. As we got closer and closer to the game with Texas, the coaches probably felt the pressure more than the players did."

After the Tech game, because some of the players left Little Rock with their families or headed home, the team's chartered flight back to Fayetteville had plenty of open seats, so Broyles told the players they could have guests on the plane if they wished. Linda Holmes rode with Bill Burnett, and they talked about the upcoming game. "It was exciting to know that we were going into that final game ranked second," Burnett says.

Linebacker Lynn Garner, who like Terry Stewart came from Fort Smith, went home for Thanksgiving. Garner was one of the bigger free spirits among the Razorbacks, and he made a pact with himself. As hard as it would be, he wasn't going to have a beer or any alcohol until after the Texas game. "I went with my buddies to the honkytonks, but I couldn't drink anything." That's when Garner's buddies realized how important this game was to him.

"Monster" Bobby Field had two interceptions against Texas Tech, and when he got back to Wilson Sharp House, he couldn't sleep. Rather than heading to his parents' farm—they had moved from Farwell, Texas, to southern Missouri—on Friday morning, he left in the middle of the night. He drove through the ranch's gate at about six in the morning, and ran into his dad, on his way out to work the land. He turned around, and the Fields had a big breakfast, excitedly talking about Bobby's big game the day before—on television no less—and the upcoming showdown.

Defensive end Bruce James, who came from Moss Point, Mississippi, on the Gulf of Mexico near the Alabama border, was desperate for some home cooking. "I told my parents I had to have some gumbo," James says. "I told them I didn't want any turkey. We flew to Little Rock for the game, but I had a friend of mine drive my car to Little Rock and park it at the stadium. I probably set an all-time world record from Little Rock to Moss Point after that football game to get my shrimp gumbo."

Arkansas kicker Bill McClard drove from Little Rock to his family's home in Norman, Oklahoma. On Friday morning, he got in a touch football game with buddies in the front yard, and he took an accidental head butt that made it seem as if he had taken a pop from Joe Frazier. He took six stitches at the emergency room, and was thinking: *God, if it had been worse, how would I have explained that?* Despite the shot to the head, he might, just might, have a shot at making a kick to win the national championship.

FIFTEEN

New York, New York, and Points Elsewhere

LONGHORN ALL-AMERICANS Bob McKay, Bobby Wuensch, and Steve Worster had a few beers on the plane to New York on the day after Thanksgiving. When they threw their bags into the trunk and climbed into the taxi, squeezing into the backseat, Wuensch decided the driver looked like a nice guy.

"You know," Wuensch said, "we're just a bunch of country bumpkins from Texas who need to go to the Americana Hotel."

The driver turned around with a gleam in his eye. Worster thought it was because this guy was excited to have the boys in his taxi. "We were shooting the bull with him, treating him like a good old Texas boy," Worster says. They chatted—and chatted and chatted—on the long drive in from the airport. McKay says, "I think we crossed the same bridge about forty-five times."

Worster says that when they pulled up in front of their Manhattan hotel, with their necks craning up, they reached for their wallets to pay the eighteen-dollar fare on the meter.

That's right, boys; eighteen dollars apiece covers it.

Worster says that Wuensch and McKay pulled out money, but that he was starting to get suspicious. He says he walked over to the doorman, who was fooling with some other luggage.

"How much should the cab ride be in from the airport?"

"About six bucks, son."

"So six apiece for three of us?"

"No, six total."

As Worster turned, the cab pulled away, tires squealing. The doorman, adding it up, took a couple of steps toward the street, then stopped.

Worster says that Wuensch, good ol' Bobby, said not to worry: He had paid Worster's share, too.

NOT FAR FROM THE LONGHORNS' HOTEL, Dr. Edward Beattie emerged from the operating room in Memorial Hospital, on Manhattan's Upper East Side. A few minutes later, he called Chicago Bears owner George Halas.

In Chicago that afternoon, Halas announced that Beattie told him the surgery to remove all of the cancerous material from the chest of Bears running back Brian Piccolo had been successful. Beattie was "delighted with the results," Halas said.

Piccolo, the former Wake Forest University player and close friend of fellow Bears running back Gale Sayers, had entered a Chicago hospital on November 18, two days after playing against the Atlanta Falcons, and was transferred to Memorial after cancer was diagnosed. He was twenty-six years old.

WUENSCH WAS ABLE TO HAVE FRIENDLY CONVERSATIONS with Arkansas Razorbacks Chuck Dicus and Cliff Powell, his fellow Kodak All-Americans. "They seemed like normal guys, real nice fellows," Wuensch says.

On Friday night, the Texas boys were taken to dinner at Toots Shor's, but they didn't see either Jackie Gleason or Mickey Mantle.

The boys didn't hear about it, but back in Texas on Saturday morning, Jack Gallagher's column in that day's *Houston Post* said that President Nixon was expected to attend the game in Fayetteville. Talk of Nixon's imminent appearance—an appearance Frank Broyles says Bud Wilkinson had "guaranteed" months earlier—reached the press box at War Memorial Stadium during the Texas Tech–Razorbacks game. Asked to comment by the wire services in the wake of Gallagher's column two days after the game, the White House neither confirmed nor denied the report, and Henry Kissinger didn't even step forward to be quoted as "a senior administration official." Arkansas governor Winthrop Rockefeller sent a telegram to Nixon, asking the president to "turn these rumors into fact and join us for this battle for the national championship. We look forward to the possibility of being able to extend our hog-calling brand of hospitality to you."

That Saturday afternoon, Penn State's Charlie Pittman—another All-American—ran for three touchdowns as the Nittany Lions beat North Carolina State 33–8 to finish the regular season undefeated and extend their winning streak to twenty-one. Pittman was the Nittany Lions' best running back, better than sophomores Lydell Mitchell and "blocking back" Franco Harris. Penn State was set to play Missouri in the Orange Bowl.

In New York Saturday night, Steve Worster and Bob McKay went to the banquet honoring the *Look*/Football Writers Association All-Americans. Before the dinner, during the cocktail hour, Worster spotted a familiar figure. Among all these football players, among all these stars, Worster was most excited to see Howard Cosell, the lawyer-turned-sportscaster who had gotten to sit at ringside to watch Cassius Clay/Muhammad Ali fight, then talk to him as if there was nothing he couldn't say to the champ. Heck, Cosell probably still could, even with the champ in fighting limbo because of his little match with the draft board.

Much to Worster's surprise, Cosell noticed his interest and walked over. "Well, if it isn't the Bridge City Bomber! How . . . ya . . . doin' . . . Steve?"

Famous in high school as the Bridge City Bomber, Worster hadn't been called by the nickname much during his college career. But Howard Cosell knew!

In Fayetteville, Razorback defensive tackle Terry Don Phillips was working out, prodded by Coach Charley Coffey. "I died about a million times," Phillips says. Part of him hoped he wouldn't be needed to play against his home-state Longhorns and his pal, James Street; part of him wanted desperately to be on the field the next Saturday.

In New York, the All-Americans stayed in a couple of hotels—the Arkansas and Texas contingents weren't in the same one—but the players wandered the streets for sightseeing in groups. On the way out of the Americana, the doorman told the Texas boys to "have a good time, but watch out for the hookers on Forty-second."

"What are hookers?" Worster asked.

The doorman laughed and waved them off.

The Texas boys were walking on the street when a man chased down another man and shot him. "What fascinated me was here's a man chasing him down the street, and everyone just parts like the Red Sea," Worster says. "He shoots the guy down and then the people come right back together, with everybody just be-bopping along."

Dicus and Powell walked by another shooting after the fact. Dicus marveled that when the policemen decided an ambulance couldn't get through the traffic just off Broadway, they slid the shooting victim in the squad car and turned it into an emergency ambulance.

McKay and Worster joined a group of about a dozen All-Americans on a subway ride to Greenwich Village. "You should have seen us idiots," McKay says. "All of us have short haircuts, we've got coats and ties on. There wasn't anybody who was going to screw with us. We looked like a bunch of giants walking on that thing. There was shit going on we never had seen in our lives. There were two girls kissing right there on the train."

The players said they also saw a derelict woman asleep in a subway station, and were feeling sorry for her, until she woke up and urinated in front of them—and everyone in the station.

IN WASHINGTON, Republican congressman George Bush and his close friend, Arkansas U.S. representative John Paul Hammerschmidt, a member of the same House Republican freshman class as Bush, pondered attending the Texas versus Arkansas game. Meanwhile in Houston, Apollo 12 astronauts Pete Conrad, Richard Gordon, and Alan Bean—in quarantine after their return to earth from the second moon mission—showed off their collection of moon rocks. Bean, a former wrestler and gymnast at the University of Texas, already was considering what to say in a telegram to the Longhorns. Apparently, he never considered: "Moon 'em."

BACK IN NEW YORK, Razorbacks Chuck Dicus and Cliff Powell went to the AFL game at Shea Stadium between the New York Jets and the Oakland Raiders. What struck Dicus more than anything else was the crowd: The New Yorkers seemed to relish getting on the Jets. The World Champions! This was the team that shocked the world the previous January, living up to Joe Namath's poolside guarantee, and the fans were taunting the Jets! That shocked Dicus as much as seeing a wounded man thrown into the back of a police car. With Daryl Lamonica throwing two touchdown passes to Warren Wells, the Raiders won 27–14. The Jets were flat; they had the AFL East all but wrapped up.

The night of the Jets' loss to the Raiders, Bob McKay, Steve Worster, and Ohio State fullback Jim Otis went to Namath's nightclub, Bachelors Three. Former Longhorn Jim Hudson, a Jets defensive back, invited them, telling them not to worry about the line outside the door. They should go to the front and say who they were, and they would be ushered right to a table for the Jets.

"Hell, we get over there and there are people lined up around the block to get in," McKay says. "God, we go up there and walk in the front door like we have good sense. We ended up sitting there with all those idiots after their game, and you talk about different worlds. You got the whole team in there, drinking, raising hell, having a good time. There were more women than you've ever seen in your life. For a kid from Crane, it was a pretty big shock. But I didn't leave. I sure stayed there and watched."

The Jets' roster listed several other former Longhorns, including tight end Pete Lammons, defensive lineman John Elliott, and wide receiver George Sauer, whose early exit to sign with the AFL had embittered Royal. (Sauer eventually wrote the introduction to *Meat on the Hoof,* Gary Shaw's acidic 1972 book about his experiences as a Texas reserve in the mid-1960s.) The Jets' former Longhorns were there to greet the present Longhorns, and so was Namath. Worster was embarrassed to find out Namath and the Jets seemed to know a lot more about college football, including the impact of the upcoming game in Fayetteville, than Worster did about the pros.

On Monday, December 1, Worster and McKay wore their uniforms and filmed the *Look* All-American team's bit with Bob Hope for his December 18 special. Razorback Rodney Brand, the *Look* All-American center, was back in Fayetteville. "I got the ring and everything, but they just put my picture up on the TV on the special," Brand says. "It really upset my mother that I didn't go, but it didn't upset me." Without Brand, the other All-Americans rehearsed several times without an audience, then did it for real with an audience in the seats and the film rolling. *Trot onstage. Stop next to Mr. Hope. Say your name, position, and school. When Hope gets off a one-liner, you laugh. Or at least hunch your shoulders and smile. Then trot off.* Bob McKay didn't have to fake his laugh. "He was funnier than a rubber crutch."

The cab ride back to the airport was cheaper.

SIXTEEN

Defensing the Wishbone

ALL SEASON LONG, the Arkansas coaches preached about not looking ahead. The players knew what they meant: Don't get caught thinking about Texas. When Arkansas struggled early in the November 8 game against Rice, several seniors made sure the coaches were out of earshot at halftime, then warned that if the Razorbacks didn't get going, they were going to "screw up that last game"—the showdown with Texas. But in truth, the coaching staff was planning for the Horns. During the bye week leading up to the game's October 18 original date, the coaches acted as if the Razorbacks were going to play the Longhorns as scheduled. Charley Coffey and the defensive staff started looking at film of the Texas wishbone—including the Longhorns' 39–29 victory over the Razorbacks in 1968—and pondering ways to try to slow it down. The Razorbacks also had an overqualified "scout" available. Bob Ford had coached at Alabama, Georgia, and Mississippi State as a young assistant, but when the entire Mississippi State staff was fired, Ford decided the instability of the coaching game wasn't for him.

A native of Wynne, Arkansas, he applied to the UofA law school. After he was accepted, he called Frank Broyles and asked if he could work as a graduate assistant while he was in law school to help support his wife and three children.

Broyles said he would arrange it, and in 1969, his final year of law school, Ford worked with the varsity, and Broyles assigned him as the primary Texas scout. Ford went to two Texas games, the second at College Station on Thanksgiving, and studied the Longhorns on film. "Bob Ford did a good job of describing what we had to do if we were going to win the ballgame," Broyles says. With Ford making suggestions, and Coffey putting together a game plan, the Razorbacks had an innovative defensive strategy for the Longhorns. Arkansas came in giving up a national low 6.8 points per game, but the Razorbacks knew they needed to adjust their scheme to defense the wishbone.

The plan, which the coaches outlined even before the actual game week, involved a fine-tuning of the usual 4-3 defense. The four Razorback linemen would play a half-step farther off the line of scrimmage than usual, giving them a bit of a "run" at angles and more of a shot at creating piles, and they also would vary their spacing and alignment. Lynn Garner, usually the left linebacker, often would pop up onto the line in a standup stance—and not always in the same place. Linebackers Cliff Powell and Mike Boschetti would be freed up because of all the traffic in front of them to chase down ballcarriers. But the most glaring adjustment for the wishbone was to have "monster" back Bobby Field usually on the line of scrimmage. Field always was going to be on the same side of the formation as Texas tight end Randy Peschel, so he would hover as the offensive huddle broke, then follow Peschel and line up just outside the tight end in a coiled, upright stance. Depending on how tight to the line of scrimmage Garner and Field got, the alignment could have a 6-2, 5-3, or 4-4 look.

Regardless, eight Razorbacks were going to be within a couple yards of the line of scrimmage. Loading up the line against the wishbone was far from revolutionary, and there were risks. If fullback Steve Worster, for example, popped through on the quick handoff and none of the eight defenders up close could get to him, then Worster had only three defensive backs between him and the goal line—with those fast Texas linemen trying to get downfield to blow defenders off the movie screen.

Coffey says the plan involved more "wrinkles" of existing Razorback concepts than major change. "It wasn't really complicated," he says. "We had three ways of playing it, rather than making it easy for them to read us. We moved our defenses around at the last moment. Then we forced them to pitch the ball or we forced them to keep the ball. We wanted to try to make the decisions, not them."

Coffey told the linemen that in many of the defensive calls, they would shift shortly before the snap, making it more difficult for the Texas linemen to quickly decide who to block. "Usually, we'd use our speed and our slants to disrupt offenses," defensive tackle Roger Harnish says. "In this game, we moved back and caused piles. We weren't supposed to be blown off the line or interfere with the linebackers. That allowed the linebackers to run more from side to side to make more tackles."

In general, the defensive tackle was supposed to fill a gap and create that pile. The defensive end—often unblocked in the wishbone scheme—crashed to the fullback, even if that meant trying to fight across the front of one of the Texas All-American tackles or simply diving at Worster's feet.

"I had the fullback probably 80 percent of the time," defensive end Rick Kersey says. "I know during the game, I tackled him almost every play. My job was to kind of slant in and take the fullback to cause a problem with the exchange."

A defensive halfback usually had the pitch man, and if the Longhorns ran the option to the strong side, where Bobby Field was aligned, the Razorbacks had an "extra" defender there.

One of their goals was when Street looked ahead, to force him to cut up and run right into the linebacker popping into the "keep" hole. Also, on certain calls, the defensive backs knew that the other Razorbacks were trying to force Street to pitch the ball, so the DBs could "cheat" toward the pitch man. All of this defensive aggressiveness made the Razorbacks vulnerable to the play-action pass.

Coffey showed a lot of faith in the ability of his defensive players to intelligently grasp and implement the defensive scheme changes. But he understood that he was coaching an extraordinarily intelligent defensive unit, and that he placed a tremendous amount of responsibility and trust in his star linebacker, Cliff Powell.

The Razorbacks—and Powell especially—were up to the challenges.

POWELL CAME OFF THE FAMILY FARM IN EUDORA, and as a member of the Future Farmers of America, he gave every indication that he wanted to go right back after graduation. His major was agricultural engineering. He was one of the top middle linebackers in the country, as the coaches recognized by voting him to their All-American team, but the realigned defense for the Texas game was going to tinker with his usual role.

"I was lined up over a tackle and I usually was over a guard," Powell says.

The other linebacker, Mike Boschetti, hadn't even played football until his freshman year at Pine Bluff High. During Texas's national championship season, 1963, the fourteen-year-old Boschetti went with his father to the Longhorns-Razorbacks game in Little Rock. It was Dads' Day, with the Razorbacks' fathers assembling on the sideline before the game. Out of nowhere, Mike told his father: "You're going to be down there someday." Marius Boschetti, an instrument mechanic at the paper mill, rightfully considered it an impudent statement from a kid who wasn't even playing football. "He just looked at me," Boschetti says. He might as well have said, "Dad, I'm going to be the first man to walk on the moon."

But Boschetti started to grow, went out for football in the ninth grade, and ended up starring as an all-state player for those Pine Bluff Zebras. ("Wear your stripes proud!" Boschetti says, smiling.)

Boschetti considered SMU and The Citadel and was crushed when his high school coach told him that Arkansas sent a letter saying the Razorbacks regretted informing him that they wouldn't have a scholarship for him. Later, Boschetti suspected that letter was bogus, perhaps part of a plot to steer him to SMU, where the Pine Bluff coach ended up the next season. But at the time Boschetti was shocked when Mervin Johnson, the offensive line coach on the staff that hadn't wanted him, showed up at school, offering him a scholarship. So Marius got to be down there on Dads' Day and Mike was entrenched as a starter as a junior.

The third starting linebacker, Lynn Garner, was a highly sought high school linebacker, starring at Northside in Fort Smith, and Darrell Royal paid him a recruiting visit. Garner's high school coach, Bill Stancil, was with them. "All I said was, 'Hi, Coach Royal,' and then the coaches did all the talking," Garner says.

Royal said, "We'd like you to come to Texas, Lynn."

Stancil, the high school coach, countered, "If he goes to Texas, they'll burn his house down."

A half-hour later, Royal left, knowing his pitch probably had been fruitless. Sure enough, Garner was in his third year as a Razorback starter by the '69 game. There had been some rough moments, such as when Garner—like Terry Don Phillips—temporarily was thrown off the team, along with linebacker Guy Parker. But when Garner and Parker went to Broyles and told him they had lined up scholarships at the University of Houston and were transferring, Broyles acted as if all was forgiven. "No, you're back on now," Broyles said.

For the Texas game, Garner would be stepping into a defensive line that started four underclassmen. Bruce James, the junior left end, was the gumbo lover from Moss Point, Mississippi. Roger Harnish, the sophomore left tackle, was from Little Rock. Right tackle Dick Bumpas was a junior from Fort Smith's Southside High. Rick Kersey, the junior right end, was from Conway.

Kersey was known for his ability to play either tackle or end, but also for going after both quarterbacks and his teammates, asking the Razorbacks if they had Christ on a throne or if they were dating good Christian girls. His father worked for the Arkansas Children's Colony, a home for retarded children, and the Southern Baptist Church was the center of Kersey family life. Rick was an all-state player, but because he weighed only 180 pounds, his high school coach in Conway refused to forward films of him to the UofA staff, and told Kersey to be realistic about his future. But the Razorbacks' Wilson Matthews came on a recruiting trip to Conway, concentrating on a star Conway tailback but also spotting Kersey. "I guess Wilson Matthews saw something in me," Kersey says.

Kersey started at defensive tackle as a sophomore and the first part of 1969 as a junior, but moved over from tackle to end when Gordon McNulty, the regular end, tore knee cartilage on November 1 against Texas A&M. A month later, McNulty was able to play on the bad knee if needed, but not at full effectiveness. "It was a real letdown to know that I wasn't going to be able to play at the top level," McNulty says. McNulty's problems were another reason the Razorbacks also hoped to have Terry Don Phillips available again, as they were pondering trying to rotate the defensive linemen, to keep them fresh.

NcNulty desperately wanted to play, because he was a senior and it was going to be his final home game as a Razorback. To get to that point, he had taken the most circuitous route of all his teammates. He was one of the lesser-recruited players on a celebrated Pine Bluff Zebras team (briefly playing with Bruce Maxwell), and he started his college career at Vanderbilt. After McNulty had a strong Arkansas high school all-star game, Razorback coaches at the game admitted to him they probably didn't recruit him hard enough and wished him luck at Vanderbilt. He decided the Vanderbilt program—including its coaching, facilities, and attitude—was second rate, though, and transferred to UofA after his freshman year.

"I wasn't really sure I could compete on that level, but I decided to give it a shot," McNulty says. He was on the B team in 1966 because he was ineligible to play, sitting out one season under transfer rules, assuming he would be able to suit up for the Razorbacks in 1967. Vanderbilt coach Jack Green, though, had resigned from the Commodores and joined the Baylor staff, and when he contested McNulty's transfer before the Southwest Conference eligibility committee, arguing he had never released McNulty, the committee ruled that the defensive end had to sit out a second season at Arkansas. McNulty was livid. "I had a copy of that letter releasing me, but he said, 'Naw, that's not what that meant,' and he took a stand, so they made me lay out two years," McNulty says. "I was on the 'meat' squad for two years—best training in the world. You just got beat on every day, but you got to go up against some great athletes, and I think it builds a good relationship with coaches because they get to where they can depend on you." He essentially never had a sophomore season: He was able to play only two seasons at Arkansas.

McNulty started in 1968 for the Razorbacks and had a great game against Georgia in the Sugar Bowl. He also was prominent on campus, serving as student body senior class president in the 1969–70 school year and taking a high-profile role in the Campus Crusade for Christ.

If McNulty was able to play against Texas, he was going to line up a lot of the time next to Dick Bumpas, the junior defensive tackle from Fort Smith who already intended to go into coaching, too. The other defensive tackle, Roger Harnish, was grateful to have all the students of the game around him. He had bounced around as the son of an Air Force officer, and played only two years of high school football. He even was a soccer player while his dad was stationed in England, so as a football player, he still was raw when he left Little Rock Catholic to head to Fayetteville.

Defensive end Bruce James, from Mississippi, had turned his back on the Southeastern Conference schools. "I was a running back in high school and all these other coaches were talking about what position I'd be and all, and Frank Broyles was basically talking about academics," James says. "He told me, 'I don't really know where you'll play if you come here, but you'll play somewhere if you're good enough. But I don't want to recruit anybody if you're not interested in coming here to get a degree.' That really impressed me. I went to the University of Arkansas specifically because of Frank Broyles."

As a freshman, James still was a running back when he talked with the freshman team's defensive line coach, graduate assistant Jackie Sherrill. Sherrill also was from Mississippi, and they agreed James should give the defensive line a try. James started as a sophomore in 1968 as a member of the young front four that was a cohesive unit through the next season as well.

THE AGGRESSIVE PLAY UP FRONT, and the move of the "monster" back up to the line of scrimmage, put a lot of pressure and decision making responsibility on the remaining three defensive backs—halfbacks Terry Stewart and Jerry Moore, and senior safety Dennis Berner. The halfbacks were supposed to come up quick to play the run, especially if the tight end was to their side. The pass coverage on that side generally would be zone, with the halfback on the other side man-to-man on Speyrer.

If the halfback on the strong side rolled up to play what looked like a run, but the play turned into a pass, it meant that the safety and the "off" halfback covering Speyrer had to be responsible for coverage. If the halfback on the tight-end side could quickly read any play-action fakes by Street and get back into zone coverage with the safety, Berner, that would decrease the chances of getting burned. But the emphasis for the defensive halfback on the tight-end side was on aggressively playing the run, and that made perfect sense, given the Longhorns' preference to run the ball—and throw deep passes to Speyrer.

That all meant Berner needed to be quick in deciding which side might need his help in pass coverage, because the Razorbacks had come up with a strategy that—among other things—*dared* Texas to throw. And it showed a lot of trust in those defensive backs, who all were heady players.

The left halfback, Stewart, was valedictorian at Fort Smith's Northside High School and was one of Lynn Garner's teammates. Terry's father, Victor, was the principal of rival Southside High, meaning the elder Stewart watched over Southside football star Dick Bumpas. Terry was Gordon McNulty's predecessor as president of the UofA senior class and carried a 3.7 grade point average in chemical engineering. He had tact, too, which was why the Razorbacks willingly shoved him forward as the spokesman in their midseason attempt to get the coaches to stop making in-season practices torture. As the Texas game approached, Stewart yearned to get back at the Longhorns after being burned on a 51-yard James Street touchdown pass to Cotton Speyrer in Texas's victory in Austin the year before.

The safety, Dennis Berner, was sailing along in premed. On the field, he was quiet and imperturbable, and the only doubt about him was whether he was emotional and passionate enough about the game. Berner was a gifted track hurdler as well, and he considered going to Alabama to specialize in track. Instead, he competed in a few meets for the Razorbacks, running a decent 14.6 in the 120-yard high hurdles. He started out as a wide receiver and had ten catches as a sophomore, then was switched to defense. To him, it was all a rest stop on the way to what he hoped was a career in medicine.

The other defensive halfback, junior Jerry Moore, Bobby Field's roommate, was an Arkansan in terms of family roots, but not in terms of his own experience. J. P. Moore, his father, was raised in Arkansas and was recruited to Vanderbilt by a young assistant coach, Paul "Bear" Bryant. Bryant liked the fact that J. P. Moore ran an eye-popping 9.8-second hundred-yard dash on a cinder track in 1939, and J.P. was a star for the Commodores before he entered the U.S. Army Air Corps and worked in research during World War II. Later, as J.P. stayed in the service and advanced to lieutenant colonel, the Moores moved around, but talked of Arkansas often. J.P. was a strict father, driving home the point to Jerry that perfection was the goal and near-perfection was barely tolerable. Jerry spent most of his teenage years in Virginia, when his father was stationed at the Pentagon, but J.P. left the Air Force and brought the family back to his native Benton, Arkansas, about twenty miles southwest of Little Rock, for Jerry's senior year of high school.

At Benton, Jerry immediately was the star—the star quarterback; the star defensive back; the star, period. He considered Virginia Tech and also his father's alma mater, Vanderbilt, but J.P. made it clear he would be more honored if his son stayed close to home. "It all boiled down to one thing," Jerry says. "I was going to go to school where my dad told me to go to school, where he encouraged me to go to school. He didn't tell me what to do, but I knew what he wanted. My dad was very much a disciplinarian and ruled the roost."

At Arkansas, Jerry competed with Bill Montgomery for the right to be considered *the* quarterback prospect. But Montgomery's recruitment had been heralded, and when the Razorbacks installed their pro-style offense under Don Breaux, it was another sign to Moore, who was an option QB in high school. During spring training in 1968, before his sophomore season, Moore asked to be switched to defensive back—with some regret.

"It was apparent to me I wasn't going to be given a fair shot at playing quarterback, and I didn't want to waste any more time doing that," Moore says. "I didn't want to sit on the bench."

Was he as good as Montgomery?

"Well, in my opinion, yeah," Moore says. "I really felt I could have played quarterback." But Moore's playing style became an issue. "I was not a pocket-type passer. I didn't grow up in that kind of offense, I was more of an option-type quarterback."

He started in the defensive backfield as a sophomore, and at six-three and 198 pounds, he was by far the biggest defensive back for either Arkansas or Texas. He also was the best.

EVENTUALLY, as the wishbone spread and became more familiar, defensive coaches around the country fine-tuned and conferred and successfully neutralized the offense, often "crashing" at the guards to take them out of the downfield blocking and fine-tuning the assignment of one defender to each of the options—the fullback, the quarterback, and the pitch man. But in December 1969, Coffey came up with a series of ideas and approaches that gave the revolutionary Texas wishbone more problems than it had ever encountered before. And he had the right players for it all.

SEVENTEEN

Defensing the Razorbacks

TEXAS DEFENSIVE END BILL ATESSIS usually played host to the card games in Jester Center. The game of choice was Bourre, a Cajun-style poker game that rewarded recklessness—or guts. The sessions could last overnight during the off-season, and were scaled back—only in terms of hours, not competitiveness—during the season. The Longhorns who didn't play marveled that these guys ever passed enough classes to stay eligible. (Sometimes, they didn't.) But Atessis, for one, was famous for being able to wedge naps in during the day, around classes.

In Bourre, if you won the hand, you got the pot; if you didn't catch a "trick" at all, you had to match the pot. "That probably sums up our attitude for playing football, as well," Atessis says. They played on credit, with extensive records kept on yellow legal pads, and everybody had to periodically settle up.

Mike Campbell didn't coach the "Split 6"—the name didn't change even after the defensive ends were put into upright stances and renamed outside linebacker and rover, officially changing it into a four-man front—as a gambling defense, but it sometimes worked out that way. The defensive tackles lined up on the outside shoulders of the offensive guards, angled in. The two inside linebackers, senior Glen Halsell and junior Scott Henderson, usually hovered a couple of yards off the ball. One or both could be in the gap between the defensive tackles; regardless, the defense was overloaded in the middle.

Against the running game, the theory was that the Longhorns had four defenders—two defensive tackles and two linebackers—against the center and two guards, making it difficult to run inside. That's where the fierce Arkansas fullback, Bruce Maxwell, would be crucial in The Big Shootout—primarily as a lead blocker to mitigate the mismatch up the middle.

The deployment of the four defenders in such a confined area so near the center, and the use of only three defensive backs, could make the Longhorns more vulnerable to the passing game, especially against a quarterback as good as Bill Montgomery. The Longhorns planned to use their standard man-to-man coverage package—called "Baylor," after the most pass-happy team in the Southwest Conference—in sure passing situations.

Coach Campbell decided that in passing situations against Arkansas, he frequently would have one of the inside linebackers blitz. The plan was to have one of them pop up to the line and fake the blitz to draw All-American center Rodney Brand's attention, then have the *other* linebacker blitz instead.

Halsell and Henderson had complementary strengths. Halsell was the terrific run linebacker. Henderson was better at reading the pass and scrambling into coverage. After all, they did call him "Professor."

————————

RALPH HENDERSON worked for 3M in the Twin Cities and was transferred to Dallas when Scott was in grade school. "We had a frozen pond down the street in Saint Paul, and if I had stayed there, I would have been a hockey player," Scott says. "I'd have been a grinder."

Scott was a devout Catholic and as he developed into a star football player at Dallas's Hillcrest High, his dream was to play for Notre Dame. He took game film over to the home of a family friend, Lancaster Smith, who played for the Fighting Irish in the immediate post–World War II years. "They wrote back and said, 'Sorry we have no place for you,'" Henderson says.

He visited Stanford and met with Dartmouth coach Bob Blackmun before making the Southwest Conference circuit and settling on the Longhorns. Because of his knee surgery, Henderson only watched those tough 1968 spring workouts. He opened 1968 as a backup and got a chance to play when Halsell became violently ill during the third game, against Oklahoma State. Henderson played so well, the Longhorns decided to play him with Halsell, and the two-man inside linebacking team was formed.

As The Big Shootout loomed, there was some doubt about whether Henderson would be available. He was kicked in the foot against TCU and suffered a slight break. Team doctors, suddenly conscientious, wanted to put Henderson in a cast, but he vetoed that, sat out the Texas A&M game and pronounced himself ready to play against the Razorbacks. But Royal wanted to check, and at the start of the Monday practice, the coach approached Henderson.

"Scott, can you run?"

"Sure."

"Well, Scott, run down there to the fifty and come back."

Henderson followed orders.

"Well, that looks OK," Royal said. "How does it feel?"

"Fine, Coach."

That's the last they talked about it all week. "Trust me," Henderson says. "If I hadn't been able to play, I would have said so. And they wouldn't have taken the chance putting me in there if they thought I couldn't perform."

Henderson was both impressed with and highly concerned about Montgomery, his Dallas-area high school contemporary. The Longhorns, he says, "watched a lot of film and Bill Montgomery was the focal point, the gun, and he had done a pretty darned good job against us in 1968. Everything started with Bill. It was a passing offense and our defense was stop run, stop run. We only played three deep with a rover back and you can't do that now. Our whole defense was geared to stop the run. We did that pretty successfully, but there was always a concern that against a good passer, things could fall apart. Coach Campbell was concerned about Montgomery and his short passing in particular."

Henderson couldn't spot any evidence of Montgomery's alleged loss of arm strength because of his injuries.

Coach Campbell harped on reacting to the slants across the middle and the dumps to the backs, but of course, it would help if the linemen put pressure on Montgomery. Bill Atessis put down the cards and went after the quarterback, along with tackles Greg Ploetz and Carl White, and fellow defensive end David Arledge. The Longhorns were still adjusting to the midseason loss of star defensive tackle Leo Brooks, and they wondered if this was the game in which his absence would be glaring.

————————

ATESSIS WAS the Longhorns' most talented defensive lineman, and at six-three, 257, he was the biggest to play for Royal up to that time. His major weakness was his inability to undergo a Bobby Wuensch–style transformation from off-the-field affability to on-field fierceness. It's not that he didn't have a chance to learn that from Wuensch, either: The two of them went to high school together, at Jesse H. Jones High in Houston, before going to Texas.

Atessis's father, James, came to Texas from Greece and eventually landed a job as the banquet maitre d' at the Shamrock Hilton in Houston. Bill began working in the kitchen at fourteen. "My father thought it was cheaper to put me to work so I could eat over there," Bill says.

When Bill grew up on all that banquet food and became a high school star, one wing of the Hilton family—Texas A&M supporters—put mild pressure on James to deliver his son to the Aggies. When Darrell Royal pressed him for a commitment on his UT visit, Atessis said sure, he wanted to be a Longhorn, and when Royal called his parents to congratulate them, Bill hadn't yet broken the news. James Atessis, with all those Aggie boosters around him, wasn't happy.

Bill agreed to take his scheduled trip to College Station. Bill's nonbinding commitment to Texas was no secret, so Texas A&M coach Gene Stallings had nothing to lose. When Atessis walked into his office on his visit, Stallings had his back to the door and was facing the wall. He kept Atessis waiting for a minute that seemed like an hour. Then he turned and looked Atessis in the eyes.

"Son, you don't have the *guts* to come to A&M."

Dumbfounded, Atessis didn't respond. Eventually, he made it clear he didn't know about the guts, but he definitely didn't have the desire to be an Aggie. Before he showed up at Austin, though, he suffered a broken ankle in the Big 33 all-star game in Pennsylvania and didn't play at all as a freshman. He started as a sophomore at defensive tackle, but felt more comfortable when he was switched to end for 1969. There, he played next to a real artist.

REALLY, LONGHORNS DEFENSIVE TACKLE Greg Ploetz *was* an artist. He didn't try to hide it, either, and his teammates learned to appreciate it when he came back from his life drawing classes, with his sketches of nude women models. The boys would be waiting for him.

"Let's take a look at them!"

They grabbed his pad and flipped through.

You get to look at naked women every morning?

You get credit for this stuff?

You get her phone number?

He was the big-time prospect Royal was going after when he went to Sherman, winning over Mike Dean's mother and landing the little guard. Like Arkansas's Roger Harnish and Jerry Moore, Ploetz was an Air Force brat, and he moved from Colorado Springs to Sherman just before high school. He was leaning toward going to Oklahoma after some heavy recruiting pitches from Sooners assistant Barry Switzer, but he and Dean ended up a Sherman-to-Austin package deal. Angry when he was listed as the fifth-team defensive end on the freshman team depth chart during the no-pads workouts, Ploetz had passion to burn when the Longhorn freshmen players finally put on pads.

"I thought, 'God, I'm going to have to kill somebody,'" Ploetz says. "Sure enough, there's a tackling drill called 'eye-opener,' when they set four bags on the ground in a line. The [ballcarrier] can run in the first hole or the second hole or the third hole, but if he fakes into one hole, he has to run into the next hole. I think this kid's name was Bobby White, he never played much for Texas, but he got the ball and I just tried to kill him. They picked him up and I got up and somebody asked me, 'Now what's your name again?' The next day, my little ring is hung at starting linebacker."

During the 1968 spring practices, Ploetz also had the "good" fortune to get a reprieve because of an injury. He got caught in a pile and got up hobbling.

"I think I hurt my ankle," he told Coach Pat Patterson. In fact, it was broken.

"All right," Patterson said, "go in and dip it in something and get back out there."

Ploetz didn't come back out to practice the rest of the afternoon. The next day, he pointed to the cast and told Patterson, "I dipped it in plaster."

In the art department, Ploetz looked as out of place as a Haight-Ashbury refugee on Jester Center's football floors. "I was pretty sympathetic with the antiwar movement, but I was required to wear my hair short and I never participated in any rallies or walks," Ploetz says. "I had lots of friends who did in the art department. It was kind of a joke over there. I only weighed about 205, but I was pretty hulked up. With short hair, I'd go into a painting class and people would look and say, 'Who's that?'"

After practice sometimes, Ploetz would head back over to the art department to paint, which was his homework and release. It was as crowded as football practice. "Your class was just a staging zone for painting," Ploetz says. "Typically, I'd leave [the canvases] on the floor to dry and then in the morning, when I got up, I'd run over there and roll them up and put them in the rack. One time I forgot a painting on the floor. Mr. Spruce, a teacher I had, came in and said, 'What the hell's this?' He started to grab it, and the kids said, 'Do you know whose that is? That big guy with short hair!' And he said, 'Oh really?' And he put it to the side very carefully."

During the 1969 season, Ploetz suffered a cracked ankle against Oklahoma. He missed one game and wasn't expected to play in the next one, either, against SMU on November 1. But Leo Brooks, the star defensive tackle, went out with a season-ending knee injury, and in the shuffling, Ploetz soon went back in. "On the film, during a pass play, you could see me hopping on one leg," Ploetz says.

He kept playing. "They kind of said, 'Well, you played on it, how's it feel?' It was kind of sore, but I played."

So in The Big Shootout, Scott Henderson played with a cracked bone in his foot and Greg Ploetz had a cracked bone in his ankle. They should have compared X-rays with Arkansas guard Jerry Dossey, who took the injections in his foot.

CARL WHITE, the big sophomore defensive tackle from McKinney who tried to tear Steve Worster's foot off in the state high school championship game, was from a Texas family well-known in the automobile business. He was all set to go to UT when he competed in the state track meet in Austin in the spring of 1968. On the same day those infamous 1968 spring practices ended with the Orange and White intrasquad game, White won the discus title on his last throw, with a handful of Texas football players watching. Guard Ken Gidney was from McKinney, too, and he hit several of the Longhorns and said, "That's our boy. He's coming here this fall!"

By his second year, he was the protégé, backup, and roommate of star defensive tackle Leo Brooks, the giant from little Kermit, Texas. "We were good friends," White says. "We did everything together. I was like his little brother."

Brooks's season-ending injury came when an SMU blocker tore up his knee. "Dadgum SMU," White says. "It was a chop block. SMU was famous for it back then. You always had a sprained ankle or two or tore a knee up against SMU."

White moved into the No. 1 right defensive tackle spot. He was one Longhorn who had mixed feelings about starting in The Big Shootout.

———————————

THE LONGHORNS labeled the defensive end combination "Big A and Little A." The former was Atessis, the latter was David Arledge, who calls his college career "a real Cinderella story." But Cinderella at least was considered big enough for her position—the belle of the ball.

Coming out of high school in Richardson, near Dallas, Arledge—then a hefty 155-pounder who played offensive guard and defensive end—at first was told he was too small for college football by everyone except Texas. Once there, he so impressed the freshman team coaches that after lining up at guard in the first no-pads offensive practice, he found himself listed on the next depth chart as the fourth-team split end. In the afternoon workout, he lined up at defensive end. The next depth chart had him as the fourth-team safety. Don't worry, he was assured, freshman football was an experimental process. "We know the cream will rise to the top," Coach Pat Patterson told him.

Arledge didn't play in the first couple of games and was watching on the sideline when the freshmen played SMU in Dallas. The SMU freshmen used crackbacks and chop blocks, too, and Arledge says four Texas defensive ends were injured in the first thirty-five minutes of the game. "As each one fell, I got a little closer and a little closer to Bill Ellington," Arledge says of the head freshman coach. "Every time Bill turned around, I'm standing there. When a fifth guy went down, one of the assistant coaches, Jim Helms, said, 'Coach, Arledge played defensive end in high school.' I was a battlefield promotion."

Ellington sighed. "Son," he told Arledge, "get in there and rush the passer, and keep containment, and good luck."

Arledge played well, grading out at a solid 88 percent on film. He started the last two freshmen games. "I weighed 163 pounds," he says. "We roll into spring training and I'm the backup defensive end on the varsity. Of course, they don't think they need me because I'm backing up Bill Atessis and Bill Zapalac, both all-Southwest-Conference defensive ends as sophomores."

But when Zapalac was shifted to strong side outside linebacker at midseason—during the two-week break caused by the move of the Arkansas game—

Arledge became the starter. Because of his size, or lack of it, the 170-pound Arledge was given license to play his position differently than the traditional style coached by Mike Campbell in which defensive ends were expected to take on the blockers and overpower them. But Arledge was extraordinarily quick and small for the position; he tried to slip blockers, not fight them off. On the first play of the Rice game, his first as a starter, Rice ran a sweep. Arledge skirted the blocker and made the tackle. At the defensive film study the next week, Arledge says, "Coach Campbell runs that play and just before I'm going to make the tackle, he stops it and runs it back. He did this about four times and each time I'm getting lower and lower in my chair."

"Arledge!"

"Yes, sir?"

"If you ever miss that tackle, you'll do it my way!"

"Yes, sir!"

"Coach Campbell just had a way of saying things," Arledge says. "You always knew where you stood. He never belittled a player as an individual, but you never wondered how he felt about it."

EIGHTEEN

Draft Lottery and the View from Oxford

BOBBY FIELD remembers a Razorback student manager wearing a sign on his back on the sideline at The Big Shootout.

WE'RE NO. 1

I'M NO. 365

Everybody understood what he meant and the nature of his relief. Everybody, including the group of politicians sitting in the stands, on the same side as the Arkansas bench. Everybody, including President Richard Nixon.

On Monday, December 1, less than a week after Nixon signed the enabling legislation, and five days before the Texas-Arkansas game, U.S. Representative Alexander Pirnie, R-N.Y., the senior member of the House Draft Subcommittee, stepped up to a glass jar in the Selective Service headquarters in Washington. Looking straight ahead, he reached into the jar and pulled out a blue capsule, one of 366 in the jar. The slip of paper in the capsule read "September 14."

The draft lottery that night was the nation's first in twenty-seven years, or since World War II. In theory, it was an advancement in fairness: Student deferments weren't eliminated, but the numbers represented prioritization for the draft of all able-bodied men who were at least nineteen and not yet twenty-six on January 1, 1970. To college students, such as the Arkansas and Texas football players, and Rhodes Scholars, it summed up in a number the likelihood of being called into the Army once their student deferments ended. The worst number was 1, virtually guaranteeing a draft notice for the able-bodied; the best was 366, virtually assuring draft immunity. Thousands of young men pondered their futures, based on the numbers assigned to their birthdates.

Representatives of state Selective Service Youth Advisory Committees were called in to draw numbers, and some gave speeches or flashed peace signs when it was their turn; four balked altogether. Yet the drawing of the dates took only ninety minutes, ending during the first half of the Texas-Mississippi basketball game in Gregory Gym. A few of the Longhorns, including Freddie Steinmark, were at the game. Many of his teammates were watching the lottery on television at Jester Center. In Fayetteville, the Razorbacks also watched with great concern in the lounge at Wilson Sharp House.

"A bunch of us were glued to the TV," Texas center Forrest Wiegand says. Wiegand drew number 158, a "gray-area" number. "We knew we were going to have to weigh our options. Everybody was talking about what we were going to do, join this and join that, get in the reserves and hope the war was going to end."

Freddie Steinmark's birthday—January 27—was number 355. His teammates congratulated him for being so lucky.

Defensive end Bill Atessis drew number 14. "I decided I'd cross that bridge when I came to it," he says.

James Street was number 45. "So I might as well have been number 1," he says.

Steve Worster was unlucky 13. "I said the hell with that, I'm playing ball right now, so I'm not concerned about it," he says.

At first, Cotton Speyrer believed he drew number 2, but the actual number for his birthday, April 29, was 191. The confusion occurred because April 24 was number 2, but he was nervous nonetheless. "I'm a patriot, but I didn't want to go," Speyrer says. "I had aspirations to be a pro football player. Had I been called to serve, I would have."

Tackle Bobby Wuensch, back from New York ahead of Worster and Bob McKay, watched the draft lottery with defensive tackle Carl White. They leaned forward on the edge of the dorm room bed and peered, listening for a specific date. The reason: Wuensch and White both had the same birthday, November 1. They drew number 19. They didn't congratulate each other.

In Fayetteville, the results were similarly mixed, the concerns virtually identical. Razorbacks guard Jerry Dossey was among those who knew he was barely healthy enough to play football and not fit enough for any draft board. So when he drew number 103, he didn't worry. Linebacker Mike Boschetti honored the centennial year of college football by drawing number 100. Defensive halfback Jerry Moore, who passionately supported U.S. involvement in South Vietnam, checked in at number 122. Safety Dennis Berner was number 171, but wasn't concerned about whether that number would be called: He already had plans to attend medical school. Defensive tackle Roger Harnish, the son of a career Air Force man, was number 338. "I was relieved, but then I started worrying about my brothers," he says.

Bruce James, the defensive end from Mississippi, also already knew he wouldn't have a problem. "When I didn't go to Ole Miss, the local draft board in Pascagoula, Mississippi, harassed me from the second I went to Arkansas," James says. "I got called up for my physical before the lottery and I just had undergone knee surgery. I was happy to go." He was classified 1-Y, meaning he would be called up only in the case of an extreme emergency. "And then my draft number was 361," James says.

And so it went. On Tuesday morning, at the dining hall, the Razorbacks either discovered or confirmed their draft numbers in the newspapers at breakfast. Tailback Bill Burnett, a notoriously late riser among a group that was *required* to be at breakfast, sauntered in. Somebody asked what number he was. He didn't know.

"What's your birthday?"

"January 11."

"You're number 329! Oh, man!"

That week, *Northwest Arkansas Times* photographer Ken Good snapped a picture of Burnett, wearing his letter sweater, helping his girlfriend, Linda Holmes, affix a BEAT TEXAS placard to the back window of her car.

Bill Clinton had just written a letter to her father.

THE LOTTERY BEGAN AT 1:00 A.M. Monday Oxford time, and Clinton's birthdate, August 19, drew number 311. He knew that his gamble—renouncing that 1-D deferment, backing out of his professed plan to take advanced ROTC at Arkansas, and allowing himself to become draft-eligible again—had paid off. His flirtation with the ROTC program enabled him to quash that July 28 induction notice, and now his high draft number was a godsend.

On December 2, Clinton mailed his application to Yale Law School.

Clinton also felt the need to explain himself to Colonel Eugene Holmes, so he sat down and wrote a letter to the head of the ROTC program. He dated it December 3, or the Wednesday before The Big Shootout in Fayetteville. Years later, Holmes said he considered the letter insulting, in part because Clinton thanked him for "saving" him from the draft and admitted that he hadn't been forthcoming about his anti–Vietnam War and antidraft sentiments. Clinton also was startlingly candid about not wanting to poison his future political "viability." Yet Clinton's letter also was a coherent expression of angst many in his generation felt at the time.

Clinton's letter began:

> *Dear Col. Holmes,*
>
> *I am sorry to be so long in writing. I know I promised to let you hear from me at least once a month, and from now on you will, but I have had to have some time to think about this first letter. Almost daily since my return to England I have thought about writing, about what I want to and ought to say.*
>
> *First, I want to thank you, not just for saving me from the draft, but for being so kind and decent to me last summer, when I was as low as I have ever been. One thing which made the bond we struck in good faith somewhat palatable to me was my high regard for you personally. In retrospect, it seems that the admiration might not have been mutual had you known a little more about me, about my political beliefs and activities. At least you might have thought me more fit for the draft than for ROTC. Let me try to explain.*

Clinton described his distaste for the war, saying he had worked against it while serving as a student aide to J. William Fulbright's Senate Foreign Relations Committee. He said he had "written and spoken and marched against the war," and claimed to have helped organize American student protests in London, in conjunction with the Moratoriums held after his summer visit with Holmes. He argued that no government "rooted in limited, parliamentary democracy should have the power to make its citizens fight and kill and die in a war they may oppose." Clinton continued:

> *I decided to accept the draft in spite of my beliefs for one reason: to maintain my political viability within the system. For years I have worked to prepare myself for a political life characterized by both practical political ability*

and concern for rapid social progress. . . . When the draft came, despite polit-
ical convictions, I was having a hard time facing the prospect of fighting a
war I had been fighting against, and that is why I contacted you. ROTC was
the one way left in which I could possibly, but not positively, avoid both Viet-
nam and resistance. . . . After I signed the ROTC letter of intent I began to
wonder whether the compromise I had made with myself was not more objec-
tionable than the draft would have been, because I had no interest in the
ROTC program in itself and all I seemed to have done was to protect myself
from physical harm. Also, I began to think I had deceived you, not by lies—
there were none—but by failing to tell you all the things I'm writing now.

Clinton told Holmes that he wrote a letter to his draft board on September 12, begging to be drafted, but never mailed the letter because he "didn't
see, in the end, how my going in the army and maybe going to Vietnam
would achieve anything except a feeling that I had punished myself and gotten what I deserved."

The letter closed with: "Merry Christmas. Sincerely, Bill Clinton."

By the time he opened the letter, Holmes barely had thawed out after attending The Big Shootout.

NINETEEN

Turmoil and Tragedy

THE RUMORS ABOUT RICHARD NIXON'S ATTENDANCE at the game circulated for weeks. In fact, Orville Henry of the *Arkansas Gazette*—who was close to Broyles—even mused about Nixon appearing at the Texas game in a whimsical August column, discussing the possibility of the final game being a showdown for the national championship. As the game approached, Governor Winthrop Rockefeller's entreaty to the president was one of several issued. John Mooney of the *Salt Lake Tribune*, the president of the Football Writers Association, also "invited" Nixon to the game after Bud Wilkinson "suggested" it. Jack Gallagher's Saturday, November 29, column in the *Houston Post* was the first public indication that the president's visit was a *fait accompli*, and several stories over the next few days—including a story in *The New York Times*—said the president would attend The Big Shootout. Some of the reports said he would arrive in the area on Friday and stay overnight at the Bella Vista resort, thirty-four miles north of Fayetteville. Those reports were free advertising for the resort, and as it turned out, Bella Vista owner John A. Cooper provided the game tickets for the Washington contingent.

Nixon knew he would be traveling to the home territory of one of his major antagonists. In fact, the president considered Senator J. William Fulbright, the chairman of the Senate Foreign Relations Committee who still called Fayetteville home, a thorn in his West Wing.

Or worse.

On Monday, December 1, a few hours before the Selective Service draft lottery, Fulbright announced the Foreign Relations Committee was sending investigators to Vietnam, presumably in advance of critical Senate hearings. The next day, Fulbright admitted he didn't have enough support on his committee to commission a full-blown investigation, but it was obvious he would continue to torment Nixon about Vietnam at every opportunity. Moreover, more details and charges emerged about what was being labeled the "My Lai Massacre," providing further fodder for the anti–Vietnam War critics. Lieu-

tenant William Calley, Jr., was charged with murdering 109 South Vietnamese men, women, and children in March 1968. The new edition of *Life*
magazine hit the newsstands, with eight alarming color photos taken at My
Lai by ex-Army sergeant Ron Haeberle. Quoted in the accompanying story,
Army sergeant Michael Bernhardt called the My Lai deaths "point-blank
murder." Calley was set to testify before an Army board of inquiry on Friday.

And while Fulbright's denunciation of both Nixon's policies and the war
itself continued, plans were being made to have the senator and president sit
together—or at least near each other—in those seats provided by Cooper.

News of the draft lottery and My Lai filled the front pages, but there was
yet more competition for Americans' attention: A Monday *Los Angeles Times*
story by Jerry Cohen reported that police believed they had solved the August 8 murders of actress Sharon Tate, the wife of director Roman Polanski,
and four others in Benedict Canyon, and the killings of Leno and Rose Mary
LaBianca the next day. Police targeted a bizarre cult, led by drifter Charles
Manson. As the week unfolded, more details about the gruesome murders—
and Manson's messianic hold on his cult—emerged.

Amid the dark news, the official announcement about Nixon's weekend
trip to Fayetteville came on Tuesday, December 2, from UofA director of information William Hughes. The president was coming to the game—just to
the game. He would not make political appearances; he would not stay
overnight. The president would award a plaque, symbolizing the executive
branch's anointing of a national champion, much to the chagrin of Penn
State fans and coach Joe Paterno.

The Texas and Arkansas congressional delegations were signing up for
rides on *Air Force One*, and in Washington later in the week, at meetings of
the House Ways and Means Committee, the staffs of committee chairman
Wilbur Mills, D-Arkansas, and George Bush, R-Texas, staged pro-Razor-
back and pro-Longhorn demonstrations. Bush even left his seat in the committee room and carried a BEAT ARKANSAS sign to Mills's office. Senator
Ralph Yarborough bet Texas steaks against Fulbright's Arkansas pork
spareribs.

On Thursday, December 4, the White House released the list of those attending the game with Nixon. The roll call included nine members of congress: Senators Fulbright and John L. McClellan of Arkansas, both
Democrats; and Republican John Tower of Texas. The representatives:

Texas Republicans Robert Price and Bush, Texas Democrats Jim Wright and J. J. Pickle, plus Mills and John Paul Hammerschmidt of Arkansas. The White House entourage included Henry Kissinger, H. R. Haldeman, counsel Bryce Harlow, and press secretary Ron Ziegler.

Nixon would be coming to a Fayetteville in turmoil—on two different levels. The anti–Vietnam War sentiment in the northwest Arkansas college town remained fervent, but the movement was neither well-organized—Vietnam War veteran Don Donner and the others were almost proud of their often chaotic passion—nor violent. But the mix of demonstrators and football fans, most of them for the Razorbacks and many of them well-lubricated, was a fight waiting to happen. Beyond the anti–Vietnam War protest, though, Nixon was dropping into another dispute with which he had no direct involvement—but which might boil over as he watched.

———————

TWO OF THE MOST PROMINENT anti–Vietnam War faculty activists on the UofA campus, Arthur Hobson and Bud Zinke, were both physics professors. "In Fayetteville," Razorbacks safety Dennis Berner says, "a protest consisted of one physics professor standing on a sidewalk, holding a sign on Wednesday at noon." Arthur Hobson was the chairman of the Fayetteville Peace Group. He spoke at a Tuesday, December 2, news conference, saying the group would stage a "propeace" demonstration at the game. At another news conference on Wednesday, Sonny Keys, a spokesman for the New Coalition for Peace, said his group would protest as well. Donner took over the role as chief spokesman for the anti–Vietnam War forces as the week went along. The movement wasn't into titles and structure, but Donner operated as the de facto chairman of a joint meeting of the Fayetteville Peace Group and the New Coalition for Peace on Wednesday night and then spoke at a news conference. (A news conference in Fayetteville sometimes meant walking over to meet the few local and campus reporters and asking, "Got any questions?") "The New Coalition protest is directed not so much against the game as against President Nixon's Vietnam policy," Donner told the *Traveler.* Donner was the spokesman for the groups again at another news conference on Friday night. He emphasized both times that the protest would be peaceful and that there were no plans to disrupt the game or confront fans.

A major concern, though, was that even if Donner believed what he told reporters—and he did—nobody could guarantee that all protesters would remain nondisruptive or even nonviolent. The campus anti–Vietnam War movement "was about as governable as a group of chimpanzees," Bud Zinke says. "We'd say, 'No sitdowns, right?' Someone would always sit down. We'd say, 'No violence!' Somebody would always start a fight."

That week, Zinke began working behind the scenes as the liaison for the anti–Vietnam War groups and the university administration. The physics professor also was friends with Donner, and they had something significant in common—they had both served in wars.

Zinke was the rare World War II veteran who militantly opposed the Vietnam War virtually from the start. Raised in the St. Louis suburb of Webster Groves, he enlisted in the Navy after finishing high school in 1944. He ended up a second-class radar technician on a destroyer in the Pacific, was detached to the Marines, and was braced for the invasion of Japan when the atomic bombs were dropped on Hiroshima and Nagasaki. Zinke was ticketed for invasion duty on one of the Japanese islands.

"Truman saved my ass," Zinke says. "My chore was to set up a shore-to-ship radio transmitter on Honshu. In that job, your average survival [time] was about five minutes." So Zinke was strongly supportive of Truman's decision to green-light the use of the atomic bombs. "If this country had found out after an invasion of Honshu that Truman had not used that bomb, he would have been lynched on the front lawn of the White House."

After the war, Zinke attended Washington University in St. Louis, and his first job in academia was at the University of Missouri. He says he was fired for giving speeches about the dangers of nuclear weapons testing in the atmosphere. He quickly had job offers at Arkansas and Ohio State. "I came down here," he says of Fayetteville, "because it was a lovely spring, and I came down just to look. I didn't think there was any way I would come to this university. I got here and just fell in love with the place, and they promised me I could teach whatever courses I wanted to teach."

In 1969, he was a tenured associate professor who publicly fought against segregation and for free speech, and was a regular on the letters-to-the-editor page of Little Rock's *Arkansas Gazette*. The university administration didn't try to shut him up. "Missouri was a lot more reactionary than this place," he says.

Given his World War II service, Zinke was no peacenik. He simply was adamant that the United States had no business in Vietnam, and that the cause wasn't worth the loss of American lives. "I was against it from the time it escalated. Hubert Humphrey was running against Richard Nixon, and I was really pissed off. If he had taken a position against the Vietnam War, he would have won the election." When Humphrey made a speech at the UofA, Zinke found himself next to him at one point and ignored the vice president's extended hand.

After it was clear that there would be some sort of anti–Vietnam War protest on game day, UofA president David W. Mullins and Zinke set up a meeting. Publicly, Mullins asked the anti–Vietnam War activists not to embarrass the university by staging a game-day protest with the nation watching; privately, he accepted the inevitable and wanted to keep it under control.

"We were concerned about the fact that football games bring in cops from all over the damn county," Zinke says. "The Fayetteville police were used to this. The others weren't. When they saw a demonstration, they were going to freak. So President Mullins and I sat down, and we both had the same thing in mind—that nobody's ever been hurt on this campus, and we don't want anybody hurt. The problem was, the movement could be like a roomful of squirrels and how were we going to contain these people? The burden fell on me. He couldn't ask them. So we sat down and kind of orchestrated it."

Zinke promised to do his best to keep the demonstration confined to the hill between the stadium and the new administration building, where the protest would be in full view of the west stands—and Nixon's seat. Zinke promised to try to have the demonstrators off the hill by the time the game ended. "We had three or four different groups that wanted to do different things, and we cautioned them all, 'You can't go near the stadium.' I think President Mullins was totally pragmatic."

Unaware of the Zinke-Mullins negotiations, Donner was angered by the university president's original public posturing that no demonstrations should take place on the campus that day. Administration underlings told the activists that the Secret Service wouldn't allow the protests. Donner wanted to know: Was this why he had gone into combat? Hadn't he been willing to die to preserve such rights as freedom of speech? So Donner, brash and impudent, took matters into his own hands.

It was an open secret by early in the week that the presidential advance party, including Secret Service agents, had taken over the fifth floor of a dormitory near the administration building as a command post. Donner went to the dormitory and rode the elevator to the fifth floor. When the door opened, two men were sitting there, on watch, and Donner reconstructs the conversations that ensued.

"Take me to your leader," Donner said.

"Who the hell are you?"

"I'm the one who's going to have a demonstration here and I heard you guys won't let me. I want to talk to somebody about it."

The two men took Donner down the hall, to a room where a man was sitting at a student desk, doing some paperwork. Donner introduced himself and asked, "Why the hell can't I have my demonstration?"

"What?"

"Look, I've been in Vietnam and I want to have a demonstration there at the game."

"Whereabouts?"

"Across the road from the stadium, by the administration building."

"Hey, as long as you're not within two hundred feet of the president, we don't care."

"But they said you were stopping—"

"We don't care! As long as you don't get near the president, we don't care."

That seems a surprisingly cavalier reaction, but Donner swears it was re-emphasized to him that the Secret Service's job was to protect the president. It would work with the administration and police, and be alert if demonstrations seemed to be on the verge of threatening the president, but wasn't going to get involved in a discussion about a nonviolent protest taking place outside the stadium. Donner says he actually left the dormitory thinking the Secret Service agents he encountered "were pretty cool. I guess I was naïve, though, because that was before hard times and I expected Americans to be that way. Later, I went through more experiences [in the antiwar movement] and I became more suspicious."

On Thursday, after the discussions with Zinke, Mullins issued a statement, and the *Arkansas Traveler* ran it verbatim on the front page of its Friday edition. Mullins again publicly asked that "no demonstrations occur on the campus this Saturday." Yet he added that if students and faculty members were "compelled to conduct peaceful, nondisruptive manifestations," they must do it in that confined area and nowhere else. He made no mention of the agreement with Zinke, and in private neither he nor Zinke pretended that the physics professor could guarantee cooperation from all those in the mood to protest.

Zinke thought he could trust Donner, though. With a couple of friends, Donner went to work in the shop at the Methodist Assembly Grounds on Mount Sequoyah, making tiny wood crosses from black slats to symbolize American deaths in Vietnam, and helped compose a treatise on the cost of the war to the average American household. And the loosely organized—if organized at all—antiwar groups made plans to meet on that hill on Saturday. The emphasis was on not disrupting the game or provoking a confrontation. "We didn't want to storm the gates, because that would have been counterproductive," Donner says.

They probably wouldn't have been as passive in Berkeley. Or Austin.

As PREPARATIONS FOR THE GAME and the presidential appearance continued, the excitement in Fayetteville was palpable. Beyond the Razorbacks' chance at a second national championship in six seasons, there also was a sense of pride, a feeling that for one day, northwest Arkansas would be the sporting capital of the country. This was the centennial season of college football, the last game on the last day, 1 vs. 2, Hogs and Horns and Nixon coming.

On the Fayetteville campus, the Arkansas Booster Club set up tables in front of Walker Library and began selling BEAT TEXAS stickers for five cents apiece. BEAT TEXAS posters were distributed to all the dormitories and fraternities on Wednesday and were placed in windows. The Booster Group asked that everyone on campus greet one another with "Beat Texas." In downtown Fayetteville, BEAT TEXAS banners stretched across the streets.

Dr. Andrew Hall, the pastor at First Baptist Church in Fayetteville, posted a message on the church marquee that first appeared in the Wednesday *Northwest Arkansas Times* and then around the country in a wire-service picture. The message: "Attention Darrell Royal—Do Not Cast Your Steers Before Swine." Before the 1965 Texas-Arkansas game, the previous Fayetteville meeting (the '67 game was in Little Rock), Hall's marquee message was: "Football Is Only a Game. Eternal Things Are Spiritual. NEVERTHE-LESS, BEAT TEXAS!"

Billy Graham dropped hints through friends, and it was announced Tuesday that he had accepted an invitation to give the pregame invocation.

Fayetteville merchants announced a citywide "Hog-Wild" sale, saying in an ad that they were "HOG WILD TO BEAT TEXAS."

On Friday night, the Razorbacks' Almer Lee played his first varsity basketball home game, against Oklahoma State. The pep band didn't play "Dixie." Nor did the marching band play the song at the pep rally that night in the Chi Omega Greek Theatre.

THE BLACK STUDENTS' OCCUPATION of the Chi Omega Greek Theatre seats and the disruption of the pep rally the previous week was somewhat underplayed, because many students had scattered for Thanksgiving. The student newspaper, the *Arkansas Traveler*, took a holiday publishing hiatus, and a story about the black students' pep rally protest didn't appear until a week after the fact—on Tuesday, December 2. When BAD leader Eugene Hunt and the contingent of about sixty black students visited Mullins's office on November 26, the day after the pep rally incident, that signaled the students' continued militancy on the issue. Rumors—well-founded rumors—spread that the black students would protest on game day if "Dixie" remained the school's unofficial anthem.

"It had evolved to the point where we decided that during halftime at the Texas-Arkansas game, we would go out on the football field," Eugene Hunt, the law student and BAD president, says. "That had been decided. We were trying to bring the issue to a head, so it would be dealt with, rather than have individuals saying, 'I don't understand why you're upset.'"

On Tuesday, December 2, shortly after school officials confirmed that President Nixon would be at the game, the "Dixie" issue publicly was back on the front burner. A University Faculty Senate Equity and Grievances Committee, involving both faculty members and administrative personnel, held an open forum in the law building. That night, the Student Senate took up the issue, and Eugene Hunt was one of the speakers in the two hours of debate. The *Arkansas Traveler* reported that he told the other students, "You don't want to realize that your grandfather might have been my grandfather's master." Then the Student Senate voted 28–6 to recommend that "Dixie" shouldn't be played at any university events. The vote was nonbinding, so it didn't settle anything.

On Wednesday, December 3, UofA dean of men John Stefferud told the *Arkansas Traveler* that the individuals responsible for the pep rally disruption would be called before the University Discipline Committee in the near future. That night, the University Faculty Senate Equity and Grievances Committee held another forum. A group of students presented the committee with pro-"Dixie" petitions signed by more than twelve hundred students. The petitions argued the Student Senate vote ignored sentiment of a majority of the student body. William Denman, the dean of student affairs, represented Mullins and re-emphasized that the administration believed that the students should decide what to do about the "Dixie" issue.

During the debate, students held a pep rally downtown, near campus. The chants were familiar: "BEAT TEXAS!" and the stirring calling of the hogs, "Wooooooooooo, Pig! Sooie!" Many of the students also waved Confederate flags.

After the debate, the Equity and Grievances Committee suggested a compromise. In a letter to Dr. Richard A. Worthington, the band director, the committee recommended that the band should stop playing "Dixie." Yet the committee suggested a final curtain call, so to speak, recommending that the band could play "Dixie" during the first half of the Texas game before throwing the song out of the repertoire. Instead, Worthington on Thursday announced that he would honor the Student Senate vote and drop "Dixie" from the playlist. That announcement didn't come out of nowhere; shortly after the black students began the anti-"Dixie" campaign, Worthington said he would abide by any decision made by a legitimate student body.

Eugene Hunt says he "considered it to be a heightening [of] sensitivity on the part of the university because it was in response to a request from a relatively small number of human beings."

Thumbing its nose at the decision, radio station KFAY announced it would continue its game-week tradition of playing "Dixie" every ninety minutes. It did, and the radio station reported it received telephone threats for doing so.

The black students weren't convinced that the band would go along with Worthington's policy announcement. They went ahead with their plan to protest at the game, in effect occupying the field, but only if "Dixie" were played. And they feared backlash if they disrupted the game. "We were fearful, concerned about retaliation," Eugene Hunt says. "We were fearful, yes, and that's probably an admission very few of us are willing to make."

"We just figured that something was going to happen," says Darrell Brown, the onetime Shoats football walk-on who was in law school in 1969. "We'd go by the Greek houses and 'nigger' was a commonly used word at that time. There were some people who were not too happy about us."

Jimmy Wilson, another member of BAD, announced on Friday that the black students had asked for National Guard protection because of harassment. The request wasn't taken seriously. But everyone involved was aware of the continuing campus tensions around the country: Earlier that day in Cambridge, Massachusetts, seventy-five black Harvard students seized control of the administration building to dramatize their demands for higher black enrollment and black employment on campus. They stayed six hours, then left after reaching an agreement with an administration-appointed negotiator—Harvard law professor Archibald Cox. The school said it would honor the agreement to establish a joint committee to implement change, but that it still would punish the occupying students. Given the black Arkansas students' frustrations, including their visit to Mullins's office the previous week to drop off demands, the Harvard occupation struck a chord.

On Friday, at the 6:30 P.M. pep rally at the Greek Theatre, Worthington assured the crowd, estimated at five thousand, that the decision to accept the Student Senate vote and ban "Dixie" was the band director's alone. The band didn't play "Dixie," but some students—not officially affiliated with the pep rally—set up a portable phonograph and played a record of the song, and one lone trumpeter performed it as well. (He wasn't a band member.)

At 9:40 P.M., after the Arkansas–Oklahoma State basketball game, Darrell Brown went from Razorback Hall, where he and his wife were resident advisors, to a strategy session at the BAD House on Buchanan Street. He says he was jogging down Buchanan Street, near the Greek Theatre, as he frequently did when he was in a hurry.

"A couple of cars passed by, somebody hollered out, and it never really dawned on me that anyone was shooting or whatever," Brown says. "I heard a sound and it didn't stop me from running. I reached down and felt some blood and that's when I realized what had happened and panicked."

He had been shot on the inside of his left leg.

Years later, he calls it "a chapter I've tried to put out of my life. It was, 'Nigger this' or something like that. I know the racial slurs were used, and someone might even have said something about 'Dixie, try this on,' that kind of stuff. I know I never was sure where the shot came from."

Brown limped toward the BAD House, and several friends spotted him and brought him in. Hiram McBeth, the B team defensive halfback, already was there. McBeth was talking with fellow student Wendell Griffin when Brown arrived. The shout went up: "Somebody shot Darrell!" The BAD students put Brown on the couch and checked his leg. Someone called the police and Dean William Denman. McBeth grabbed a pistol. "I thought I needed it because people were going to be shooting up here." Others armed themselves as well. "A few of us who had pistols were standing in the window, like Malcolm X," McBeth says. "People were making phone calls to their homes, saying, 'Come get me,' or, 'Bring a pistol up here.'"

Realizing Brown's wound wasn't serious, Eugene Hunt and Jimmy Wilson took him to the nearby hospital. A police car arrived as they were leaving, and the officer escorted the car to the hospital. Two others rushed to the nearby home of Dr. Gordon Morgan, the first-year sociology professor. "Since I was the only black faculty member on the campus at that time, they thought I could say something or do something, which I did," Morgan says.

Morgan first came to the BAD House, then went with graduate student Edward Hill to nearby Washington General Hospital. By the time Morgan arrived, the attending physician had said the gunshot wound probably came from a .22-caliber weapon, and the bullet had grazed Brown, going from just below to just above the knee. Two university representatives already were there—Palmer Pilcher, the vice president for academic affairs, and Dean Denman. Morgan checked on Brown, then talked Pilcher and Denman into going to President Mullins's Mount Sequoyah home with him.

It was after midnight, and Mullins was in his bathrobe. Morgan pleaded with Mullins to take a dramatic stand with an appearance on television or radio, decrying the violence. "He said he thought the local authorities would take care of the situation and there wasn't anything he thought he should do about it," Morgan says.

Morgan returned to the BAD House and was alarmed to see it had become an armed camp. Morgan says the rules against personal weapons on campus largely were ignored. "A lot of the Anglo boys brought weapons that they claimed they were going to use for deer hunting. That had been a customary part of the university culture. So if a youngster brought a deer rifle, nobody said very much." That night, Morgan acknowledges, many of the black students were carrying guns. Overnight, he shuttled back and forth between his home, checking on his family, and the BAD House. "I tried to calm them down," the sociology professor says. "We said we should not be provocative, so that the others would not be."

Hiram McBeth admits to being scared. "Sure, but only from the standpoint that they might have had more guns than we had." At about three in the morning, McBeth and several others left the BAD House and returned to their dormitories. "We ran. We knew Darrell got shot, we knew he wasn't dead, but you knew you might be next."

Eugene Hunt returned to his house, rejoining his wife and two-year-old son. Guarding his family, he slept on the floor of the living room, near the front door. "I thought it was safer," Hunt says. "And I had my shotgun by me on the floor."

Kickoff was only a few hours away.

And the president was preparing for his Saturday trip to Fayetteville.

TWENTY

Horns Getting Ready

JAMES STREET HAD BEEN GOOD ALL FALL; he really had. Since his rabid-dog story on press day and the "smartass" lecture from his head coach, the Texas quarterback had been calculatingly bland. Yet Street didn't see anything wrong with telling reporters that playing in Fayetteville couldn't be worse than playing at some of the other trouble spots in the Southwest Conference, such as at Texas A&M's Kyle Field, the home of: *Hullabaloo, Caneck! Caneck!*

Of course, the scribes brought it up with Darrell Royal at his Monday news conference: *Say, Coach, James kind of downplayed the disadvantage of playing in Fayetteville. What do you think of that?*

Royal didn't say he would attempt to strangle his quarterback after his session with the reporters was over, but he made it clear he wasn't thrilled. "Street hasn't quarterbacked in Fayetteville," Royal said. "When those cheerleaders go out there on the middle of the field and yell, 'Sooie, pig!' it comes from all directions." Then Royal reminded reporters of what Coach Mike Campbell said earlier. "Playing in Fayetteville," Campbell said, "is like parachuting into Russia."

When Street was a sophomore, the Longhorns met the Razorbacks in Little Rock, and the 1968 game was in Austin. "You've never played in Fayetteville, James," Royal lectured. "It's going to be different."

Street watched the Razorbacks play Baylor on film, and he confidently told Royal, "We're gonna kill 'em, Coach." That set off Royal again, and he never stopped sounding the refrain all week. "He must have told me a hundred times, 'This game is going to be different than anything you've gone through,'" Street says.

Freddie Steinmark was hoping he would make it through the week and play. In *I Play to Win*, the Longhorn safety wrote that he went to trainer Frank Medina after the Monday practice and confessed his leg still bothered him. He said he didn't want to reveal too much to Medina, but he told the trainer the pain was causing him to wake up in the middle of the night. Still, it's apparent Steinmark understated his level of pain to everyone—and perhaps even to himself. Steinmark wrote that Medina showed him how to put analgesic balm between two pieces of gauze and tape that to his leg, and also advised him to put a pillow under his knee at night. Steinmark also said he took Darvon, a painkiller earlier supplied to him by team physician Joe Reneau, every night. He wrote that he skipped all his classes and spent most of the day in bed.

The next day, only hours after the Longhorns learned their draft lottery numbers, they had what Royal told reporters was "the worst practice we've had in about seven games." Halfback and cocaptain Ted Koy mused that preoccupation with the draft lottery probably had something to do with it.

Royal was far more happy with the Wednesday workout, which helped the Longhorns get into a good mood for the pep rally—officially, the Texas Victory Rally—at Texas Memorial Stadium that night. Nobody was particularly concerned that Worster, fresh from his New York trip, wasn't able to fully participate in practice either Tuesday or Wednesday because of a pulled groin muscle. His teammates teased him about his tendency to be hurt early in the week, then recover in time to play. Freddie Steinmark's aching leg wasn't a secret: He was listed in news accounts as having a "bruised leg." It didn't seem significant.

At the rally, the players rode onto the track in convertibles, and the captains were in a car with Royal. Only one side of the stadium was open for seating, and crowd estimates ranged from twenty-five thousand to thirty thousand. Street addressed the crowd, saying, "This is the most important game of my life. All those past victories are meaningless, just building up to this game. I wish we could take you with us." Master of ceremonies Wally Pryor read telegrams from Governor Preston Smith, plus several famous UT grads—including Apollo 12 astronaut Alan Bean, still in quarantine after America's second lunar landing mission ("You can bet your moondust I'll be watching the game on TV").

The Longhorns say their limited memory of practice that week underscores that Royal stuck to the usual routine. "We knew they had a very, very good football team," defensive halfback Tom Campbell says. "I don't think we prepared for them any different." But the Longhorns' defensive plan was coming into focus: Blitz far more than usual, keeping Montgomery under pressure and hurried. The defensive linemen were exhorted to keep Montgomery in the pocket, preventing him from scrambling to make the big play. That meant that the undersized defensive end, David Arledge, knew he couldn't take the inside route much, because that might chase Montgomery into scrambling. The Longhorns were concentrating on Montgomery and containing the running game, but they weren't studying the offense player by player. "We just knew the guy on the other side of the line had a different color jersey on and he was the enemy," Arledge says. "It was a matter of Coach Campbell saying, 'This is what we're going to do, this is the defense we're going to run, this is the place I want you when we run this defense.'"

Early in the week, Freddie Steinmark came to defensive backs coach Fred Akers, who says Steinmark reported he felt sluggish, and asked if there were extra drills he could do on his own to try to regain some quickness. Steinmark mused to Akers that his heavy studying for the upcoming final exams might have affected him, and at the end of practice, after everyone else was done running, Steinmark put himself through extra sprints, plus agility and footwork drills. "Freddie didn't know what was wrong," Akers says. "He was working hard, preparing for the ballgame. I thought he might be working too hard. You need to be fresh. At the time, no one knew what he was thinking and doing, but I was convinced later that he knew something was wrong and he was trying, in his way, to solve it."

The Texas band—the 250-student "Show Band of the Southwest"—departed for Fayetteville in a seven-bus caravan Friday morning. The team left at noon on a chartered Braniff Airlines plane. The Fayetteville region had an airport, Drake Field, but it wasn't suitable for larger planes, so the flight landed in Fort Smith, and the Longhorns made the final part of the journey on buses.

On guard Bobby Mitchell's bus, the Longhorns joked about arriving in "hillbilly country." Mitchell didn't remind everyone that his girlfriend, Honor Franklin, was a UofA student. "The first farm we passed by, there was a guy standing there," Mitchell says. "He had his big old dirty overalls and a hat with the flappy ears sticking out. Tobacco juice was coming out of his mouth. He really fit the stereotype, and that cracked everybody up."

The ride up winding and scenic U.S. Highway 71, along the Ozarks, was breathtaking. The Texas players who hadn't been to Fayetteville—and most hadn't—started asking themselves: *Where are we going?* The ride "scared me to death," Tom Campbell says. "I was looking out the window, straight down hundreds of feet, or thousands of feet. You're thinking if this bus just turns to the right a little bit, you're never going to stop rolling."

The buses went straight to Razorback Stadium, where the Longhorns had a brief no-pads workout on the Astroturf field, the same surface they played on in Austin. The players were struck by how small the stadium—which seated forty-four thousand with temporary stands—seemed, and how close the fans would be.

Freddie Steinmark told Frank Medina his leg still was bothering him. The trainer tried taping it a little differently, but the defensive coaches noticed the little safety was limping slightly in the workout.

Kicker Happy Feller tried some placements off the sort of pad the holders—in this case, backup quarterback Donnie Wigginton—then were allowed to place on the turf. Feller decided that—virtually regardless of the weather conditions the next day—the Astroturf was going to provide good enough footing for his two-step, straight-on approach. Because of the way the Longhorns had been blowing out opponents, Feller hadn't kicked under intense pressure all season.

His teammates, though, just assumed the kicker who seemed to chuckle virtually every time he talked would be impervious to the tension. What else could they expect from a guy who had been known as "Happy" since he was in diapers?

"I'm really James Patrick," Feller says, smiling (of course), "but very few people know that. When I was an infant, I laughed all the time. I had two older brothers, one seven years older and one five years older, and they said I was a happy baby, so they started calling me Happy and it stuck all the way through. You'd even see Happy Feller under my picture in the first grade."

Dr. Lorence Feller, the general practitioner and surgeon in Fredericksburg, was the president of Texas Lutheran College's board of regents. He was unhappy when Happy said he wanted to attend UT and, at the invitation of the Royal staff, walk on and try to win both the kicking job and a scholarship. Dr. Feller went with Happy to Austin and told freshman coach Bill Ellington, the guru for first-year players beloved among the Longhorns even as they moved up, that he was concerned that UT might be too big for his small-town son. Happy played end and defensive back in high school, and probably could have played at Texas Lutheran. Ellington put his arm around the small-town physician, saying, "Doc, don't worry, we'll take care of him."

Happy took over the kicking job from Rob Layne in the middle of the 1968 season, cementing the position with a 53-yard field goal against Oklahoma. By the end of 1969, he was one of the top kickers in the country.

———————

THE LONGHORNS LEFT THE STADIUM and headed for the Holiday Inn in nearby Rogers. As the Longhorns had on the ride to the stadium, they saw more signs of the Arkansas fans' loyalties and fanaticism as they traveled to the hotel. Bobby Mitchell says, "The thing that amazed me as we were driving around is that these people would paint their storefronts and sidewalks in red—'Go Hogs!' It was such an event to them, the only thing in the whole state to these people."

"I knew *we* had avid fans, but I had never seen anything like that," Steve Worster says. "There was hog calling as we went by, red everywhere, and signs that basically said we were going to die."

"*Woooooooooo, Pig! Sooie!*

"*Wooooooooooo, Pig! Sooie!*

"*Woooooooooo, Pig! Sooie! Razorbacks!*"

Tom Campbell was amazed, too. "Those fans were just absolutely crazy. We didn't have 'University of Texas football team' taped to the side of the bus, but they knew who we were, and man alive, they would start calling the hogs each time they saw the bus. If there was one guy on the corner when the bus went by, he would be calling the hogs. They were hollering at you, cussing at you, calling the hogs!"

When the buses arrived at the hotel in Rogers, the Holiday Inn marquee read, "WELCOME COACH ROYAL AND THE LONGHORNS." Earlier in the day, it had looked ahead to an Arkansas victory and a Cotton Bowl berth, proclaiming, "GO HOGS GO, BEAT NOTRE DAME."

As the Longhorns walked through the hotel, offensive coach Emory Bellard found himself walking with split end Cotton Speyrer, who was uncharacteristically tightly wound. "If somebody had pinched me, I probably would have gone through the roof," Speyrer says. "Coach Bellard looks at me and says, 'Hey, how do you think this jacket looks with my eyes?'"

Speyrer laughed and loosened up. Bellard had a glass eye.

The Longhorns had a team meal at the hotel—steaks, the trimmings, and suspicions that cooks were planted by Frank Broyles. "Dinner wasn't worth a crap, and they treated you like a bunch of turds," center Forrest Wiegand says.

It got worse. Royal considered taking the players to a movie, but decided against it. The Longhorns had position meetings with assistant coaches, then adjourned to their rooms. Although the Razorbacks weren't staying very far away, at the Town and Country Motel in Rogers, their fans got wind of where the Longhorns were and serenaded the visitors through the night with honking horns. Some fans also threw snowballs at the windows and doors.

Greg Ploetz, the painting defensive tackle, got up to answer a knock on his door. Probably a coach or a trainer or a teammate, he thought. Instead, it was a buddy from Sherman High School who lived in Rogers. "I heard you guys were here and thought I'd drop by and say hello," the buddy said. Ploetz liked the guy and didn't mind seeing him, but what kind of security was this? Was the front desk telling Razorback fans what room James Street was in, too?

On road trips, the Horns were assigned roommates by position, so defensive halfbacks Tom Campbell and Danny Lester were together. Instead of counting sheep, they went over defensive assignments and tested each other. *Rees and Morrison come to their right and we're blitzing?* Answer: The three defensive backs were entrusted with straight man coverage, including Lester on Chuck Dicus, Freddie Steinmark on Morrison, the tight end, and Tom Campbell on Rees.

After midnight, they finally fell asleep.

In another room, Steinmark took a Darvon and went to bed.

James Street usually fell asleep in less time than it took to ride the fullback, pull the ball out, and make the pitch to the trailing halfback. "It was a little harder that night," he says. "I was thinking a little more." Plays, situations, conditions—all kept running through his mind.

Texas assistant sports publicity director Bill Little was sharing a room with San Antonio newspaperman Dan Cook, because Cook hadn't been able to find space in Fayetteville. As the two men talked about what might happen in the game, Little told Cook: *If we have to hit a big pass, mark my words, it's gonna go to Randy Peschel.*

Texas coach Darrell Royal diagrams the Longhorns'
virtually unstoppable wishbone offense.

Razorbacks head coach Frank Broyles keeps his eyes
on the action as he relays instructions up to the booth.

Heavily recruited out of high school, Arkansas quarterback Bill Montgomery became a star in Frank Broyles's sophisticated pro-style offense.

Despite his slight stature (and being listed as the ninth tailback out of ten on the Arkansas depth chart before his sophomore season), Bill Burnett became an extremely effective runner for the Razorbacks.

A notorious party animal off the field, in cleats and pads no one was more determined—and more intimidating—than Arkansas fullback Bruce Maxwell.

Courtesy University of Texas Sports Information Office

Longhorns quarterback (and unlikely star) James Street hands off to
All-American fullback Steve Worster. Never the biggest, strongest,
or fastest guy, Slick Street just knew how to *win*.

A study in contrasts: Though they starred in the same Longhorn backfield, the hell-raising Steve Worster (right) and quiet, studious halfback Ted Koy couldn't have been any more different.

Named to the Kodak All-America Team, Hogs linebacker Cliff Powell and split end Chuck Dicus journeyed to New York before the big showdown with Texas.

Vietnam veteran Don Donner enrolled in 1969 and quickly became a leading figure in the antiwar movement on the Arkansas campus. One of the principal organizers of the game-day protests that accompanied Nixon's visit to Fayetteville, Donner is seen here in both '69 and 2001.

Nixon Coming: Marine One touches down in Fayetteville before the game.

"Wooooo, pig! Sooie!" Not just another face in a very animated crowd,
the president and football-fan-in-chief watches the "game of the century."

In the Longhorns' locker room, Richard Nixon presents
Darrell Royal with a presidential plaque proclaiming Texas
the number one team in all of college football.

Hook 'em Horns: Randy Peschel, whose 43-yard reception on fourth and three with time running down gave Texas new life and a first down at the Razorback 13-yard line, celebrates as halfback Jim Bertlesen scores the game-winning touchdown.

Courtesy University of Texas Sports Information Office

As the clock expires, the Texas bench celebrates their enormous victory.

Longhorns' safety Fred Steinmark played the entire 1969 season despite the unbearable pain from an undiagnosed bone tumor in his left leg, which was amputated six days after the Arkansas game. Steinmark, who succumbed to cancer in 1971, is still remembered by his teammates and the entire Texas football program for his faith and courage. Below, Texas players touch an image of Steinmark before heading onto the field.

As midnight approached, Darrell Royal was restless. He says he called the room of defensive coach Mike Campbell. Royal went to Campbell's room and chatted a bit. Finally, he asked a question.

"Mike, what's the hardest play to stop in a goal-line defense?"

"Oh, the counter option."

Arkansas used a typical goal-line defense, with the defensive line submarining and creating obstacles as the linebackers followed the ball. Royal wasn't just thinking about a potential third-and-goal from the 2. "I made up my mind to run the counter option for two points if we needed to, if the game called for a two-point conversion," Royal says.

The two tackles, Bobby Wuensch and Bob McKay, were in one room. Around three, McKay woke up with a start. Wuensch wasn't in his bed. *What the hell?* McKay looked around. The sliding glass door was open and Wuensch was out on the deck of their second-floor room, looking around and thinking. McKay climbed out of bed and joined him. For a few minutes, they shivered as they watched the light snowfall. Then they went in and went back to sleep.

In the tight ends' room, backup Jay Cormier heard the horns in the middle of the night and, annoyed, got up and looked out the window. "It's snowing," he told Randy Peschel. Conventional wisdom was that terrible weather would favor the Longhorns and their ground game, but that wasn't necessarily true: The ball-handling in the wishbone was tricky, and a wet ball and slips made turnovers more likely.

Game day dawned. The Longhorns had steak and eggs and pancakes at eight. "Breakfast wasn't worth a crap, either," Forrest Wiegand growls. "It wasn't on time and the steak was like a piece of leather."

The Longhorns went into a meeting room. The lights went out. Royal went to one of his favorite pieces of equipment—the overhead projector. The Longhorns knew exactly what he was going to say and how he was going to say it, and it was all written out on the transparencies, anyway. Royal read a transparency, then replaced it with another and read that, too. They were his commandments. He started out by stressing the kicking game, "for it's here the breaks are made." He read off the charges about avoiding turnovers, avoiding penalties, keeping your poise. The boys could close their eyes and know what was coming next, but Royal knew that, too. Then he added something: *Boys, there's going to be a winner and a loser out there today; we aren't play-*

ing for a tie! Bob McKay took it to mean his coach had bigger balls than Ara Parseghian. "Hell," McKay says, "that's the only reason to go out there and play."

Bill Zapalac, the strong side linebacker, wondered if Royal was saying the Razorbacks had declined to agree to play sudden-death overtime in case of a tie. But all the boys got the message: If it came down to it, the Longhorns wouldn't accept a tie. There were no guarantees, but a tie most likely would have kept the Longhorns the No. 1 team in the nation in the polls, because they were on the road against the AP's second-ranked team. But the teams would be Southwest Conference cochampions, and Arkansas would go to the Cotton Bowl to play Notre Dame because the Longhorns had gone to the Cotton Bowl the season before. At 9–0–1, Texas would play Mississippi in the Sugar Bowl. The Longhorns probably could have lived with that, if they retained their No. 1 ranking, but a tie's effect on the rankings might have depended on the perceptions of which team looked better that day. There even was the possibility that a tie could cause AP and UPI voters to put undefeated and untied Penn State ahead of both SWC teams.

As the Longhorns were about to board their buses, Street stood in the lobby, waiting for his brother, Sewell, and a friend, Andy Malone, who were going to pick up tickets. Boosters and fans kept approaching Street, wishing him luck. (Later, Street would think of this morning when he spoke with his friend, Elvis Presley, on the phone and said he might come over to see Elvis that afternoon, before that night's show. "After," Elvis said. "After. I don't see anyone before the show. I'm getting ready.")

On the bus ride, Royal called Street up to sit next to him. Street had heard the talk about not playing for a tie, too, but he hadn't thought too much about it.

"If we get in a situation where we need a two-point conversion, this is the play I want," Royal said.

Counter 49.

"Coach, we're not gonna need a two-point play!"

"All I'm telling you is *if* we're going to need a two-point play, that's what we're going to run."

"OK, Coach."

Street says Royal never had summoned him on the bus before, nor specified a two-point call. But at least it gave Street something to do on the ride besides look at the Razorback fans. "It was nothing but a sea of red," Forrest Wiegand says. "And the gestures weren't like they were welcoming Mama home."

The buses had a police escort, and the only way to get to the stadium was to go down the *wrong* lane on Highway 71. The Razorbacks did it, too, but they were used to it, and the Arkansas fans recognized the difference between the home-team and visiting-team buses. "We're going down the wrong lane and it's sleeting and raining and there's really no shoulder on that road," guard Mike Dean says. "The cops were making the cars coming at us go off the road, and they're going into the mud. That made them even madder."

Ted Koy was sitting by a window. The bus went by a drive-in hamburger place and Koy noticed that the parking lot was barricaded. Then he read the signs draped across the barricades: "CLOSED, GONE TO TEXAS FUNERAL."

In the tiny visiting dressing room, the Longhorns got ready in virtual silence. Tom Campbell thought it was maybe too quiet, but then smiled as he thought back to something his father, the defensive coach, told the boys after the warmup at the Oklahoma game earlier in the season. "Men, you're too tense out there! There's only one thing a man can do all tensed up and we're not going to be doing that this afternoon!"

In the warmup, the Longhorns marveled that the stands were already nearly full. In the drizzle and cold, the Longhorns had a hard time with their footing and deciding which shoes to wear. They had brought two kinds—one pair with molded rubber cleats on the bottom of the shoe, designed for Astroturf, and their regular football shoes with screw-in cleats. The regular Astroturf shoes didn't seem to give them much traction on the wet turf. Most of the Longhorns tried both during the game before settling on their football shoes, with the shortest screw-in spikes available. It wasn't good for the carpet, but afforded better footing.

Then the Longhorns went back into the dressing room, waiting. The president of the United States was on his way, in the *Marine One* helicopter. ABC's Bud Wilkinson and Bill Fleming were on the sideline, talking their way through a "College Football Today" preview of the game, complete with an explanation of the wishbone's three options and the Razorbacks' pro-style offense.

As the time approached for the Longhorns to take the field, Darrell Royal stood in the middle of the room. Maybe the boys were a little nervous, he said, and that's fine. Again, Royal talked about not taking a tie, and again, some Longhorns inferred the coach was saying that the Razorbacks had turned down a chance to agree that overtime would settle any tie. (There was no overtime option in the rules.)

But what of the Razorbacks? "Their assholes are so tight," Royal told the Longhorns, "they couldn't pass a pumpkin seed right now."

TWENTY-ONE

Hogs Getting Ready

WHEN BOB FORD PRESENTED THE UPDATE of his Texas scouting report to the Razorbacks in the team meeting room, the graduate assistant coach and law student sensed the tension. He opened with, "Well, I don't know how many of you guys have ever attended a national championship scouting report before . . ."

That lightened the atmosphere, and then he went over not only what the Longhorns did in general, but each Texas starter, including the strengths and weaknesses of each offensive lineman. The Razorbacks were impressed, and the other assistants decided they pitied the poor attorneys opposing Ford in the courtroom after he got through law school.

On Monday, as the Razorbacks awaited the draft lottery, they practiced in pads—a departure from the usual no-pads routine at the beginning of the week. But because they hadn't played since Thanksgiving and especially because the coaches wanted the defense to do contact work against the wishbone, the pads came on. The B team, though, struggled to get the wishbone down, and the workout was ragged. But Charley Coffey's defensive strategy was on display. "I was getting phone calls and letters that week, just people constantly making suggestions," Coffey says. "It was an amazing atmosphere."

Offensively, as the week progressed, the Razorbacks worked on running up the middle just enough to keep the Texas inside linebackers, Glen Halsell and Scott Henderson, honest. If the linebackers froze half a count each play, that could open up the passing game, especially if Henderson, the better pass defender, had to hesitate before dropping into coverage.

The Razorbacks were certain they could find other ways to take advantage of the fact that the Longhorns used only three defensive backs. "They had a talented secondary, but there were some things we thought we could do," split end Chuck Dicus says. "We didn't feel like they could cover us locked up man-for-man, that's for sure. We also liked that there were some areas between the linebackers. We thought that if [I was] in the slot, we could get into those areas with a curl route."

Dicus was the All-American receiver, but the flanker—John Rees—was dangerous as well, and offensive guru Don Breaux hoped to make the Longhorns pay if they concentrated too much on Dicus. He didn't expect that to happen, though, because the Longhorns under Mike Campbell tended to be democratic in their pass coverage—not drastically changing anything to react to a single receiver. When the Longhorns played zone coverage, they often employed the unusual approach of four linebackers and a defensive back in short zones and only two backs covering deep.

Rees, however, had the pedigree to be a Razorback hero. His dad, Harold, or "Greasy," had been a star running back at Arkansas, and his mother was the homecoming queen. John was raised in Jonesboro, and the family made it a holiday weekend to attend the Razorback home games in Little Rock. After John ended up a second-generation Razorback, he and Greasy frequently were frustrated by John's initial lack of playing time, and then by the number of passes thrown his way. "I always felt like I was a decoy and that Chuck was getting more passes than he should—although he did a good job," Rees says. "You know how it is. You're always wanting a few more passes to go your way. I'm telling Montgomery, 'Now, Bill, Chuck's not open all those times! Throw me the ball!' But that year, I felt pretty good. We were winning, by big margins."

As the week progressed, Arkansas tackles Mike Kelson and Bob Stankovich worked on slanting quickly to their inside on selected plays, trying to knock the defensive tackles—who were on the offensive guards' outside shoulders in the Split 6 alignment—off balance enough to enable the guards to get after the linebackers. It took a lot of quickness from the offensive linemen, and while the Razorbacks' linemen weren't as quick as the undersized Texas blockers, they were quick enough to make the scheme work. All-American center Rodney Brand would go after one of the two linebackers, depending on the play, or just peel back and look for "strays" when pass blocking.

"The preparations for this game weren't like any other," Bill Montgomery says. "It was notched up another 20 percent." The Razorbacks worked on several audibles at the line of scrimmage, giving Montgomery the option to change from a running play to a Dicus slant across the middle if the Longhorns appeared to be locked in man-to-man coverage on the star split end. Everybody could hear the audible in practice, and the play change went smoothly.

The Razorbacks' preparations also were more personal than those in Austin: The coaches gave each Arkansas starter a scouting report, complete with a press guide biography, newspaper clippings, and pictures of the Longhorn—or Longhorns—they most often would be going against. By the time the game arrived, for example, Mike Kelson felt as if he knew Longhorns defensive end David Arledge. "David Arledge is going to kick your butt!" Don Breaux challenged. Guard Jerry Dossey studied Texas defensive tackle Leo Brooks, but was also alerted that the injured Brooks still probably wouldn't be able to play, and that he most likely would face backup Carl White. Dossey had White's picture taped to his bathroom mirror.

On Wednesday, as writers' access to the players was about to be cut off, Montgomery met reporters and talked over lunch. (In sports writing, then as now, there always is a free lunch.) Montgomery said this game was so big, he was reminded of a *Peanuts* cartoon. In the strip, Montgomery said, someone tells Charlie Brown about "the 70-yard run that won it, the scoreboard lighting up, the thousands of fans rushing on the field, and the players carrying the coach off and the celebrations. And Charlie Brown said, 'What'd the other team feel like?'"

The Razorbacks hoped they wouldn't be "the other team."

In the defensive work, Bobby Field was going through a new experience. As a defensive back, he never had to take part in the interior run drills because they were held in the practice period when the DBs worked against the passing game on another part of the field. But because he was deployed virtually on the line of scrimmage in the scheme against the wishbone, Field—all 162 pounds of him—worked all week with the linemen and linebackers. Bob Ford, helping implement the recommendations in his scouting report, was Field's personal coach. Field also studied the Longhorns on film. The first thing he noticed was the sheer volume of film. Usually, the two reels of offensive plays in each game would take up about two-thirds of the reel. But when Field slipped the cover off the reel of the Longhorns' offensive film, it was so full that the film spilled off as it uncoiled slightly. To Field, that emphasized how many plays the Longhorns ran every game. They ate up the clock, and they always seemed to have the ball.

At the practices, the coaches preached that linebackers Cliff Powell and Mike Boschetti had to be especially conscious of the counter options. If Steve Worster goes one way, but James Street does a reverse pivot and heads the other way with the ball, *it's big trouble if the linebacker has been sucked in!* At one point, Boschetti, assigned to the quarterback on most of the calls, took the bait, assuming the fullback's movement guaranteed the quarterback was going to the same side, too. But the play was the B team's rendition of the counter option, so when the quarterback quickly did a reverse pivot and went the other way, Boschetti had taken himself out of the play. Broyles charged down his tower. "What's Boschetti doing in there?" Broyles barked. Boschetti vowed not to let it happen again—in either practice or the game.

One afternoon, Montgomery and Field walked together from Wilson Sharp House to the dressing room. "Bill was talking about a meeting he had been in with Don Breaux, talking about how they felt there were some holes in the secondary, and there were different play-action things they could do to get guys open," Field says. "I was confident, too. There was just a feeling on both sides of the ball, that we could move the ball and at least slow them down."

At one point, fullback Bruce Maxwell got into a discussion with Terry Don Phillips, his former roommate. Phillips said the Razorbacks shouldn't underestimate James Street. "Bruce, I'm telling you," Phillips said, "he's not the greatest athlete in the world. He's not big. He's a winner. He's just a winner." That was the Phillips message all week, to anyone who would listen—and to some who wouldn't.

The Razorbacks worked out both in the stadium and on the fields to the south of Razorback Stadium that week. The coaches already knew that while the stadium Astroturf carpet was resilient, players tended to get hurt more often on it. There also was a chance the presidential helicopter was going to land on the practice field Saturday, and even if it didn't, the president's presence required security vigilance. So there were a few distractions for the Razorbacks. As they walked through Barnhill Arena to practice, they noticed the men in dark suits in the smoke-filled assistant athletic director's office. At first, some of the Razorbacks assumed they were from ABC. But after some of these men walked through the dressing room both before and after practice each day, unchallenged, saying nothing, glaring, surveying as the Razorbacks walked through with towels around their waists, the players figured it out. They were Nixon's men. Secret Service.

As the Razorbacks practiced, they noticed the sharpshooters, scouting out vantage points on the tops of the nearby campus buildings. The Razorbacks also hoped that none of them were spying for Texas on the side. The players who walked by the stadium area during the day watched helicopters repeatedly landing on and taking off from different areas around the stadium, including the practice field, as the sharpshooters watched. "Hell, a lot of us hadn't ever seen a helicopter before," linebacker Lynn Garner says.

STEVIE D. WAS ABOUT TWENTY-FIVE YEARS OLD, the Razorbacks guessed. He was a diminutive black man who carried around a shoeshine kit and seemed to show some idiot-savant tendencies. Stevie loved to hang around the football field and the team offices, watching practice and making friends with the players. He memorized their birthdates and astounded them by saying "Happy Birthday!" on just the right day. The Razorbacks didn't know his entire story, but it was an open secret that Broyles's administrative assistant, Wilson Matthews, helped out Stevie. Matthews gave him money—far more than the shoeshine was worth—and food and clothes. If asked about it then, Matthews probably would have bellowed: "GODDAMMIT, WHAT THE HELL ARE YOU TALKING ABOUT?" But everyone knew he was Stevie's buddy.

Matthews says, "He came around all the time. He had the damndest memory for athletics I'd ever seen. Right now, if I ran into him—and he's not well—I could ask him, 'Stevie, what was the score of the Baylor game in 1960?' Shit, he wouldn't hesitate. He could tell you the score and he could tell you where it was played."

On Thursday of the Texas game week, at a team meeting before practice, Matthews stood in front of the Razorbacks and said, "OK, boys, Coach Broyles wants to talk to you."

Stevie D. walked in, wearing a miniature Razorbacks road-game wardrobe. Gray slacks, white shirt, navy blazer, Razorback tie. The Razorbacks broke up. But that was just the start. In a perfect imitation of Broyles's stooped mannerisms, his hand gestures, and his Georgia drawl, Stevie paced and went through the start of Broyles's usual speech—the players called it "the sermonette"—which always began with the five commandments of the kicking game. Stevie put his hands behind his back, he folded his arms, he rubbed his chin, all at the right moments.

Stevie preached:

Thou shalt not be offside.

Thou shalt not clip.

Thou shalt not let the ball hit the ground.

Thou shalt not . . .

Guys were having trouble staying on their stools, they were laughing so hard. At least that afternoon, the Razorbacks were loose enough to pass pumpkin seeds.

THE COACHES CUT OFF ALL INCOMING CALLS to the players' rooms in Wilson Sharp House, and the Razorbacks didn't mind. (*"AUNT WHO? NO, I DON'T HAVE ANY TICKETS!"*) The Razorbacks moved into the Rogers Hotel on Thursday night, a day early. "It was a twenty-four-hour party on campus," Field says.

On Friday, the Razorbacks worked out at Rogers High School. Then most of them went on the arranged trip to see *Butch Cassidy and the Sundance Kid*, back in Fayetteville. As the bus pulled up to the theater, students and fans cheered, called the Hogs, and chanted, "Go Hogs Go!"

Back at the hotel, the assistant coaches passed out brief written quizzes about the game plan, assignments, and strategy, tailored for each position. They would go over the answers in the morning. The Razorbacks ate their late-night snack of Hershey bars and apples, and tried to get to sleep. They also were given sleeping pills, if they needed them.

The next morning, the Razorbacks had a team breakfast. Frank Broyles didn't want to depart from the norm, either, so he went from table to table, saying hello—but also taking a look at the steaks. The Broyles mandate was that steaks must be cooked at *least* medium-well or better, and if the players were caught trying to coax the cook into leaving some red in the darned things, they went right back to the grill. That morning, Broyles caught guard Jerry Dossey eating a pink steak. Back it went. Terry Don Phillips, after weeks of eating both his own steak and the leftovers on game morning because he wasn't going to suit up, was back in a pregame mood: One steak was enough. He still didn't know how much he was going to play against the Longhorns, if at all, but he was going to be back in uniform.

In a hotel meeting room, the defensive players were grouped by position and seated in a semicircle. The coaches raised flash cards showing a formation and a down and distance, and each player had to call out his responsibility on that play.

The Razorbacks were accustomed to the wild bus ride down the wrong lane of Highway 71. Once or twice a year, somebody would freeze in the other lane as police waved them off the road, and the bus drivers would have to hit the brakes and screech to a halt. It didn't happen on Big Shootout Day.

As the Razorbacks dressed in silence in their locker room in Barnhill Arena, a few tried to decide whether to wear the cotton turtlenecks over their T-shirts and underneath their shoulder pads. "Coach Coffey walked through and said we wouldn't need the turtlenecks," defensive tackle Roger Harnish says. "And we didn't. With the adrenaline in that game, you never felt the chill."

As they always did, the Razorback specialists went out first. "It usually would be my parents and four other people there," kicker Bill McClard says. "God almighty, we came out to warm up and there wasn't an empty seat. It was like it was time to kick off. It's usually, 'Oh, well, here come the kickers,' but this time, there were banners everywhere and the band started playing."

When the other Razorbacks came out to warm up, the atmosphere was even more electric. Tailback Bill Burnett says, "The hair stood up on the back of my neck. That was the only time it ever happened to me."

Frank Broyles spotted one of his former quarterbacks—Texas assistant coach Fred Akers. Both were out on the Astroturf, checking out the carpet conditions after a tarp was rolled off the field. Broyles wished Akers luck, but not too much of it.

Tackle Mike Kelson, who was about to go against his home-state team, didn't feel very nervous until then. "I walked through the gate for warmup and the crowd was going crazy and the damn ground was shaking," Kelson says. "That's when it hit me what was going on. I got scared. I got nervous. I said, 'Please, God, don't let me screw up.'"

Lynn Garner worried that the "form tackles" in the warmup—where defenders were supposed to make the first "pop," then back off—were a little too serious. "They were almost like game tackles," the linebacker says.

There was one block of empty seats.

The Washington contingent was on its way.

TWENTY-TWO

The President Has Landed

UNIVERSITY OF ARKANSAS PRESIDENT David W. Mullins never stepped in front of the television cameras and radio microphones to make a public statement about Darrell Brown's game-eve shooting. That disappointed Dr. Gordon Morgan, the sociology professor who visited Mullins's home late Friday night. Mullins did issue a statement in a press release on Saturday morning, but it got lost amid the excitement of the game, and Morgan had hoped for something more dramatic. By the time the *Northwest Arkansas Times* story based on the press release was on the streets in the Saturday paper, attentions were focused elsewhere—at Razorback Stadium. For the record, Mullins's statement called Brown "one of our most respected and capable black students." After that condescension, Mullins said, "We have requested and received the assurance of the police that they are doing all in their power to apprehend the guilty party or parties. . . . Criminal acts such as these are thoroughly reprehensible and out of keeping with the civilized principles and high traditions of the University of Arkansas and of the Fayetteville community."

Morgan got to the stadium before the teams arrived for the scheduled 12:20 P.M. game. He found the ABC production trailer, opened the door, and approached the first man who looked as if he had some power. Morgan asked that at some point on the broadcast the ABC sportscasters—Chris Schenkel, Bud Wilkinson, and Bill Fleming—acknowledge the racial tensions on the campus, the Brown shooting, and the "Dixie" issue. Morgan doesn't know the name or the title of the ABC employee, but he remembers the response: *Sorry, we don't get involved in politics; we just show the games.*

That morning, *Air Force One* brought President Nixon and the Washington contingent from Andrews Air Force Base to Fort Smith, sixty-three miles south of Fayetteville. Governor Winthrop Rockefeller greeted Nixon with a bunch of Razorback red and white carnations. After a local high school band played "Hail to the Chief," the *Air Force One* and Rockefeller contingents climbed onto three Marine helicopters.

Most of the high-profile politicians were on *Marine One*, including two Republican congressmen from Texas and Arkansas—George Herbert Walker Bush and John Paul Hammerschmidt, who both were elected to Congress for the first time in 1966 and were close friends. Bush was a Yalie, but a confirmed Texan by the late 1960s. Hammerschmidt attended the University of Arkansas before serving in World War II (he graduated from Oklahoma State after the war), so he had more at stake emotionally at the game. Hammerschmidt was from Harrison, seventy-nine miles east of Fayetteville, and the campus was in his district. For one afternoon, Hammerschmidt and Bush would be on different sides of the aisle, so to speak. On the helicopter, they sat together.

"The weather was just absolutely terrible in Fort Smith," Hammerschmidt says. "So we got up in the helicopter, and it started circling three hundred or four hundred feet above the ground."

As the helicopters hovered over the Ozark foothills, the ceiling was low, the skies were threatening, and even two decorated World War II pilots wondered whether it was a wise trip to make. Bush had flown 58 missions as a torpedo bomber pilot in the Pacific; with the Third Combat Cargo Group, Hammerschmidt had flown 217 missions over "the hump" in the China-Burma-India Theater. Both Bush and Hammerschmidt had earned the Distinguished Flying Cross. "I remember worrying about the weather as the chopper groped to its destination," Bush says. "I was used to flying, but the weather was worrisome."

Hammerschmidt says that Bush turned to him and said, "When this thing goes down, there's so much brass who outrank us on this thing, we won't even get our names in *The Congressional Record*!"

Hammerschmidt looked out the window and noticed that the helicopters were scaring livestock. "I saw cattle running around down below," Hammerschmidt says. "I said, 'You know, we're running a lot of pounds off that cattle, I sure hope that guy doesn't know who it is up here. That's my constituent!'"

Bush joked, "How do you suppose we let the president get in a hairy situation like this?"

Bush and Hammerschmidt were on one side of the aisle in the helicopter, and Nixon and Rockefeller were directly across from them, near Arkansas U.S. senator John McClellan.

Bush says, "McClellan turned to me and said, 'Who's that man on the end down there?' It was Kissinger."

Up to that point, Dr. Henry Kissinger, the president's national security advisor, had kept such a low profile, a senator didn't recognize him.

On the ride from Washington, Hammerschmidt says, President Nixon showed a stunning depth of knowledge about football and the teams he would see that afternoon. On the helicopter ride, Hammerschmidt says, "Nixon was very impatient. He never wanted to be late to anything."

Two alternative plans had been formulated. One was to have the helicopters land at Fayetteville's Drake Field. The other was to land on the practice field next to the stadium. Hammerschmidt says that during the delay, the decision was made: They were going straight to the practice field.

In Razorback Stadium, groups of black students and friends—the potential "Dixie" protest included some white sympathizers—settled into their seats. They were scattered, mostly through the student section. Hiram McBeth says the potential protesters numbered about two hundred students, friends, and sympathizers.

The automatic halftime occupation of the field was off because of band director Richard Worthington's official disowning of "Dixie" after the Student Senate vote that week. Now they were waiting to see if the band would perhaps decide to go along with the Equity and Grievance Committee's recommendation to play the song during the first half, or if renegade band members would ignore Worthington's directive and play the song anyway.

"We had agreed we would head to the field and lie down, all of us," McBeth says. "We made sure we were all placed at various places so we could get down there. As soon as the first note was played, we were heading down there and lying on the field, and they were going to have to get all two hundred of us off there. And they were not going to be able to do it in a commercial break."

McBeth watched from a seat a few rows from the field. "I was torn, really torn," he says. "I was concerned with both my obligations as a black student and my loyalty to the team. I still felt loyal to that team. I would have loved to be an Arkansas Razorback. But we knew what the plan was. We weren't going to have this kind of political presence in Fayetteville to help make our point."

Eugene Hunt, the law student and BAD president who had slept on the floor the night before with his shotgun, decided against trying to go to the game after the occupation of the field at halftime was called off. For one thing, he didn't have a ticket. He thought he should stay with his wife and child.

On the field, with the Arkansas band forming "USA" and the Texas band forming a "shield" around the letters, Dr. Billy Graham delivered the invocation. He prayed for God to bless the game. He prayed for "both sides, that not only will we exhibit great sportsmanship, but that we will remember that there's a greater game in life." He prayed for the president and "all of the leaders. And we pray that if it be thy will, that we might have peace in our time." Finally, he asked that the players be protected and that none of them suffer "serious injury." After the "Amen," he strode down the sideline with his young son, Ned, and went to his seat. On the sideline and in the stands, Secret Service agents were scattered, wearing ties, trenchcoats, and tiny earphones, with binoculars hanging on straps around their necks.

As the helicopters headed toward the stadium, the starters for the Arkansas defense and the Texas offense, plus their head coaches, lined up single file down yard stripes on each side of ABC's Bill Fleming. Darrell Royal and the Longhorns were to Fleming's left, Frank Broyles and the Razorbacks were to his right. "Now," Fleming said, "you guys stand here and run up and just pause for a second and run off." The lines were close together, yet there was no yapping back and forth. They quietly waited during a commercial break. Fleming was facing the single camera, holding sheets with the starting lineups.

In the Texas group, Longhorns left guard Bobby Mitchell—recovered from his sternum injury—had a thought: Did Fleming's sheets still have Randy Stout listed as the starter, as did the program and the official press releases that week? When it was Bobby Mitchell's turn, would Fleming introduce him to America as Randy Stout?

"Can I see your list a minute?" he asked Fleming.

Sure enough, the list had Stout as the starter.

"By the way," Mitchell said, pointing, "that's wrong, I'm Bobby Mitchell."

"I'm glad you told me," Fleming said. Frantically, the ABC technicians got Mitchell's graphic ready to superimpose on the screen when he was introduced. (All afternoon, the white lettering and numbers all looked as if someone held up a clear piece of plastic in front of the camera, and couldn't quite hold it still.)

Fleming was on. With his voice broadcast over the stadium public-address system, he introduced eleven Hogs and eleven Horns. All Fleming said was position, number, and name. The head coaches were at the end of each line.

The Horns wore their white pants and white jerseys, with the burnt-orange numbers. On the back, the numbers rode high on most of the Longhorns, stretching down to only about the middle of their backs, making them look a little, well, clunky. The burnt-orange Longhorn symbol on the side of their white helmets was adorned with a single-season addition—the football decal with the number 100 inside it, symbolizing the centennial anniversary of Princeton and Rutgers meeting in the first recognized game, in 1869. Arkansas didn't have the centennial symbol on its red helmets, which featured the white Razorback hog on the sides, huge numbers on the back and white facemasks that stood out, especially against the red. The jerseys were simple, with white numbers on red, no stripes, but the numbers both in front and on the back were so large, they screamed.

Texas tight end Randy Peschel, the first player introduced, didn't step far enough over to the yard stripe the cameraman was using as his "mark." America saw only Peschel's shoulder and arm. His teammates didn't step any farther, but the cameraman compensated. The others slid sideways into the camera view, most of them smiling tightly, and then moved off. Guard Mike Dean especially looked as if tackle Bob McKay had just told him a joke, but McKay—next up—looked grim, so maybe that wasn't it. The camera rose and fell, going from the tall (McKay and Arkansas linebacker Cliff Powell) to the diminutive (James Street and Bobby Field, who looked as if he should be throwing newspapers on porches). To honor him as a senior, the Razorbacks arranged to have injured defensive end Gordon McNulty introduced as a starter, instead of junior defensive tackle Roger Harnish.

Arkansas's captains were Bruce Maxwell, Rodney Brand, Cliff Powell, and Dennis Berner. They met Ted Koy, James Street, and Glen Halsell at midfield, and after all the reach-across handshakes ("*Cap'n Maxwell . . . Cap'n Halsell*"), referee Carl Landiss introduced the other officials. Street called tails, the coin came up heads in Landiss's hand and the Razorbacks' Lynn Garner said Arkansas would defend the north goal and take advantage of a roughly north-to-south wind that periodically reached around ten miles per hour. The rain, which had fallen in the morning, had stopped. But it was so damp and wind-whipped chilly, in the high thirties, that ballboys were instructed to bring in a dried-off football after every play. (That became more important when a freezing mist fell later.) The captains shook hands again, Landiss called out, "Good luck, gentlemen!" and The Big Shootout was about to start.

Gradually gaining volume, the unmistakable noise of whirling helicopter blades and growling engines could be heard above the anticipatory din in the stadium.

"It sounded like the militia was coming in," Razorback Terry Don Phillips says.

"They came down the draw, along the hills from the south," Chuck Dicus says. "I looked, you bet. That's a sound you don't hear in Fayetteville, Arkansas."

As the teams broke their final sideline huddles and the kickoff and return teams trotted onto the field, the helicopters in the presidential party began landing on the practice field, just to the south of the stadium.

Bill McClard, the Hogs' sophomore kicker, teed up the ball on the 40. Years later, McClard looked at the tape, trying to confirm his memory, but the ABC shots left him after he put the ball on the tee. The nation saw Longhorns Jim Bertelsen and Cotton Speyrer down on the goal line, and the Texas band playing. McClard swears that as the Arkansas fans called the Hogs, the ball fell off the tee.

"*Woooooooooo, Pig! Sooie!*

"*Woooooooooo, Pig! Sooie!*

"*Woooooooooo, Pig! Sooie! Razorbacks!*"

"It stunned me because it was almost like a clap of thunder," McClard says. "It fell off the tee, I picked it up, and the official was standing there, and he looked at me and said, 'I never would have believed that if I hadn't seen it.' I swear, it wasn't the wind."

With the Washington contingent stepping off the helicopters, McClard approached the ball straight-on, and kicked it with his square-toed shoe. The ball landed over the Longhorns' heads, near the back of the end zone, and bounced up against the bleachers. The Longhorns had the ball on the 20.

The Arkansas interior linemen—Rick Kersey, Dick Bumpas, Roger Harnish, and Bruce James—waited before getting in the poised, four-point stances taught by Charley Coffey. Spotting Texas offensive tackle Bob McKay, Harnish muttered loud enough so James, the end next to him, could hear. "Damn," Harnish said, "he's the biggest son of a bitch I've ever seen." It broke the tension. "I fell out laughing," says James, who was going to be across from McKay most of the game. James recovered, though, and carried through what would be his assignment on most plays—slanting at fullback Steve Worster.

On that opening play, Street got his first hint of the Razorbacks' defensive unpredictability. Linebacker Cliff Powell jumped up to the gap between Bumpas and Kersey. Street feinted a handoff to Worster, then turned the other way and gave the ball to Jim Bertelsen. The counter action was a test, to see how heavily the Razorbacks would respond to Worster's move. Bertelsen gained only one yard, with Powell in on the tackle.

On the next play, in line with the plan the Razorbacks had practiced all week, monster Bobby Field trotted over to the same side as Peschel, the tight end. Field lined up outside Kersey, the defensive end, standing up on the line of scrimmage. Field wasn't about to strike fear into anyone trying to block him, but he was *there*, giving the Razorbacks one more man defending the various option possibilities to the strong side—the way the Longhorns preferred to go. Bobby Wuensch, the Horns' left tackle, blocked in, and Kersey scraped between him and Peschel and had a free run inside. He was assigned to Worster, but he got there so quick, he went at Street instead. Street faked to Worster, but they weren't in sync. When Street yanked the ball out and reached to give it to Koy for a straight power play off left tackle, Kersey already had made contact with Street. The ball went off Koy's arm—and onto the Astroturf. Linebacker Mike Boschetti tackled Koy, and Field fell on the ball at the Texas 22.

"It was no great play on my part," Field says. "It wasn't like I made a crushing tackle and made the ball pop loose. It popped out on the ground and it was relatively close to me and I was able to get in and get on it."

As the Razorbacks jumped up, and the officials signaled the change of possession, the ABC shot switched to Nixon striding into the stadium. A youthful-looking, forty-five-year-old George Bush was just off the president's right shoulder and a step back. He was walking with John Paul Hammerschmidt, whose loyalty was unmistakable, announced by his bright red jacket.

(On the broadcast, neither Schenkel nor Wilkinson identified the Razorback who came up with the ball at the time. A few minutes later, when Schenkel—who otherwise was adept at trying to get as many names mentioned as possible—recapped the play, he twice gave the credit for the recovery to the wrong Razorback, reserve end Bill Powell, no relation to Cliff. Bill Powell, who didn't play in the game, wore number 40, while Field was number 49.)

As they walked toward the stadium, "We heard this tremendous roar in the stadium," Hammerschmidt says. "I said, 'Hell, Bush, we've already scored!'"

Not quite.

Street, meanwhile, was alarmed as much by the defensive alignment he faced as he was by the fumble. "There was an indecision on my part and Worster's part," the Longhorn quarterback says. "Usually, when I put it in there riding, he would automatically clamp down on it if the defensive guy disappeared because he was supposed to get the ball. But if the guy's coming at him, he keeps it loose and I pull it out. On this one, it was kind of half of both, because we never faced the defense like they were running it."

The Longhorn offense went to the sideline, perplexed and angry. "Usually after the first series, I go back and talk with my linemen about what they felt they could do with their guys, and talk to Coach Bellard upstairs," Street says. "We didn't really have enough plays in the first series to determine what they were going to do and weren't going to do. So we didn't have anything."

Mike Boschetti charged to the sideline, amazed by the way this game was affecting him. "The butterflies usually are there for the first play," he says. "Then they go away. But they never went away this game."

So the Razorbacks offense came on, trying to take advantage of the turnover. The Longhorn defenders weren't used to this; typically, they could stand and stretch and gather their thoughts if the offense got the ball first. "We were not particularly ready," linebacker Scott Henderson says. "We were settling in and Coach Campbell yelled, 'Defense! Go!'" Defensive tackle Carl White was concerned that this was a sign that the offense might have trouble all day hanging on to the ball in the wet and cold. "It was, 'Oh, shit,' here we go," White says.

Bill Montgomery threw two wild incompletions, one toward Maxwell, and the second—rushed because of pressure by a blitzing Henderson—on the sideline to Chuck Dicus. On third down, Montgomery rolled left. Both rover Mike Campbell and inside linebacker Glen Halsell blitzed, but the rollout action left them chasing Montgomery from behind. Defensive end David Arledge came off blocks from tackle Mike Kelson and then Bruce Maxwell, and leaped at Montgomery, his arms extended. "I thought I had a sack," Arledge says. "I closed my eyes and I hit Montgomery when he still had his arm behind his head. And I'm getting off the ground and everybody's cheering, and I'm shocked he got the pass off and somebody caught it."

The "somebody" was flanker John Rees, who had a step on defensive half-back Danny Lester. Rees made a great diving catch, and while it was excruciatingly close, he never got the necessary one foot in-bounds as he flew over the sideline at the 2, but the linesman, Shorty Lawson, a resident of College Station, called it complete.

"I caught it, came down, and rolled up against the fence," Rees says. "Pat Morrison came over and congratulated me. 'Man, great catch! Way to go!' I thought I was out of bounds, because when I rolled, I rolled so far."

So did he get one foot in?

"Uh," Rees says, smiling, "I'll let the official make the call. He was from Texas A&M, so maybe he had an ax to grind. It was close. He was standing on the sideline. He had as good a view as anyone."

Although it should have been called incomplete, that terrifically athletic 20-yard play was the start of an eventful afternoon for Rees. He wasn't in the goal-line offense, so he was on the sideline when Nixon and his entourage began walking up the aisle to their seats about a third of the way up the stands, around the 35-yard line on the west side.

Arkansas went to its proven goal-line approach: Give the ball to Bill Burnett, let him follow Bruce Maxwell and dive over the pile. The Razorbacks had to do it twice this time; on second down, Maxwell dove, too, and Burnett followed in his wake. Glen Halsell hit his legs, but Burnett catapulted into the end zone. "With Bruno in front of me, I knew there was going to be a hole," Burnett says. "I did a somersault, which is pretty much what I always did. To me, it didn't seem like anything big. We just scored a touchdown, and the game was just getting started."

McClard kicked the extra point, off the pad and out of the hold of defensive back Gus Rusher, and the Razorbacks led 7–0—only eighty-seven seconds into the first quarter.

Nixon sat down just in time to see the touchdown. Rockefeller was between Hammerschmidt and Nixon, and Hammerschmidt later teased Bush that many pictures cropped out the Texas congressman, who was farther down the row.

Through the game, the bantering went back and forth. "We were among rabid Razorback fans, but the cocoon around the president kept us from heavy abuse by them," Bush jokes. He says the reaction around them showed something else: "They were thrilled to see the president at the game."

Others considered it an opportunity.

TWENTY-THREE

Flagged!

THE RAZORBACKS' early touchdown was the first major test for the banishment of "Dixie." The band hadn't played the song through the rallying and pageantry of the pregame activities. But when the Razorbacks scored, would the emotions bubble over, would some members of the band ignore director Richard Worthington's directive and start the song, which might have brought along the rest of band? "If they had played it, we would have been out on the field," Hiram McBeth says.

By early afternoon, wounded law student Darrell Brown was out of the hospital and was watching the game in his dormitory. Who was he rooting for? "I was rooting for these guys I thought were getting ready to march down into the middle of that field," Brown says. "I was hoping it wouldn't happen because I could not imagine what fifty thousand red—"

Brown pauses there for a second, then continues.

"—wearing Razorbacks would do."

(Brown laughs. "You were waiting on that one, weren't you?")

The band director's ruling was honored. The Razorbacks were ahead a little over a minute into the national championship game, and "Dixie" seemed to be in exile.

In the stands, the black students didn't know whether to celebrate the death of "Dixie" or be relieved. But they knew there would be other posttouchdown or postvictory chances for the band to play the song. Or at least that's what the red-wearing fans in Razorback Stadium were hoping.

Shortly after the game started, on the hill above the northeast corner of the stadium, in Nixon's line of sight, the anti–Vietnam War protesters showed up and pieced together their visual demonstration. Shortly before the game, as the Razorbacks were about to run onto the field from the southeast corner of the stadium, ABC panned the area, showing the hill, and it was deserted.

"I had told them not to get there until the game started, and why they listened to me, I don't know," says physics professor Bud Zinke, the anti–Vietnam War veteran of World War II.

Vietnam vet Don Donner picked up other members of the coalition at the Presbyterian Center, then drove to the campus and began unloading the tiny crosses and the sheets he and others would lay out on the hill to form a peace sign. Other protesters met at the library. The peace sign ended up visually striking, and Nixon couldn't have missed seeing it. "Have you ever seen a skywriter, and you can't figure out what it is until it's almost done?" Zinke asks. "It was like that. A friend of mine who was sitting behind him told me Nixon couldn't stop looking, he was fascinated."

The crosses inside the peace sign, representing war dead, were ineffective, though. The dark wood couldn't be spotted from the stands.

Arthur Hobson, the other activist physics professor, came with two huge hand-painted signs. One said, "MY," the other "LAI." In that order, he leaned them up against the administration building. Other signs said: "Give Peace a Chance" and "Can Your Conscience Stand Another My Lai Slaughter?" Bud Zinke stood with an American flag, waving it, then sticking it in the ground. "I was telling myself I was about to get pneumonia," Zinke says. "My feet were wet. I was thinking, 'Couldn't we demonstrate on concrete somewhere?'"

Only about fifty protesters were on the hill, and at no point did the demonstration come close to turning violent. It was crucial that it didn't begin until after most of the fans were in the stadium, lessening the chances of angry taunts and confrontation causing trouble. At one point early in the game, a state representative, Paul Meers of Little Rock, approached Donner and thanked him for the calm nature of the protest. Nixon had been subjected to far worse abuse, of course, and it was so low-key, George Bush has "no recall of demonstrations. I wasn't in sympathy with the insults to Nixon that took place across the country, having served in a different war at a different time."

During the second quarter, the protesters left the hill and placed the "cost of the war" sheets on car windshield wipers. The sheets said that the price of the aircraft alone lost in Vietnam could have built and supplied 750 schools, and it blamed the cost of the war for inflation. After leaving the sheets, the protesters left the stadium area. Zinke had promised Mullins to nudge the protesters away from the stadium before any fans exited, and he delivered.

"We were deathly afraid of the fans interacting with those kids, and the local police trying to break it up," Zinke says. "The Secret Service men were cool; they were up on the buildings with guns." Donner went back to the Presbyterian Center, then to his girlfriend's apartment.

ON THE SECOND TEXAS POSSESSION, a pattern emerged: The Longhorns could chip away, but couldn't break a big play on option action against the Razorbacks, with Cliff Powell making a lot of the tackles. On the drive, Steve Worster had five carries for 21 yards and Ted Koy two for 7. James Street kept it twice for 8 yards. After all of that, the Longhorns still were only on the Razorback 44, faced with a second-and-8. Street faked to Worster and took a shallow drop. Cotton Speyrer did a hesitation step, then broke down the sideline against defensive halfback Terry Stewart, with safety Dennis Berner breaking over. Street's pass was a floater. Stewart wasn't fooled, and he jumped with his back to the goal line and came down with the interception at the Arkansas 8. In the Longhorns' 39–29 victory at Austin the year before, Street had hit a 51-yard touchdown pass to Speyrer on a similar play. This time, as he came off the field, Stewart told his teammates: "I can't believe they really would think I would be suckered in again." Again, the Razorbacks' defensive backs weren't coming up to play the run when the action went to the split-end side.

Montgomery took the Razorbacks right down the field, using both Bruce Maxwell and Bill Burnett in the ground game. Twice, the Razorbacks used a rolling pocket, pulling center Rodney Brand as Montgomery's protector. Montgomery's elusiveness, quickness, and poise already were frustrating the Longhorns. Once on the drive, Montgomery scrambled for 8 yards, and the Razorbacks even ran a straight option on another play, with Montgomery cutting up for 14.

In their pass-blocking schemes, the Razorbacks showed the most respect for Bill Atessis, the junior defensive end from Houston, usually having Maxwell go over to help out if the Longhorns weren't blitzing. "I prided myself at keeping containment and not getting knocked off my feet, and those guys were coming at me like mad dogs," Atessis says.

David Arledge, the other defensive end (and the "Little A" to Atessis's

"Big A"), did force Montgomery to step up on one play, and Atessis made the 5-yard sack. But the Montgomery-to-Dicus connection looked formidable. On a third-and-13, Montgomery hit Dicus across the middle for 22 yards, just behind Glen Halsell and in front of Danny Lester and Freddie Steinmark. That got the Razorbacks to the Texas 45.

Two plays later, on third-and-7, Dicus lined up in a slot, inside of John Rees, and rover Mike Campbell stayed with Dicus across the middle. Montgomery pirouetted and scrambled to his left to buy time, then made a dangerous across-the-field throw, connecting with Dicus before Steinmark could get there. The pass was good for 16 yards.

Upstairs, offensive coach Don Breaux noticed how the Longhorns covered Dicus man-to-man with the rover, Campbell, when he was in the slot. "They were trying to exploit what they perceived to be a weakness on defense," Campbell says. "Unfortunately, that was me. They had such a balanced attack. They still believed in running the ball, but they passed it better than anyone else we played. I think Chuck Dicus could run about a 9.9 hundred-yard dash, and it was him up against me. That was not a good matchup." Dicus also tried to run his pattern so a linebacker, either Halsell or Scott Henderson, inadvertently might "pick" off Mike Campbell. As the game went on, Montgomery's uncanny accuracy for most of the afternoon took advantage of the matchup. Ultimately, Coach Campbell started calling more zone coverage and variations.

"Sometimes we had combination coverage, with zone on one side of the field and man-to-man on the other side, toward Dicus," defensive backfield coach Fred Akers says. "Montgomery was good enough to throw the ball against pure zone coverage. When you're playing zone, you give them certain things and count on misthrows. Maybe you'll hit them and punish them when they catch the ball and try to knock it loose. But the problem was, Montgomery just kept throwing the ball in there. And with a guy like Dicus, a route runner and a sure-handed guy who also was quick, it was tough."

The Razorbacks had a first down at the Texas 26. In the huddle, Montgomery called a handoff to Burnett to the weak side—away from the tight end—with an asterisk. The word "read" added to the call alerted everyone that there could be an audible. All week, the Razorbacks had worked on changing out of that play on the line of scrimmage. Dicus was the split end to the left, and Rees, the flanker to the right, outside tight end Pat Morrison.

If there was double coverage on Dicus, or Montgomery wasn't intrigued by what he saw, the Razorbacks would stick with the run. But if Montgomery spotted single coverage on Dicus, he would call an audible. In this case, safety Freddie Steinmark popped up and looked to be involved in man-to-man coverage on the tight end, signaling to Montgomery that the Longhorns probably were blitzing a linebacker—or two. Linebacker Glen Halsell indeed looked as if he was about to come after the quarterback. It also meant that Steinmark was vacating the middle of the field, opening up the post route for Dicus.

Because of the formation, with Dicus split to one side alone, Dicus wasn't working against Mike Campbell, but was getting man coverage nonetheless, from halfback Danny Lester.

Montgomery called the audible. He faked to Burnett, then dropped to pass and hit Dicus—who had gotten behind Lester and Steinmark—in full stride on the Texas 3. One step later, Dicus was in the end zone.

"Now I'm feeling pretty good, real good," Montgomery says. "Absolutely at the same instant I get rid of the ball Atessis nails me and it's like getting hit by a truck. I see nothing except Chuck cutting across and I get a glimpse of the ball, then see nothing—and then hear cheering."

The Razorbacks were ahead 13–0. Or were they? Dicus turned, flipped the ball to the official in the end zone, took four steps upfield, raised his arms overhead briefly, then saw the officials behind him converging to confer.

Referee Carl Landiss got everyone's attention. An official had dropped a flag for offensive pass interference—on Rees. The breaks had evened out. Rees didn't get a foot in bounds on the first catch, and now he had made a crucial error, but the call was petty.

On the play, Rees slanted in from the right, attempting to block the Texas left defensive halfback on him, Tom Campbell. Campbell had come up to play Rees tight, lining up only 2 yards off the line of scrimmage. Rees admits he was a shaky blocker in the first place—a not particularly damning weakness for a wide receiver. But he rolled at Campbell's legs, and Campbell fended him off, dodged him, and stayed on his feet. "While the ball is still in the air, Rees is still trying to block on me," Tom Campbell says. "Number one, it was very innocuous, and it didn't have anything to do with the play. Even if he hadn't been blocking on me, I couldn't have made a play on Dicus. But after seeing Dicus in the end zone, I turned to an official, who was looking at me."

What the hell, it was worth a shot.

"Sir," Campbell said to the official, gesturing to the prone Rees, "this guy was blocking on me!"

The official dropped the flag.

(Was the call technically correct? Yes. A good call? No. Good football officiating is discretionary, and this would have been a shaky call in The Big Shootout or in an Ivy League game.)

"If the official's back was to me," Tom Campbell admits, "I probably wouldn't have said anything. It had nothing to do with anything. I'm 100 percent convinced they win the football game if that stands up."

Frank Broyles calls the play a coaching error. "We just didn't do enough coaching to tell [Rees] he wasn't involved in the play, just to stay over there," Broyles says. "The coaches accept the blame for that."

Rees says he can't "say on a stack of Bibles that I didn't hit him at all, but it wasn't anything. It should have been called if it hindered him from getting to Chuck, but it didn't."

Pat Morrison also was lined up on the right side of the formation, closer to Montgomery than Rees, and he says he tried to block Steinmark, too. "John wasn't alone on that," the tight end says. "I didn't hear the audible, either, and I was throwing a block at the same time John was. We're taught that every time we go down the field, we throw a block and leave our feet. Neither of us heard that audible and I'm sure I was closer to the play than Rees was."

Montgomery calls the coaxing of the penalty "a smart play on Campbell's part, and it was stupid on the ref's part."

Instead of taking a two-touchdown lead, the Razorbacks still were ahead 7–0. On the next play, Montgomery scrambled and retreated and finally was tackled for a loss of 24 by Bill Atessis and David Arledge. That made it third-and-49, and after Bruce Maxwell ran for 3 yards on a draw play, the Razorbacks punted.

Darrell Royal, meanwhile, was getting wind of a problem. Shoes. Many of the Longhorns were switching from Astroturf spikes back to the regular grass shoes, with the nylon screw-in spikes. And the Texas coach decided that all his players needed to do that. "Dammit, Atessis, change shoes!" he hollered at one of the last holdouts, the defensive end who came off the field after the punt. Atessis says he wasn't having any problems, but he obliged.

ON THEIR SECOND POSSESSION of the second quarter, the Razorbacks threatened again. Bill Burnett broke a 16-yarder through a huge hole off right guard to get Arkansas a first down at the Texas 41. On the next play, Montgomery rolled right and escaped a blitzing Mike Campbell, but was pressured into throwing an ill-advised pass toward Dicus near the sideline. Freddie Steinmark stepped in front of Dicus at the Texas 33 and got his hands on the ball, but couldn't hold it when Dicus turned defender and tackled him. Steinmark slid across the sideline into a group of photographers, then climbed up and trotted back onto the field. He was hurting, but not limping.

After defensive tackle Carl White sacked Montgomery for a 10-yard loss on third-and-6 from the Texas 37, the Razorbacks had to punt. For years, guard Jerry Dossey blamed himself for the sack and the loss of opportunity, chewing himself out for trying to cut White instead of just staying in front of him. "That was my one horrible mistake," Dossey says. "I didn't need to put him on the ground. He was a big strong kid. He could push me back, but not enough to cause Montgomery problems." White says Dossey "was a good player. He had a tremendous first blow. There were some guys who could hit you from five or six inches away, and he was one of them. But after it was over, you could get away from him sometimes." On this play, Dossey popped into White's right shoulder with his helmet and got caught off balance, and White got by. Dossey dove to "cut" White as he went past, attempting to recover. White says coaches later told him that Arkansas had John Rees open deep on the play, if Montgomery had been able to throw the ball.

After the punt, Dossey talked with offensive line coach Mervin Johnson— "Jerry, what were you doing?" Johnson asked—and then threw on a parka and waited on the bench. Dossey's foot was shot up, and he liked to rest it— and contemplate—between series. He trusted the crowd noise to tell him what was happening.

Texas had the ball back, and the next drive again demonstrated the potential problem of the wishbone: Without a big play or two in a possession, which was easier to produce against Texas Tech than Arkansas, it could gain yardage, eat up time, but ultimately not yield any points. Texas had the ball for nearly seven minutes, but only got as far as the Arkansas 31. Street's fourth-down pass—hurried by a blitzing Cliff Powell—fell incomplete and the Razorbacks took over with 1:32 left in the half.

During that drive, Razorback defensive tackle Terry Don Phillips—who two weeks earlier thought his college football career was over—got the news he was both dreading and wanting to hear: He was going to play. He spelled Roger Harnish and played left defensive tackle on Texas's possession, lining up within a few feet of his Longview buddy, James Street. He alternated with Harnish the rest of the afternoon. "I thought I was going to die about a thousand times," Phillips says. "Number one, I wasn't in shape. Number two, I was an average player at best when I wasn't hurt. I was fortunate to get to play, but I went from average to somewhere way below that."

On the other side of the line of scrimmage, the Texas offensive linemen were frustrated, trying to figure out whom to block, and, just as important in the wishbone, not block. "It was frustrating because we didn't know what they were doing," guard Bobby Mitchell says. "We knew we could handle them if we just knew where to go." The problem was that with defensive tackle Dick Bumpas and end Rick Kersey varying where they lined up, the Longhorns' Mitchell and Bobby Wuensch were having a hard time making their blocking "reads." Randy Stout, who came in for Mitchell when the Longhorns wanted to send in a play, or give Mitchell a break, says, "Everybody was convinced somebody wasn't blocking who they were supposed to be blocking. You'd get in the huddle and somebody would start yelling, 'Are you blocking the guy you're supposed to be blocking?' and you'd say, 'Damn right!'"

The same thing was happening on the Longhorns' right side, with Mike Dean and Bob McKay. Center Forrest Wiegand, who almost never had a Razorback lined up over him, was similarly confused. "The first half, I'm sitting out there blocking air," he says. "They'd gotten into that eight-man front, the wide-tackle look, and I'm running out like a chicken with my head cut off, trying to figure out who the hell I was going to block."

As Royal had noticed, the Longhorns were also having trouble with traction. "You can't imagine the conditions," Mike Dean says. "Every time we came off the field, we'd change shoes. You'd fire out, and your feet would just go out from under you."

The defense acknowledged the offense's unprecedented struggles. "Coach Campbell is wearing our butts out," Carl White says. "He's saying things like, 'Boys, we're gonna have to win this game, we cannot depend on the boys on the other side of the ball to win it, and the way we win it is by not letting them score anymore!'"

After that drive, Royal approached Randy Peschel and asked the Longhorn tight end why he hadn't blocked Razorbacks defensive back Terry Stewart on an option play to the strong side. Jim Bertelsen had gained 3 yards, and Bobby Field and Stewart made the tackle. That play was indicative of the problem the Longhorns were facing with the "monster" back always moved up to the line: Peschel had Field on his outside shoulder, and they brushed each other, so by the time Peschel got past Field cleanly to go after Stewart, he already was charging up, full-steam, and Peschel couldn't get to him. So Peschel was right when he told Royal that the defensive halfbacks—either Stewart or Jerry Moore, depending on the side—were coming up brazenly fast. The fact that Peschel was held up by a half-count because of the contact with the "monster" outside him didn't seem to register or trigger significant adjustments. Also, because Field was a defensive back moved up to the line of scrimmage for this game, there was some confusion over whether *he* was one of the defensive backs "coming up fast." He wasn't. In this scheme, Field was more of a standup defensive end.

Texas's best chance to score was on the final play of the half. Linebacker Scott Henderson came up the middle, dove straight at the leg of Arkansas punter Cary Stockdell, and blocked the punt. The ball bounced sideways, and Longhorns outside linebacker Bill Zapalac fell on it near the sideline at the Arkansas 17. Though he could have picked the ball up easily, there were enough Razorbacks in the neighborhood to probably prevent him from scoring. But the clock had struck all zeroes; the half was over.

"I thought we had enough time to line up and score," Zapalac says. "People were screaming at me. I had teammates telling me how stupid I was. My dad came up to me later and said, 'What the hell are you doing?' For a long time, I never saw the replay, not up until about ten years ago. I thought I was wide open and if I had picked the ball up, I would have scored. As it turns out, there were people right there with me, and I wouldn't have scored, and I can't tell you how relaxed that made me feel. I carried that for twenty years."

DURING HALFTIME, the Texas band played a medley of Christmas songs, and then—as it transformed its "TEXAS" formation into "NIXON"—"Hail to the Chief." That came just as Richard Nixon entered the ABC booth for his halftime interview with Chris Schenkel. ABC college football guru/publicist Beano Cook was in the booth, too, and he remembers that Nixon stepped to the window and waved to the band in acknowledgment.

Nixon's advisor, Bud Wilkinson, abstained from the interview, and was nowhere in sight. It's also entirely possible that Wilkinson—as good advisors do—briefed Nixon about what he could say. Then again, it's possible that Nixon just talked off the top of his head. There was no doubt that he followed football.

Not surprisingly, Schenkel—known in the business as one of the nicest men ever to work in a broadcast booth—didn't grill the president with the seriousness of a moderator in the 1960 presidential debates.

Nixon complimented Arkansans for the spirit he witnessed that day in Fort Smith and Fayetteville, and noted that he received considerable flak from Penn State partisans about his intention to award his national championship plaque to the winner of the game. "Penn State is the team that will have the longest undefeated streak for the year," Nixon told Schenkel. "You've covered them and I know they're a great team. Maybe we ought to have a super college bowl after this, whatever the case might be. Looking at these two teams today, either one is going to be number one by vote of the writers. But what is more important is the tremendous spirit that they generate. It's good for people to be for somebody, to be for a team. You can learn a lot from losing as well as winning. I've had a little experience with that."

When Schenkel said, "Boy, you came back a winner," Nixon joked he "was down more than 7–0, I would say. It was sort of a fourth-quarter finish and a pass perhaps in the last thirty seconds to win; that's what counts."

Schenkel asked whether Nixon, as a noted observer of the college game, had an opinion about what might happen in the second half.

"I sat on the bench when I was in college, and you learn a lot from the coach when you sit on the bench," Nixon said. "As I look at this game in the first half, I think that Texas has enormous power that is really not unleashed yet. And in the second half, they are likely to be much better offensively. However, they're not going to run over Arkansas. They can't do it by just going that three yards and a cloud of dust, the old Woody Hayes formula . . . I think they're going to have to throw more. They have an excellent passer. They're going to have to throw to open up the Arkansas defense. I think under those circumstances, they're likely to score once or twice. But also I would suggest that Arkansas looks better offensively than I had realized. They could score in this second half. They have a fine passer. I don't think I've seen a cooler passer than Montgomery. He's really cool under very great pressure and Texas has a great pass rush . . . I'd rather say that I expect both teams to score in the second half. The question is whether Texas's superior manpower, and I mean probably a stronger bench, may win in the last quarter. That's the way I see it."

Schenkel told Nixon that "if Bud Wilkinson, our analyst, ever falters, we at ABC may call on you to do our commentary. Excellent."

"I'm not thinking, Chris, of what I'm going to do when I finish my present job. But there's nothing I'd like better than to have Bud's job, right with you."

DURING AND AFTER THE NIXON INTERVIEW, the Arkansas band stuck to its script, playing "Music That Rocks—Past and Present," and then the school's official fight song as the members marched off the field. The script didn't include "Dixie," and nobody broke ranks for an impromptu chorus, either. More and more, it seemed that Daniel Decatur Emmett's 110-year-old song was history on the UofA campus, at least officially.

THE RAZORBACKS' HALFTIME DRESSING ROOM was the "half-house," between the field and the bigger locker room in the basketball arena. They were ahead, but more important, they were convinced they were the best team on the field. At first, the offense met at one end, the defense at the other.

"It wasn't like we couldn't believe what was happening," Bobby Field says. "We were feeling like this is what *should* have happened."

Field's roommate, defensive halfback Jerry Moore, also was confident. "They couldn't do anything," Moore says. "We had a super defense for the wishbone. We had a lot of guys in the box and when they tried to run a sweep, we had the corners coming up supporting. We just all felt very confident that we had stuffed them in the first half and there was no reason we wouldn't do the same thing in the second half."

That was the point: The Razorbacks' defensive focus was to keep doing what they were doing. "We felt good, we felt like we were controlling the front and we hadn't given up the big play," Terry Don Phillips says. "If they're going to beat you, make them go the long way."

The other senior defensive lineman, Gordon McNulty, still hadn't played because of his torn knee cartilage—and was going to continue to sit out unless the Razorbacks were desperate. But as he watched, he was excited. "We had these coaches coming up with this new defense, and we were going up against a team rushing for 376 yards a game," McNulty says. "We probably didn't know if it would work or not. There was this tremendous feeling of exhilaration that, 'Hey, this can work! We're shutting these guys down!' They were supposed to be unstoppable and invincible, and it was a great feeling."

"The excitement was at such a peak," Chuck Dicus says. "I couldn't help but think, 'My gosh, we're going to win this game, we're going to win the national championship, how much better can things get?'"

The Razorbacks met in their position and unit groups.

"We got real quiet, the quietest I've ever seen us," tackle Mike Kelson says. "The coaches didn't say much, didn't have to say anything. It was just, 'Any problems?' 'No, Coach.' We knew we had the opportunity, we knew we were better than they were. We knew we had the defense. We knew we could definitely score on them. There's no way they could cover our wide receivers, and we had Bill Burnett, who was our ace card."

Broyles talked briefly to the entire team. Some of the players felt his voice had an edge to it they hadn't heard before. "There was incredible tension in the dressing room," Jerry Dossey says. "To me, he was always the consummate class gentleman. But that day, he was excited, he was keyed up, he was fired up. He was impressing on us that we had another half to play, that we needed to avoid mistakes, play with intensity, play smart—and keep doing what we were doing."

Confident that the Longhorns were confused, the Razorbacks seemed more than halfway home.

IN THE VISITING DRESSING ROOM, the Longhorn coaches conferred, trying to decide how to adjust.

"Sure, I was worried," Darrell Royal says. "They're not Little Sisters of the Poor. They're number two. They were shutting us down offensively. We were doing a good job on defense, though."

Emory Bellard, the wishbone's inventor, maintains that "the scheme wasn't the biggest factor. They had an excellent defensive football team. But we probably didn't exploit the things that they were doing."

Some of the Longhorns are convinced they didn't sufficiently adjust to the Razorbacks' use of the "monster" back on the tight-end side of the line of scrimmage or to the defensive back coming up fast on that side as well. "Even if everybody blocked who they should on that side, there would be an extra man," guard Randy Stout says. The alternative would have been to run the option more often to the split-end side, with either straight or counter action.

"I didn't know exactly what they were doing," Royal says. "I couldn't tell from the sideline [what adjustments to make]."

The one change the Longhorns' offensive line made was to decide that once they made their blocking call at the line of scrimmage, they would stick with it—even if the Razorbacks slid over before the snap. Guard Bobby Mitchell and tackle Bobby Wuensch talked it over. "We had an option, I would get the guy on the gap and Wuensch would get the linebacker," Mitchell says. "Or we would call a switch where he would crash down and I'd go around and get the linebacker. But we decided that once we called it, that was it. Once we got that worked out, we started playing our normal ball."

Otherwise, the halftime discussion involved minor tweaks and emphasis on avoiding turnovers.

"We were saying we've hurt ourselves, stopped ourselves every time," James Street says. "We're OK, we have to score a touchdown, we will score a touchdown, we have to stop killing ourselves with interceptions and fumbles."

Center Forrest Wiegand says, "We were shooting ourselves in the foot. We were turning the ball over. We felt like if we got situated and calmed down, we'd be OK. And then everybody was kind of looking at each other. That was the first time we'd been in that situation for a long time. We were asking each other what was happening, what we were going to do."

Yet for all the hand-wringing, the Longhorns had outgained the Razorbacks in the first half—by one yard, 124–123. In part because of Tom Campbell's coaxing of the flag out of the official's pocket, both teams had played an efficient bend-but-not-break half.

"They scored seven points when they had to go only twenty-two yards, and twenty of them were on a miracle catch," Tom Campbell says. "The way I look at it, the score should have been 7–0 at the half—but on that Dicus catch."

Royal asked Peschel one more time about whether the defensive backs were coming up on the option. They're charging up there, Coach, Peschel said.

As the Longhorns were about to go back on the field, Royal spoke. "He just told us what we needed to do—keep trying," Bob McKay says. "We had fumbled and thrown an interception, and we needed to stop that. Nobody was desperate or anything. I just figured that if we played well enough, we'd win. I don't think anybody was scared that we would lose." McKay laughs. "Well, maybe the coaches were."

TWENTY-FOUR

Back and Forth

RICHARD NIXON WAS BACK IN HIS SEAT when Arkansas's Bill McClard put the ball on the tee. (The Razorbacks kicked off both halves because they won the opening toss and elected to defend the north goal and take the wind. Texas elected to receive to open the second half.) Unlike the start of the game, this time the ball stayed on the tee—all three times. On the first two attempts, McClard kicked the ball out of bounds inside the 5, drawing 5-yard illegal procedure penalties. That *never* happened to McClard, who was shaken and angry as he teed the ball up a third time at the Arkansas 30. The Longhorns seemed on the verge of having great field position. McClard's third kick went to Cotton Speyrer on the 9, who was fighting for extra yardage at the 37 when Bobby Field's backup, Steve Birdwell, and reserve linebacker Richard Coleman hit Speyrer from behind and the ball popped loose. Backup tailback Paul Blevins recovered for the Razorbacks. (ABC got that one wrong, too.)

It wasn't the way the Longhorns had been hoping to start a second-half comeback, but the defense held, with Bill Atessis forcing Montgomery into a David Arledge sack on third-and-10, resulting in a Razorback punt.

The Horns got one first down on the next drive before James Street was faced with a third-and-7 from the Longhorns' 35. Texas wasn't used to facing third-and-long, and it was beginning to look as if Street was going to have to be effective throwing the ball to make Arkansas pay for so brazenly packing the line of scrimmage. Ted Koy lined up as a flanker and Street dropped to throw without any play action at all. (That was rare, too, an indication of the Longhorns' abandonment of their usual modus operandi.) Street connected with Speyrer, hooking over the middle, and safety Dennis Berner hit him before Cliff Powell reached in and knocked the ball loose. Defensive halfback Terry Stewart fell on it for the Razorbacks at the Arkansas 47. "Bobby Wuensch and I both were going for the ball," Speyrer says. "Bobby hit me and kind of knocked me out. They had to put smelling salts in front of me. I was literally dazed."

Another turnover! The tally had reached one interception and three fumbles. Two plays later, on third-and-long, Montgomery couldn't find anyone open and Longhorn defensive tackle Greg Ploetz—the artist—chased him out of the pocket. Montgomery avoided Bill Atessis, got a crushing block from Bruce Maxwell, then pump-faked another Longhorn up in the air and went down the sideline for 18 yards, to the Texas 31. Carl White, the sophomore defensive tackle playing well in the injured Leo Brooks's spot, chased down Montgomery from behind and made the initial contact, then fell hard. He felt a twinge in his knee and stayed down on all fours for a moment before getting up. Montgomery's mobility and poise were continuing to frustrate the Longhorns.

The next play was even worse for Carl White. Maxwell went for 2 yards off left guard, but White got caught in the pile. He twisted grotesquely, then grabbed his left knee. White was through for the afternoon, with torn cartilage and a sprained ligament. White was helped to the bench, but vetoed a trip to the dressing room. "The doctor gave me a shot so I could stay on the bench," he says.

As White talked with the trainers and the doctor, and with junior Scott Palmer replacing him at defensive tackle, the Razorbacks came out on the second-and-8 play from the Texas 29 with Chuck Dicus in the slot, on the same side as John Rees. The Longhorns blitzed *both* inside linebackers, Glen Halsell and Scott Henderson, increasing the pressure on both the Arkansas offensive line and the Texas defensive backfield. In the coverage, Danny Lester had Rees man-to-man, and rover Mike Campbell had Dicus. On the other side, tight end Pat Morrison split out slightly, further spreading the defensive coverage away from Dicus. With neither inside linebacker dropping back even to get in Montgomery's line of sight, Dicus had what amounted to a free run as he cut across the middle with Mike Campbell chasing him. Montgomery got the ball off an instant before Halsell leveled him, but it couldn't have been thrown any better. "I didn't see anything except Chuck cutting across and I got a glimpse of the ball on the way to him," Montgomery says. "After that, I couldn't see anything."

Dicus caught it in full stride at the 11, then ran for the flag. "I could tell it was going to be close," Dicus says. "So I headed for the corner and tried to tiptoe in the best I could."

He was trying to outrun Freddie Steinmark to the corner. Steinmark made a desperation dive and grazed Dicus, but the Arkansas receiver already was in the end zone.

Dicus turned around, carefully surveying the field for another flag. There weren't any. McClard kicked the extra point, and the Razorbacks were up by two touchdowns with 9:06 left in the third quarter.

"Now it's pretty cool," Montgomery says. "We're up 14–0 against a wishbone team, one which our defense has summarily throttled all day long. We have had some success moving the ball, particularly with our passing game. So I'm beginning to think, 'Goll, this is good.' We're in position to win a national championship, we're playing well."

On the sideline, the Texas defense was starting to get concerned—if it wasn't already. Halsell, the captain, wasn't particularly vocal, and he tried to cut off any expressions of near panic with glares. *Just shut up and play.*

And the Longhorns still couldn't effectively run the ball! Just as significant, they were starting to act as if they knew it. On the next series, Street hit Cotton Speyrer for 19 yards on the sideline to get Texas to midfield. The pass was perfect, dropped over Terry Stewart, and Speyrer made a catch reminiscent of John Rees's diving grab on the sideline on the first series—except Speyrer got a foot in bounds.

After Jim Bertelsen ran for 1 yard, Razorback defensive end Rick Kersey ran off, limping slightly. So Gordon McNulty, the senior operating at less than full effectiveness because of torn knee cartilage, came on for the first time in the game, taking Kersey's spot.

On the next play, Street tried to force the ball to Speyrer again down the left sideline, but defensive halfback Jerry Moore, not buying a stop-and-go fake, was running step-for-step with Speyrer. The pass hung and safety Dennis Berner came over, too, stepped in front of Speyrer, and made the interception at the Razorbacks' 24. If Berner hadn't picked it off, Moore probably would have. For the second time, the Razorback defensive backs didn't buy a short fake and let Speyrer run by them, because of their recognition that Speyrer was the Longhorns' only deep threat.

The Horns' turnover count had reached five. Another touchdown would put the game out of reach, and the Razorbacks went after it. The big plays in the following drive were a Montgomery-to-Dicus wide-receiver screen for 14 yards and an 18-yard Bill Burnett run off an option pitch from Montgomery—with Bruce Maxwell throwing a huge block. But on first-and-10 from the Texas 41, Montgomery tried to call an audible and ran out of time and the Razorbacks drew a delay-of-game penalty. The 5 yards lost were crucial.

On third-and-6 from the Texas 37, Montgomery rolled right and couldn't spot an open receiver, and Bill Atessis finally made the coverage sack near the Arkansas sideline for a loss of 5. The Razorbacks were driving south, in the direction of the wind, and anything but a sack would have left Frank Broyles pondering whether to give Bill McClard a chance to kick a long field goal. But faced with the fourth-and-11 from the 42 (which would have made the field goal attempt 59 yards), Arkansas punted and Cary Stockdell drove it straight through the end zone.

So with 3:24 left in the third quarter, Texas had the ball, trailing 14–0.

"We're still in the game," defensive halfback Tom Campbell says. "But I do remember starting to think negative thoughts on the sideline as the third quarter is coming to an end. I was thinking the offense has got to score some points. They're not even coming close."

As the Longhorns were about to form their huddle, James Street decided it was time for another pep talk. The Longhorns knew Street's speeches almost as well as Royal's transparencies. "Stay steady in the boat, guys! We're all right! We're still going to win! Keep working! Everything's going to be fine!"

That set off Bob McKay, the big offensive tackle.

"No, we're not all right!" thundered McKay. "We're going to get our asses beat if we don't do something! We're running out of time, and it's time to get going! We gotta make something happen! NOW!"

In the first eight plays of the drive, Texas only threw once—when Street hit an 8-yarder to Speyrer on the next-to-last play of the quarter. Other than that, the Horns ground out the yards. After gaining 7 on his second carry of the drive, Steve Worster went limping to the bench, and Bobby Callison replaced him. Street hit a slant to Speyrer for 8 yards to get another first down before Callison gained a yard on the final play of the third quarter.

Going into the final fifteen minutes, Arkansas was still up 14–0. The Longhorns were facing a second-and-9 from the Razorbacks' 42, but the way they were eating up the clock, it heightened the pressure to score—and soon.

DURING THE LONG QUARTER BREAK, Arkansas center Rodney Brand and guard Jerry Dossey sat together on the bench. "The year before we had gotten Southwest Conference championship rings," Brand says of the 1968 team, officially cochampions with Texas. "If you won it again, they'd put a diamond in the top of the ring. So Jerry and I were sitting there saying, 'How big of a diamond are you going to put in your ring?' It was going that good for us."

———————

THE LONGHORNS HUSTLED UP TO THE LINE for the first play of the fourth quarter, but the officials still were holding up the game, thinking—incorrectly—that ABC's commercials weren't over. The network appeared to be confused, too, because there was about thirty seconds of silence on the broadcast. The Longhorns rehuddled briefly, then came back up to the line.

With the Longhorns on the left hashmark, Ted Koy flanked out to the right, with Speyrer. Street dropped to pass, looking for tight end Randy Peschel across the middle for a first down. Defensive tackle Dick Bumpas squeezed through, between center Forrest Wiegand and right guard Mike Dean, as the Longhorns still weren't quite sure of their blocking scheme on the play. Lynn Garner, the linebacker often dropped into the line for this game, burst inside McKay, the right tackle, who essentially overcommitted and overran him. But the key was that Bumpas and Garner both were coming from Street's right, and he could see them. If they had been coming from the blind side, Street wouldn't have stepped up. As it happened, Street took a step to his left, and then up, to avoid Bumpas. Bumpas reached out with his right hand and brushed Street, but couldn't get a grip on him. "I literally had him with my fingertips, and that was all I could get on him," Bumpas says. Wiegand made a heady play to scramble back and chase both Garner and Bumpas, getting between both of them and Street after the quarterback stepped up. "I'd beaten the blocker," Bumpas says of Wiegand, "but . . . he did a good job of pushing me by and I reached and couldn't get anything to hold on to."

Though he missed Garner, who was a half-step behind Bumpas in the race to Street, McKay took off and made a block downfield on defensive halfback Jerry Moore. "I told James, shit, I couldn't afford to let him throw the ball anymore because he'd thrown three or four interceptions," McKay says.

"But I damn sure didn't miss [Garner] on purpose, I promise you. That was the best thing that could have happened to us, though. We screwed up and scored."

After cutting up, Street headed diagonally to the right corner. At the 35, Cliff Powell got an arm on him, but couldn't hold on, and as he lost his grip, Powell collided with defensive end Bruce James. "I dropped back for coverage," Powell says, "and I hit him, but I didn't wrap him up. And he kept going."

Before the collision, James was thinking he was going to nail Street from behind, at an angle. "Because he was cutting back into me, I'm thinking, 'Do I try to strip this ball, or do I try and put him out of the football game?'" James says. "I made the split decision that I'm going to hit him with everything I've got. The next thing I know, I'm upside down from the contact with Cliff Powell. And the rest is history."

Peschel came back to block defensive end Rick Kersey, who was back in the game, and Speyrer rolled and took out both Jerry Moore, coming off the Bob McKay block, and safety Dennis Berner.

A third block on the play still has the Razorbacks screaming *clip!* As Mike Boschetti angled toward Street, halfback Jim Bertelsen closed on the Arkansas linebacker from the side and dove at his legs. When Bertelsen made contact, Street was at the 27, Boschetti at the 28, but also to the side. Bertelsen's dive carried him at Boschetti's side, and he initially appeared to have his helmet in front of Boschetti's feet. But Bertelsen's major contact was a scrape of Boschetti's ankles, and ultimately his heels. Boschetti went down.

"I knew I was going to be clipped on that play as soon as Street started running," Boschetti says. "I went back to my hook zone [where receivers run 'hook' routes]. Bertelsen kind of flared out and went down the sideline behind me, so I knew he was there. As Street broke the line and took off to the other side and I started after him, I just knew Bertelsen was right there. Sure enough he got me on my right ankle. It kind of sprained my ankle slightly. I didn't need to go out of the game, but I did feel a little hitch. I've seen one view of it where it looked like he might have had a good block because he kind of got in front of my left leg, but by the time he got to me, my left leg was up. And so he ended up hitting the back of my right leg."

Was it clipping?

Frank Broyles answers quickly. "Yeah, but that's part of the game," the

Arkansas coach says. "You don't get every call. On a broken play like that, you're going to see players change responsibilities, and we should have made the play. You shouldn't be able to scramble up the middle for a touchdown, but he had the ability to pull it off."

Should the clip have been called? No. It was behind the play, and it would have been a trivial call. But that's based on the same discretionary standard that rules out the tacky offensive interference call on Rees that nullified Dicus's second-quarter touchdown. So the converse point of view—if the call on Rees was made, the clipping call should have been made, too—is eminently defensible.

"Boschetti got clipped," says Rees, who was watching from the sideline. "He got knocked down. I don't think mine was as bad as his. Mike might not have been able to catch Street, but it should have been called."

Boschetti second-guesses himself on one point. "I should have got up and told the referee he clipped me. He probably wouldn't have called it, but I've heard since that's what they did to John. I just wish I had at least pointed it out, and they might have said, 'You know, I saw it!'"

As Street headed toward the flag—at the same corner Dicus had reached only a few minutes earlier—Terry Stewart and Bobby Field both tried to chase him down, but the geometry didn't work. Stewart says, "He cut back and had the angle to the flag and I guess I committed myself too much to the inside. Even though he didn't have great speed, he had good moves."

Field also got caught trying to reverse direction. "A few years ago," Field says, "a friend of mine, a coach, came up with a picture of that play. Street is cutting back and there I am, behind him. My friend wrote on it: 'Poor pursuit angle.' I do remember James Street was faster than I was."

Street says he "was thinking a couple of things. Number one, it sure would be embarrassing to get caught from behind. And number two, can I get stopped before I run into that fence down there? I'd really look stupid if I fell on my ass."

He made it and he stopped a stride before the fence, among a handful of police officers in orange rain slickers. Street turned and looked for penalty flags and didn't see any. After Street's 42-yard touchdown run, the first Longhorn to get to him was Forrest Wiegand—the center who had scrambled back to make a block *behind* Street in the pocket.

"We had to get something going," Wiegand said to Street. "And you did it!"

As Street started back toward the bench, he crossed paths with Stewart—and reached out and handed the ball to the Razorbacks' defensive back. Street insists it wasn't a taunting gesture. "I don't think there was any thought to that, I was just giving the ball to him." Stewart didn't react beyond dropping it and continuing to the preconversion defensive huddle.

Street was headed to the sideline to give way for holder Donnie Wigginton. Quickly, he saw Darrell Royal holding up his hand, gesturing Street to stay out on the field. Street could read his lips. "Two-point play!"

"That's where I give Coach Royal a lot of credit," Street says. "He totally had us prepared, he had me totally prepared. Instead of total confusion, I was ready to go. And I also knew what the play was going to be."

Counter 49.

So why was Royal going for two? Before there was overtime in college football, the most pressure-packed—and often second-guessed—decision for a coach came when his team scored a touchdown to close within one point in the final minutes of a game. Do you kick and take the tie, or do you go for two and the win?

In 1964, the Longhorns were the defending national champions and lost 14–13 to Arkansas when they failed on a two-point conversion attempt with 1:27 left in the game. Royal wasn't the only one with reason to remember it, either. The touchdown that brought the Longhorns to within one point came on a 1-yard run by Ernie Koy, Ted's older brother. And the Longhorns' quarterback whose pass fell incomplete on the two-point attempt was Marvin Kristynik, the older brother of '69 senior reserve defensive back Paul Kristynik. The undefeated '64 Razorbacks claimed a share of the national championship, winning the Football Writers Association's top spot, while Alabama was No. 1 in both wire-service polls before losing to—of all people—Texas in the Orange Bowl and causing the Football Writers Association to designate the Razorbacks the national champs. Royal didn't forget the sense of disappointment of losing that game to Arkansas.

In the '69 game, what Royal did was such a wise preemptive strike that the biggest surprise was that coaches didn't do it more often when their teams were down by 14, then scored a touchdown.

First, consider the scenario if Texas *failed* on the two-point conversion. The Longhorns would have been down 14–6, desperately hoping for a second touchdown. And with a full quarter left, the Longhorns also could have accepted a field goal on the next possession to get within 14–9, and be right where they would have been with a successful two-point conversion, needing another touchdown to win. But if the score stayed 14–6, and the Longhorns scored late in the game, there was no decision at all: Texas would have to go for two and the tie. If the Longhorns made it and the game ended in a tie, nobody could second-guess Royal. He wouldn't have *taken* the tie; he would have *gone* for it. If the Longhorns scored twice, and then twice failed on two-point conversions, and there was no other scoring, they would have lost 14–12. But that potential downside was outweighed by the positives.

"If you're down 14–0 and you're thinking of winning or losing with the two-point play, to me the obvious time to do it is the first time you score," Royal says. "If you miss it, you can come back and have the second time to tie. If you wait until the last touchdown, it's all or nothing."

Street scampered to the huddle, told the Longhorns they were going for two, and called the play. *Counter 49.* There was only one problem with the call. "They weren't in the defense that I anticipated," Royal says, smiling. The two-point planning in Coach Mike Campbell's room the night before was based on the assumption the Razorbacks would be in a tight goal-line defense. Instead, the Razorbacks lined up in a fairly straight 6-5, which they considered a goal-line alignment, but Royal expected the Razorbacks to have as many as eight men in down stances, on the line. Street didn't audible out of the play, though.

At the snap, Street did a quick circle pivot to his right, as Worster—back in the game now—and Ted Koy both took quick fake steps toward the right, mimicking the usual action of the triple option to the right. Then Street, Worster, and Koy all headed left. Jim Bertelsen charged straight ahead to the left-guard hole, and Street faked a handoff to him and ran a couple of steps down the line. His option was a pitch to Koy, who had Worster in front of him to block. The counter actually was going to the strong side, since Peschel lined up to the left, with Field outside him, and Peschel made an effective block inside on the play. Street cut up just outside the tackle and inside the hashmark. Defensive end Rick Kersey was drifting a step, playing the pitch, and Cliff Powell had burst through the right side of the Longhorns' defensive line on a stunt and was chasing Street from behind. As Street cut up, Powell dove, got his arms around Street's legs and dragged him down. As they both rolled, Powell's arms ended up under Street's legs, preventing the quarterback's knee from hitting the turf, and Street's arms—and the ball—ended up in the end zone. "I just barely fell over the line," says Street. Royal calls the gain "three yards and a foot. It was a tight squeeze." As Powell and Street fell, Kersey got caught up in the pile.

Kersey knew his knee was torn asunder, but as he lay facedown on the Astroturf, his good friend, Mike Boschetti, mistakenly thought Kersey was moping because the Longhorns had made the two-point conversion. "He said, 'Get up, Kersey, get up, get up!'" Kersey says. "I'm thinking, 'Man, I'm trying.'"

Kersey had played a terrific game, slicing in from his defensive end spot, but now he had suffered a torn medial collateral ligament in his right knee and, like Texas's Carl White, he was done for the day. (He was helped to the bench, then to the half-house, where trainers taped his knee. He came back out and tried to trot for the coaches, but couldn't. He took a pain pill, sat down on the bench for the rest of the game, and didn't see a thing. He was in both pain and a fog.)

So it was 14–8 with nearly a full quarter to play. "I was thinking, 'OK, great, now we're going,'" Ted Koy says. "It was going to be kind of like an old engine that's not starting and then, boom, it starts up."

On the sideline, the Longhorns' defense hoped the Street run meant the offense had awakened. "Thank you, James," linebacker Scott Henderson says. "It was going to take something like that, and James made a terrific play."

But Texas had to stop the Razorbacks again.

TWENTY-FIVE

Going for Broke

BECAUSE ARKANSAS KICKED OFF TO OPEN BOTH HALVES, and the Longhorns went for two, Texas's Happy Feller didn't kick in the game until the kickoff following the Longhorns' first touchdown. It had been a strange afternoon of inactivity for the junior from Fredericksburg, but he drove the ball through the end zone.

Bill Montgomery started picking apart the Longhorns again. Against zone coverage on the second play of the drive, Montgomery dropped the ball over Glen Halsell to Chuck Dicus, in front of Danny Lester. The play was good for 20 yards, to the Razorback 41.

On third-and-4, Montgomery found Dicus down the middle for 18 yards, but the play was called back because of illegal procedure and the Razorbacks seemed to have gotten another bad break. On the next play, though, Dicus was back in the slot, inside John Rees, and ran another slant across the middle. There was no pressure on Montgomery, and he came right back to throw another strike through traffic to Dicus for 21 yards and a first down on the Texas 37. "Bill could have cooked a steak back there," tackle Mike Kelson asserts.

Montgomery rolled right and hit Rees near the sideline for 13 yards, and the Razorbacks quickly reached the Texas 24. They were going into the wind, so they probably needed a few more yards to give Bill McClard a chance at the field goal that would put them up by nine. On first down, Montgomery didn't like what he saw at the line of scrimmage and called a timeout, the Razorbacks' first of the half. He came over to the sideline and spoke with line coach Merv Johnson, who was talking with his fellow offensive coaches, Don Breaux and Richard Williamson, upstairs. The gist: Keep going at them.

The Longhorns came with an all-out blitz. Again, Rees and Dicus were on the same side—this time the left—so Danny Lester was covering Rees. Because rover Mike Campbell and linebacker Scott Henderson both were blitzing, that left safety Freddie Steinmark alone on Dicus. Steinmark didn't retreat and seemed frozen as Dicus approached him, and it looked as if the little safety was thinking the blitz would force Montgomery to throw quickly. As Dicus cut inside, Steinmark realized the ball wasn't coming and he was about to get beat. So he reached out and grabbed Dicus at the 20, slowing him down. Montgomery lofted the ball down the middle; it landed in the middle of the end zone, well over Dicus's head. Steinmark was called for defensive holding, and the Razorbacks had a first-and-goal from the Texas 9.

From the coaches' booth upstairs, defensive backfield coach Fred Akers reluctantly told Coach Mike Campbell, down on the sideline, that the Longhorns couldn't stick with Steinmark. "That play was so plain, we had to change," Akers says. "We were talking about it, because there were some other plays, too." Steinmark wasn't benched completely, but backup Rick Nabors came in for Steinmark after that play and was on the field much of the rest of the game.

Arkansas now was in field-goal range. McClard began warming up his kicking leg and stretching in earnest. "It's one of those things I can't explain, like there was something that was supposed to happen in my life I had always waited for," McClard says.

On first down, Montgomery rolled right, looking downfield to pass, then kept the ball and ran for 2 yards. Why weren't the Razorbacks just giving the ball to Burnett or Maxwell? They were going for the jugular.

But Mike Kelson would kick himself about the second-down play for years. Montgomery rolled left, and David Arledge beat Kelson and hit Montgomery's arm as the Razorback quarterback released the ball, trying to get it to Dicus. The ball fluttered, dangerously, but it fell to the Astroturf in front of both Dicus and Nabors. The Razorbacks assert Dicus was held again on that play, before the ball went in the air. "They gave Steinmark a holding penalty down on the goal line, but they were holding Chuck all day long," Montgomery says. "But having said that, that's not whining. Texas was the cleanest team of any team I ever played against. They were the hardest-hitting, and the cleanest. But on the goal line, I think their strategy was clear. I'd hold Dicus, too. I'd rather get a holding penalty than give up a touchdown."

Now it was third-and-goal. After looking to the end zone on the first two downs, the safe play would be to run left, get the ball to the middle of the field and—unless Burnett or Maxwell broke the run to the end zone—accept the McClard chip-shot field goal. That would make it 17–8 and force the Longhorns to get at least a touchdown and a field goal to win.

"I thought the game was over then," Darrell Royal says. "I thought they'd run to the middle of the field and McClard will kick the field goal and the game's over."

In the Arkansas coaches' booth, offensive guru Don Breaux and defensive czar Charley Coffey were sitting together. Coffey says he quickly lobbied for a running play. "We had the best field-goal guy in America," Coffey says. "I wanted to get the ball in the middle of the field and kick the field goal. I said, 'We're holding them, it's obvious, and it's going to be hard for them to drive on us.'" Coffey says Breaux ignored him. "I was mad as hell. We were great friends and still are, but during that time, I was really raising sand because he didn't call for the field goal. He just put his head down and shook his head. Look, when I'm thinking and calling defenses, I'm not hearing what Don is saying, so I'm sure he wasn't hearing what I was saying. I'm sure he was thinking of the way he was going to get it in the end zone. But the thing you have to know is that offensive coordinators, especially the good ones, think every damn play is going to be a touchdown, anyway."

Bob Ford, the graduate assistant coach and law student, and another Razorbacks graduate assistant coach, former Baylor quarterback Ken Stockdale, also were in the crowded coaches' booth. They remember the exchange differently. Ford says Breaux reacted to the run-the-ball suggestion vehemently. "Don Breaux took his fist and hit the table and said, 'Damn it, I'm calling 'em!' He hit that table with his fist and the paperwork bounced on it." Breaux called down a rollout pass, and the play was signaled in to Montgomery.

Stockdale, who wrote a book about Southwest Conference rivalries called *The Classic 60's*, says he was the first one to question the call after it went in, asking about a field goal, and that the defensive coaches then reacted. Stockdale says Breaux came back with, "We'll get it next down!"

Breaux since has been through many games, including being on the coaching staff for three Super Bowl championship teams, so it's entirely understandable that he doesn't remember the sequence of events in the coaching booth before that one play. "Charley's got a pretty good memory," Breaux says, in all sincerity. "I have to be truthful, I just don't remember the circumstances surrounding that."

(Stockdale also says Breaux tossed his headset out the booth window, then pulled it back with its cord, after the apparent touchdown pass to Dicus in the second quarter was called back, which alarmed the Secret Service agents watching President Nixon below. None of the others remember that, either.)

Some of the Razorbacks recollect a timeout before the third-and-goal play, and recall that Montgomery and the coaches talked over the play, but they're mistaken. There was no timeout; in fact, only about twenty-five seconds passed between the instant Montgomery's second-down incomplete pass hit the Astroturf and the moment Montgomery, after being signaled in the play, stepped into the huddle to relay the call to his teammates.

Twenty-five seconds, and that even includes the few seconds it took Merv Johnson to signal in the call, using gestures that first specified the formation and then the play. (It was a digital code, with spots on the body representing numbers.) So there was no time for debate, and this much is clear: Any exchanges in the coaches' booth must have been very brief.

The case for Breaux's call: The Razorbacks were moving the ball. Breaux had been brilliant in both coming up with a game plan and then adjusting it on the fly to take advantage of the Texas defensive schemes. All game, he maneuvered to get one of the best receivers in the country—Dicus—into single-coverage situations, whether against Danny Lester or Mike Campbell. Even Texas defensive end Bill Atessis says he wasn't shocked by the call because "they called a great game. They kept us off-balance all day." This was Don Breaux, the modernist, continuing to go against the grain of conventionality.

"In a critical time, we called on two of our best players," Breaux says. "I think I would do it again under those circumstances."

Merv Johnson doesn't remember his reaction when he got the play call from Breaux. Given the time frame, of course, he had to be most concerned about translating it into the signals for Montgomery. "I think we had a lot of confidence in Montgomery and probably after the fact regretted having him throw a pass with that amount of risk to it," Johnson says. "A field goal would have been so big then. Hindsight tells us we should have been more conservative."

The play was a sprint-out pass, with Montgomery coming to the left.

"By then, I knew the coaches so well, I usually knew what was going to be called, and I wasn't surprised," Montgomery says.

Guard Jerry Dossey says that when Montgomery called the pass, "he had a Cheshire grin. I'm stunned. We were all stunned. But then instantly, I'm thinking, 'They're never going to expect that! It's six points! Texas will never believe we're calling this play!'"

That was Breaux's point.

Guard Ronnie Hammers recalls thinking, "'What did they call? Why are we doing that?' But there again, it happened so fast, even though you're wondering, you don't doubt because everything's worked so far."

Tight end Pat Morrison is emphatic that he "thought that was probably the right call to make. We were trying to score a touchdown and really put the game away. I never had any question or problem with that."

Others, including an always-winded Bruce Maxwell, didn't think much about it. "I was a guy who just got in the huddle and ran the play that was called," Maxwell says. "I wasn't thinking about the field goal. In retrospect, I wish we had taken it, but I'll tell you one thing I know all of us feel—Billy Montgomery played so good for us, we wouldn't have been anywhere without him."

If the pass worked, the Razorbacks would pretty much clinch the national championship—at least the prebowl championship and Nixon's plaque. The theory was that if Dicus wasn't open, the incompletion would leave the Razorbacks with fourth-and-goal, and McClard would kick about a 24-yarder from the right hashmark.

In the Texas defensive huddle, the Longhorns were screaming at one another, to be heard. "This is another one of those things where you almost have to believe that the Lord took some goofy thing and put it in Frank Broyles's mind," Tom Campbell says. "We were yelling that they're going to run the ball and we have to stop them and then block the field goal! There's absolutely no doubt in our minds that they're going to do a quarterback sneak up the middle or run, then kick the field goal."

But the Longhorns also reminded themselves of one of Coach Mike Campbell's mantras: *Even if you think you know what they're doing, stick to your own responsibility!* In practice and film work, he preached that he didn't like it when defensive backs didn't honor the threat of the pass, coming up to try to make tackles in the running game. So the defensive halfbacks—Lester and

Tom Campbell—reminded themselves not to come up fast. Besides, if the Razorbacks were simply going to run a little dive play or a quarterback sneak to the left, they weren't going to be involved, anyway.

On the sideline, Texas split end Cotton Speyrer was doing the math. "Hmmm," he thought, "17–8? Tough duty."

In the stands, a former Houston high school football coach—Ed Kelson—was glowing. With his son at left tackle, the Razorbacks were on the verge of clinching the national title. "I was just thinking about the man I had to block," Mike Kelson says. "But my dad told me later, he was sitting there saying, 'That's it! That's the end of the game! All they need to do is kick the goddamn field goal and the game's over!'" At that point, Ed Kelson and Darrell Royal were thinking a lot alike.

In her seat behind the Texas bench, Kathy Pulley wondered whether her son's team was going to be able to pull off a miracle, and she watched her boy—Danny Lester—trot out to work against Dicus man-to-man, clear across the field from the Texas sideline.

Third-and-goal from the 7.

Breaux got exactly the coverage he foresaw. "We wanted to get man coverage outside, and hoped for [Lester] to be a little bit inside," Breaux says.

Both Morrison, who split out slightly from his usual tight-end spot, and Rees went to the right. Dicus was split left, going one-on-one with Lester. The kid who could party into the night and run windsprints four hours later, who lost both a father and a stepfather, lined up only 2 yards off the line of scrimmage, on Dicus's inside shoulder, all but daring Dicus to break outside.

"When the play's called, I knew I had limited yardage to work with and I needed to beat this guy on an out route," Dicus says. "I wanted to make sure I didn't give it away with my alignment. I needed to [line up far enough inside] to give me room for an out, but I couldn't do it too much because I might tip something off."

Montgomery rolled to the left, cocked, and threw for Dicus, who had broken toward the side of the end zone. Lester still was on his inside. But twisting to make the right-handed throw going to his left, Montgomery slightly underthrew and floated the pass. If Lester hadn't been there, Dicus would have been able to turn on the move and catch the ball on his inside shoulder. It didn't work out that way.

As Dicus turned back to reach for the ball to his inside, Lester cut up and made the interception a step inside the end zone. He took off down the sideline. In the stands, his mother couldn't see a thing. "Everybody stood up in front of me," Kathy Pulley says. Montgomery made the tackle on the Texas 20.

"Dicus, in my opinion, was open on the play," Montgomery says. "In one of those stricken moments of fate, the ball was underthrown. It's been described in various ways. People go, 'Did you choke, did you shortarm it, did you do this?' I mean, who knows? I had only thrown at this time eight bazillion passes and football is unlike golf, it's kind of a hard sport to choke in because things are happening so fast. In that split instant, in that incredibly fine split instant that goes from the brain to the arm, was there something that made me throw it differently? I don't know. It was not a very well-thrown ball from me. If it had been well thrown, I think Chuck would have caught it and we would have scored. I threw a bad pass. It was poor execution. Calling the play doesn't cause me to have poor execution."

On the Texas sideline, James Street yanked off his orange jacket and hollered, "This is it! Here we go!" The offense charged onto the field.

WHAT WAS FRANK BROYLES THINKING when he didn't overrule the call? Some of the players believe the Arkansas coach was trying to put to rest, once and for all, his reputation for conservatism. Three years earlier, the Razorbacks were going after their seventeenth straight Southwest Conference victory against Baylor, when on a fourth-and-3 from the *Baylor* 29, Broyles ordered a "pooch" punt to pin the Bears back in the still-scoreless game. The snap went over the punter's head, Baylor took over at midfield, and the Bears drove down for the only touchdown of the game to win 7–0. After that, for all his success, Broyles had to hear himself called, "Pooch Kick Frank." And although he had hired Breaux and the Razorbacks' 1969 offense was inventive and more like what some schools were running in the Southeast and the West, Broyles still was sensitive to the charges.

The argument makes sense, but it also is overly analytical. Because there was no timeout, the call and the play unfolded quickly, and Broyles was more than anything sticking to his practice of delegating authority and trusting his bright staff. Broyles was a great head coach *because* of his confidence in his staff and delegation of authority, not despite it. He knew what was coming, but he didn't overrule it.

Broyles notes that Montgomery hadn't thrown an interception since the fourth game of the season, against Baylor. "We felt that was even a better chance to complete the pass than our field-goal kicker making the field goal," Broyles says. "We'd had some bad snaps. In the back of my mind, there was always that possibility of a bad snap, or missing the field goal, or getting it blocked, and I thought we had two chances to win the game."

If the Razorbacks *had* taken a timeout, it might have been different. Even if they called the pass, everyone—especially Montgomery—would have been reminded that it either had to be complete for a touchdown or thrown harmlessly away, or Montgomery could have dived to the middle of the field himself. The timeout also might have enabled Coffey and the others to get Broyles's ear and argue for the field goal, or even for Breaux to further ponder the call—and the dissent—and change his mind.

The players, though, have long considered Broyles's mention of snapping problems—something he brought up in his 1979 autobiography—to be off-target. Center Rodney Brand, the All-American, also snapped for punts and placements. He laughs about hitting McClard in the helmet on an extra point against Texas A&M, then being met by Merv Johnson as he came off the field and hearing: "If we lose this game 7–6, you better find a bus back to Newport." But at the implication that the Razorbacks had season-long problems with snaps and holds, Brand explodes—incredulously, not angrily. "Naw, I don't think so! I don't remember that being a problem." In fact, he says his nailing of McClard in the helmet "was the only bad snap I had all year." The Razorbacks already had kicked two extra points in the game, in the cold and damp conditions, and this field goal would have been only 4 yards longer than a conversion.

McClard also says there weren't significant problems. "Gus Rusher was a real good holder," he says, adding that Brand "got it back in a hurry and we didn't get a single kick blocked all year."

Fred Akers watched the play unfold from the Texas coaches' booth. "You have to scratch your head a little bit about why they even would try it," the Longhorns' defensive backfield coach says. "What's the old saying? In coaching, more games are lost than won? I'm not so sure that wasn't the case right there."

Judged with conventional wisdom, the play was an awful call. Yet as Merv Johnson points out, that's easy to say in hindsight. If the Razorbacks had taken the safe route, made the field goal, and gone ahead 17–8, Texas would have needed a touchdown and a field goal to win, and while that seems unlikely, it wouldn't have been impossible. A 21–8 Arkansas lead, forcing the Longhorns to get two touchdowns, would have been even more secure.

This play was not the only daring risk taken in the game. When dangerous—even inexplicable—calls work, they're brilliant. When they don't, they are moronic. The third-and-goal pass play was an ill-advised gamble. But if it had worked, Don Breaux would have been toasted as a go-for-broke genius.

Did he ponder running the ball and taking the field goal? "No," says Breaux, "and in retrospect, that would have been great. We were criticized later, but that's part of it. But we had confidence that play would work, and it was just one of those things."

This much is indisputable: While trying to put the game completely out of reach, the Razorbacks kept the Longhorns in it. After Lester's interception, the Longhorns still were down 14–8, with 10:34 remaining.

———————

WITH RICK KERSEY out with the injured knee, Gordon McNulty—the senior from Pine Bluff who started out at Vanderbilt—knew he would have to finish out the game at defensive end, playing on his torn knee cartilage. He wasn't brimming with confidence. "It wasn't so much pain as it was instability," he says. "It just didn't work quite right."

On many plays, the Longhorns were using either Jim Bertelsen or Ted Koy as a flanker and going with two backs behind Street, because Arkansas was playing only the three defensive backs and controlling the running game. On a third-and-4 from the 26, Street hit tight end Randy Peschel across the middle, just past Cliff Powell, for 15 yards and a first down. It was Peschel's first catch of the day. Then Speyrer went 14 yards on an end-around. The Longhorns were pulling out all the tricks now. Two plays later, on a third-and-3 from the Arkansas 39, the Longhorns finally went back to the basic triple option, going to the left—again to the tight-end side, into the "monster" side of the defense. Bobby Field had been banged on the knee, and his backup, Steve Birdwell, was spelling him. Birdwell did a good job of fighting off Peschel, who didn't brush by him this play, and then going after the pitch man, Ted Koy. Street was tackled by Dick Bumpas as he pitched to Koy, who couldn't hang on, and Gordon McNulty recovered at the 42. It was Texas's *sixth* turnover.

The Razorbacks had another chance to put it away.

Two Bill Burnett runs gained only 1 yard, and Montgomery took a third-down sack after he didn't see a receiver open and held the ball in the pocket. Cary Stockdell punted the ball high and short against the wind, and Speyrer made a fair catch of the 28-yarder at the Texas 36.

The clock showed 6:10 left in the game.

Koy ran for 1 yard, then Steve Worster gained 4 and 2 yards on consecutive carries, and the Longhorns faced fourth-and-3 from their own 43. The ball was on the left hashmark, to the same side as the Texas bench. Quickly, it was obvious that Texas wasn't going to punt.

With 4:47 remaining, Street called timeout and trotted over to the sideline to talk with Darrell Royal.

TWENTY-SIX

Right 53 Veer Pass

As tackle Bob McKay frequently noted, Darrell Royal did not run a one-man, one-vote democracy. But as the quarterback and captain, James Street at least had a voice in the decision-making process. As he arrived at the sideline, he knew what he would call, given the choice—another counter option, this one to the short side of the field and away from what Street by now recognized was the defensively overloaded tight-end side. It had worked on a fourth-and-2 on the Longhorns' final possession of the first half, when Street cut up for 3 yards, and this play was going to be from the same hashmark, going the same direction.

"I wanted to go strong to the wide side of the field," Street says. "I knew they would overshift to the wide side, and that would make it easier for me to get three yards the other way. All I have to do is get inside that end."

So Street lobbied Royal. "Coach, if we set the formation up, I can make three yards on the outside option!"

In the pressbox, offensive coach Emory Bellard was talking over the headset phone to Royal. Street always has presumed Bellard was arguing for an option play as well, but Bellard says that isn't true. Bellard's call was going to be a pass—a play-action delay to tight end Randy Peschel over the middle, theoretically underneath the coverage after Cotton Speyrer went deep and linebackers took the play-action fake.

Just as Broyles rarely vetoed play calls, Royal rarely overruled Bellard. This time, he did. "No, we're going deep!" Royal said to Bellard, with Street standing there.

Royal turned to Street. "All right," he said, "tell you what we're going to run. Right 53 veer pass!"

Street was dumbfounded. In the Longhorns' parlance, the "right" was the formation call. It meant the split end—Speyrer—was to the right, and the actual strength of the formation was to the left, where Peschel lined up. The "53" meant Street would go left, faking the 53 veer running play, then dropping to pass. That, coupled with the formation, meant he had one receiver going deep—the tight end, or "TED" in Texas terminology. *Deep to 'TED'?* That's just *not* the way the Longhorns did it. Peschel was counted on as the solid blocker and short-game receiver. Hell, he still wore his old wingback number—40, which looked weird as hell on a tight end. Everyone knew *anything* deep went to the speedy Speyrer; everyone, including the Razorbacks, whose defensive scheme quite reasonably incorporated that assumption. And that was exactly why Royal called Peschel's number.

"OK," Street said, and took a couple of steps back toward the huddle. "I'm sitting here, registering, 'right 53 veer pass,'" Street says. "Randy Peschel is the only guy going out and he's going deep. I have one receiver to hit, and if this son of a bitch doesn't work, I don't have anyone else to throw to. So I'm wondering if Coach Royal means 'left,' which means Cotton going deep. That might make more sense to me."

Street came back to Royal and ran through it one more time. "Right 53 veer pass," Street said to Royal. "We got one receiver going out, Coach, and that's 'TED'? He's going deep? Are you sure that's what you want to run?"

"DAMN RIGHT!"

Defensive coach Mike Campbell heard the call and wasn't exactly brimming with confidence. Instantly, he turned and approached the members of the defense. Tom Campbell, the defensive halfback, wasn't even sure of the fourth-down circumstances. "All of a sudden my dad is standing in front of me and the other guys on the defense and saying, 'Defense, get ready! We gotta get the ball back!'"

Linebacker Scott Henderson smiles and shakes his head, remembering. "'Defense, get ready!' That's exactly what he said. So I got up."

Upstairs, Longhorns defensive backfield coach Fred Akers had the same initial reaction as Street. *Could Coach Royal have the formation fouled up?* "We thought he had got turned around," Akers says. "That happens, you know!" Like Street, Akers wondered if Royal had meant the play to go to Speyrer. "I asked Mike Campbell, 'What'd he say?' He had called the veer pass to the wrong side, I thought," Akers says. "I thought, 'Oh, my God, no!' But, man, he knew what he was doing!"

Royal remembered Peschel talking about how fast the Arkansas defensive backs were coming up to play the run. And, finally, he had a gut feeling that he needed to gamble. "That was the time to put it all on the line," Royal says.

"If we had run for a first down, we'd have lost the game. We weren't moving the ball. It was one of those situations where you have to swing from the floor and hope you put a square peg in a round hole."

Street headed back to the huddle, thinking, *Man, the guys aren't going to believe this one! I've got to sell it!*

The Longhorns were all kneeling in a loose imitation of their round huddle, waiting through the timeout. For all the struggles the Longhorns had that afternoon, theirs was a great offensive line, and the five men up front still were thinking: *Run the damn ball! Let us go after these guys!*

As Street arrived at the huddle, Peschel had just gotten up and was putting on his helmet. "Peschel, don't look at me!" Street said, conspiratorially.

Peschel asked himself: *What the hell is he saying that for?* But he didn't look at Street. "James's eyes were as big as saucers," guard Mike Dean says. Street looked first at Speyrer, and kept returning his gaze to the split end through his spiel. If the Razorbacks were watching, he wanted them to think he was going over a pass route with Speyrer.

"Guys," he said, "you aren't gonna believe this call, but it's gonna work! It *will* work! We're gonna run right 53 veer pass, and that means you're the only receiver, Peschel, and you're going deep!"

Memories differ on the reaction. Several players—including Peschel, center Forrest Wiegand, and tackle Bobby Wuensch—recall that Bob McKay said something along the lines of, "You gotta be shittin' me!" McKay says that isn't true, and others—including Street and Mike Dean—back him on that. Whether McKay said it or not is almost irrelevant, as Steve Worster points out. "We all kind of looked at each other and said, just by looking, 'What?'" Worster says. "I thought it was all or nothing right there. I don't remember Bob saying anything, but I guarantee you, *everybody* in the huddle was *thinking*, 'You gotta be shittin' me!'"

But all agree, Street took control and sold it. *They won't be expecting this! It will work!*

(It's a good thing this was a long timeout.)

Finally, though, Street tried to leave himself a safety net. He told Peschel that if he decided he couldn't get deep, if the defensive backs didn't bite on the fake, he should cut the route short, come back, and Street would get him the ball. *No matter what, we gotta get the first down!* He says he had some nightmares later in which Peschel broke off the route, Street threw the ball about 25 yards over his head and had to explain that to an irate Darrell Royal.

Speyrer trotted out to the right, to his split-end position, with mixed feelings. "Personally," Speyrer says, laughing, "I thought it should have gone to *moi*, if we're going to throw the ball. But then I thought it could be a great call. I thought Randy Peschel would be wide open. I'm going to run down the field, congratulate him for scoring a touchdown, the whole bit."

The Razorbacks didn't watch Street stare at Speyrer, or at least they didn't buy it. The coaches' defensive call, relayed to Cliff Powell, was "80 short," a goal-line defense designed to stop the run.

At the start of the play, the two buddies from Longview were only a yard or so apart—James Street, taking the snap, and Terry Don Phillips, the Razorbacks' defensive tackle. In 80 short, Phillips says, his job was "to execute a goal-line charge and build a pile, and your linebackers run up and go to the football."

Powell got ready to play the Longhorns' straight triple option. "That was what we were geared for," he says.

Peschel says his first concern was getting off the line of scrimmage. Steve Birdwell still was in for Bobby Field at the "monster" spot, and he lined up outside Peschel. Street took the snap and started the triple-option action, riding a fake to Worster to his left. Carrying out the fake, Worster leaned forward and fell onto his knees, just short of the first-down marker.

On his first step, Peschel made a slight blocking motion at Birdwell with his left shoulder and forearm. It was as if he coiled to make the block, but didn't uncoil. The Longhorn tight end and the Razorback monster back brushed one another. As he was supposed to do in this defense, Birdwell stepped across the line of scrimmage to play the option. Peschel was off the line of scrimmage and into the pattern, heading downfield and angling slightly toward the sideline. That route was designed to give him more breathing room if the safety—Dennis Berner—came over. Peschel made the decision to go deep, even though right defensive halfback Jerry Moore hadn't significantly bought the fake and turned around to run after Peschel.

This is a crucial point, especially in light of the misconceptions that abounded later: If Peschel was on his side, Moore was *encouraged* to read the tight end's first move and rush up if it looked as if Peschel was blocking. And on this play, in a short-yardage defense, with the expectation that the Long-horns would run the option, it would have been understandable if Moore had *sprinted* up to play the run, even though it would have been a mistake.

Moore didn't make that mistake.

After Peschel's feinted block, Moore made a smart play to spot the pass soon enough to recover, turn, and run with Peschel, which didn't leave Berner as the only defender. (Nobody remembers if the Razorbacks were playing man-to-man or zone on the tight-end side on that specific play, but the way it worked out, Peschel ended up being double covered.)

"We have our defense set to defend the run," Moore says. "We've got everybody packed in there to stop it, thinking that they're going to run the ball. My read is through the tight end." Moore noticed Peschel's coiling move at Birdwell. "In watching the film, I think I did initially take a step up when he blocked down or whatever," Moore says. "But he released and I re-covered and got back."

Berner also reacted quickly, angling over from the middle of the field to chase Peschel. "I just took off for the guy Street was looking at," Berner says.

After the fake to Worster, Street dropped diagonally, taking five quick steps and setting up to throw. Jim Bertelsen threw a block on Birdwell, in case he decided to charge at Street. Terry Don Phillips and Gordon McNulty both went low and ended up on the turf, and McNulty jumped back up to reach for the pass. He didn't come close. But he wasn't worried, either. "When Street put the ball up there, I was thinking, 'He ain't got a prayer!'" McNulty says.

Street threw the ball from the Texas 39; it wasn't a laser, and it wasn't a soft rainbow. It was an arching quasi-spiral with just the right touch, and he led Peschel slightly toward the sideline, which was crucial.

"When I first looked back, I thought, 'This is overthrown,'" Peschel says. "I just kept running and looked back again, and there it was."

By the time the ball came down, Moore was *less than a step* behind Peschel, a couple of feet closer to the sideline. Berner was there as well, about a half-step back. On the run, sensing the ball was arriving, Moore reached out with his right arm, raising his hand slightly. Berner reached around Peschel's back, to the inside, with his left arm.

"Actually, I think I touched the ball with the tip of my [left] ring finger," Berner says. "Barely a touch."

For several strides, Peschel was looking over his outside shoulder. "This is what I see here, one hand from each of them," he says, crossing his own wrists. The ball made it through the maze, into Peschel's hands.

The pass was perfect, and the play gained 43 yards. In the clutch, with the national championship on the line, with his teammates wondering what the hell was going on, James Street put the ball exactly where he had to. If thrown shorter, or with a minuscule flattening, the pass would have been incomplete, probably knocked down by either Moore or Berner. Maybe a foot longer, it would have been incomplete. A foot more to the center of the field, Berner would have batted it down—or even gotten hit by the ball. A quarterback not known for his passing ability, with it all on the line, made an absolutely perfect pass. It was the only way it would have worked.

The catch was clutch as well. As he angled slightly toward the sideline, Peschel focused on the ball through the hands and caught it at the Arkansas 18, holding on as Berner dragged him down at the 13 and Moore fell on him. All three slid over the sideline.

"I remember faking through the hole, and naturally being knocked down to my knees, which I always was," Steve Worster says. "I was looking at the pass and Randy making that phenomenal catch. And, yeah, I *was* going, 'You gotta be shittin' me!'"

The entire play was based on the assumption the Razorbacks would be fooled, but they weren't.

"Three guys go for the ball and, give the guy credit, he makes a miraculous catch," Jerry Moore says.

Razorbacks linebacker Mike Boschetti was distraught. "I had gone back to my hook zone, and then kind of turned and followed the ball," he says. "It sickened my stomach when he caught it. They teach you as linebackers to play the run first and then get back in your hook zone, but if you ever commit too far, just go ahead and rush the passer because you'll never get back anyway. I've looked at the film since and there was a big opening where I could have gotten to Street. If I had actually continued on that path I could have been in his face."

Boschetti probably couldn't have gotten to Street, but that's the kind of *what-if* mind game the Razorbacks have been playing for years.

Back upfield after the play, Street was still standing. He noticed his buddy, Phillips, prone at his feet. He reached down and tapped Phillips, and nudged him, as if he was trying to help him up. "Come on, Terry Don," Street said. "The ball's down there! Come on, buddy!"

Phillips laughs about that. "'Come on!'" he says, shaking his head. "It was a great call, a great throw, a great catch. How many times out of ten could they execute that? That might have been the only time. But you only need to do it once."

Peschel rolled over onto his back and, while prone, flipped the ball to the official marking the spot. Berner quickly got up and trotted toward the huddle. Moore had done a somersault, and he was a little stunned. He struggled to his feet and wobbled a bit, walking toward the center of the field to join the other Razorbacks.

"We had the safety man and the halfback there," Frank Broyles says. "We don't know why odd things happen, but they happen in sports."

Charley Coffey, the defensive coach, doesn't fault the coverage, either. Never has, never will. "It seemed like there was something miraculous about it," Coffey says.

Royal calls it a "perfect throw and a great catch, and both of those things had to happen." And if the play—a daring gamble—hadn't worked? "Oh, man, I'd have been the biggest idiot of all time," Royal says.

The first four Longhorns to get to Peschel were offensive linemen—in quick succession, Bobby Wuensch, Forrest Wiegand, Bob McKay, and Mike Dean. "McKay and I were like little kids let out into the schoolyard," Dean says. McKay belted Peschel and—using Peschel's nickname among his teammates—said, "Nice catch, Pasquale!"

The Longhorns still were 13 yards away from the potentially game-winning touchdown. "All I know is that our sideline was celebrating, so I figure we've scored a touchdown," Tom Campbell says. "Then I realize we're only down to the 13. So I went back and sat down."

The next play was a run off left tackle, with Jim Bertelsen leading the way through the hole for Ted Koy, slanting across from his right halfback spot. It started out with Street faking to Worster, who went over left guard. Wuensch and Mitchell both blocked inside, leaving McNulty able to slant in from left end and hit Worster. Rather than joining that pile, Bertelsen went right past McNulty and took on Boschetti, the linebacker, driving him back. Koy burst through the hole, broke arm tackles from Bobby Field and Moore, and finally was dragged down by Boschetti. "Bertelsen gets a good block, and I come off of that, and I thought for a moment I had carried it all the way in," Koy says.

The play went for 11 yards, and the Longhorns had both a first-and-goal from the 2 and a better idea of how to block the Coffey-designed defense—have a lead back bypass the pile and go after the linebacker.

The Longhorns didn't fool around, and Bertelsen, whether inadvertently or intentionally, was rewarded for that block. On the next play, Street turned to his right, did a quick feint toward Worster, who headed over right guard, then did a reverse pivot and handed off to Bertelsen. The halfback from Wisconsin went between Mitchell and Wuensch, on the left side. Boschetti and Moore dragged him down, but he fell over the goal line. Boschetti confesses he also grabbed Bertelsen's facemask, but there was no flag. Cliff Powell stood over Bertelsen, distraught and looking down. Gordon McNulty was on his knees in the end zone, watching Bertelsen cradle the ball. Peschel raised both arms, giving the "Hook 'em Horns" sign.

But the score was only tied, 14–14. Now it was up to Happy Feller. This extra point was the Longhorns' first placekick of the game. The holder was his roommate, reserve quarterback Donnie Wigginton.

When Feller and Wigginton went on the field, Feller made a mistake: He started thinking. "My heart's pumping," he says. "If I miss this kick, I'll be exiled from the state of Texas. I probably won't be able to go back. I might as well go over to the other team's bench and join the Arkansas team."

Wiegand's snap was slightly high and into Wigginton's body, and the reserve QB did a good job—especially under the pressure-packed circumstances—of reaching over, then putting the ball down on the pad. The kick sliced slightly to the right, but was good enough. Wigginton leaped high. Feller turned around and trotted back upfield.

"I wanted to give the impression to the rest of the team that, 'Hey, this game isn't over!'" Feller says. "If there were three seconds left in the game, that would have been one thing. But there were three minutes left in the game."

Actually, the clock showed 3:58.

Texas led 15–14.

TWENTY-SEVEN

To the Finish

HAPPY FELLER'S KICKOFF was going to fly in the same direction as all the others in the game so far—north to south, toward the football practice fields and the presidential landing pad, and away from the hill between the stadium and the administration building. The ABC representative who told Dr. Gordon Morgan that the network only showed the games and didn't get into politics was wrong, of course, because the halftime and pending postgame appearances of President Nixon weren't exactly third-and-8 draw plays, either. Yet the network never showed the huge peace sign or protest banners that still were visible on the hill and were impossible to miss from most of the pressbox, even long after the demonstrators left.

As physics professor Bud Zinke checked the progress of the game and asked around, he figured out that ABC hadn't acknowledged that Nixon's appearance generated the anti–Vietnam War protest—and he assumed the network wouldn't do so during the rest of the game, either. On this day, even Spiro Agnew couldn't have complained about negativism in the coverage of the administration.

Feller again kicked the ball through the end zone. The Razorbacks were on their own 20, needing to drive at least 55 yards to have a realistic shot at the game-winning field goal. Arkansas's Bill McClard had a strong leg but was honest with the coaches about his range against the wind. He thought he could kick a 40-yarder, maybe one even from 42. "I could have kicked one 55, 56 yards, no problem, without any wind," he says. So as Bill Montgomery trotted on the field with the offense, the quarterback knew he needed to get the Razorbacks to at least the Texas 25 to give McClard a chance against the wind.

Montgomery exuded confidence, and the rest of the Razorbacks shared it. Hadn't they moved the ball? Weren't they capable of doing it again? Didn't they have one of the best kickers in the country—if they needed the cocky, bubble-gum-popping sophomore to make the game-winning field goal? Wasn't the nation about to witness one of the all-time great clutch drives?

The precipitation had turned from a mist to an open-the-umbrellas rainfall. Montgomery began the drive with a 5-yard completion to Chuck Dicus across the middle. Scott Henderson made the tackle, then calmly and immediately turned to the bench to get the defensive call for the next play. On second down, tight end Pat Morrison couldn't hold on to a short pass over the middle when he was hit by linebacker Bill Zapalac as the ball arrived. A 4-yard completion to Dicus, with Glen Halsell nailing him over the middle, left the Razorbacks facing a fourth down and less than a yard to go at their own 29. As the Razorbacks came up to the line, several Texas defenders signaled for a timeout: The Longhorns hadn't been able to make their defensive call. After the timeout, Bill Burnett dove over left guard behind Bruce Maxwell for 2 yards and the first down at the 31. The clock was running, passing 2:40 left in the game.

On the sideline, McClard was getting ready, which for him mostly meant light stretching and mentally challenging himself. "We didn't have little nets to kick into in those days," McClard says.

Hootie Ingram, who coached the defensive backs, approached the kicker.

"Get loose! Get ready!" he hollered at McClard.

"I'm fine, Coach. I'm ready."

The Razorbacks continued chipping away. Montgomery started flaring the ball out to Bill Burnett. Most of the game, Bill Zapalac was responsible for Burnett and the flares didn't seem open, but now the Texas outside linebacker was dropping into the middle, trying to help against the slants. Burnett was supposed to make sure he wasn't needed to block Zapalac or any other blitzing linebacker. "If the outside linebacker is going back to cover the curl, which is what Dicus is doing, then I take off in the flat," Burnett says.

On first down, Montgomery had plenty of time to survey the field and hit Burnett along the left sideline for 9 yards.

Between plays, the Arkansas band played, "Charge!"

Montgomery cut up on an option for the first down at the Arkansas 42. His shoe came off his heel, though, and after he put it back on and got back to the huddle, he didn't have enough time to decipher the play being signaled in and had to call the Razorbacks' second timeout with 2:21 left.

By now, McClard knew he was ready, and he took a knee on the sideline to watch, occasionally dropping his head in contemplation.

Hootie Ingram came back to McClard. "You sure you're ready?"

"Yeah, Coach, I'm fine!"

On first down, Bruce Maxwell gained 2 on a draw play, with Scott Henderson making the solo tackle. Then Montgomery threw twice more to Bill Burnett, both times on a play called "66 Special." The Razorbacks had enough faith in the offensive line, which generally had protected the mobile Montgomery, to send both Maxwell and Burnett out in the pattern after they checked for the blitz.

The first to Burnett went for 10 yards and another first down at the Texas 46, with Burnett making the catch with his back to the sideline and then falling out of bounds. The second was along the left sideline, again, and Bill Zapalac this time came over to nail Burnett after a 7-yard gain.

"Montgomery was just uncanny," defensive halfback Tom Campbell says. "We weren't making it easy on him on that drive. The moment he releases the ball, he gets clobbered by a defensive end or linebacker or maybe the ball is thrown and it literally goes off the tip of one of our linebackers. The entire day was like that."

The Razorbacks had second-and-3 from the Texas 39. Montgomery came to the line of scrimmage, didn't like what he saw—an apparent blitz—and called Arkansas's final timeout rather than an audible. He came over to the sideline, talking to Mervin Johnson with Broyles next to them, minus a headset.

Hootie Ingram spotted McClard, still kneeling. The coach approached the kicker, reaching out and grabbing him by the shoulder pads. "McClard! Do you realize that we're fixing to give you a chance to win the national championship? AND I DON'T THINK YOU'RE WARMED UP YET!"

McClard got up, not saying anything, and walked away. He knew he was ready—if the Razorbacks got a little closer. A field-goal attempt at this point would have been 56 yards, impossible against the wind. By the kicker's calculations, the Razorbacks needed at least another 14 yards. The Longhorns could do the math, too, and knew they had to take away the Razorbacks' short passing game. Still, some of the Razorbacks question why they just didn't keep dumping the ball to Burnett, or otherwise stick to the short game.

"In my mind," Montgomery confesses, "I'm going, 'Why don't we just keep doing this?'"

Even Frank Broyles says, "We should have stayed with short passes in hindsight and could have gotten down there. One more completion would have gotten us in field-goal range."

The call coming out of the timeout was a rollout to the right, with Rees and Dicus both split to that side.

Tom Campbell was on Rees and Mike Campbell was covering Dicus. Before the snap, Tom Campbell barked to his brother, "Don't let him inside!" Tom lined up on Rees's inside shoulder, only 3 yards off the line of scrimmage. They had help deep from safety Rick Nabors.

The Arkansas backs, Burnett and Maxwell, both swung to the right, too, to block on the rollout for Montgomery. First Maxwell and then Burnett threw blocks at Bill Atessis.

Dicus ran about a 12-yard out, Rees about a 20-yard route on the same sideline. The two receivers *were* close together, and while that stands out, it probably didn't have anything to do with what happened next because Tom Campbell was locked onto Rees, disregarding Dicus.

Rees ran downfield, with Tom Campbell turning and running with him. One Horn, one Hog. It looked similar to the play earlier in the fourth quarter when Rees ran a route along the same sideline and came back to the ball, making a catch for 13 yards in front of Tom Campbell. This time, it worked out differently.

"You talk about a guy being in someone's hip pocket?" asks defensive backs coach Fred Akers. "Well, Tom was *in* his hip pocket. I tell you, Tom and Mike both were smart. They could read things so quickly and they weren't afraid to take risks."

"[Rees] starts putting on the brakes, and when he does, I was expecting him to go to the inside," Tom says. "But I wasn't leaning to the inside, and when he stopped and cut to the outside, I was absolutely in a perfect position to stop that play because I was a half-step behind him, pretty much between him and Montgomery. A lot of times you'll see the defensive back in the right position, but the footwork isn't quite right. As soon as Rees's foot hits the ground, mine hits the ground, and I cut at the exact moment he did. When I did, I just turned to the outside and I was looking at the receiver's eyes. Rees looked back, and [I did too]."

The ball already was on its way. Montgomery was trying to get the Razor-backs within field-goal range with this one throw. The ball was going to be in line with Rees's inside shoulder. Rees leaped, and to his credit, he jumped back toward the ball, realizing he had company and might have to fight for it or knock it down himself. But Campbell's quick reaction—he was slanting back toward the ball as well—had put him in the ideal spot at just the right moment. He outfought Rees for the ball and made the interception, then tumbled to the Astroturf as Dicus moved in for the tackle and Rees was at his feet.

Rees still can pantomime the action of the play with vivid recall. "The ball was like this," he says, reaching slightly to his right. "When I was trying to get the ball, he came up and caught it. He had the leverage and he took it away. If the pass had been out here"—now, he acts out his first diving catch of the game, with his arms extended to the outside—"hopefully I could have caught it and we would have had first down on the twenty-two."

Campbell, though, bristles whenever he hears that Montgomery under-threw the pass.

"If he had thrown it this much further to the outside," he says, holding his hands about a foot apart, "I wouldn't have intercepted it and maybe he would have caught it. All I'm saying is that don't tell me that you underthrew a ball a foot and tell me that's underthrown! That's asking for perfection. When I turned, maybe I saw a blur, but the ball was right there, and Rees would have caught it if my hands weren't there."

Tom's brother, Mike, was important on the play because if he hadn't been close to Dicus, Montgomery might have spotted that and thrown to his fa-vorite receiver instead of Rees. The gain would have been shorter, but the Razorbacks still had time.

"Dicus made his cut right when I thought he would," Mike says. "I'm right with him." Mike laughs. "This is the only time in the game I thought, 'I hope they throw to Dicus.' I'm ready to be the hero and make the big play. As soon as I turned my head, and I was disappointed that he hadn't thrown to Dicus, Tom intercepted it. I couldn't even get to him because everybody was mob-bing him. He made a great play."

Defensive end Bill Atessis was trying to get to Montgomery. "When Bill released the ball, I turned and looked, and it was like I couldn't tell who was running the route," Atessis says. "Tom shadowed the guy that well. It was one of the prettiest defensive positioning interceptions I've ever seen. That was just, 'You're not going to catch this damn ball! We're going to win this game.'"

Tom Campbell, the coach's son, the walk-on whose own father hadn't thought he could make it as a big-time college football player, was one of the heroes.

The other coach's son on the defense, Bill Zapalac, charged over to congratulate Tom, too. And when he had time to contemplate, he considered it the highlight of the Campbell boys' remarkable journey from scrubs to starters. "I see Tom when he's a sophomore and I'm kind of giggling because he had no talent—except the talent of really wanting to succeed," Zapalac says. "In those days, you could overcome more things with desire than you can now. His progress was unbelievable, it was unbelievable the way he came away with that pass. He literally takes the ball away from him. If there ever was a play where a champion was crowned, it was that play."

The Longhorns led 15–14 and they had the ball back, on their own 22, with 1:13 remaining in the game, and Arkansas couldn't stop the clock. Unless the Horns did the unimaginable and fumbled, the game was over. The Razorbacks and their fans knew it. "The thing I really remember is the silence," Tom Campbell says. "The decibel level had been so high all game, and suddenly it was just so quiet."

As the Longhorns celebrated on their sideline—the interception came on the same side as their bench—Montgomery and Maxwell walked toward the Razorbacks' sideline, their helmets off and their heads hanging. Maxwell reached over and put his arm around Montgomery as they walked, then patted the quarterback on the back as they neared the sideline.

"I felt sick for Bill, so bad for Bill," Maxwell says. "I wanted to let him know I was going to live and die with him."

A few of the embittered Arkansas fans were throwing garbage—including empty liquor bottles—at the Longhorns' bench area, which happened intermittently throughout the game, and the coaches told the Longhorns not to take off their helmets when they were on the sideline. Now, with the outcome assured, the garbage came in torrents. Steve Worster and the offense went whooping onto the field, out of the line of fire. "Fortunately, the idiots up in the stands throwing the whiskey bottles were nerds," Worster says. "They couldn't even reach the field. All they were doing was knocking their own people out in the stands."

Amid the tumult, the Longhorns had some communication problems. As Street went onto the field, Royal grabbed him and said, "Run out the clock!" He assumed Street knew what he meant. Yet on first down, Street *handed off* to Worster, for no gain.

On the sideline, Royal was screaming and gesturing to get Street's attention. The quarterback scurried a few yards toward the bench and stopped to get the message, which clearly was: DON'T HAND THE BALL OFF!

On second down, following orders, Street kept the ball. Instead of kneeling, though, he charged ahead for 7 yards, as if the call was a quarterback sneak on a fourth-and-goal from the 5 with the game on the line. Now Royal was roaring. He grabbed the player nearest to him, shoved him toward the field, and told him to tell Street: "Don't advance the ball! Just fall down!"

On the opposite sideline, Montgomery watched helplessly. "As the clock was ticking down, I was numb," he says. "I wasn't mad. I wasn't running around having a temper tantrum. I was just numb. I was completely and totally in shock. To some degree, it would be like the feeling of having someone come up and give you the most precious gift that anybody ever could give you, and then fifteen minutes later have somebody come back up and say they made a mistake. It really wasn't yours, it belonged to the next guy."

Danny Lester, who made the other key interception, hugged Tom Campbell. Then Campbell scrambled over to embrace Carl White, the injured defensive tackle.

The Longhorns came up to the line of scrimmage, with Street lining up behind center Forrest Wiegand as the clock counted down the final seconds.

But referee Carl Landiss had to step over the ball and signal the timekeeper to stop the clock with six seconds remaining. A bottle had just been fired out of the stands, onto the field. "It flew right by my head," Mike Campbell says.

After a few moments, Landiss gave the "winding" signal to start the clock again.

"It seemed like it was taking forever," Wiegand says.

The clock hit all zeroes. Wiegand jumped in the air.

"I put that ball in my arms and I took off," Wiegand says. "I'd never been so excited in my whole life. I've still got the dadgum thing."

The Longhorns had won 15–14. The field became a madhouse, with fans charging out of the stands and the Longhorns mobbing one another as refuse still flew at them.

BACK IN AUSTIN, Julius Whittier—the freshman from San Antonio destined to be the first black letterman at Texas—was watching the game in the TV room at the girls' wing of Jester Center. He was prone on the floor in the crowded room, his elbows on the carpet and his chin resting on his hands.

When the game ended, he jumped up, hollering, and went charging out to celebrate.

TERRY DON PHILLIPS was a few feet from his Longview buddy, James Street, when the game ended. Phillips stepped across the line of scrimmage, reached out his hand and told Street, "Good luck in the Cotton Bowl." Unfortunately for the Razorbacks, Phillips's warning about Street's "winning" traits had been deadly accurate. Street told Phillips, "It was a great game, man, a great game." Phillips told him the Longhorns better beat Notre Dame.

Street couldn't understand why during the postgame chaos on the field, including that handshake with Phillips, he felt a little disconnected from reality. "It was a totally different feeling from any other game when I walked off the field," Street says. "I felt for Terry Don, I felt for them."

Street spotted Frank Broyles's eleven-year-old twin daughters, Betsy and Linda, running up to the Arkansas coach and hugging him. "They both were crying," Street says. "I'm thinking, 'Oh, man.'"

Then around him, Arkansas fans were yelling.

"Bill Montgomery's a better quarterback than you," one fan said.

Street responded, "He's a great quarterback, a fine quarterback. You're probably right."

Worster went through a similar experience. "It was such a well-played game and they did such a phenomenal job against us, doing what nobody else in the nation had been able to do, I was in a really weird state of mind," he says. "It seemed like we had won, but lost. Or lost, but won. I couldn't believe we had won the game, and I just felt bad for them because they were a class act. We played against teams that were the dirtiest scungeballs in the world—the Notre Dames of the world that pulled every trick, broke every rule in the book, knew every underhanded way to hurt you. These were good, solid athletes and good sportsmen. That's the way we were taught and the way we played, too. They'd bust your ass and help you get off the ground. They'd knock your dick in the dirt and then help you up. It was just a shame. I put them on the same level as us."

Worster played in high school all-star games with and against some of the Arkansas players, including Montgomery. He searched out the Razorback quarterback and shook his hand. "I'm sorry, man," Worster said. "Nobody should have lost this game. You guys should not have lost this game."

Texas tackle Bob McKay was happy, but not completely triumphant. "I couldn't believe that after all the crap that went on that day, we pulled it out of the hat," McKay says. "We didn't play worth a shit. They had us boxed and we couldn't do anything." McKay then compliments the defensive end near him most of the afternoon, Bruce James. "We ran a reverse and I finally hit the kid," McKay says, referring to Cotton Speyrer's 14-yard end-around, which enabled him to nail James as the Razorback defensive end focused on Speyrer. "Other than that," McKay says, "I had to shake hands with the kid at the end of the game to say I touched him. It was [my] worst game."

With his self-deprecating sense of humor, McKay is greatly overstating his own problems that day. "The reason I frustrated McKay was that I just never got up and let him get near me," James says. "I was going to hit him and be gone." But there was no denying how confused the Longhorns looked at times. "They did a hell of a job on us," McKay says. "So when it was over, I didn't talk to anybody, I just went to the locker room. I was the happiest son of a bitch in the world to get the shit out of Arkansas."

PERHAPS THE LONGHORNS didn't play "worth a shit," by their own high standards, but they played just well enough to win, surviving the six turnovers. The coaching staffs battled to a push, in effect. The Razorbacks were much better prepared: The defensive game plan was ingenious, especially considering the wishbone's freshness in the game, and the Razorbacks' offensive approach took advantage of the Longhorns' early insistence on trying to cover Dicus man-to-man. The Longhorns were confused offensively, but made clutch plays—the type that win championships—at the right time. And the Longhorns' sideline and coaching-booth decisions were crucial. Royal's wisdom in going for two after the first touchdown was undeniable. The pass to Randy Peschel was such a high-wire risk, it made no "sense" at all. All the same, it worked.

For all their problems, the Longhorns actually outgained the Razorbacks, 368 yards to 308. Texas had 19 first downs, Arkansas 18. Worster had 94 yards on 25 carries. The biggest dropoffs from Texas's normal production were that Ted Koy—partially because he was "credited" with losses on two fumbles that weren't completely his fault—was limited to 28 yards on 13 carries, and Jim Bertelsen only gained 29 yards on 10 carries. The Longhorns had eaten up yards all season, but on this afternoon their two longest runs were Street's touchdown scramble and Speyrer's 14-yarder. Street was 6–10 passing, for 124 yards, with 2 interceptions, and gained 73 yards on 8 carries. The Razorbacks' Cliff Powell was in on tackles on 21 of the 70 plays, with 7 unassisted and 14 assisted tackles.

Montgomery finished 14–22, for 205 yards and 1 touchdown, plus the 2 crucial interceptions. Dicus caught 9 passes for 146 yards. Bill Burnett carried 19 times for 82 yards, and also had the 3 receptions on the final drive—his only catches of the game—for 26 yards. The Texas defense played a classic bend-but-don't-break game, coming up with the clutch interceptions and getting a break on the offensive interference call on Rees. Bill Atessis, Greg Ploetz, Carl White (until he was injured), and David Arledge for most of the game kept pressure on Montgomery, and Scott Henderson had a strong game at linebacker. Finally, Tom Campbell made a huge, perhaps game-clinching play.

Royal says the game "never has been the highlight" of his coaching career. "I don't think we played well. I'm just saying we were confused and didn't play well and Arkansas played a heck of a game. It was really about three plays that we won the game on."

LEAVING THE FIELD, Mike Campbell was stopped by one Arkansas fan in red. The fan said he was the Campbell twins' cousin and congratulated Mike on a good game. The Campbells *did* have distant cousins in Arkansas, but the twins never had met them. "I'm sitting there listening to my cousin talk to me, and tell me what a great game it was," Mike says. "To this day, I still don't know his name and I haven't spoken to him since. All I could think about was that Richard Nixon is in our dressing room, and I'm standing here talking to a cousin I don't know."

TWENTY-EIGHT

Presidential Addresses

IN THE VISITING DRESSING ROOM, Texas tackle Bob McKay tempered his disgust with the way he had played long enough to join in the celebration. He didn't have much choice: The temporary stage set up in the dressing room was wedged against his locker.

The noisy party began. Players hollered and hugged, popped each other on the shoulder pads, and squeezed among one another to celebrate.

The president's on the way, ABC's Bill Fleming told the national television audience. Behind Fleming, McKay reached down from the platform and stowed his helmet in his locker, then walked past Fleming and spotted Darrell Royal on the floor. The big tackle reached down and pulled Royal onto the platform.

Royal peeled off his orange Texas jacket, then helped Randy Peschel up on the platform and planted an emphatic kiss on the tight end's left cheek. McKay grabbed Peschel from behind, around the collar of his shoulder pads, then hugged and lifted him. Ted Koy jumped up on the platform, too.

Royal signaled for quiet. Between Peschel and Koy, he led the Longhorns in the Lord's Prayer. They said amen, and then they cheered to high heaven.

Fleming grabbed Royal for a quick interview, and the coach—looking stunned—wouldn't confirm the broadcaster's assertion that this was "one of the greatest victories in all of Texas history."

"We just kept turning the ball over," Royal said. "I really . . . I just don't know what to say."

Fleming said, "I know in just a few minutes, Darrell, President Nixon will be here to congratulate you and your boys. I'm sure during that time, you'll have a chance to reflect and think about what this really means to you."

Royal laughed. "Well, I already know."

Tom Campbell looked like a president in a receiving line, accepting congratulations from the Longhorns gathered around him. McKay squeezed into the tiny space between the platform and his locker, tossing gear onto the stage and then taking off his number 62 jersey, baring his midriff on national television, and peeled off the arm pads. He was still wearing his shoulder pads and a cut-off T-shirt. "I got a lot of letters about that," McKay says. "A lot of 'em were from Notre Dame people talking about what a turd I was. 'No respect for the president.' I looked at it like he had more important people to talk to than me."

Now Nixon was in the room, and it quieted. The president filed through, shaking hands, and he stopped at the base of the platform to greet Royal. Bud Wilkinson, broadcaster and presidential consultant, was behind Nixon. McKay was right there, too, undoing the string on his neck ring. The big tackle reached in front of the president and his coach to James Street, shaking the quarterback's hand. Street had a Coke bottle in his hand through the rest of the ceremony.

Nixon walked up the little steps, up onto the platform, triggering more cheers. The three Texas captains—Street, Koy, and Glen Halsell—were standing to the president's left and Royal joined them.

"You can't describe that tug of emotions," Ted Koy says. "Here's the president of the United States, and he's just a human being, standing and talking in front of you. Here I am, a little kid from small-town Bellville, Texas, standing here shaking the president's hand on national television."

Fleming gushed to Nixon, "You chose yourself a football game to attend, didn't you?"

"One of the great games of all time, without question," Nixon said, turning to face Royal. "I was up in the booth, the ABC booth, at halftime and incidentally, I got to brag a little. They asked me what was going to happen in the second half, and I said, 'Both teams are gonna score,' but that I thought what would really determine the second half would be whether Texas had the ability in the fourth quarter to come through. And you did!" He put a hand on Royal's shoulder. "How do you feel?"

Royal said, "I've got to be the happiest man in America tonight."

Nixon turned toward the cameras and said he knew Texas would be rated No. 1 in the wire-service polls, and someone reached up and handed him the presidential plaque. "What convinced me that Texas deserves that is the fact that you won a tough one," Nixon said. "For a team to be behind 14–0, and then not to lose its cool and go on to win, that proves you deserve to be No. 1 and that's what you are!"

The Longhorns cheered.

It was Royal's turn. "Mr. President, it's a great thrill to win the football game. But the big thrill, I know I speak for all of our squad, is for the president of the United States to take time to endorse college football and to honor us with your presence in our locker room. This is a big moment in all of our lives."

Linebacker Scott Henderson, the son of liberal Democratic activists, says it "didn't seem odd to me that Nixon and Royal were talking to each other. That's not to say that Royal admired Nixon, but he had that presence and it seemed right."

Nixon now tried to mend some political fences. He said the plaque had a blank spot for the name of the winning school, because he hadn't known who would win, and he would take it back to Washington and have it engraved. Then he pointed out, "Penn State of course felt that I was a little premature in suggesting this, so we're gonna present a plaque to Penn State as the team in the one-hundredth year with the longest undefeated, untied [streak]. Is that fair enough?"

"Fair enough," Royal said.

Nixon turned and shook more hands from the platform as Fleming tossed the broadcast back to Schenkel, upstairs. Bobby Wuensch, the shy tackle who turned into a monster on the field, jumped up on the stage. From behind, he called out to the president of the United States. "Mr. President," he said, "my name is Bobby Wuensch." Nixon shook his hand.

Down on the wet floor of the tiny locker room, the identical Campbell twins each shook the president's hand about five times. "He probably thought, 'Man, this kid really likes me,'" Tom says.

Fred Akers, the defensive backfield coach, told Nixon that they had met before, when Nixon was vice president and Akers was a high school junior. He didn't try to explain that he was *Arkansas's* representative to Boys Nation.

Bobby Mitchell, the guard whose brother was killed in Vietnam three days before Nixon took office, wasn't thinking politics. "You were so elated, on such a high, it's kind of like you're on equal footing with the president and Billy Graham and we're national champions," Mitchell says. "Your frame of mind is that the whole world is watching and cares about football and nothing else exists, you're king of the heap. So why *wouldn't* the president be here?"

Greg Ploetz, the artist–defensive tackle, knew that a lot of his friends in painting classes would have preferred that he throw paint—and not water-colors, either—on the president. "I wasn't that crazy about the president at the time, but I shook his hand and got to meet Billy Graham, too," he says. "I sensed that because the president was there and he had come down to see us, this was a special deal. So I shook his hand."

But some other Longhorns never fought their way to that side of the locker room; Freddie Steinmark was one of them. He stayed over in the corner, and Steve Worster spotted him crying. Worster found himself crying, too, and in line with his confused reaction immediately after the game, he wasn't exactly sure why. Steinmark later wrote that his were tears of joy, but Worster wonders if there wasn't some pain involved, too. That definitely was the case with injured defensive tackle Carl White, who gave up trying to get up and make it across the dressing room to meet the president because he was hurting so badly.

When Billy Graham indeed came into the dressing room, James Street politely cut off a talk with reporters, explaining he never had met Graham, and rushed over to have Royal introduce him. When Graham spoke to the team, he said he had tried to be neutral, but that he was a member of a Dallas church, then signaled, "Hook 'em Horns!"

Guard Randy Stout was one of the many Horns who also made a point of approaching Graham. That night Stout called his mother, a devout Baptist and serious Democrat.

"Not to worry, Mama, I didn't shake Nixon's hand," he said. "But I did shake Billy Graham's hand and he's a really nice man. I couldn't get his autograph, Mama, but I shook his hand."

To Randy Stout's mother, it was like a Catholic hearing her son had had an audience with the pope.

The Longhorns excitedly talked with reporters, explaining the key plays.

Finally, some of the Longhorns got undressed and started to step into the shower room. But the yelps in there had nothing to do with triumph.

There wasn't any hot water.

Danny Lester was one of the first Longhorns out of the dressing room, because he knew his mother and his stepfather were waiting and he wanted to talk with them before getting on one of the team buses. He hugged his mother warmly, and then he talked about his interception and a postgame conversation he had with Darrell Royal.

"I told Coach Royal, 'When I saw them line up the way they did, I couldn't believe my eyes,'" Danny told his mother. "I thought they can't be stupid enough to throw a pass. I knew they didn't need me down the middle for that run. I thought, 'Boy, if they're stupid enough to throw that pass, I'm either going to intercept it, knock it down, or have Dicus out of the end zone.'"

Lester told his mother that Royal looked at him and said, "Danny, you didn't have those three choices. The only choice you had was to intercept, because if you hadn't, they would have kicked a field goal and won it."

After seeing Freddie Steinmark outside the dressing room, Rosemary Henderson—Scott's mother—told her son Freddie didn't look good.

IN THE ARKANSAS "half-house," Frank Broyles paced, periodically reaching up to rub his chin. The Razorbacks were silent, except for the sniffling and the scraping of spikes on the cement. Their coach had made a brief speech, telling the Razorbacks he was proud of them and they had nothing to be ashamed of, but now they were waiting, and they knew why: Nixon was congratulating the Longhorns and awarding them the plaque. The Razorbacks couldn't even start to get undressed; all their clothes and equipment bags were in the regular dressing room in Barnhill Arena.

"It was just complete devastation," Chuck Dicus says. "How did it happen? Why did it happen? We're told the president wants to come over and it's going to be a few minutes and we have to gather ourselves and wait."

"Oh, it was awful," tailback Bill Burnett says. "I was over in the corner, blubbering."

And it wasn't only the players. Assistant coaches, including Don Breaux and Richard Williamson, "were just bawling," Bill Montgomery says. "The season was long and the pressure had been on the coaches. To go into that final game of the season like that, and then have it end the way it ended, to go into that final quarter ahead 14–0 and lose 15–14, it was just overwhelming. No other loss was like that loss."

Defensive guru Charley Coffey admits he had a unique attitude. "I wasn't down in the dumps at all, like I typically would be when we lost a game," Coffey says. "I was excited about how well we played. I was telling our defensive players they played a great game. In my eighteen years of coaching, I never had a defense play better. Now, we shut teams out and other things, but this was a team that was so awesome offensively. Against other teams, Texas ran up and down the field like they were out early to practice. It was kind of unrealistic that we played as well as we did as long as we did, and with two or three exceptions, it was the whole game."

As word came that the president was on his way, the Razorbacks' four captains—Lynn Garner, center Rodney Brand, safety Dennis Berner, and fullback Bruce Maxwell—obediently lined up with Broyles. They had mixed feelings, and as the wait continued, they climbed back off the platform to stand with their teammates.

"It was an honor that he recognized us that way," Berner says of Nixon. "I was not a big fan of President Nixon, but I still was glad he was there and glad that his office and what it represented was at that game."

Maxwell is less charitable, growling, "They made us stand up there and that bullshit." Garner felt the same way. "I didn't care that the president of the United States was there," he says. "I wanted to get out of there and be with my buddies."

ABC's Bill Fleming was the traffic cop again, and he interviewed Broyles while Nixon made his way from the visiting dressing room across to the half-house, through the rain and the mobs. Broyles told the national television audience that they had watched "a great ballgame" and that he was "very proud of" his team.

When Nixon arrived, he stepped up on the platform and shook hands with Broyles. "It's an honor to be here with a great team," Nixon said.

"Thank you, we feel that way, too," Broyles said.

The president turned toward the players. "I'd like to say something to the team, because I know how you feel," Nixon said. "In my field of politics, I've lost some close ones and I've won some close ones. But I want you to know that in the one-hundredth year of football, in the game to prove which was to be number one, we couldn't have had a greater game. Arkansas was magnificent throughout the game. Texas, in order to win, had to beat a great team. On any Saturday, if we were to make a bet, I would say we wouldn't know which team to choose, whether it would be Arkansas or Texas."

Nixon congratulated the Razorbacks on having great fans and rallying "the whole state behind you." After Broyles said he agreed, the Arkansas coach added that the Razorbacks were "doubly proud that you're a big sports fan and believe in our program across the state. This will mean a lot to football for years to come."

Nixon turned back toward the players. "I know how the fellows feel," he said. "After being right up there, and being right down there on that 8-yard line ready to go over and then losing the game after what they've done." He concluded by saying he "wouldn't have missed" the game. "I'm only sorry that both teams couldn't have won."

Stepping off the side of the platform, Nixon reached out to the first player he saw—flanker John Rees, who looked as if someone had just run over his dog. Broyles stood with Nixon and waved the four captains over, then introduced them one by one. Maxwell was a good boy and didn't say anything about this being "bullshit." "Of course, he acted like Texas was going to win before the game," Maxwell says. "He was like, 'You all played them good, but you shouldn't have won anyway.' That was my impression." Nixon brightened when he was introduced to Brand. The president congratulated the All-American center on a good game. Brand, too, bit his tongue. He took Nixon's remarks to mean that the president was saying there always would be other chances. "We were all thinking, 'Shit, there ain't goin' to be another chance.' The seniors, anyway."

Then Broyles introduced Nixon to Chuck Dicus. "I tell you what you reminded me of," Nixon said. "[All-Pro and former Razorback Lance] Alworth. I've seen him play for San Diego. You've got his hands and you've got his moves. And I tell you, it was really terrific."

Next up was Bill Montgomery. "I tell you, you've got a lot of poise under fire," Nixon told the quarterback.

Montgomery was remarkably composed. "Thanks for coming by, sir," he said. "It's quite an honor to meet you."

"Both teams couldn't win," Nixon said, "but I tell you, you were as close as you can be without winning it. Good luck to you now."

Montgomery moved on to shake hands with the man next to Nixon, former Razorback player and ex–University of Arkansas president J. William Fulbright. In a football dressing room, the severe critic of the administration's Vietnam policy and the president of the United States stood side by side.

"You played a great game," the powerful U.S. senator said to Montgomery. The Razorbacks started filing by, meeting Nixon. Defensive back Terry

Stewart, who vehemently opposed the Vietnam War, willingly got in line. "I wasn't a big fan of his in terms of his politics and the Vietnam War, but I don't think that made his presence any less special," Stewart says. "I think you separate the office and the man from his politics."

Linebacker Cliff Powell, who had just played the game of his life after being entrusted to do so by the defensive scheme, still was in an aggressive mood. "I got to shake hands with him and I was a little surprised by how limp of a handshake it was," Powell says. "I thought, 'Gee, he's the president of our country; give me a grip.'"

Bruce James, the defensive end, was struck that the president had prepared for the television lights. "All I can remember is how much makeup he had on and how his mascara was running," James says. "I was thinking, 'Man, the president of the United States has more makeup on than my date does.' I guess it was impressive that he was there, but it was anticlimactic to me."

Linebacker Mike Boschetti never approached Nixon, but it wasn't a political statement. "Everybody else for the most part at least got the composure to say, 'Hey, this is an opportunity to shake the president's hand.' I was sitting in the corner and crying, saying I couldn't care less."

Billy Graham also addressed the Razorbacks. Rick Kersey, the good Southern Baptist boy, was in such pain after suffering the torn knee ligament on the two-point conversion that he didn't even get up from his seat in the back of the room to meet Graham.

The Razorbacks also quietly went over the game with reporters. With great poise, Montgomery answered question after question, including the ones about Danny Lester's interception. "I guess I'll be second-guessing that play the rest of my life," he said. "If the pass was incomplete we definitely would have gone for the field goal. He just stepped in there and took it away." When Bill and his father, Catfish, finally left the half-house and started back to the Barnhill Arena dressing room in a lightly falling snow, the quarterback finally broke. The father-and-son conversation was reported the next morning in the *Arkansas Gazette*.

"I just blew it, Dad, just blew it," Bill said.

"No, now you didn't blow anything, just walk along."

"We'll get them next year."

"We got them this year, son. Now come on."

A few minutes later, Bill Burnett finally was showered and dressed. He walked out to Linda Holmes's car, climbed in, and kissed her. Linda had been trying to think of something, anything, to say—and she had had plenty of time to ponder it.

"You know that tooth that was bothering me?" she asked.

"Yeah?"

"Well, it's still bothering me."

It was lame, and that was the beauty of it. Bill laughed. Linda started the car and they headed toward her parents' house. "They had a party set up, with a cake and punch and everything that goes with it," Burnett says. "But it didn't turn into a party. Everybody moped around and ate cake."

In a few more days, Colonel Eugene Holmes would be angered by a letter he received from Rhodes Scholar Bill Clinton—the envelope was on the way from Oxford—but on this night, he was simply disappointed. Colonel Holmes, after all, was a Razorback.

TWENTY-NINE

All Quiet

HIRAM McBETH, THE B TEAM DEFENSIVE BACK, didn't go to the half-house or the dressing room in Barnhill Arena after the game. Instead, he went to the BAD House to check in with his fellow black students. They confirmed that Darrell Brown had gone home and wasn't seriously hurt, and they talked about not hearing "Dixie" all afternoon at the game.

They considered it Arkansas's only victory of the day.

They also knew that with running back Jon Richardson on the verge of joining the varsity the next season, the loss to Texas was the last time the Arkansas Razorbacks would play a home game without a black player.

Brown was resting in Razorback Hall, where he was the resident advisor. "There was still tension," he says. "It was a real tense period as far as I was concerned, and I think everybody felt that."

———

SEVERAL HOURS AFTER THE GAME, Don Donner and a couple of the other anti–Vietnam War protesters returned to the hill between the stadium and the administration building.

As they approached, they stopped and surveyed the mess.

The peace sign was ripped apart, the pieces of the sheets scattered. The crosses were torn up and tossed all over. The brochures about the cost of the war littered the nearby parking lots.

Donner was incredulous that ABC hadn't shown or referred to the protest. "How could they do that?" he asks. "On the other hand, it shook Nixon. This wasn't on one of the coasts. This was the heartland. This is Nowhere, Arkansas."

Arkansas newspapers ran stories about the protest the next day, and Donner was quoted. Pictures of the peace sign also ran, so the local media didn't ignore the protesters. But the sports media, including the many reporters and columnists who came from around the country for the game, didn't consider it worth mentioning. That was the dilemma: Peaceful dissent often didn't get attention, but if more elements in the anti–Vietnam War movement had followed the lead with civilized dissent, more minds might have been changed sooner. To think that it affected Nixon, one way or another, is unrealistic, though. Maybe he even wondered why he couldn't get the television networks to ignore the protesters all the time.

Nixon and the presidential party traveled back to Washington on *Air Force One* that night.

In his journal, White House chief of staff Robert Haldeman crowed that Nixon's appearance at the game was a resounding public relations success, and with the exception of the wrath it earned the president from Penn State fans, that was right. Haldeman, the former public relations executive, exclusively cared about the PR mileage earned in the trip to the game. Nixon also considered the political favor gained from the jaunt to Fayetteville, but the president also clearly enjoyed himself. He handled the entire day deftly. His halftime remarks were vague, yet prescient; the self-deprecating comment about learning as a benchwarmer seemed to humanize him much more than an awkward "sock it to me" on *Laugh-In*. His postgame talks to both teams were slightly stilted, but except for the wince-inducing remark about the Razorbacks' ill-fated fourth-quarter drive, they also mostly struck the right chords. Nixon never was a warm man, and familiarity required blasting through many barriers. But on the afternoon of December 6, 1969, Richard Nixon was a fan, too. As Arkansas "monster" Bobby Field would discover nearly sixteen years later on a run past the Hotel Bel-Air, Nixon never forgot this game, either.

THIRTY

Agony

FRANK BROYLES, as most college head coaches did after home games, entertained at his house that night. The custom was to have boosters and friends over, but Broyles routinely invited the reporters in town for the game.

"There wasn't any way to get out of Fayetteville at night," Broyles says. "Four o'clock was the last flight, so we entertained. The coaches and their wives and all the press that wanted to come were invited to the house, and we served a steak dinner like we always did. I don't know what I felt. I was in a daze really. I remember going to Little Rock the next day to tape my TV show and I was thinking what am I going to say? How am I going to handle this? Maybe I'll just commit suicide now before I tape the show."

––––––––––––

ARKANSAS TACKLE MIKE KELSON—the passionate Razorback from Houston—was depressed, disgusted, and looking to be consoled. When he arrived back at his apartment after the game, his wife, Linda, was having a party. And it wasn't even one of the many Fayetteville wakes going on at the time, like the one at Colonel Eugene Holmes's house. This was a celebration! Linda Kelson was a University of Texas student when she married Mike, "so she invites all her girlfriends from the University of Texas over to my little apartment," Mike says. "I went to bed and they partied all night. Next day, I got up and washed the diapers."

––––––––––––

LINEBACKERS MIKE BOSCHETTI AND CLIFF POWELL went out on a double date—and for Boschetti, it was a blind double date. Powell's girlfriend was an Arkansas student, but her twin sister went to Texas and had come up for the game. The sister didn't gloat, so Boschetti never had to bring up the alleged clip. "She was very gracious, I have to say that," Boschetti says.

FULLBACK BRUCE MAXWELL wasn't going to let a crushing loss scrub the party at the rental house off-campus. "It was a big drunk, with probably fifteen or twenty of the boys and girlfriends and whoever wanted to come," Maxwell says.

Center Rodney Brand and guard Jerry Dossey were among those who showed up, with their wives. "We listened to a lot of people talk about what a great game it was and how we should have won," Dossey says.

Brand's wife decided to go home ahead of her husband, but as she was trying to leave, she drove their Chevrolet Impala over a curb and an embankment and it got stuck. So with the snow falling, Brand and several of his teammates had to go out and shove the car back onto the street.

When Dossey got home later—much later—the telephone was ringing. It was his cousin, asking what the hell happened there at the end, Jerry? Dossey hung up. The phone rang again. It was someone telling him: "You guys got robbed!"

ROOMMATES BOBBY FIELD AND JERRY MOORE went out to dinner with their families. Many of the other Razorbacks went to fraternity parties. Linebacker Lynn Garner says he probably just *started* at the fraternities, then hit the clubs on Dickson Street. "I think I stayed drunk for a week."

BILL MONTGOMERY AND CHUCK DICUS had dates and spent subdued evenings. Tight end Pat Morrison and his fiancée, homecoming queen Ann Hartenstine, went to dinner. Defensive tackle Terry Don Phillips, who hadn't even expected to play, was so sore—and disappointed—he went straight home and to bed. The other defensive tackle, Dick Bumpas, says he "didn't want to be with people for about a week."

INJURED RAZORBACKS DEFENSIVE END RICK KERSEY was trying to get around on crutches. He made it over to a party at the home of the director of the Arkansas chapter of the Campus Crusade for Christ, Don Meredith. ("Not *the* Don Meredith," Kersey says.) He was so groggy, he went into a bedroom at the house, went to sleep, and stayed overnight.

ANOTHER PLAYER CAME OUT OF THE DRESSING ROOM at Razorback Stadium, hugged his girlfriend, then went with her to a couple of fraternity parties and a club—and was introduced to her friends. But Arkansas coed Honor Franklin never mentioned that her boyfriend, Bobby Mitchell, was Texas's starting left guard. Some of her friends knew, but most of those they came across that night didn't. Bobby was just "with Honor."

"I asked Coach Royal if I could stay behind and he said, 'Sure,'" Mitchell says. "That night, I was still elated and high from winning the game, but at the same time, I was in an environment there that was totally depressed. It was very strange. People were having fun, but it was very subdued at the same time. I just didn't feel like saying I played for Texas, and it was partly a safety issue, too. Some people were throwing bottles and they were not serving gasoline to people with Texas plates. They were so fanatical, I was incognito."

The rest of the Longhorns, including Mitchell's roommate and high school buddy, Freddie Steinmark, had headed back to Austin.

THIRTY-ONE

Ecstasy

THE HORNS' BUSES were far from silent as the team headed down to Fort Smith to catch the chartered flight back to Austin, but the celebration was cranked down a notch after the dressing-room exhilaration. It was an eerie ride, down the curving roads in the shaky weather and the dark.

On the plane, team manager Bill Hall went down the aisle, asking each player which kind of Cotton Bowl watch he wanted—male or female. Because the Longhorns had gone to the same bowl the season before, most of them already had a Cotton Bowl watch, and many ordered female watches for their girlfriends.

James Street was claustrophobic and nervous on planes, and he liked to wander the aisles, both to be social and to keep himself occupied. He went into the cockpit, and the pilot grabbed the microphone and said: *Here! Talk to the boys!*

Street identified himself as the captain and congratulated all the Longhorns, but said he sure hoped the defense would toughen up for the Cotton Bowl against Notre Dame. Most of the boys laughed; a few others already felt the defense wasn't getting enough credit for the victory over the Razorbacks. That feeling lingers in some of the Longhorns.

"What's so irritating about this football game is that in all probability, it was the worst offensive performance our team gave in three years," Tom Campbell says. "A lot of that was due to Arkansas, but not only was it the worst offensive performance for our team, I think it was without a doubt our best defensive performance in three, four, five, six, seven years. And all they talk about is Peschel and Street."

As the plane approached Austin's Municipal Airport, news of a problem came from the control tower and the pilot passed it along. "The pilot told us we were going to circle because there were people out on the tarmac," Darrell Royal says. "They needed to give the police time to clear them out."

"It wasn't Lindbergh," Tom Campbell says, "but they wanted to get those people out of the way."

The pilot took the team past the campus, and the players looked out of the plane and saw the Bell Tower—as was the custom after victories—lit up in orange. This time, though, there was an addition—a huge number "1."

Finally, the plane landed at about 7:30 and taxied toward the gate area. When the plane stopped, there was another delay while it sat on the runway and waited until the pilot was told the crowd was far enough back. The plane was towed in as far as the pilots thought prudent, and the ladder was hauled up to the back door. The crowd rushed up to the jet. "You could actually feel the plane move!" guard Mike Dean says.

One by one, braced for the reception, the Longhorns walked down the stairway and stepped into the crowd.

"I got hurt worse getting off the plane than I did in the ballgame," tackle Bob McKay says.

Mike Dean was scared, too. "It was a sea of heads. When you got down to the bottom, the guy in front of you disappeared. It startled me. I kind of stopped for a second. I had family there and I had to hunt for them."

Ted Koy, the cocaptain and *Daily Texan* columnist, couldn't have taken notes if he wanted to. "That's the only time I've had a true fear of a crowd," he says. "One time I literally picked both feet off the ground and I didn't drop, because of the compression of the people. For a second or two, I was held sardine-style. That's scary, because if something happens—gee, if somebody falls down, there's no way to get up."

Peschel was scared, but he also had to smile a bit when he saw a sign in the crowd: "STREET FOR PRESIDENT, PESCHEL FOR VICE PRESIDENT!" After making it down the stairway, the vice presidential candidate looked for Sue, his fiancée, but couldn't spot her.

Street and tackle Bobby Wuensch were among the last players off the plane. They made "Hook 'em Horns" signs and pleaded for the crowd to make a lane. But Wuensch had one more blocking assignment to complete: As he and Street tried to get through the crowd, several fans, including a woman, grabbed at the quarterback and wouldn't let go of his coat collar. Wuensch blocked them out of the way, and Street made it through the crowd. Then the strangest thing happened. Street was in the terminal, virtually alone, and he walked to his car in peace.

Darrell Royal waited as long as he could. Everyone was off the plane except the head coach, the medical staff, and injured defensive tackle Carl

White. Once the mob disappeared, White was loaded into a van and taken to the Student Health Center, to spend the night. "I missed everything," White says, laughing.

Royal finally walked down the stairway. "This real tough-looking guy with a half-beard was there," Royal says. "I really was a little nervous, he looked a little sinister to me. I was kind of jumpy and he reached out and grabbed me and kissed me on the cheek. It was the first time I ever was happy some guy kissed me."

———————

BY THEN, THE "DRAG"—Guadalupe Street, running down the west side of the campus—was jammed. Traffic was impenetrable. Horns honked, students walked up and down the street, screaming "Hook 'em Horns!" hugging complete strangers and even climbing lightpoles.

Many of the Longhorn players went to a party put on by local politicians and boosters at the Terrace Club in a hotel on South Congress. At the club, the players were greeted as heroes, and the beer flowed. Freddie Steinmark shocked James Street. "He said, 'I may just have a beer tonight and see what it feels like,'" Street says. "I always wondered in my own mind if he knew more than we knew."

Bill Zapalac says he teased Freddie about limping. When Steinmark was leaving later, he told Scott Henderson the beer hadn't deadened the pain in his leg.

Finally, James Street jumped into his car and headed back to Jester Center. Arriving at a blinking red light on the largely deserted street, he didn't come to a complete stop. Next thing he knew, he saw blinking lights in his rear-view mirror and pulled over. The police officer had a civilian riding with him, and both recognized Street. *Way to go, James! What a great win!*

"He gave me a ticket, anyway," Street says. "I got out of it, though. The judge said, 'There were circumstances that caused you to be anxious.'"

THIRTY-TWO

Courage

WHEN THE POLLS CAME OUT the next week, the Longhorns indeed remained No. 1. In the final United Press International coaches' poll, Texas was No. 1, Penn State No. 2, and Arkansas No. 3. The coaches didn't vote again after the bowls; the writers who had ballots in the Associated Press poll did.

ON MONDAY MORNING, RANDY PESCHEL walked into his statistics class. He wasn't wearing his number 40 jersey, of course, but everyone knew who he was. Professor Carl Henion started out by saying the students had just seen what teamwork, whether in sports or business or anything else, could accomplish. No one individual, he said, was responsible, and the students could be proud of what the football team accomplished. An embarrassed Peschel felt the eyes on him, and he was relieved when Henion announced, "All right, let's get down to statistics!"

Henion took off his sport coat, draped it on his chair, then turned around to face the blackboard.

"The class just went bonkers," Peschel says.

Henion had a homemade number 40 on the back of his shirt.

LATE MONDAY MORNING, FREDDIE STEINMARK went to see Frank Medina and, for the first time, leveled with him about the magnitude of his pain. Medina sent Freddie to see the team physician, Dr. Joe Reneau, for X-rays. Steinmark volunteered to take the film over to the Student Health Center, to Dr. Jerry Julian, on the way back to the dorm. Driving Linda Wheeler's car, he pulled over, took out the X-rays, and tried to decipher them himself. He couldn't, and dropped the film off.

THE LONGHORNS were going to receive the MacArthur Bowl, symbolic of the national championship, at the National Football Foundation's awards banquet on Tuesday night in New York. The captains were going to travel to New York on Tuesday, but Royal left Monday to appear on the *Today* show Tuesday morning.

On Monday night, the Longhorns were honored at halftime of the basketball team's game against Tulane in Gregory Gym. Freddie Steinmark and Linda Wheeler got there early, and Steinmark later wrote that Dr. Reneau gave him the news just after the Texas freshmen finished the preliminary game.

It might be a bone tumor. More X-rays and tests tomorrow.

At halftime, captain Glen Halsell thanked the students for their support and asked that they give the same kind of backing to the basketball team. James Street then introduced about fifty of his teammates—including Peschel and Steinmark. Street called Steinmark by one of his nicknames: "Fast Freddie Steinmark!"

Steinmark dropped Linda off back at her dorm, the other wing of Jester Center, then went to the Catholic Student Center and sat in the front row. He prayed and he cried. He walked past the campus fountain on the way back to the dorm and again sat, thinking. When Steinmark got back to the room, Bobby Mitchell still was out, so Freddie called home and talked with his dad, Freddie Gene, filling him in. Don't tell Mom, the son said. But after they hung up, Freddie Gene couldn't keep it from his wife, and then they called their son in Austin and talked it through again.

RANDY STOUT, THE LONGHORNS' GUARD, had a final exam Tuesday morning. He got up at about 5:00 A.M., took his books into the hallway commons area in the back of one floor and started cramming.

Just before seven, Freddie Steinmark slipped out of his room, wearing blue jeans and a T-shirt.

"Where are you going?" Stout asked quietly.

Stout says Steinmark told him his leg "really, really" hurt and that he was going to see the doctor for X-rays.

A little later, after more X-rays, Dr. Julian told Steinmark that because of the spot on the film—just above his left knee—he was being sent to M. D. Anderson Hospital and Tumor Institute in Houston. Dr. Charles A. LeMaistre, the university's vice chancellor, was going to escort him to Houston on a leased jet.

———————

AT THE WALDORF-ASTORIA HOTEL in New York that night, Darrell Royal and the three captains accepted the MacArthur Bowl, then smiled as they posed with it for the wire-service pictures that appeared in sports sections from coast to coast the next morning. Royal was told that afternoon that Steinmark had been sent to Houston.

The Longhorns also saw a couple of familiar faces at the banquet. Arkansas defensive back Terry Stewart was there, too, honored as the recipient of a postgraduate scholarship from the Football Foundation. And President Nixon was at the banquet, too, receiving the "Gold Medal" award for his support of and contributions to the game.

In his acceptance speech, Nixon joked that he was going to propose that a "college Super Bowl" be played following the bowl games. "But I decided I was in deep enough already, so I decided to skip it," he said. He also complimented Penn State as a team "among those who should be considered for the No. 1 spot."

Nixon saluted the Longhorns, especially because they went for two points after James Street's touchdown run. "In this one-hundredth year of football and close to the two-hundredth anniversary of our nation, I thought this was the kind of competitive spirit that characterizes our nation," Nixon said.

During the speech, an anti–Vietnam War protester started yelling at the president. Nixon "just backed off," Street says. "They carried the guy off screaming, and the president just stepped back up and talked like nothing had happened."

After the banquet's program, Royal got the news that Freddie's prognosis wasn't good and that a private jet would take the coach straight to Houston.

Royal called the captains together. He wouldn't be traveling back with them to Washington, D.C., to meet the Texas congressional delegation the next day, he told them, and here's why: *Freddie's got cancer in his leg, they might have to amputate, he's in Houston and I'm going there.*

Ted Koy was stunned.

"It was a huge emotional polarization," he says. "You're on top of the world, then you're on the bottom."

———————————

THE WORD WAS SPREADING among Freddie's teammates back in Austin, too. "You're dumbfounded, just dumbfounded," Tom Campbell says. "How can this happen? And the more I thought about it, I'm asking myself: 'How did he play?'"

Frank Medina broke the news to one of Steinmark's closest friends, Scott Henderson. "I hadn't seen Freddie in a couple, three days, but I didn't think anything about it," Henderson says. "All I knew is he was having trouble with his leg."

Henderson immediately made plans to go to Houston the next day with Linda Wheeler.

"We'd been giving Freddie shit because he was a friend of ours," Bob McKay says. "Then this deal. You talk about taking the wind out of it. You see how hard he played in that ballgame, and hell, the doctors told us they didn't know how he could walk, much less play. And you never heard word one out of him. Here's a kid who doesn't even have a bone in his leg, and he does the job."

Defensive backfield coach Fred Akers was shocked, too. "We just couldn't believe it," he says. "The doctors said he was in such great shape physically, that he had built the muscles up so well in his legs through weight work and running, that was the only thing that kept him out there. They felt a lesser man's leg might have snapped."

———————————

ON WEDNESDAY, ONLY DARRELL ROYAL was with Freddie when the doctors outlined the possibilities. The spot could be a benign tumor or a blood clot. But if the surgery on Friday showed the lump was a malignant tumor, doctors would amputate Freddie's leg.

A little later, the doctors also briefed Freddie's parents. Scott Henderson and Linda Wheeler arrived, too, and were updated.

Henderson made another trip back to Austin, and then returned the next day with Bobby Mitchell, Darrell Royal, and Steinmark's Austin priest, Reverend Fred Bomar of St. Peter the Apostle. The players got out of the car noting vulnerability in a visibly shaken Coach Royal.

More Steinmark relatives and friends came in from Denver on Thursday, and Fred Akers visited him, too.

In a private session with Father Bomar that night, Freddie joined in the Catholic *Memorare* prayer to Mary, which began:

> *Remember, O most gracious Virgin Mary,*
> *that never was it known*
> *that anyone who fled to thy protection,*
> *implored thy help or sought thy intercession,*
> *was left unaided.*
> *Inspired with this confidence,*
> *I fly unto thee . . .*

―――――――

ON FRIDAY, DECEMBER 12, six days after Freddie Steinmark played in a monumental college football game, doctors amputated his left leg because they concluded the lump was an osteogenic sarcoma—a bone tumor. Publicly, they were hopeful they had caught the cancer in time. "The boy is in great spirits," a hospital spokesman said. "He is a fine boy—really inspirational."

―――――――

THOUGH THE MAGNITUDE OF THE GAME is irrelevant, it bears repeating that *six days after Freddie Joe Steinmark played in a football game, doctors told the world he had done it on a leg being eaten up by cancer.*

There never has been a more courageous effort on a football field. Ever.

―――――――

NIXON CALLED STEINMARK ON SUNDAY, two days after the surgery. He talked with Steinmark's parents on Saturday, and called back when doctors believed Freddie was up to talking.

"We all admire your courage and heart," Nixon told Freddie.

"The call sure picked my boy up a bit," his father, who went by Fred G., said in a United Press International story published in Freddie's hometown paper, *The Denver Post*. "His eyes got real big. I'm not sure what their exact words were. He's getting along real good. He's taking it like a champ—a lot better than I can take it. He has a lot of energy. Darrell Royal instilled a lot of things in my boy."

———————

FREDDIE'S LONGHORN TEAMMATES sent a carnation arrangement, forming the number one. Scott Henderson and Bobby Mitchell visited him often, and many other teammates stopped by, too, before practices began again.

He also received cards and gifts from other Southwest Conference teams, including the Arkansas Razorbacks, and also from the Penn State Nittany Lions. Bill Montgomery sent a personal card and a note, telling Freddie, "You are in my prayers. Congratulations on a fabulous season. You all have a really good team and deserve every honor that you are now receiving. After the game, I remember saying to myself that even though I had two passes intercepted and was able to keep the ball away from you this time, you broke our backs in Austin the year before." He said he wanted Steinmark to know he was thinking of him, and signed it: "In God's love, Bill."

Steinmark also received a letter from Chicago Bears running back Brian Piccolo, who said he watched the Arkansas game and read about Steinmark's surgery. "I guess I, more than any other football player, must have known how you felt," Piccolo wrote. Their lives "are in God's hands now," he said.

Piccolo said he hoped they would meet someday.

———————

STEINMARK WAS DISCHARGED FROM THE HOSPITAL on December 23 and spent Christmas with his family in Houston. A little over a week later, he was on the Texas sideline for the Cotton Bowl against Notre Dame, the favorite team of his childhood.

THE LONGHORNS had already received the MacArthur Bowl, President Nixon's plaque, and UPI's final No. 1 ranking, but there was one more opportunity for AP voters to weigh in after the bowl games. The problem on the public opinion front for the Nittany Lions not only was their relatively weak schedule as an independent, but the perception that Penn State could have had control of its own No. 1 destiny if it hadn't rebuffed the Cotton Bowl.

The Cotton Bowl's second choice, Notre Dame, was playing in its first bowl game in forty-five years, and only the Irish's second ever, ending the university's self-imposed prohibition. The Longhorns were stunned at how much bigger the Irish were than their Southwest Conference opponents. The contrast between the Longhorns' 195-pound guard, Mike Dean, and Notre Dame's huge defensive tackle, Mike McCoy, was the most obvious example.

Dean's play in the game against an out-of-shape McCoy became required viewing in the Longhorns' film room later. "Mike Dean whipped his ass 75 percent of the time," Steve Worster chortles. "I mean, we watched it for hours and we laughed our asses off."

Dean, however, says that's getting a little carried away. On the Longhorns' first play, Worster ran over the right guard for 15 yards. "I'm lying on the ground and Mike McCoy's lying on the ground there, too," Dean says, laughing. "Bobby Wuensch comes over and grabs McCoy's facemask, lifts him off the ground, and says, 'Dean's going to whip your ass all day long,' and shoves him back down. I'm going, 'Golly, this guy wears a 59 coat and you're making him mad at me?'"

The Longhorns fell behind 10–0 on a field goal and a 54-yard touchdown pass from Notre Dame quarterback Joe Theismann to Tom Gatewood and still trailed 10–7 after three quarters. In the fourth quarter, the Longhorns got a 3-yard touchdown run from Ted Koy and took a 14–10 lead, but another Theismann touchdown pass put the Irish back ahead, at 17–14, midway through the fourth quarter. Texas twice converted on fourth-down-and-2 on the next drive, the first when Koy took a Street pitch and made it by inches at the Irish 18, and the second when Street hit Cotton Speyrer for 8 yards, getting the Longhorns a first-and-goal from the 2. Backup halfback Billy Dale scored the touchdown with 1:10 left to put the Longhorns in the lead, and Happy Feller's extra point made it 21–17.

It still wasn't over, though. Two Theismann completions got the Irish to the Texas 39 with thirty-eight seconds remaining, but Tom Campbell—again making a big play—came up with an interception at the Longhorns' 14 to clinch it.

The Longhorn ground game had gotten cranked up again, picking up 331 yards, and Worster was the offensive star, with 155 yards on 20 carries; Theismann threw for 231 yards and 2 touchdowns for the Irish.

This time, former president Lyndon Johnson appeared in the Longhorns' dressing room and Nixon checked in with a phone call. Nixon congratulated the Longhorns on "playing like champions," and Royal came back with, "Well, Mr. President, I am glad that we didn't embarrass your selection."

Royal and the Longhorns gave a game ball to Freddie Steinmark.

THIRTY-THREE

Bourbon Street

THE MORNING AFTER The Big Shootout, Bobby Field woke up and looked out the window of the Wilson Sharp House room he shared with Jerry Moore. The window faced the stadium. "All the debris and the papers were blowing around and it was a real dreary, cloudy day," Field says. "At that moment, it all hit me, the magnitude. It was painful and life goes on, and there are lessons to be learned from it."

Moore was distraught, and even if Bobby Field had been a talker, he couldn't have gotten Moore out of it. For several days, Moore left the dorm room only to eat.

"I was depressed, just devastated about this ballgame," Moore says. "I realized that I was involved in one of the bigger plays of the game, and I don't know if anything was said or whatever, but maybe I felt I could have played the ball a little better. If I would have done a little better, maybe I could have knocked the ball down. Probably that's what it all stemmed from. I was always hard on myself, I was raised that way, that I had to be perfect. Nothing less than perfection was acceptable and that wasn't a perfect performance because the guy caught the ball."

After the word of Moore's depression got around, the phone rang in the dorm room. It was Frank Broyles, and Moore reconstructs the conversation.

"Jerry, I understand you're taking this loss pretty hard."

"Yeah, Coach, I am. I hate to lose."

"This thing is not your fault. There were a zillion plays in this game. You had the guy covered great. There's nothing more you could have done. Now I don't want to hear anything more about this. You suck it up!"

That made Moore feel a little better.

THE RAZORBACK SENIORS again approached Broyles. "We asked if we could go to the Bluebonnet Bowl in the Astrodome," Cliff Powell says. "Those people said we could go and roam the dome, so to speak. But they'd already cut a deal, and the Sugar Bowl would take the loser of our game."

So the Razorbacks were matched up against the Archie Manning–led Mississippi Rebels. The Hogs' hearts weren't in that one. The coaching staff didn't seem to be, either, and the Razorbacks never reviewed the film of the Texas loss. It would have been too painful, raised too many questions.

The Razorbacks were going to have to play in New Orleans without defensive end Rick Kersey, who underwent knee surgery in Fayetteville on the Monday after the Texas game.

Defensive end Bruce James, the only Razorback starter from Mississippi, tried to pump up his teammates to play against his home-state Rebels. "I tried to talk about what it meant to rebound," James says. "'If we don't, then we're a flash in the pan. We play one big game and lose it, and then we turn around and lose another one. If we really want to keep our credibility, we go down and beat Ole Miss.' It didn't work."

In New Orleans, some of the Razorback seniors ran wild. What was Broyles going to do, bench them? The year before, the Razorbacks had been superlative in a 16–2 upset of Georgia; this time, the Hogs, and especially the defense, which had been strong against Texas, came out flat.

"My junior year, we went to the Sugar Bowl and no one broke curfew and everything was if the coaches told you to do it, you did it," center Rodney Brand says. "My senior year, we were all twenty-two-year-old men and we were out on Bourbon Street all the time, it seemed like. It was completely different."

The Razorbacks fell behind 24–6 in the second quarter before they woke up. The funny thing was that Bruce Maxwell was blasting through big holes, right up the middle—and screaming at his linemen about it. "Ole Miss had a little middle linebacker and I was running over him and Maxwell was running up the middle," Brand says, laughing. "We were marching up and down the field."

Finally, Maxwell had enough. He threw up in the huddle a couple of times, displayed the dry heaves several other times—and Montgomery kept giving him the ball. "God damn it!" Maxwell roared. "Can't y'all miss a block one time and give me a break!"

Maxwell finished with 103 yards on the ground and also caught a 6-yard pass from Montgomery for a touchdown. Montgomery was 17–34, for 338 yards, with a second touchdown pass of 47 yards to Chuck Dicus. Kicker Bill McClard, fighting a terrible cold, missed an extra point and a field goal. At one point, Maxwell approached McClard on the sideline and informed the sophomore kicker that if he missed one more kick, the senior fullback would kill him. McClard ended up making a 35-yarder in the fourth quarter and an extra point as the Hogs climbed back to within 27–22—but that's the way it stayed.

"We should have beaten Mississippi," guard Ronnie Hammers says. "If everybody had been sober and stuff, we would have. All the seniors didn't even want to go play. Us juniors didn't want to either, but I was going to be back for another year, so I did what the coaches told me."

To a man, the Razorbacks say that wasn't their real team in the Sugar Bowl—at least in the first half. "We were very flat," Cliff Powell says. "I know that sounds like sour mick, or whatever, but it was true."

On New Year's night, the seniors were back on the prowl. "We went into Pat O'Brien's," Lynn Garner says. "A bunch of Ole Miss people were in there saying, 'Ha, ha, ha, Southwest Conference!'"

The Razorbacks' comeback?

Mindful of the Cotton Bowl score, Garner says they all held up index and little fingers and said: "Hook 'em Horns!"

THE LONGHORNS indeed remained No. 1.

On New Year's night in Miami, the Penn State Nittany Lions beat Missouri 10–3. The Penn State offense wasn't impressive, and the Lions' only touchdown—a 28-yard pass from Chuck Burkhart to sophomore halfback Lydell Mitchell in the first quarter—came on the first play following a Missouri fumble. Sophomore Franco Harris, the Nittany Lions' third-best running back (behind All-American senior Charlie Pittman and Mitchell), had 46 yards on seventeen carries. The Nittany Lions' defense had three senior All-Americans in tackle Mike Reid, linebacker Dennis Onkotz, and safety Neal Smith; plus a standout junior linebacker, Jack Ham. It wasn't a complete shock when Missouri struggled all night offensively.

In the postbowl Associated Press poll, Texas was No. 1, Penn State No. 2, and Arkansas No. 7.

The 1969 Longhorns not only were Texas's last all-white team; they also were the last all-white national champions.

They were the last of how it was.

THIRTY-FOUR

Requiem

FREDDIE STEINMARK'S DETERMINATION became a national inspiration. He re-enrolled in school and struggled to learn how to use an artificial leg. He played golf and drove his new Pontiac GTO, bought with contributions that came from around the country.

When former Longhorn great Tommy Nobis opened a fried chicken restaurant in San Antonio in the spring of 1970, he asked Steinmark to come and bring some of his teammates. Mike Campbell was among those riding along. "About halfway between Austin and San Antonio, Freddie got pulled over for speeding," Mike says. "Three or four of us were in the car and we started giggling and laughing and razzing Freddie. The officer came up and asked Freddie to get out of the car, and that's when we started howling. Freddie opened the car door and put his crutches out, and that's when the officer realized who it was. He was mortified, and he just said, 'Mr. Steinmark, would you slow it down a little bit? I'm gonna let you go this time, but slow it down.'"

AT FIRST, HIS TEAMMATES believed Freddie had cancer beaten. "He never gave you the impression, 'Why is God doing this to me?'" guard Mike Dean says.

ON APRIL 13, 1970, Steinmark went to the White House as part of the kickoff for the American Cancer Crusade fund drive. He presented President Nixon with a football signed by the 1969 Longhorns.

STEINMARK LIVED FOR A WHILE in the rectory at St. Peter the Apostle, where Father Fred Bomar became his protector. Some of Steinmark's friends resented Bomar, believing the priest reveled in the reflected attention and interfered in Freddie's friendships and relationships, including his relationship with Linda Wheeler. But the understandably and justifiably protective Bomar and the church staff were a great help in filtering Freddie's correspondence and helping him answer it. The speaking invitations were legion. Randy Peschel helped him tape his Christian testimony, and Peschel often took it to his Fellowship of Christian Athletes appearances.

———————

IN JULY 1970, during a checkup at M. D. Anderson Hospital and Tumor Institute in Houston, doctors discovered the cancer had spread to Freddie's lung.

Although the doctors were publicly optimistic, bone sarcomas are among the most devastating and aggressive of cancers. The amputation almost certainly had bought time; the question was only how much. And while it was reasonable to wonder if it might have helped if Steinmark had been encouraged to have an extensive checkup sooner, by the time sarcomas are big enough to be noticed and cause significant symptoms, it almost always is too late—even now.

Bobby Mitchell and Scott Henderson, who stayed in Austin for the summer, were among several of Freddie's teammates who briefly stayed at the rectory. After Steinmark attended the College All-Star Game in Chicago, he began chemotherapy treatments, which came in five-day sieges.

That fall, he was helping coach the freshman team as he continued to attend classes. Steinmark noticed that his hair was starting to fall out, and his friends noticed it, too. One day in the dressing room before a practice, Longhorns tackle Bobby Wuensch—the 1969 All-American who was a senior in 1970—volunteered to help when Freddie said he wanted to shave his head. Wuensch used one of the clippers the players used to shave areas about to be taped. He kept working until Freddie's head was a cue ball.

Freddie put up a brave front, but as he shaved Freddie, as the hair fell away, tears rolled down Bobby Wuensch's cheeks. "I remember shaving it quite lovingly," Wuensch says.

Finally, Wuensch did what he used to do with his five-foot-eight, bald father. Bobby rubbed the top of Freddie's head, then bent down and kissed it.

Later, word circulated that Freddie tried to fool his teammates by asking Wuensch to shave his head, and portraying the request as a self-imposed bit of hazing for the new freshman team coach.

But the boys watching that day sensed what was going on. Even if they didn't want to face it.

GREG PLOETZ DECIDED NOT TO PLAY IN 1970—much to the chagrin of the coaching staff. He married a girl from back home in Sherman and managed an apartment complex as he continued school and awaited the birth of the couple's child. "The baby was real premature and had to stay in the hospital," Ploctz says. "They didn't know if he was going to make it, so I called Fred Bomar."

Father Bomar quickly came to the hospital to baptize the baby, Chris. Freddie Steinmark came with the priest and was Chris's godfather in the baptism ceremony.

Chris survived; the doctors were shocked.

Greg Ploetz still can't talk about Chris, his baptism, and his godfather without choking up.

STEINMARK NEVER LOST HIS FAITH, and in some ways, it even was strengthened. But his friends did notice some changes.

"He had a celebrated year and a half of his life after that, I will say that," Bill Zapalac says. "He really never hardly drank before that, but the year he wasn't playing, he enjoyed himself." Zapalac says he again told Steinmark he looked like "Ratso," the scruffy Dustin Hoffman character in *Midnight Cowboy*.

Linebacker Rick Troberman called him "pirate." Bobby Mitchell says Freddie played along, wearing an earring. "I don't think he ever drank till after he lost his leg," Mitchell says. "He kept a pretty good sense of humor about it. It was a complete role reversal for him. Before, it was always go by the book, go to church on Sunday, go to mass, study."

FREDDIE AND LINDA BROKE UP, reconciled, and eventually scheduled a wedding for May 23, 1971. Invitations were printed and plans were made. Linda bought a low-key wedding dress, one without a train, and the rings were purchased.

Steinmark re-entered the hospital on April 20. The wedding wasn't held, but Linda was with him at the hospital on May 23.

Freddie Joe Steinmark died on June 6, 1971.

Linda Wheeler wore her understated wedding dress at Freddie's funeral.

Freddie was buried at Mount Olivet Cemetery in Wheat Ridge.

A statue of the Virgin Mary sits atop the monument on the family plot. And carved into the monument is the *Memorare*, which begins:

> *Remember, O most gracious Virgin Mary,*
> *that never was it known*
> *that anyone who fled to thy protection,*
> *implored thy help or sought thy intercession,*
> *was left unaided.*
> *Inspired with this confidence,*
> *I fly unto thee . . .*

"IT MAKES YOU CRY TO THINK ABOUT IT NOW," big Bob McKay says. "He was the greatest kid in the world. He wasn't quite as sorry as the rest of us."

"You can draw a tear to my eye and you can probably hear it in my voice when you say Freddie's name," Carl White says, his voice indeed catching. "He was one of the good guys. Such a quality person. He didn't raise hell, he didn't get arrested, he went to school, he didn't cuss, he went to church. That's a tough one, man."

But there was one more.

DANNY LESTER, who made one of the two key interceptions against the Razorbacks, couldn't understand it, either. He played next to Freddie, and

Freddie died so young. Danny finished up his Longhorn career, even playing both ways as a senior during a stretch when split end Cotton Speyrer was hurt. In fact, his seventeen receptions in 1970 led the Longhorns. He won the Blair Cherry Award, as Amarillo's top college football player two straight years, accepting it the second time on the same day he was drafted in the thirteenth round by the Philadelphia Eagles. But he didn't stick with the Eagles and came back to Austin, selling property for the Lake Livingston development near Houston. Then he caught on with an oil company, Dawson International, working on offshore rigs. He and his best friend, Tim Connor, lived in Livingston, Louisiana, and worked together.

On September 4, 1973, Danny and Tim had some time off from the rig and decided to head for Austin. Danny's Porsche was in the shop, so they took Tim's 1971 Ford Ranger pickup. Danny drove. The weather was turning terrible, and it officially was designated Storm Delia. Rain was pouring down and the wind was gusting. Danny and Tim were heading west on Interstate 10, near Anahuac on Houston Bay.

KATHY PULLEY had just gotten home from work when the phone rang. Monty Johnson, Danny's high school buddy, who transferred from Texas to Oklahoma, didn't know what to say after it quickly became apparent to him that nobody had broken the news to Danny's mother. He said Putt Powell, the Amarillo sportswriter beloved by anyone who ever played high school sports in the West Texas city, had called and said Danny had been in an accident.

Danny? How is he?

Monty said he didn't know. He couldn't bear to tell Danny's mom. He said to call Putt. So Kathy did, and Putt—kindly ol' Putt—gave her the runaround, too. He said he got some news from the paper's police reporter, and that Kathy should call the Amarillo police. Now convinced something horrible had happened, Kathy called the police station, and the officer wasn't going to tell her anything, either. An officer was on his way to the Pulley home, he said. Tell me, Kathy insisted to the officer on the phone. Finally, the officer did.

THE TRUCK DRIVER WAS FROM IRVING, Texas. He had a 1973 Peterbilt truck tractor and a 1965 Fruehauf van trailer. He was heading east on I-10 when, apparently caught by a gust of wind in the storm and affected by the slick pavement, the truck went sliding off the freeway, across the median, and into the westbound lanes. The back part of the truck's trailer crashed into Tim Connor's pickup. Tim and Danny were killed instantly.

"Danny was driving and this was typical, because every one of those kids, whether it was Danny's car or anyone else's, they handed the keys to Danny," Kathy Pulley says.

The newspaper stories didn't say it, but the police report obtained by a dogged Kathy Pulley did. The driver was given a test at the scene, and his blood alcohol content was .06, meaning he wasn't legally drunk—but was irresponsible. Depending on when they were consumed, it might have meant a couple of beers. Especially in that weather, it was too much. Kathy was urged to sue, but didn't. That wouldn't bring Danny back.

When Danny was buried in Hereford, Texas, he was wearing his national championship ring.

THIRTY-FIVE

Horns Revisited

No. 16 James Street, QB, Senior

(vs. Arkansas: 8 carries, 73 yards, 1 touchdown; 6–10 passing, 2 interceptions, 124 yards)

Street was the star pitcher for the Longhorns' baseball team the next spring, and he threw the last perfect game in the history of the now-defunct Southwest Conference. He suffered an arm injury at the College World Series in Omaha, so he turned down the chance to play in the Cleveland Indians' farm system that summer. He sang on the rodeo circuit, then served a stint in the National Guard. As he was deciding whether to report to the Indians' minor-league camp the next year, he visited Darrell Royal.

"James," Royal said, "if you go off and play pro baseball and you make it to the big leagues, you're going to be making $25,000 a year. But if you don't make it, and you play in those bush leagues for ten years, you'll come back to Austin and they'll say, 'Yeah, James, didn't you play ball here?' Why not quit on top and get a job, build a business for yourself?"

That's what Street did. Staying in Austin, he briefly worked at a car dealership, then got into the insurance business. He formed James Street and Associates in the mid-1970s, then the James Street Group in 1991. He is one of the most successful structured settlement experts in the country.

No. 30 Steve Worster, FB, Junior

(vs. Arkansas: 25 carries, 94 yards)

Worster was an All-American again as a senior, finishing with 2,353 rushing yards in three seasons. He tested Royal's patience with his ways off the field—if there was a party, Worster found it. As his career wound down, he and Royal were feuding, because Royal thought he was losing control of his team and believed Worster was a rabble-rouser. But as promised, he also offered to help Worster after the fullback's pro football career—a brief stay in the Canadian Football League. Worster got his degree in communications. "Coach Royal was a true class act," Worster says, "and I don't know if anybody will ever be able to equal that." Worster is a salesman for Wilson Supply in Bridge City.

No. 35 Jim Bertelsen, HB, Sophomore

(vs. Arkansas: 10 carries, 29 yards, 1 touchdown)

By the time his Texas career was over, Bertelson was the Longhorns' No. 2 career rusher—behind Chris Gilbert and just ahead of Steve Worster. After playing for the Los Angeles Rams from 1972 to 1976, Bertelsen returned to Austin. He works for Arnold Oil.

No. 24 Ted Koy, HB, Senior

(vs. Arkansas: 13 carries, 28 yards)

The halfback with the movie-star looks and the cattle posters on his wall was drafted by the Oakland Raiders and played one season under John Madden, then four seasons with the Buffalo Bills.

He already had a journalism degree from Texas, but he enrolled at Texas A&M, got a second bachelor's in veterinary science, and then attended the A&M veterinary school. Koy has his own veterinary clinic in Georgetown, Texas, just north of Austin.

No. 40 Randy Peschel, TE, Senior

(vs. Arkansas, 2 receptions, 59 yards)

Peschel married Sue, the girl he gave the ring to on Thanksgiving 1969, in 1970. He jumped right into the banking business while finishing up at Texas and worked at several banks before owning his own small construction and development firms. He then was the chief financial officer for Legend Home Builders before becoming a Compass Bank vice president in Austin. He specializes in construction financing. He and Sue have three children and Peschel still occasionally hears: "Hey, aren't you the guy who . . . ?"

No. 50 Bobby Wuensch, LT, Junior

The gentle, soft-spoken Wuensch—at least off the field—was a repeat All-American in 1970. He played four exhibition games with the Baltimore Colts, suffered a broken leg, and never went back. He returned to Houston and got into the family business, Wuensch Sales. Now he runs the company, a wholesale distributor of marine and industrial hardware.

No. 64 Bobby Mitchell, LG, Junior

Mitchell also was an All-American in 1970. After graduation, he attended the Baylor dental school in Dallas. He and Honor Franklin, the Arkansas student he dated in 1969, are married. Dr. Honor Franklin, a speech pathologist, and D.D.S. Robert Mitchell have their practices in the same two-suite office building in North Dallas.

No. 74 Randy Stout, LG, Sophomore

Stout only played one more season. Because of an injury, he was listed as second-team guard going into 1971 fall drills. "Quite honestly, they did it to see what I would do, and what I did was quit," he says. "Coach Royal wasn't happy with me and I wasn't happy with him. But I kept my scholarship that year. Coach Royal and I had a nice conversation, and I agreed I wasn't going to say anything to anybody and he said he was going to be helpful to me. My dad had suffered a heart attack, and Coach Royal knew I couldn't afford to stay there without the scholarship. He has never been anything but nice to me, he's stayed at my home, he has helped me, and I think a lot of what happened was the lack of maturity on my part. He's been unbelievably nice to me and my family."

Stout attended law school, then went to work in the district attorney's office in Galveston. After his stint as a prosecutor, he moved back to San Angelo and went into private practice. He was a district judge from 1986 to 1989, then went back to private practice.

No. 52 Forrest Wiegand, C, Senior

The scrambling center suffered a torn anterior cruciate knee ligament in the Cotton Bowl victory over Notre Dame. He served as a UT graduate assistant while finishing school, then got into high school coaching. He has been at La Porte High School since 1974, and has been the head coach since 1988.

No. 66 Mike Dean, RG, Junior

What are the odds of both guards becoming dentists? After playing one more season for the Longhorns, Dean was accepted to law school, but decided on dental school instead. Like Mitchell, he went to Baylor–Dallas. His private practice in his hometown of Sherman flourished for twenty years. He sold that operation, moved to Horseshoe Bay and opened an office in Marble Falls. In a smaller practice, his wife is his only employee and he specializes in orthodontics, works thirty hours a week, and plays two or three rounds of golf a week.

No. 62 Bob McKay, RT, Senior

At the Hula Bowl all-star game a month after The Big Shootout, Arkansas center Rodney Brand and McKay became friends. "I think we beat you guys," Brand insisted. McKay smiled. "You all played pretty good," McKay drawled, then held up his hand. "But if you all beat us, how come they gave us these rings?"

"Big 'Un" played six seasons with the Cleveland Browns and three seasons with the New England Patriots. When he retired, McKay began selling tires for GCR Trucking, and has been doing that ever since. "They pay me to ride around the state of Texas and talk to friends of mine," McKay says. One of his closest friends and a fellow West Texan—star Horns defensive tackle Leo Brooks, who was injured and didn't play in The Big Shootout—died of throat cancer in April 2002. Like Freddie Steinmark, Brooks—who was president of his own real estate firm—died at M. D. Anderson Hospital in Houston.

No. 88 Cotton Speyrer, SE, Junior

(vs. Arkansas: 4 receptions, 65 yards)

His senior season ended when he suffered a broken arm in the fourth game against Oklahoma. Speyrer played three seasons with the Baltimore Colts and one with the Miami Dolphins. He became a stockbroker in Austin, then founded a software development company, Pathways, and remains the company president. He emphasizes that Darrell Royal has "gone to bat for me in so many ways. When he was a coach, he kind of had to be a hardass. But he loves his former players and he'll go all the way with them. He's one of the finest men I've ever met in my life."

No. 77 Bill Atessis, DE, Junior

(vs. Arkansas: 6 unassisted, 2 assisted tackles)

Also drafted by the Baltimore Colts, along with his high school and college teammate Bobby Wuensch, Atessis suffered a knee injury in the exhibition season and was traded to New England. He played for the Patriots in 1971 before leaving football. He owned a nightclub briefly, then went into the construction business. A resident engineer, he is a construction project manager for PBS&J in Houston.

No. 31 Greg Ploetz, DT, *Junior*

(vs. Arkansas: 4 unassisted, 2 assisted tackles)

Ploetz was named the outstanding artist in UT's class of '71 and also earned a master's of fine arts. A movie buff—he credits those free movie tickets the Longhorns received—he managed a movie theater, and taught art at several schools, including the University of Arkansas–Little Rock. He then bought, refurbished, and resold homes, but decided he missed teaching. He has been on the faculty of Trimble Tech High School in Fort Worth since 1995. Chris Fry, Greg's son and Freddie Steinmark's godson, is a train supervisor in Omaha. Greg remarried in 1978, and his wife, Deb Hardin, is an Arkansas graduate who attended the Big Shootout as a student.

No. 70 Carl White, DT, *Sophomore*

(vs. Arkansas: 3 unassisted, 3 assisted tackles)

The big defensive tackle who suffered the knee injury against Arkansas also only played one more year and decided to leave the squad as a senior. Royal had been on him for underachieving, and he had gotten married and gained weight. He says that when he told Royal he just didn't have the desire to play any longer, Royal understood. "He had been working on me quite a bit because I disappointed him in a lot of ways, and he let it show," White says. "He was a great manager, an absolutely fabulous manager, and after running a business for thirty years, I understand what a good manager is. He hired the right people and put them in the right place. He oversaw a pretty good operation, about as good as there was. He handled all the politics and diplomacy and my hat's off to him." White eventually returned to Corsicana and began working in the family car business; he now owns Carl White Chevrolet.

No. 89 David Arledge, DE, *Sophomore*

(vs. Arkansas: 2 unassisted, 4 assisted tackles)

Arledge says he didn't play as well as a junior, "but I had an OK year." He suffered a knee injury in the 1971 opener and didn't play again. He also got into the family car business, and owns Forest Lane Motors in Dallas.

No. 80 Bill Zapalac, OLB, Junior

(vs. Arkansas: 4 unassisted, 1 assisted tackle; 1 fumble recovery)

After playing three seasons for the New York Jets, Zapalac entered the construction business in Austin in 1974. Bill is co-owner of Zapalac-Reed Construction Company in Austin.

No. 67 Glen Halsell, ILB, Senior

(vs. Arkansas: 4 unassisted, 3 assisted tackles)

The once-wild linebacker stayed straightened out. "I'm lucky I didn't get into worse situations," Halsell says.

After graduating, he worked for a while at the Texas state capitol, attended law school, and went into private practice in his hometown of Odessa. He has a general practice but specializes in bankruptcy law. Over the years, he has dropped several notes to Darrell Royal, thanking the coach for sticking with him.

No. 61 Scott Henderson, ILB, Junior

(vs. Arkansas: 5 unassisted, 3 assisted tackles; 1 blocked punt)

"The Professor" went on an NCAA-sponsored visit to meet troops in Vietnam in the summer of 1970. "I didn't see a lot of excitement from the people who were over there to be there," Henderson says. "I didn't see a lot of respect for the Americans by the Vietnamese, or for what the Americans were doing. You get out in those firecamps, and you see the way those kids were living and the patrols they had to take, it just didn't seem right. I didn't quite understand why those kids were getting killed or what purpose it served."

After his strong senior season, Henderson tried playing in the Canadian Football League but was cut by the Hamilton Tiger Cats. As he was about to start in the UT law school, Winnipeg in the CFL offered to sign him, but he passed on that. He entered private practice in 1975 and is a prominent civil trial lawyer in Dallas, where he is a partner in the firm of Henderson & Hendrickson.

No. 86 Mike Campbell, Rover, Senior

(vs. Arkansas: 3 unassisted, 1 assisted tackle)

After working for three years in the oil business in Singapore and Indonesia, Mike was brought back to Texas and went into sales. He lives in the Houston area and works for Baker Hughes Oilfield Service Company, selling products and services to major firms.

No. 84 Tom Campbell, DHB, Senior

(vs. Arkansas: 2 unassisted tackles, 1 interception)

The other Campbell twin signed a free-agent contract with the Oakland Raiders but didn't go to their camp until 1971 because of basic training and National Guard service. He was cut by the Raiders, then also by the Philadelphia Eagles, and went back to Austin. His daughter, Beth, played soccer for the University of Arkansas, and Tom was a regular in Fayetteville, made friends with many of the former Razorbacks, and even went in to see Frank Broyles. He is a printing systems specialist.

No. 23 Danny Lester, DHB, Junior

(vs. Arkansas: 4 unassisted, 1 assisted tackle; 1 interception)

Lester's mother, Kathy Pulley, was widowed for a third time in 1996. She still lives in Amarillo and occasionally hears from Danny's former teammates.

No. 28 Freddie Steinmark, S, Junior

(vs. Arkansas: 1 unassisted, 1 assisted tackle)

Texas dedicated the stadium scoreboard to Steinmark in 1971, and the Longhorns still stop and touch the plaque honoring the little safety as they head onto the field.

Freddie's father, Freddie Gene, died in 2000. He and his son are buried under the same Virgin Mary monument at Mount Olivet in Wheat Ridge.

No. 5 Happy Feller, PK, Junior

(vs. Arkansas: 2 kickoffs through the end zone, 1 extra point)

The name still fits. The gregarious Feller kicked for three seasons in the NFL, with Philadelphia and New Orleans. He worked for Bell Systems for seven years, then quit and founded his own company, TeleDynamics, in June 1981. TeleDynamics is a worldwide consumer electronics distributor and sells business telephone systems to installers.

No. 70 Julius Whittier, LB-OT, Freshman

The Longhorns' first black letterman was a solid contributor on the offensive line and at tight end in his three-season career.

Whittier says he never felt completely accepted by all his teammates, but he says he never received overt maltreatment and he was friends with many of his teammates, and emphasizes he felt the coaches treated him fairly. By the time he was a senior in 1972, he had five black teammates.

Whittier's relationship ran hot-and-cold with Royal, but he had more direct dealings and conversations with the head coach than most other Texas players, and they often were blunt with each other. Royal sometimes felt as if Whittier saw racism in any criticism of his play, and Whittier continued to feel as if Royal wasn't being perceptive enough about some of the attitudes toward the black players in the program. Yet, on the whole, they developed a mutual respect that lasts to this day.

"The athletic department became sensitized in dealing with black athletes," he says. "They discovered some of the ranges of personality, humor, etiquette, social protocol that you see among blacks. [Coach Royal] didn't know everything, but he set the tone about how we were treated."

Whittier also went to the Texas law school, and then worked in Dallas as an assistant district attorney for the legendary district attorney Henry Wade. Whittier handled many high-profile prosecutions for Wade. Shortly after Wade retired, Whittier entered a private practice in Dallas. He is passionate and respected as a defense attorney who served on the "other" side. Over half of Whittier's practice involves defending indigent clients, who are often surprised by his candor in emphasizing that they can take control of their lives by making better personal choices.

Head Coach Darrell Royal

The 1970 Longhorns went 10–0 under Royal in the regular season, beating Arkansas 42–7 in a Big Shootout reprise on December 5 in Austin. Texas won the United Press International national championship because the coaches' final poll occurred before the bowl games. The Texas winning streak was at thirty games, but the Longhorns lost to Notre Dame in the Cotton Bowl and dropped to No. 3, behind Nebraska and Notre Dame, in the final Associated Press poll.

Royal shockingly resigned after the 1976 season, but remained as athletic director. He was only fifty-two, but he decided he had had enough of coaching and remained for short terms as athletic director and as assistant to the president before completely retiring. At Texas, his twenty-season record was 167–47–5, and his Longhorns won the Southwest Conference eleven times.

Royal remains in demand for appearances and as a speaker. "I've often said I need to get a job so I can have an excuse not to be as busy," he jokes.

Offensive Coach Emory Bellard

The wishbone's inventor was the head coach at Texas A&M and Mississippi State, then retired. Restless, he came out of retirement to coach high school football for fun, then went back to a life of leisure for good in 1995. He lives in Marble Falls, Texas.

Defensive Coach Mike Campbell

The twins' father retired from coaching when he wasn't named Royal's successor by the university administration—a slight that bothered many of the 1969 Longhorns and Royal himself. For four years, he worked for the Texas Teacher Retirement System, then returned to UT as the head of the athletic department's scholarship fund-raising wing. He was inducted into the school's Hall of Honor in 1984. He died of lymphoma in 1998.

Defensive Backfield Coach Fred Akers

The administration faced a tough decision in selecting Royal's successor, and chose the younger Akers in part because he had left Texas in 1975 to gain head-coaching experience at Wyoming and had done well. The Cowboys won the Western Athletic Conference title in 1976 with Freddie Steinmark's little brother, Sammy, at safety. In ten seasons under Akers, the Longhorns were an excellent 86–31–2, but he was fired after a 5–6 season in 1986. After coaching four seasons at Purdue, he returned to the Austin area. He and his son, Danny, run Akers Performance Group, a motivational firm.

THIRTY-SIX

Hogs Revisited

No. 10 Bill Montgomery, QB, Junior

(vs. Texas: 15 carries, -2 yards; 14–22 passing, 205 yards, 2 interceptions, 1 touchdown)

In 1970, the Razorbacks' quarterback went on an NCAA-sponsored tour of military hospitals in the Pacific, visiting American soldiers wounded in Vietnam. "We'd see burn wards," he says. "We saw double amputees, blind guys, and it was just a horrible experience. And they're all our age. I was still able to think that we had this great obligation to save the world from communism and it was a noble cause. It was just a few years later, looking back again, that I was asking, 'How did we get ourselves in there to begin with?'"

With Montgomery at quarterback, the Razorbacks went 9–2 in 1970, losing the opener to Stanford and the final game to Texas. The players voted to decline an invitation to the Liberty Bowl and Frank Broyles went along this time.

Montgomery wasn't drafted and considered both free-agent offers from NFL teams and a contract offer from the Winnipeg Blue Bombers of the CFL. "But primarily because of not being drafted, I thought, 'This is enough, I've had a great career, it's time to go to work.'"

He worked for Smith-Barney and other investment firms, both in Dallas and New York, and owned a traffic safety sign firm, SA-SO, before selling the company in 1998. He is a highly successful private investor in Dallas.

No. 33 Bill Burnett, TB, Junior

(vs. Texas: 19 carries, 82 yards, 1 touchdown; 3 receptions, 26 yards)

Burnett had an injury-plagued 1970 season, getting only 110 carries for 445 yards. Broyles made sure he was named to the Hula Bowl all-star game, so he could have a honeymoon after marrying Linda Holmes in December 1970. He was drafted by the Baltimore Colts but was cut and claimed by the New England Patriots. Rather than report to New England, Burnett went back to Fayetteville and graduate school. After getting his master's degree, he worked for the Fellowship of Christian Athletes as a field representative for eight years. He studied at a seminary in Dallas and earned a doctorate in counseling. He is a Christian family counselor in Fort Smith.

No. 34 Bruce Maxwell, FB, Senior

(vs. Texas: 10 carries, 23 yards)

Maxwell played for the Detroit Lions in 1970, then returned to Pine Bluff and sold insurance and cars. He also was a guard and internal affairs officer at the Arkansas state prison, but when the state tried to turn him into a paper-pushing administrator, he quit and sold cars again for a while, then went into the landscaping business.

No. 20 Chuck Dicus, SE, Junior

(vs. Texas: 9 receptions, 146 yards, 1 touchdown)

Dicus caught 38 passes as a senior and was a repeat All-American. A seventh-round draft choice of the San Diego Chargers, Dicus was a part-time starter for two seasons and also played one year with the Pittsburgh Steelers. He sold real estate, then was receivers coach at Memphis State for three seasons under former Razorbacks assistant Richard Williamson. He went back into private business and did well in commercial real estate, development, and investment banking. He became director of the Razorback Foundation Inc., the UofA's chief athletic fundraiser, in 1991.

No. 78 Mike Kelson, LT, Sophomore

What could be worse than coming home after The Big Shootout and hearing his wife and her former Texas sorority sisters celebrating? The next year, before Big Shootout II on December 5 in Austin, Kelson was getting psyched up to face the Longhorns in a few minutes when a United Press International photographer begged Mike to pose for a picture with his sister, Karla, on the sideline. Mike grudgingly obliged.

With her brother at her side in the Razorbacks uniform, Karla held up her hand in the "Hook 'em Horns" sign. Karla was a Texas cheerleader, and she had a lot to cheer about that afternoon, when the Longhorns won 42–7.

In 1971, though, Kelson was a senior cocaptain for "The Revenge at the Rock," Arkansas's 31–7 victory in Little Rock. Because he was in ROTC, he helped make sure the cannon was overloaded when it was rolled onto the War Mamorial Stadium floor. So when the Razorbacks scored, he says, "You couldn't see the field when that damn round went off."

When Mike became a regional manager for a data firm and was transferred to Dallas, Karla's husband—UT grad Bob Shelby—said he was looking forward to showing Mike the Cotton Bowl, since Mike never got to see it as a player. Kelson works for a learning systems company in Dallas.

No. 74 Jerry Dossey, LG, Senior

Dossey left the Dallas Cowboys' 1970 camp after four days, because his foot wasn't healed, and entered the Arkansas law school the next year. In his final year, he found himself arguing virtually all term with one professor about President Nixon. The issue was whether Nixon should have the right to executive privilege, limiting the availability of administration officials to testify and restricting the availability of presidential documents and material in the Watergate investigation. Dossey says he passionately argued that "the president of the United States shouldn't have to turn over his private tapes. Executive privilege means something." The young professor disagreed, saying not even the president was above the law. But the paper Dossey wrote for the professor on the subject won an American Jurisprudence Award.

Later that year, the young law professor ran for Congress against John Paul Hammerschmidt, George Bush's close friend. Hammerschmidt won by 2 percent of the vote.

The professor, Bill Clinton, ran for other offices later.

Dossey has been an attorney in Bentonville since 1974, and he most often does tax-planning and estate work.

No. 57 Rodney Brand, C, Senior

With the New York Giants, Brand had the bad luck to make his first professional start—in an exhibition game after the usual starter was injured—against the Green Bay Packers and middle linebacker Ray Nitschke. "I wasn't big enough for pro football," he says. "I had to put some bricks in my pocket." He was cut and was a high school coach for four years, then a salesman. In 1985, he founded his own company, manufacturing and selling automatic window lift motors for Ford, then sold the company and retired to a farm near Oklahoma City in 1995.

No. 70 Ronnie Hammers, RG, Junior

The guard who had refused to commit to Texas early in the recruiting process and ended up at Arkansas gained further respect for Darrell Royal when he was on the sideline on crutches before the 1970 Texas-Arkansas game because of a career-ending ankle injury. Royal spotted him, came over, and congratulated Hammers on "a great career," adding he would have been proud to coach him as a Longhorn.

After his senior season, he did student teaching in Fayetteville, then returned to Marshall, his hometown, to coach and teach for nearly three years. He left teaching to go into the family home remodeling business, and he runs the company today.

No. 75 Bob Stankovich, RT, Senior

A Kansas City draft choice, Stankovich didn't stick with the Chiefs and went into teaching and coaching. He has coached at several places in Texas, and has taught biology at and has coached at Vidor High School since 1983.

No. 88 Pat Morrison, TE, Junior

After his senior season, Morrison was drafted by the Buffalo Bills but didn't like the contract and bonus offer and decided to get on with his life immediately. He went into banking, then into the commercial real estate business. Married since 1970 to the former Ann Hartenstein, the Razorbacks' homecoming queen, Morrison works for Harris-McHaney Realtors in Rogers, Arkansas.

No. 25 John Rees, FL, Junior

(vs. Texas: 2 receptions, 33 yards)

After an injury-plagued senior season, Rees tried out as a free agent with Pittsburgh and left camp after a week. Eventually, he founded his own real estate company in Little Rock in 1981 and then created Rees Development in 1989. Married since 1971 to the former Debbie Brasher of Dallas, he has three daughters, Amy, Lauri, and Pamela, who all attended the UofA. They once asked him if he met Richard Nixon at the game. He said no, then was flabbergasted when he watched a rebroadcast years later with his daughters and saw that he was the first player with whom Nixon shook hands after stepping off the stage in the dressing room. His daughters still tease him about being in such a fog after the loss that he couldn't remember meeting the president. He and Debbie also have a younger son, John Aaron.

No. 85 Bruce James, DE, Junior

(vs. Texas: 2 unassisted, 6 assisted tackles)

By the time he was finished at Arkansas, James had endured six surgeries, but he was an All-American in 1970. He was drafted by the Philadelphia Eagles, received a three-thousand-dollar bonus, was injured in training camp—after getting to know another rookie, Danny Lester—and returned to Fayetteville to be checked over by the doctor who did most of his surgeries. The doctor recommended he walk away from the game, and that's what James did. He went to work for International Paper as a management trainee, then moved to Little Rock in 1972 and opened his own insurance agency two years later.

No. 63 Roger Harnish, DT, Sophomore

(vs. Texas: 4 unassisted, 4 assisted tackles)

Harnish gave up football after his junior year because of a knee injury. After spending some time in Europe following graduation, he worked for a bank and caught on with Bridgestone-Firestone in 1974. A regional manager for the company, he lives in Little Rock.

No. 68 Terry Don Phillips, DT, Senior

(vs. Texas: 3 unassisted, 2 assisted tackles)

After he was through playing, Phillips was a graduate assistant with the Razorbacks. When Charley Coffey became head coach at Virginia Tech, Phillips went with him and served on Coffey's staff for eight seasons. He was an assistant athletic director at Florida and Missouri, and the athletic director at Liberty College and Southwestern Louisiana, before returning to Arkansas as the head of the Razorback Foundation. When he became an assistant athletic director for the Razorbacks, Dicus succeeded him at the foundation. Phillips left his alma mater to become athletic director at Oklahoma State in 1995, then accepted the athletic director job at Clemson in June 2002.

No. 71 Gordon McNulty, DE, Senior

(vs. Texas: 1 fumble recovery)

The folks at the Campus Crusade for Christ had a sardonic sense of humor—or wanted to test their charges' determination. McNulty was one of two Razorbacks who went to work for the Campus Crusade after graduation, and both were sent on their first assignments to the University of

Texas. In his stint in Austin, McNulty became friends with many of the Longhorns, including Freddie Steinmark, and saw Bobby Wuensch tearfully shave Steinmark's head.

Later, McNulty attended Dallas Theological Seminary and was a minister at Fellowship Bible Churches in Little Rock and Dallas. He founded a Dallas food distribution company, Grubbs Foods, in 1989, and he is the firm's president.

For years, McNulty's father, Gordon Sr., had a lithograph of Jim Bertelsen's touchdown run for Texas on the wall of his home in Pine Bluff. Gordon Jr. is in the picture, on his knees near Bertelsen.

"He was proud," Gordon says of his father. "Most of the people in Arkansas were proud that the University of Arkansas was playing for the national championship. It was such a big game and we played so well." For years, whenever Gordon Jr. visited his parents, he took down the picture and turned it around, against the wall. "If you can be proud only when you win, then at the end of the season, only the undefeated teams can be proud," he says. "We had a great year and we played well, but I was like everyone else. It took me years and years to get over that game. But looking back now, I'm proud to be a part of it."

No. 61 Dick Bumpas, DT, Junior
(vs. Texas: 4 unassisted, 5 assisted tackles)

Bumpas was the Southwest Conference's defensive player of the year and an All-American as a senior. He got into coaching and his résumé includes a one-season stint as the Razorbacks' defensive line coach in 1989. When head coach Ken Hatfield bailed to go to Clemson, Bumpas moved to Notre Dame. He also has coached at Army, Air Force, Kansas State, Tennessee, Utah State, Navy, and Houston. He is the defensive coordinator at Western Michigan University.

No. 72 Rick Kersey, DE, Junior
(vs. Texas: 2 unassisted, 8 assisted tackles)

The little defensive end who was injured on the Texas two-point conversion played for a while through a hairline leg fracture as a senior and had an understandably subpar season. After graduation, Kersey became a staff member for the Campus Crusade for Christ, succeeding Gordon McNulty as a rep at the University of Texas. "Nine months there was all I could handle," he says, laughing. He moved on to be campus director at Stephen F. Austin University, then worked for Christian Family Life in Dallas. After a brief coaching stint at the University of Central Arkansas in his hometown of Conway, he went to the Western Conservative Baptist Seminary in Portland, Oregon. In 1982, he started the Fellowship Bible Church in Texarkana, Texas. He remained active with the church after going into the business world, and he has been a salesman of hospital equipment and pharmaceuticals for twenty years.

No. 53 Lynn Garner, LB, Senior
(vs. Texas: 1 unassisted, 8 assisted tackles)

Garner admits he was a cavalier student while playing, but then he got serious. He was a graduate assistant for two years while he completed work for his degree, then was a high school coach in Texas for seven years. He left coaching and began selling environmental cleanup supplies, then founded his own company. Garner Environmental Services, Inc., in the Houston area, is the best-known company of its kind in the country. It cleans up oil spills and other environmental accidents and also was involved in the work at the World Trade Center site in New York following the September 11, 2001, terrorist attacks.

No. 64 Cliff Powell, LB, Senior
(vs. Texas: 7 unassisted, 14 assisted tackles)

Not long after The Big Shootout, Powell one day opened an envelope, and a silver dollar fell out. A man had taped a label to it: "MVP, Arkansas vs. Texas."

Powell got a degree in engineering and sold life insurance for two years before returning to Eudora to work the family farm. He sold the farm in 1990 and bought a sporting goods store. "I found out that I didn't like retail," he says. After a stint as a salesman of medical diagnostic equipment, he returned to college and studied computer programming. He was inducted into the University of Arkansas Sports Hall of Honor in 2001.

No. 59 Mike Boschetti, LB, Junior
(vs. Texas: 2 unassisted, 4 assisted tackles)

Boschetti became a CPA in Little Rock. At one point, he helped develop software to handle loans left behind by failed savings and loan institutions. In 1998, he formed his own financial-consulting business and does a lot of free counseling through his church. He volunteers as the defensive coordinator at Little Rock Christian Academy, where his son-in-law is the head coach.

He still thinks he was clipped.

No. 49 Bobby Field, "Monster" Back, Junior
(vs. Texas: 3 assisted tackles, 1 fumble recovery)

After his senior season, Field told Frank Broyles he wanted to get into coaching, but that serving as a graduate assistant elsewhere—away from former teammates—might help his development. Broyles recommended him to Bear Bryant, and Field served as a graduate assistant at Alabama. He coached there for two years, then five years at Mississippi State, before going to UCLA in 1978. He was the defensive coordinator when he left coaching in 2001 to become an assistant athletic director.

No. 18 Jerry Moore, DHB, Junior
(vs. Texas: 4 assisted tackles)

Moore was an all-Southwest-Conference choice as a senior in 1970 and had a four-season NFL career that was cut short by injuries. So in one measurable way, he turned out to be the best Razorback position player. With the Chicago Bears in 1971, he won the Brian Piccolo Award as the team's rookie of the year. He spent two seasons with Chicago, then two with New Orleans.

As the years went on, the pass to Randy Peschel continued to bother him, especially because of the ridiculous barroom misconceptions that he had either blown the coverage or been badly beaten on the play. In fact, given the emphasis of coming up to play the option on the tight-end side, he made a good play not to overreact to the play fake and get back into pass coverage.

"I've listened to this stuff for thirty years," Moore says. "That's what they remember you for. It's like, 'This is Jerry Moore, you remember him, he was the guy covering Randy Peschel in The Big Shootout.' Or, 'You remember Jerry Moore, he was the guy on the fourth-and-3 play, covering the guy.' Introduced that way! Remembered that way! It's not as bad as it used to be. But it used to be I got it all the time. It was something that would happen at least once a week.

"I felt like I had a good career in football and nobody ever brought up anything positive and even that deal, they made something negative of the deal when it really wasn't. Defensive backs have passes caught on them all the time. You can really cover a guy only so well. I understand that that was a big play in the game, obviously, but there were a lot of other big plays. There were interceptions thrown. There were field goals that should have been kicked, but were not kicked. There were clips that were not called by the officials.

"You can go back and there were probably ten or twelve plays in the course of that game that could have changed the outcome, so I got beyond it real quick. This was a big play. But you have the guy covered. Could you have covered the guy better? Yeah, maybe. Maybe not, I don't know. I really don't know if I could have or not. The bottom line is he was covered pretty well and Dennis Berner came over and we had two guys on the guy and it was a miraculous deal."

Moore works in sales for Tri-States Expedited Service, which does emergency freight shipping. He lives in Little Rock.

No. 24 Terry Stewart, DHB, Senior

(vs. Texas: 1 unassisted, 3 assisted tackles; 1 interception, 1 fumble recovery)

Stewart went to the University of Texas graduate business school for two years and helped out coaching the freshman team. He worked at Texas Instruments for a year in Dallas, then went to Minneapolis and got into investment banking. He is chief financial officer for Bioenergy, a specialty pharmaceuticals and life sciences company.

No. 36 Dennis Berner, S, Senior

(vs. Texas: 3 unassisted, 2 assisted tackles; 1 interception)

The quiet Razorbacks safety attended the Arkansas–Little Rock medical school, and served an internship in Russellville and then two years as a Navy physician. He has been in private practice in Russellville since 1979.

No. 19 Bill McClard, PK, Sophomore

(vs. Texas: 2 extra points; 4 kickoffs, 2 unreturned)

The sophomore kicker, who didn't get the chance to kick a potentially gamewinning field goal, was an All-American in both 1970 and '71. McClard kicked four seasons in the NFL, with San Diego and New Orleans. He went into real estate, working in Little Rock for twenty-one years before moving back to northwest Arkansas in 1995. In Rogers, he works for Lindsey and Associates, the firm owned by Jim Lindsey, who was a sophomore wingback on Arkansas's 1964 national championship team.

No. 15 John Eichler, QB, Senior

Bill Montgomery's backup quarterback, who tried to get Darrell Brown the ball with the 1965 Shoats, is co-owner of Eichler-Williams Insurance in Fayetteville.

Head Coach Frank Broyles

Like Darrell Royal, Broyles quit as head coach after the 1976 season. (Royal sent him a presidential Rolex watch as a retirement present.) Broyles's nineteen-season record with the Razorbacks was 144–58–5, and his reputation as a "coach of coaches" was enhanced after The Big Shootout. His assistants from 1970 to 1976 also included Joe Gibbs, the future head coach of the Super Bowl champion Washington Redskins; Raymond Berry, the future head coach of the AFC champion New England Patriots; and Bill Lewis, the future head coach at Wyoming, East Carolina, and Georgia Tech.

Broyles still is the Razorbacks' athletic director, and his latest triumph is a stunning reconstruction job on Razorback Stadium that was completed for the 2001 season.

He says he has never watched The Big Shootout on tape or film.

Defensive Line Coach Charley Coffey

The crusty Coffey was thinking about getting out of coaching altogether when he was hired as the head coach at Virginia Tech. He and a friend bought a struggling truck company—Goggin Truck Line—in his native Tennessee, and the friend ran it until Coffey left Virginia Tech. Eventually, Coffey and his partners sold Goggin for $20 million. Coffey started another company, Nationwide Express, Inc., also a successful venture. Coffey is semi-retired, living in the Knoxville area, and his sons run the company.

Offensive Backfield Coach Don Breaux

Breaux is best-known as the Washington Redskins' running backs coach under Joe Gibbs. Breaux was with Washington for twelve seasons, and the Redskins won the Super Bowl three times during the period. After The Big Shootout, he was with the Razorbacks through 1971, then joined the Houston Oilers' staff for one season. He was at Florida for two years, then—oh, the irony—was on Royal's staff as Fred Akers's replacement in 1975–76. Breaux served a second stint at Arkansas from 1977 to 1980, working under Lou Holtz and athletic director Frank Broyles, then joined the Redskins.

While in Washington, his wife, Harleen, was a scheduling secretary for Vice President George Bush. He was with the New York Giants in 1994 before moving to the expansion Carolina franchise in 1995. He served eight seasons on the Panthers' staff before retiring.

Receivers Coach Richard Williamson

Williamson served a six-season stint as head coach at Memphis State. He moved to the NFL as an assistant with Kansas City, and was the Tampa Bay Buccaneers' interim head coach in the final three games in 1990, then the head coach in 1991. He was on the Cincinnati Bengals' staff from 1992 to 1994. Like Don Breaux, Williamson joined the Carolina Panthers for the 1995 expansion season, and he coaches the wide receivers under John Fox.

Offensive Line Coach Mervin Johnson

The popular assistant stayed at Arkansas until 1974, then went to Notre Dame as offensive coordinator. With the Fighting Irish, he coached Joe Montana. He moved to Oklahoma in 1979, joining the staff of former Razorback player and assistant Barry Switzer. Johnson has been with the OU program ever since as a coach and, most recently, the director of football operations. In that job, he coordinates the off-the-field details for head coach Bob Stoops and also serves as the analyst on the OU radio broadcasts. Official records aren't kept on such things, but he might be the only man to have been on the coaching staffs of national championship teams at three different schools. In his case, the national titles came at Arkansas in 1964, Notre Dame in 1977, and Oklahoma in 1985 and 2000.

Administrative Assistant Wilson Matthews

The former Little Rock Central High and Razorbacks coach—who was an administrative assistant to Broyles and ran the Fourth-Quarter Program in 1969—continued to work for the athletic department for years. He is credited with coming up with a season-ticket priority program that helped support the athletic department's ambitious projects and budgets. He still lived in Fayetteville and was associate athletic director emeritus when he died in May 2002. He was 82.

Graduate Assistant Coach Bob Ford

The author of the critical scouting report on the Longhorns stuck to his plan to get out of coaching and is a lawyer in his native Wynne, Arkansas. Not long ago, Charley Coffey was on a cross-country drive and stopped to visit

Ford. When Coffey pulled into the parking lot at Ford's office, the attorney saw the coach and ran out, yelling, "Kick the field goal!"

Jon Richardson, TB, Freshman

The Razorbacks' first black scholarship football player backed up Bill Burnett on the varsity in 1970 and Dickey Morton in 1971–72. His best game was against Oklahoma State in 1971, when he rushed for 154 yards and two touchdowns. In his three-season career, he ran for 1,237 yards, a total that placed him eighth on the Razorbacks' career list when he finished his eligibility. After also getting a master's degree, he worked for Southwestern Electric Power Company in Fayetteville for many years, then moved to Tulsa and ultimately to Chandler, Arizona. He died of a heart attack, at age forty-nine, on January 18, 2002.

Hiram McBeth, DB, Sophomore

The little B team defensive back never lettered, but he suited up and got into games on special teams in 1970–71.

McBeth went to the Arkansas law school, and he had both Clinton and Hillary Rodham as professors. As a corporate attorney in private practice in Dallas, he has worked with utility companies, banks, and mass transit firms.

Durrell Brown

Brown, the law student who was shot on the night before the game and tried out for the Razorback freshman team in 1965, entered the bar and was a magistrate in the Panama Canal Zone from 1972 to 1979. He briefly worked in the Arkansas attorney general's office in 1979, shortly after Bill Clinton left the post of attorney general, then went into private practice in Little Rock.

He was on the defense team for Arkansas governor Jim Guy Tucker in the "Whitewater" trial of Tucker and Susan and James McDougal, the Clintons' former partners in a failed real estate investment. As such, Brown was among those who questioned President Bill Clinton in the White House on April 28, 1996, for videotaped testimony that was shown at the trial in Little Rock on May 8. Tucker and Jim McDougal were accused of conspiring to acquire $3 million in illegal loans. David Hale, the head of the company that arranged the loans, said Clinton had pressured him in 1986 to push through the deal.

During his examination of the president, Brown eventually asked: "Did Governor Tucker ever ask you to do anything at any time to help him obtain loans from David Hale or any of his companies?"

"No, sir," Clinton told Brown, "he did not ever ask for that kind of help."

Brown's daughter, Dee, is a scholarship track star at the University of Arkansas. "I had some mixed emotions about it," Brown says. "The institution had tested me. But the institution that tested me had a black assistant coach involved in its recruiting program. I sat down with him and shared a little bit of my history and my reservations about encouraging my daughter to attend. I assured him that because he was there and the university had in good faith made some strides toward integration and leveling the playing field, so to speak, I would not discourage her."

Brown still wonders if he could have been the Razorbacks' first black varsity player in 1966 if he had stuck with it after his freshman walk-on experience. "It should have been done earlier," he says of the program's integration, "and I was bitter about that. I wanted to play football. I wanted to give myself a chance. Even now, I sit and look at football players, athletes running up and down that field, and I look back on my experiences at the University of Arkansas and tears come to my eyes—literally come to my eyes."

Eugene Hunt

The head of the Black Americans for Democracy finished law school in 1971 and served nine months as a UofA assistant dean of students before opening his law firm in Pine Bluff.

Dr. Gordon Morgan

Arkansas's first black faculty member—in his first school year at the time of The Big Shootout—still is a sociology professor on the Fayetteville campus.

Colonel Eugene Holmes

The much-decorated head of Arkansas's military sciences department—or ROTC—retired in the early 1970s. Holmes and his wife live in Fayetteville.

Bud Zinke

The physics professor continued to be active in the anti–Vietnam War movement and fought for civil rights and free speech issues on and around campus. He retired in the mid-1980s and still lives in Fayetteville.

Don Donner

The former Army combat engineer in Vietnam and organizer of the protest on the hill above the stadium, Donner got more heavily involved in the

Vietnam Veterans Against the War national organization and was an unindicted coconspirator in the 1973 trial of the "Gainesville Eight," anti–Vietnam War activists acquitted of conspiring to violently disrupt the 1972 Republican convention at Miami Beach. After getting a biology degree, he also went to the Arkansas law school and took the Clinton-taught Criminal Procedures course.

After graduating law school, Donner became an oil-well geologist, based in Oklahoma City. He was very successful, but when the oil boom ended, he opened a private law practice in Fayetteville in 1991 and is active in the Veterans of Foreign Wars post. He is best known for doing election law work for the "Shiite" insurgent wing of the Arkansas Republican Party and has served as a special justice on the Arkansas State Supreme Court, standing in when judges withdraw from specific cases because of potential conflicts of interests or for other reasons. In 2000, he enthusiastically campaigned for fellow Vietnam War veteran John McCain for president. Still a vigilant free speech absolutist, he has worked for conservative churches in danger of losing their tax-exempt status. Laughing, he notes, "They say, 'That Donner's going to hell for sure, but he sure is a good-hearted guy.'"

Rhodes Scholar William Jefferson Clinton

Former thirteen-term U.S. representative John Paul Hammerschmidt, who presented tapes of The Big Shootout to the Razorbacks at their 1989 reunion, laughs when he is reminded that Bill Clinton wrote the now infamous letter to Colonel Holmes the week of the game. "It's kind of ironic," he says. He adds he spoke with Colonel Holmes "when that letter became public. They wanted me to give that to Bush, and I did." Hammerschmidt also says that Bush "didn't want to use it. . . . He didn't use it. He didn't think it was a good thing to do. But I let him know there was such a letter."

However, the letter to Holmes was leaked to ABC during the 1992 Democratic primary campaign, just days before the New Hampshire primary. ABC's Ted Koppel read the entire letter on *Nightline* on February 12, 1992, as Clinton appeared on the show to discuss it. Koppel said on the air that *World News Tonight* "got its information from Colonel (Clint) Jones, who was an aide" to Holmes.

Clinton told Koppel on the air: "I think the important thing is that the letter is consistent with everything I've been saying for the past thirteen years, since I was first asked about this in 1978. I was in the draft before the lottery came in. I gave up the deferment. I got a high lottery number and I wasn't called."

Clinton said that when he wrote the letter he was "a deeply agitated twenty-three-year-old boy, a young man. At least I was involved in the issues of my time, I cared deeply about them. That's the way I felt. If I were writing that letter today about how I felt, I'd still disagree with our policy in Vietnam but I wouldn't say the same things in the same way." He said he had come to believe that "when you have a general draft, at least there ought to be a declaration of war."

Bill Clinton, the forty-second president of the United States, lives in Chappaqua, New York, and has an office in New York City.

AFTERWORD

Nearly two years after the publication of the hardback edition of *Horns, Hogs, and Nixon Coming*, I can get away with a confession.

Originally, after literary agent Randy Voorhees asked if I could expand my 1994 *Sporting News* silver anniversary article on "The Big Shootout" into a book, I had a fallback plan. If I didn't find enough material on Texas vs. Arkansas, I was going to make it the centerpiece of a work on the 1969 college football season in that tumultuous summer and fall. Even now, I believe that would have been a worthwhile approach as well. Because my father, Jerry Frei, was the head coach at the University of Oregon in Eugene in 1969, I had a unique perspective on football and on the campus atmosphere. That year, the UofO president, caught in the crossfire between radical students—many of my father's football players were political activists—and the public, drove his Volkswagen Beetle head-on into a logging truck. The national turmoil was winding down when my father became the Denver Broncos' offensive line coach in 1972, and I transferred to Wheat Ridge High School—the alma mater of 1969 Texas starters Freddie Steinmark and Bobby Mitchell.

However, after again looking through my magazine article research material and starting the new and far more extensive wave of interviews in 2001, I realized that with the 1969 Texas–Arkansas game not only could I deliver a book, but I could also write an epic. Actually, that's what I did—before Simon and Schuster editors Jeff Neuman and Jon Malki wisely counseled restraint, and we considerably trimmed the manuscript.

After publication, both on the book tour and in e-mail communication, I heard from many readers who, like me, considered this game a time marker in their youths. The 1969 players told me they learned a lot from the book about the game, about each other, and about the events of that week and that fall. Darrell Royal gave it his stamp of approval, saying that he didn't know his players feared him that much—but adding that he had to assume that was true, too. As the 2003 game between the two programs approached, Frank

Broyles said in a conference call with reporters that he hadn't read the book—the memories of the loss were still too painful—but that he had heard it was good. I consider that high praise. At the University of Arkansas' Black Alumni Reunion in Fayetteville in April 2003, I appeared on a symposium panel and heard additional details about that game week. Judge Wendell L. Griffen of the Arkansas Court of Appeals, who is also a reverend, told me he was the flagbearer for the ROTC color guard that day and was prepared to throw down the U.S. flag and storm onto the field if "Dixie" was played. UofA journalism professor Gerald Jordan, a student journalist on the Fayetteville campus in 1969, talked during the symposium about the BAD meetings during the week of the game. Both Griffen and Jordan believed I underestimated the potential for violence against the black students if they had staged an on-field protest. They also said I hadn't given band director Richard Worthington enough credit for his courageous stand for making sure "Dixie" wasn't played. Consider those views added to the record.

Some readers believe I should have ruthlessly applied today's standards to condemn Royal, and especially Broyles, for not integrating their programs sooner. Others didn't understand why the material about the pending integration of programs and the campus unrest needed to be in the book at all. I believe I have been fair and have left many judgments up to intelligent readers. I also consider excessively self-righteous hindsight to be one of the scourges of modern journalism, especially in this era of staking out extreme, exaggerated, hand-waving, finger-pointing positions in the hope of gaining attention—and even of selling books. So this is my story, and I'm sticking to it.

— Terry Frei
   Denver, Colorado
   January 1, 2004

SOURCES AND CREDITS

Author Interviews (1994, 2001, 2002)

Fred Akers

David Arledge

Bill Atessis

Emory Bellard

Dr. Dennis Berner

Mike Boschetti

Rodney Brand

Don Breaux

Darrell Brown

Frank Broyles

Dick Bumpas

Dr. Bill Burnett

George Herbert Walker
Bush *written correspondence*

Mike Campbell IV

Tom Campbell

Charley Coffey

Carroll "Beano" Cook

Dr. Mike Dean

Chuck Dicus

Don Donner

Jerry Dossey

David Edwards

John Eichler

Happy Feller

Bobby Field

Bob Ford

Dr. Honor Franklin

Lynn Garner

Glen Halsell

Ronnie Hammers

John Paul Hammer-
schmidt

Roger Harnish

Scott Henderson

Colonel Eugene Holmes

Eugene Hunt

Bruce James

Merv Johnson

Mike Kelson

Rick Kersey

Dr. Ted Koy

Wilson Matthews

Bruce Maxwell

Hiram McBeth III

Bill McClard

Bob McKay

Gordon McNulty

Dr. Bobby Mitchell

Bill Montgomery

Jerry Moore

Dr. Gordon Morgan

Pat Morrison

Randy Peschel

Terry Don Phillips

Greg Ploetz

Cliff Powell

Kathy Pulley

John Rees

Darrell Royal

Cotton Speyrer

Bob Stankovich

Terry Stewart

Randy Stout

James Street

Carl White

Julius Whittier

Forrest Wiegand

Steve Worster

Bobby Wuensch

Bill Zapalac

Bud Zinke

BIBLIOGRAPHY

Ambrose, Stephen, *Nixon: The Education of a Politician 1913–1962*, Simon & Schuster, 1987.

Ambrose, Stephen, *Nixon: The Triumph of a Politician 1962–1972*, Simon & Schuster, 1989.

Banks, Jimmy, *The Darrell Royal Story*, Shoal Creek Publishers, 1973.

Blanton, J. Neal, *Game of the Century*, Jenkins Publishing, 1970.

Brodie, Fawn M., *Richard Nixon: The Shaping of His Character*, W. W. Norton and Co., 1981.

Broyles, Frank, *Hog Wild*, Memphis State University Press, 1979.

Evans, Rowland Jr., and Novak, Robert D., *Nixon in the White House: The Frustration of Power*, Random House, 1971.

Haldeman, H. R., *The Haldeman Diaries: Inside the Nixon White House*, G. B. Putnam's Sons, 1994.

Hubbell, Webb, *Friends in High Places*, William Morrow and Co., 1997.

Maraniss, David, *First in His Class*, Simon & Schuster, 1995.

Morgan, Gordon D., and Preston, Izola, *The Edge of Campus: A Journal of the Black Experience at the University of Arkansas*, University of Arkansas Press, 1990.

Morris, Roger, *Richard Milhous Nixon: The Rise of an American Politician*, Henry Holt and Company, 1990.

Nixon, Richard M., *R.N.: The Memoirs of Richard Nixon*, Simon & Schuster, 1978.

Shaw, Gary, *Meat on the Hoof: The Hidden World of Texas Football*, St. Martin's Press, 1972.

Steinmark, Freddie (with Blackie Sherrod), *I Play to Win*, Little, Brown and Co., 1971.

Stockdale, Ken, *Southwest Conference Football: The Classic 60's*, Companion Press, 1992.

Publications

Amarillo Daily News

Amarillo Globe

Arkansas Democrat

Arkansas Gazette

Arkansas Democrat-Gazette

Arkansas Traveler

Austin American

Austin American-Statesman

Austin Statesman

The Daily Texan

Dallas Morning News

The Denver Post

Houston Chronicle

Houston Post

Mizzou Illustrated

Northwest Arkansas Times

The Rag (Austin)

St. Louis Post-Dispatch

San Antonio Express-News

Archives/Research/Editing Assistance

University of Arkansas sports information office; Kevin Trainor, director; Mary Lynn Gibson

University of Arkansas, Mullins Library, Special Collections Department; Andrea Cantrell

University of Arkansas, Razorback Foundation; Harold Horton

University of Arkansas, Alumni Association; Deborah Hughes

Austin Public Library

Jim Beseda, *The Oregonian*, Portland

Mike Burrows, *The Denver Post*

Dr. Robert Dougan

Fayetteville Public Library

Little Rock Public Library

University of Missouri sports information office; Jeremy McNieve, football sports information director

Dr. Orderia Mitchell

The Richard Nixon Library, Yorba Linda, California; Susan Naulty

Neal Rubin, *Detroit News*

University of Texas sports information office; John Bianco, director; Brian Hernandez, football assistant; Bill Little, assistant athletic director

University of Texas, Center for American History

ROSTERS AND 1969 RESULTS

TEXAS LONGHORNS

Starters vs. Arkansas

QB—16 JAMES STREET, Senior, 5-11, 175, Longview

FB—30 STEVE WORSTER, Junior, 6-0, 208, Bridge City

HB—35 JIM BERTELSEN, Sophomore, 5-11, 197, Hudson, Wis.

TE—40 RANDY PESCHEL, Senior, 6-1, 195, Austin

LT—50 BOBBY WUENSCH, Junior, 6-3, 221, Houston

LG—64 BOBBY MITCHELL, Junior, 5-11, 206, Wheat Ridge, Colo.

C—52 FORREST WIEGAND, Senior, 6-1, 200, Edna

RG—66 MIKE DEAN, Junior, 6-0, 195, Sherman

RT—62 BOB McKAY, Senior, 6-6, 245, Crane

SE—88 COTTON SPEYRER, Junior, 5-11, 169, Port Arthur

DE—77 BILL ATESSIS, Junior, 6-3, 257, Houston

DT—31 GREG PLOETZ, Junior, 5-10, 205, Sherman

DT—70 CARL WHITE, Sophomore, 6-4, 216, McKinney

DE—89 DAVID ARLEDGE, Sophomore, 5-11, 177, Richardson

OLB—80 BILL ZAPALAC, Junior, 6-4, 206, Austin

ILB—67 GLEN HALSELL, Senior, 5-11, 202, Odessa

ILB—61 SCOTT HENDERSON, Junior, 6-1, 213, Dallas

ROVER—86 MIKE CAMPBELL, Senior, 5-11, 186, Austin

DHB—84 TOM CAMPBELL, Senior, 5-11, 183, Austin

DHB—23 DANNY LESTER, Junior, 5-11, 174, Amarillo

S—28 FREDDIE STEINMARK, Junior, 5-10, 166, Wheat Ridge, Colo.

Specialists and Reserves*

PK—5 HAPPY FELLER, Junior, 5-11, 173, Fredericksburg

HOLDER—18 DONNIE WIGGINTON, Sophomore, 5-9, 180, Spring
Branch

DHB—19 PAUL KRISTYNIK, Senior, 5-9, 174, Bay City

PUNTER—20 SCOOTER MONZINGO, 6-2, 183, Del Rio

HB—22 BILLY DALE, Junior, 5-10, 190, Odessa

HB—33 TERRY COLLINS, Junior, 5-6, 181, San Angelo

ILB—34 DAVID RICHARDSON, Junior, 6-0, 192, Abilene

S—41 RICK NABORS, Junior, 6-0, 169, Austin

FB—46 BOBBY CALLISON, Junior, 5-10, 190, Abilene

DT—65 SCOTT PALMER, Junior, 6-2, 224, Houston

LG—74 RANDY STOUT, Sophomore, 6-2, 241, San Angelo

Remainder of Game Program Roster

10 ROBBIE PATMAN, E, Senior, 5-9, 164, Texarkana

13 JIMMY GUNN, LB, Sophomore, 6-0, 180, Carrollton

14 EDDIE PHILLIPS, QB, Sophomore, 6-0, 188, Mesquite

21 DICKIE JOHNSTON, DHB, Senior, 6-0, 190, Clovis, N.M.

26 JOHNNY ROBINSON, DHB, Junior, 6-1, 177, Plano

27 TOMMY ASAFF, DHB, Senior, 5-11, 188, Marshall

29 ROBERT PAINE, HB, Sophomore, 5-11, 182, Houston

32 MIKE HUTCHINGS, LB, Senior, 6-0, 191, Mt. Pleasant

36 DAVID BALLEW, DHB, Sophomore, 5-11, 177, Clarksville

37 ROB LAYNE, PK, Senior, 5-10, 196, Lubbock

38 JAY CORMIER, TE, Sophomore, 6-0, 209, Freeport

42 MACK McKINNEY, LB, Senior, 6-3, 195, Cameron

44 RAYMOND FONTENOT, LB, Junior, 5-11, 215, Port Arthur

45 KEN EHRIG, E, Senior, 5-11, 173, Gonzales

47 PAUL ROBICHAU, HB, Sophomore, 5-10, 189, Beaumont

48 RICK TROBERMAN, LB, Sophomore, 5-9, 175, San Antonio

51 JEFF ZAPALAC, C, Sophomore, 5-11, 185, Austin

54 RICK MARTIN, LB, Sophomore, 6-2, 195, Odessa

55 RONNIE TYLER, T, Sophomore, 6-2, 219, Jefferson

57 JIM ACHILLES, C, Junior, 5-11, 204, Spring Branch

60 SYD KEASLER, G, Sophomore, 6-0, 205, Hallsville

63 GEORGE COBB, DT, Senior, 5-10, 186, Amarillo

69 CHARLES ROGERS, G, Sophomore, 6-2, 206, San Antonio

71 LEO BROOKS,[†] DT, Senior, 6-6, 244, Kermit

72 JIM WILLIAMSON, DE, Senior, 6-0, 198, Dallas

73 TRAVIS ROACH, DT, Sophomore, 6-3, 225, Marlin

75 CHARLES CRAWFORD, G, Sophomore, 5-11, 208, Spring Branch

76 CHRIS YOUNG, DT, Senior, 6-1, 219, Houston

78 TOMMY LEE, T, Sophomore, 6-2, 215, Belton

79 PAT MACHA, DT, Sophomore, 5-11, 225, Orchard

82 TOMMY WOODARD, LB, Sophomore, 6-1, 201, Abilene

83 DERYL COMER,[†] TE, Senior, 6-2, 225, Dallas

85 STAN MAULDIN, DE, Sophomore, 5-11, 195, Azle

1969 Results

September 20, at Berkeley—Texas 17, California 0

September 27, at Austin—Texas 49, Texas Tech 7

October 4, at Austin—Texas 56, Navy 17

October 11, at Dallas— Texas 27, Oklahoma 17

October 25, at Austin—Texas 31, Rice 0

November 1, at Dallas—Texas 45, Southern Methodist 14

November 8, at Austin—Texas 56, Baylor 14

November 15, at Austin—Texas 69, Texas Christian 7

November 27, at College Station—Texas 49, Texas A&M 12

December 6, at Fayetteville—vs. Arkansas

Nine-Game Statistical Leaders

RUSHING: Bertelsen 94 carries, 711 yards, 7.6 average; Worster 111–555, 5.0; Koy 71–413, 5.8; Street 68–339, 5.0 yards

PASSING: Street 34–71, 8 interceptions, 575 yards, 3 touchdowns

RECEIVING: Speyrer 26 catches, 427 yards, 3 touchdowns; Peschel 12 catches, 169 yards, 1 touchdown; Ehrig 10 catches, 167 yards, 1 touchdown

TEAM AVERAGES: 44.3 points scored, 9.8 points allowed, 24.8 first downs, 376 yards rushing, 108 yards passing, 484 yards total offense

ARKANSAS RAZORBACKS

Starters vs. Texas

QB—10 BILL MONTGOMERY, Junior, 6-1, 180, Carrollton, Tex.

TB—33 BILL BURNETT, Junior, 6-0, 185, Bentonville

FB—34 BRUCE MAXWELL, Senior, 6-1, 218, Pine Bluff

SE—20 CHUCK DICUS, Junior, 6-0, 172, Garland, Tex.

LT—78 MIKE KELSON, Sophomore, 6-4, 225, Houston

LG—74 JERRY DOSSEY, Senior, 6-3, 230, Lawton, Okla.

C—57 RODNEY BRAND, Senior, 6-2, 218, Newport, Ark.

RG—70 RONNIE HAMMERS, Junior, 6-3, 230, Marshall, Tex.

RT—75 BOB STANKOVICH, Senior, 6-4, 230, Bentleyville, Pa.

TE—88 PAT MORRISON, Junior, 6-2, 205, Little Rock

FL—25 JOHN REES, Junior, 6-1, 180, Jonesboro

DE—85 BRUCE JAMES, Junior, 6-3, 216, Moss Point, Miss.

DT—63 ROGER HARNISH, Sophomore, 6-2, 206, Little Rock

DT—61 DICK BUMPAS, Junior, 6-1, 215, Fort Smith

DE—72 RICK KERSEY, Junior, 6-0, 200, Conway

LB—53 LYNN GARNER, Senior, 6-2, 200, Fort Smith

LB—64 CLIFF POWELL, Senior, 6-1, 210, Eudora

LB—59 MIKE BOSCHETTI, Junior, 6-1, 195, Pine Bluff

MONSTER—49 BOBBY FIELD, Junior, 5-11, 180, Farwell, Tex.

DHB—24 TERRY STEWART, Senior, 6-0, 185, Fort Smith

DHB—18 JERRY MOORE, Junior, 6-3, 198, Benton

S—36 DENNIS BERNER, Senior, 6-2, 187, Little Rock

Specialists and Reserves*

HOLDER—17 GUS RUSHER, Sophomore, 6-2, 180, Brinkley

PK—19 BILL McCLARD, Sophomore, 6-0, 190, Norman, Okla.

DB—21 DAVID HOGUE, Sophomore, 6-1, 180, Eudora

TB—26 PAUL BLEVINS, Junior, 5-9, 175, Norman, Okla.

FB-TE—27 BOBBY NICHOLS, Sophomore, 6-1, 200, Tulsa

FB—29 DICK FULLER, Junior, 6-0, 190, Manchester, N.H.

DB—30 STEVE WALTERS, Junior, 6-0, 189, Springdale

MONSTER—31 STEVE BIRDWELL, Sophomore, 6-0, 205, Murfreesboro

LB—32 RICHARD COLEMAN, Senior, 5-11, 202, Holly Grove

LB—35 RONNIE JONES, Sophomore, 6-2, 195, N. Little Rock

FB—38 RUSS GARBER, Sophomore, 6-0, 210, Riverton, Kan.

PUNTER—43 CARY STOCKDELL, Senior 6-5, 225, Richmond, Va.

DB—46 ROBERT DEW, Sophomore, 5-11, 170, Warren

C—50 TERRY HOPKINS, Junior, 6-0, 200, Lawrence, Kan.

C—54 BILL CARTER, Sophomore, 6-1, 193, Little Rock

G—65 JIM MULLINS, Senior, 6-1, 220, Warren

DT—68 TERRY DON PHILLIPS, Senior, 6-1, 220, Longview, Tex.

DE—71 GORDON McNULTY, Senior, 6-4, 215, Pine Bluff

E—FRED EDWARDS, Junior, 6-0, 200, Blytheville

Remainder of Game Program Roster

15 JOHN EICHLER, QB, Senior, 6-1, 190, Stuttgart

16 WALTER NELSON, QB, Sophomore, 6-0, 180, Little Rock

22 STEVE HOCKERSMITH, SE, Sophomore, 5-11, 180, Little Rock

23 MIKE HENDREN, TB, Junior, 6-3, 205, Muskogee, Okla.

37 LOUIS CAMPBELL, DB, Sophomore, 6-1, 175, Hamburg

42 STEVE VESTAL, LB, Sophomore, 5-11, 194, Houston

45 RUSSELL CODY, TB, Senior, 5-11, 175, Russellville

51 DON WUNDERLY, DT, Sophomore, 6-4, 225, Fort Scott, Kan.

52 ROBERT LEWIS, LB, Sophomore, 6-3, 195, Ruston, La.

58 STEVE BENOIT, DE, Sophomore, 6-1, 210, Shreveport, La.

60 RICK VICKERS, DT, Sophomore, 6-2, 210, Dumas

62 DeWITT SMITH, G, Senior, 6-3, 209, Forest City

69 DONNIE BENNETT, G, Sophomore, 6-3, 225, Osceola

73 TOM MABRY, T, Sophomore, 6-6, 250, Conway

77 GARY PARSON, T, Junior, 6-9, 260, Huntsville

79 JOHN TURNER, T, Junior, 6-3, 240, St. Louis

80 DAVID COX, SE, Senior, 6-0, 180, Dallas

83 TIM WEBSTER, K, Junior, 6-1, 190, Grove, Okla.

87 TOMMY DEW, DE, Senior, 6-0, 200, N. Little Rock

1969 Results

September 20, at Little Rock—Arkansas 39, Oklahoma State 0

September 27, at Fayetteville—Arkansas 55, Tulsa 0

October 4, at Little Rock—Arkansas 24, Texas Christian 6

October 11, at Waco—Arkansas 21, Baylor 7

October 25, at Little Rock—Arkansas 52, Wichita State 14

November 1, at Fayetteville—Arkansas 35, Texas A&M 13

November 8, at Houston—Arkansas 30, Rice 6

November 15, at Dallas—Arkansas 28, Southern Methodist 15

November 27, at Little Rock—Arkansas 33, Texas Tech 0

December 6, at Fayetteville—vs. Texas

Nine-Game Statistical Leaders

RUSHING: Burnett 190 carries, 818 yards, 4.3 average; Maxwell 96–559, 5.8; Garber 49–219, 4.5; Cody 47–195, 4.1

PASSING: Montgomery 79 completions, 151 attempts, 5 interceptions, 1,128 yards; Eichler 49–90–0, 566 yards

RECEIVING: Dicus 31 catches, 548 yards, 3 touchdowns; Rees 19 catches, 268 yards, 3 touchdowns

TEAM AVERAGES: 35.2 points scored, 6.8 points allowed, 24.3 first downs, 224 yards rushing, 192 yards passing, 416 yards total offense

*Reserves and special teams players listed for both teams are those who played in the December 6 game, according to the official participation chart in the postgame statistical package issued to the press. Those charts were notoriously unreliable.

†Injured and not able to play.

INDEX

ABOUT THE AUTHOR

TERRY FREI is a sportswriter and columnist for *The Denver Post* and ESPN.com. He has been voted the state Sportswriter of the Year multiple times, in both Oregon and Colorado. He also is the author of the forthcoming *Third Down and a War to Go*. His website is www.terryfrei.com. He lives in Denver.